A Debutante's Passion—
A Coach's Erotica

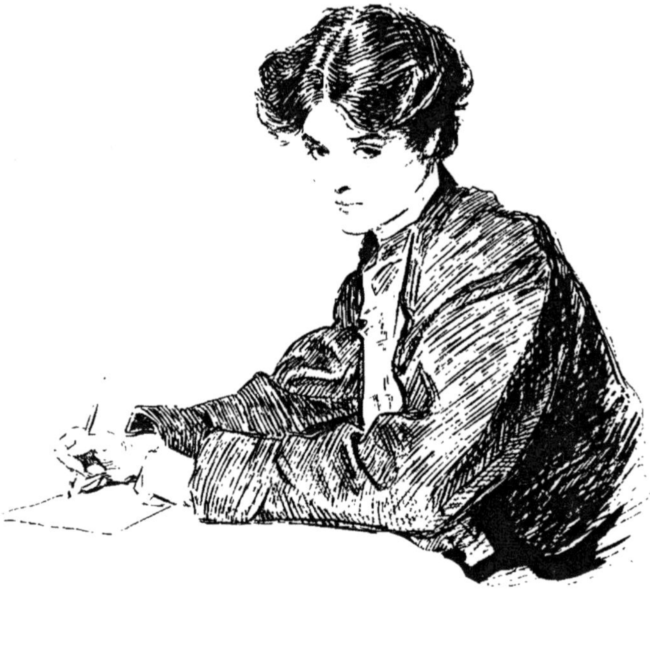

A Debutante's Passion—
A Coach's Erotica

Love Letters of a Harvard Man and a Boston Elite

Edited by

Ronald A. Smith

Eifrig Publishing
Lemont   Berlin

© 2009 by Ronald A. Smith
Printed in the United States of America

All rights reserved. This publication is protected by Copyright, and permission should be obtained from the publisher prior to any prohibited reproduction, storage in a retrieval system, or transmission in any form or by any means, electronic, mechanical, photocopying, recording, or likewise.

Published by Eifrig Publishing,
PO Box 66, 701 Berry Street, Lemont, PA 16851.
Knobelsdorffstr. 44, 14059 Berlin, Germany

For information regarding permission, write to:
Rights and Permissions Department,
Eifrig Publishing,
PO Box 66, 701 Berry Street, Lemont, PA 16851, USA.
publish@eifrigenterprises.com, 814-235-1501.

Library of Congress Cataloging-in-Publication Data

Smith, Ronald A., 1936-
   A debutante's passion—A coach's erotica:
   Love letters of a Harvard man and a Boston elite
   / edited by Ronald A. Smith.
   p.   cm.
   Includes timeline

   ISBN 978-0-9795518-0-2

     1. Correspondence—United States. 2. Love-letters.
     3. 19th-20th centuries. 4. Harvard.
     5. William T. Reid, Jr., 1878-1976.
     6. Christine Williams Lincoln Reid, 1881-1924.
   I. Smith, Ronald A. (Ronald Austin), II. Title.

13 12 11 10 2009
5 4 3 2 1

Printed on acid-free paper. ∞

*With love to my half-century partner and friend,
Susan Catherine Bard MacFarland Fernald Smith*

R.S.

CONTENTS

Acknowledgments *ix*
The Editorial Method *xi*
Introduction *xiii*

Chapter 1   1
Prep School - Early Harvard: "Remember Love Is for Life"

Chapter 2   33
Courtship: "I am Hunting for a Team, You Are Too"

Chapter 3   63
Engaged, Voyage, and Steamer Affair: "Are You Engaged or Not?"

Chapter 4   115
Return, Marriage, and Honeymoon: "A Double Bed and You"

Chapter 5   139
Love and Children: "If You Were Here Now We'd be in Bed"

Chapter 6   169
The Call to Harvard: "Anxious To Have All You Can Give"

Chapter 7   203
Heading West—Again: "There's a Girl Waiting To Be Loved"

Chapter 8   219
Mrs. Jackson—Lake Tahoe Summer: "It's All or Nothing for Me, Dearie"

Chapter 9   247
The Western Family Crisis: "Let's Clear Out"

Chapter 10   263
East Over West: "A Cloud Between Us Is Just Plain Torture"

Chapter 11   299
Hard Times: "You Are a Household Aren't You?"

Chapter 12   317
The End of a Love Affair and a Life: "This Isn't a Love Letter"

Epilogue   337
Life After Christine: "How Far Short I Have Fallen"

Timeline   343

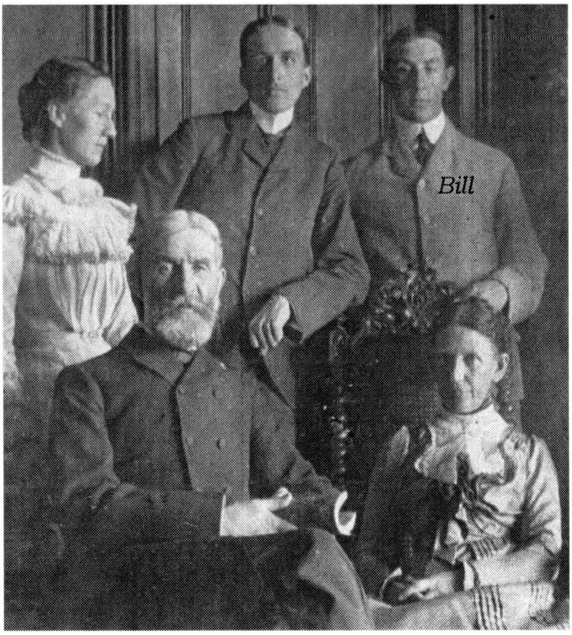
Bill

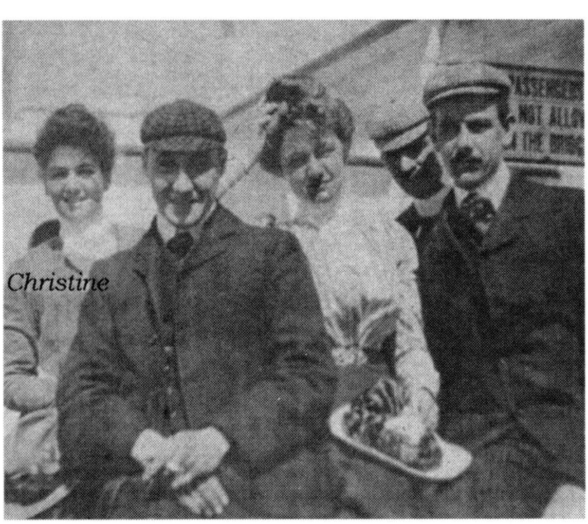
Christine

ACKNOWLEDGMENTS

Some years ago, a member of the Penn State University faculty, Earl "Buzz" Graham, Jr., with whom I have skied and played squash, tennis, and golf, suggested that if I wrote another book on the history of sport I should add more sex to the narrative. "Sex is what sells books," he opined. At the time, this geophysics professor, who spent his academic efforts in the College of Earth and Mineral Sciences studying the nature of planets, didn't know that in the pursuit of editing a diary of Harvard University coach I had come across the love letters of Coach Bill Reid and his socially elite wife, Christine Lincoln Reid. I spent considerable time in quoting extensively from these letters, but for more than a decade, the excerpts lay idle in my computer while I worked on other projects. Finally I decided to take Buzz Graham's advice and put the intimate letters together in book form, not a sport history volume but one of passionate love letters.

I greatly appreciate Bill and Christine Reid's grandson, Thomas Stetson, for allowing me to read the collected, lifetime letters saved by Bill and Christine. Mr. Stetson graciously allowed me to peruse the extensive collection of letters and to use them in my research and writing. In addition to the principal source for this love letters volume, I owe a debt to the Harvard University Archives for collecting other papers of Bill Reid, including the 440-page diary of the 1905 football season at Harvard. I used material from the diary in my *Sports and Freedom: The Rise of Big-Time College Athletics*, published by Oxford University Press in 1988. Later, in the process of publishing the 1905 diary with the University of Illinois Press in 1994, I came in contact with Thomas Stetson and the collection of love-letters. Another valuable source for this book was the University of California Archives, for it holds the papers of Bill's father, William T. Reid, Sr., a former president of the University of California.

A number of years ago, I was fortunate to receive a grant from the National Historical Publications and Records Commission to attend an institute at the State Historical Society of Wisconsin. Of particular importance was a statement by Sharon Macphearson, who was an editor of the Andrew Jackson papers. She emphasized that when editing, keep the material "in the form it was originally written." I have attempted to keep this piece of advice in the present volume.

Acknowledgements

Finally, I want to acknowledge the Department of Kinesiology at Penn State University, for allowing me to pursue for three decades my academic interests by providing reasonable teaching loads and the granting of four sabbaticals. I was fortunate to be in a fine university, including a library in which service to patrons was foremost and archives that placed an emphasis on preserving material in my area of study.

Lemont, Pennsylvania
January 2009

THE EDITORIAL METHOD

In publishing the love letters of and about Bill Reid, Jr., and Christine Lincoln Reid, I have tried to retain the original prose as much as possible while producing a work that would read well. Because the original material is well written for the most part, only minor editorial changes were required.

Letter form. The city locations and dates at the head of the letters have been standardized. Where no address or date is included, an approximate location or date is provided.

Spelling. There are several misspelled words in the letters that have been corrected. For instance "realise" has been corrected to "realize" throughout the document. When words that are used, such as "dearie," that are generally not accepted as correct English but are easily understood, they have been allowed to stand.

Grammar and syntax. The grammar and syntax have been allowed to remain in nearly all instances. If a serious ambiguity existed, it has been corrected with square brackets. When a word has been repeated inadvertently, it has been omitted.

Capitalization. Capitalizations were standardized. For example, "papa" and "mama" became "Papa" and "Mama."

Paragraphing. Original paragraphing remains in nearly all cases, though some extremely long paragraphs have been divided for reading comfort. All paragraph forms have been standardized.

Punctuation. Most punctuation marks have been allowed to stand. However, a dash (—) has been used when a dash was clearly intended when using a hyphen (-). When additional punctuation was needed for clarity, particularly commas, it has been added.

Underlining. All the prevalent underlining in original letters has been eliminated for aesthetic purposes, being too intrusive.

The Editorial Method

<u>Abbreviations and contractions</u>. Most abbreviations and contractions have been allowed to stand, unless ambiguity existed.

<u>Illegible matter</u>. In the rare situation where material is unreadable, suspension points inside square brackets "[. . .]" replace the unclear words.

<u>Eliminated material</u>. Many letters have been severely edited by eliminating pages and whole or partial paragraphs to make it more readable, to create a clearer story, and to eliminate redundancy. Omissions have been identified by the use of ellipses (. . .). Some entire letters have been included to give a sense of the entirety of communications, not only the love interests.

<u>Editorial insertions</u>. Material added by the editor was placed in square brackets. Full names of important individuals who could be identified have been added when they are encountered for the first time with square brackets. Thus "Haughton" became "[Percy] Haughton."

<u>Chapter Titles</u>. All chapter titles include a quote taken from one of the letters in the chapter.

I have included a total of 516 letters, two-thirds of which are from Bill to Christine (176) or Christine to Bill (154). To make the story more complete I have included excerpts from a number of other letters including those from Bill's father, mother, sister, and aunt, and Christine's father, mother, and sister. There are also letters from Bill and Christine's two daugters, as well as from friends of both Bill and Christine. In addition, several letters from those associated with Harvard University are contained in the collection.

INTRODUCTION

Bill Reid wrote to his wife in March of 1905, just as he took over the head football coaching position at Harvard: "I'd just like to have you here now to take you in my arms first, & squeeze you tight against me & then in my lap for a good hugging and a passionate kissing. And perhaps, my hand might get up your dress—um—so warm and soft!!! And then I'd undress you gradually, kind of teasing myself by taking my time until I had you absolutely stripped. . . ." Christine Lincoln Reid, a day later and without the above promptings from Bill, sent a letter to her husband of nearly three years: "It is cold, and I am just comfortably tired enough to want to snuggle and be 'loved.' I am going to take a hot bath, and I know after that I shall feel—well—you know how! Don't you wish you were here? I'd guarantee you a good time!"

The love letters of Bill and Christine give a glimpse of the inner life of two passionate individuals at a time in the early twentieth century when the inner life of sexual obsession was often covered up by an outward life that appeared prudish and sexually repressed. Beyond the loving letters of a sensuous debutante from Brookline, Massachusetts and an erotic athlete and sometimes scholar from Belmont, California, there is an intriguing story of a Western boy who traveled East to attend Harvard and compete in athletics, who then met and married an elite from the Boston area. Could an individual from the West return to the West with an Eastern woman with strong attachments to her family, friends, and Eastern sophistication and live in happiness?

This book, consisting mostly of love letters, began in the 1980s when I was seated in the Harvard University Archives, researching the early development of intercollegiate athletics in America. On my last day in Cambridge, I came across a 440-page diary of Bill Reid, a 27-year-old Harvard football coach, who recorded his impressions of the Harvard program from spring training in 1905 until Harvard played Yale in the final game the following fall. I obtained a copy of the Reid diary, and after attending a two-week seminar sponsored by the National Historical Publications and Records Commission for Editing of History Documents at the University of Wisconsin-Madison, the diary was readied and published in 1994 by the University of Illinois Press. The volume, *Big-Time Football at Harvard, 1905: The Diary of Coach Bill Reid*, in my opinion, is the best single source of understanding how Big-Time intercollegiate athletics were commercialized and professionalized from

INTRODUCTION

an early period. My interest was, then, the history of college sports, not in the private letters of lovers. Material from the Bill Reid diary became important in my early history of intercollegiate athletics, *Sports and Freedom: The Rise of Big-Time College Athletics*, published by Oxford University Press in 1988.

In pursuing the possibility of making a documentary or a full-length movie on the 1905 football season and Bill Reid's place in it, I came in contact with Bill Reid's grandson. He said that he had two suitcases full of Bill Reid materials, including the letters that Reid had saved for a lifetime. I was given permission to read the entire collection and to use them in my research and writing. There were over 1000 letters, some as early as 1885 when Bill was seven years old. Most were from the period from 1896 to the 1920s, but they covered nearly his entire lifetime from 1878 to 1976. The letters beginning in 1896 often centered on the love interests of Bill, and especially was this true when he began attending Harvard in the fall of 1897. In his junior year, Bill met Christine Williams Lincoln, a stunning 19-year-old debutante from Brookline, Massachusetts, near Boston. Most of the letters between them from 1900 for the next quarter century have been preserved. Quoting from nearly all of these letters forms the core of this book.

Bill's family lacked a strong elite Eastern pedigree, something that was there for Christine dating back to colonial New England. Yet, there was a kind of Western prestige in the Reid family. Bill's father and mother were highly educated for the 1800s, and they placed much emphasis on educating their two children, Julia and Bill. Bill's father, William T., Senior, had volunteered during the Civil War while attending Harvard University and graduated following the war. His mother had a degree from Elmira College. Following Harvard, William T., Senior went into public school administration, eventually becoming principal of the Boy's High School in San Francisco public school before being hired as the president of the University of California, Berkeley in 1881. That was a politically contentious position, for when the Democrats came to power in California, he was forced to leave the presidency and to find other work. He and his classically educated wife, Julia, started a prep school in 1885, the Belmont School, about 25 miles south of San Francisco. Bill, Jr., attended the Belmont School in preparation for Harvard, the only college his dad wanted his son to attend.

Bill's father had enjoyed the prestige that came with being the president of the University of California, even though the University was second or third rate to the Eastern colleges of the time. But heading the Belmont School was a step down, and he wanted Bill to attend Harvard and achieve something more than what he had attained. When the senior Reid had gone to Harvard, he was something of a social outcast, if for no other reason than that he had come from the farmlands of Jacksonville, Illinois. He was both poor and a non-Easterner. He wanted to live his life vicariously through Bill at Harvard, and this time he wanted the

INTRODUCTION

Reid name to mean something socially. Thus, when Bill passed his entrance exams and became a freshman at Harvard in the fall of 1897, he presented Bill with a series of letters advising him how to win the social game at the elite institution. One of the ways was to be introduced to the social set in and around Boston. He wanted Bill to be invited to the homes of some of the best families, to join an elite dancing club, to be invited to the top eating and social clubs on campus, to find success in writing for the school newspaper, *The Crimson*, and to improve these opportunities by becoming prominent on campus through Bill's athletic abilities in football and baseball. "Accept some invitations to dances in Dorchester," he wrote to his son, so that he would "get a look into the best society, in one of the neighboring towns as well as in Boston."

The elder Reid also cautioned Bill about the "fast set" of irresponsible social elites at Harvard and of the moral degeneration that he might be exposed to while there. Only weeks after Bill had starred as fullback on the Harvard freshman football team in its victory over the Yale, his father cautioned Bill about the "looseness of life" in Boston and "the Bawdy house" where "girls are for sale." There, he warned Bill, "is where your battles are to be fought." Bill's father knew that because Bill had visibility though athletics, he would be more exposed to women than he had been a generation before as a little-known student from the Midwest. "Your sexual passions," he wrote Bill, will give you "the most serious struggle of your life." He told his son, "buckle on your armor and wear it always."

Christine Lincoln did not need to improve her social status as she was born with it and had it conferred officially when she became a debutante as a teenager. Her mother was a socialite and her father was a prominent lawyer in Boston. Her mother's brother, Uncle Moses Williams, was on the Board of Overseers of Harvard University, a position of prominence. If Christine had been born a male, she would likely have attended Harvard, but she decided that she would prefer not to go to college. She was active in the social life of the elite in the Boston area and attended activities at Harvard University, including football games. She was in attendance when Bill, a sophomore, starred in the 1898 Harvard-Yale game in which he scored two touchdowns in a 17-0 defeat of Yale. No Harvard man had ever scored two touchdowns against Yale, and 17 points was the largest score ever achieved against Yale, the greatest "jock school" for the first half-century of American football. Yale, it should be noted, only lost 10 football games in the last quarter of the nineteenth century. Bill was an immediate hero and was displayed in his football uniform in a full-page picture in the Christmas issue of *Harper's Weekly*. The 18-year-old Christine did not then know the star Harvard fullback. She would, however, in just a little over a year.

In the meantime, Bill's father, especially, and his mother were trying to get Bill to date some of the Boston social elites and other women who would be attending local colleges such as Radcliffe or Wellesley. The

XV

INTRODUCTION

letters of correspondence between Bill's parents and Bill in the first three years of his Harvard experience noted a number of young ladies they wanted Bill to meet. At the same time, they tried to discourage Bill from getting more highly involved with females in the Belmont, California area, whom Bill had known since the Belmont School days. Assuming that Bill would be a prominent individual after college, they both wanted Bill to meet a woman with good connections who would eventually become his wife. Bill's athletic prominence brought him a certain social position at Harvard, but he disliked the "fast set" at Harvard, the rich men who controlled the social scene at the university. The antagonism between Bill and the Harvard "fast set" stymied his social acceptance, but his success in football in addition to his starring role as catcher on the Harvard baseball team contributed greatly to his Harvard prestige in his sophomore and junior years. His athletic prowess brought him into contact with a number of the elite females who sought out Harvard men.

In the winter of his junior year, Bill met Christine and invited her to several social affairs at Harvard. By this time, he had been chosen captain of the baseball team. He almost immediately fell in love with Christine, though she was much less sure of her feelings. She had been dating a local elite, Eben, but when Bill began dating her and taking her to such Harvard events as the prominent Hasty Pudding supper and dance, she moved away from Eben toward the prominent Harvard athlete. In the first preserved letter from Bill to Christine, Bill redrew an ox yoke, which Christine apparently had drawn previously, with two openings for oxen. In one opening he wrote "taken" and the other "to let." He wrote: "'To let' isn't already filled (and from what I hear I was not so sure it isn't) I should like to buy it. Renting isn't satisfactory, for the tenant may be turned out and I want to feel secure." Three months after meeting Christine, the Reid-captained baseball team was coming to its season climax with the first game of the Yale series. Bill had just visited Christine at the Lincoln's summer ocean home in Cohasset. "I have been sort of dreaming," he wrote Christine, "ever since I came back—visions of Buggy, the Lighthouse, etc., keep bobbing up in my mind." He took her to Harvard Class Day activities and took pride in being with beautiful Christine as any star athlete or any other one might have.

In July 1900, Bill left Christine and began his trip to the West coast to be with his parents for the summer. He had known Christine for about a half-year, and he had essentially made up his mind that she was the woman with whom he would like to spend the rest of his life. He needed to test her long-term commitment to him, as his senior year at Harvard was about to begin, and a lifetime job was on the horizon. While in California, Bill wrote Christine saying that she had "always been surrounded with plenty and with luxury. . . ." Knowing this, would a move to California and a less luxurious setting "not be pretty hard for you?" He then added a somewhat surprising comment that he undoubtedly penned to draw a stronger reply of commitment from

INTRODUCTION

Christine. "Why," he asked, "are you fond of me? I am not man enough for you to be fond of—I wish I were." Strange, because the meaning of man and manliness at the turn-of-the-century had much to do with physicality. And, of course, Bill's athletic success and captaincy of the baseball nine gave him this status. The manliness issue was never a large one for Bill, at least from a physical standpoint. Whether Christine would be happy in the West was continually on his mind—and probably on Christine's mind also. In one of his many letters from Belmont, California, he asked Christine: "If you should learn to love me, then you'd be willing to come out here wouldn't you?"

As the summer came to a close, Bill said that he would return to Harvard early, presumably to work on details related to Harvard baseball, but actually to be with Christine a short while before she left for an eight-month family journey to Europe and Egypt. In one of his last letters before leaving California, he wrote: "I may ask you a question I've never asked before—so just think up the possible questions. This one— "yes" or "no" simply will answer fully and satisfactorily." Previously she had hesitated about answering the marriage question because she was unsure of her love. However, when Bill arrived, she decided to answer "yes," though on the night before she sailed, the two did not inform her parents of their decision. As Christine left on a steamer for England with her mother, father, aunt and uncle, and two younger sisters and a brother, Bill returned to Harvard for his senior year. Bill chose not to play football, claiming a leg injury from baseball as the explanation, but the major reason was that he felt both the captain and the young coach were prejudiced against him. In any event, Bill spent much of his time and energy writing to Christine through the fall and winter, the letters being both lengthy and searching.

And, despite Christine's steamer incident with a young French artist on the way over to England, the passion grew. Christine came to fantasize about Bill as she came to feel freer in expressing her physical attraction to him, something Bill wanted her to do. From Germany, Christine confided: "I am glad that you are so big and strong. I like to think that you could kill me if you wanted to. There is a certain fascination about it, I suppose," she told him. "It is sweeter to be caressed by the hand that could kill, than by one that at its worse and strongest could only scratch." Bill felt good about that, and not long after he received her letter he told Christine that he was "just ravenous for you" and wanted to "wrap you up" in bed. That he could not do so "was regular 'torture,'" he told her.

It was likely anguish for the next year and a half, for there is little reason to believe that he was not true to Christine, nor to think that their own sexual lives were consummated at any other time than on their wedding night. Bill once confided to Christine, while she was in Europe: "It is a big comfort to be decent after all—even if it does take a struggle. You girls don't realize just what a fellow has to fight against." I suspect that Christine knew, for she had her own struggles. She looked

xvii

INTRODUCTION

forward to fully loving Bill, being "quite anxious" as she said "to know for myself just how it feels. . . . What's mine is yours in the future you know." Christine commented on a book she was reading in which it was stated that men chiefly wished to be loved while women wished to love someone. Christine reacted: "I know of one girl anyway who wants to be 'loved' very much indeed, quite as much as to 'love.'" Christine thought it would be blissful "loving each other, sleeping together. . . . Somehow," she wrote, "I seem to look forward to lying in your arms all night more than to anything ever before. It is a delight to think of it ever, and I do very, very often." Bill replied as a gentleman might: "In recent letters, you 'almost wished sometimes that I had no honor' so that you can show me that it was me you loved."

When Christine returned from her lengthy stay in Europe, she and Bill no longer needed to search their hearts long distance. Bill was concluding his senior year, leading Harvard to its third series victory over Yale in Reid's four years as a baseball starter. In addition, he had been asked to coach the football team the following fall, as it was common practice then for a new graduate to lead the team upon graduation. Bill was in the graduate program at Harvard as he coached the Crimson football team to an undefeated season. In the midst of the football campaign, Christine was living at her parent's ocean home at Cohasset. Being sorry she had not been able to get to the game and see him, she wrote to Bill. "Dear Coach," she began, "I worship you, I do really. Will you kiss me a lot when you come? I want you to, just awfully. If you don't, I warn you I shall turn aggressor and unsex you," a fairly strong statement for a turn-of-the-century social elite.

Christine probably did not have to turn aggressor, for Bill searched for loving relief from the coaching tension of the football season. Near the end of his first year of coaching, he wrote Christine a "blue" letter while awaiting the game against Penn in Philadelphia. "I'm glum, . . . peevish and irritable. . . . I wish you were here in Philadelphia tonight so that I could love you, kiss you, and hug you—that would ease the strain tremendously. . . ." He made it through the Penn game and concluded the season with a resounding beating of Yale, 22-0, only the third defeat of Yale by Harvard since 1876. Reid continued his hero status at Harvard, and he found more time to be with Christine.

Yet there was little let up for Bill the next spring, as he tried to combine his version of eros with graduate study and helping to coach the baseball team. When off on a trip to Annapolis to play the Naval Academy, just a little more than two months away from their July wedding, he wrote to Christine. "I'm, crazy to see you, to love you, to hug you, to squeeze and kiss you and to sleep with you. . . . I could," he said, "kiss you within an inch of your life and hug you and squeeze you so hard that you couldn't breathe. . . ." Nearly a decade later he recalled a similar situation to his Annapolis wish. "Do you remember that night while we were engaged & how naughty we were? I can feel you tight against me now—with the same little thrills that went over me when I felt your bare legs touch mine. Whew—it makes me wriggle. How we ever stood it without just going to it, I don't see. I couldn't stand it now." And he did not have to stand it much longer. By the summer of 1902, Harvard had again beaten Yale in baseball, Bill graduated with a master's degree, and he got married—all within a week early that summer.

Their wedding trip was planned. Following the wedding day, they would spend a night at the Hotel Lennox in Boston, followed by a short trip to the White Mountains in Franconia Notch, New Hampshire. Then it was on board a ship to Europe for a half year. Bill recalled his first night with Christine at the Hotel Lennox three years later, when he returned to the Boston area to begin his second football coaching stint at Harvard. "I looked up at the window of the room in which we had so much fun that first night," he wrote Christine in 1905. "Let's see, four times was it. . . ? I'll never forget the blue dress you wore that night or how deliciously then it was & how good you felt through it. . . ."

The advice of William Reid, Sr., on early married life, given to both Christine and Bill, must have been taken. Bill's father wanted grandchildren and advised Christine, before they were married, that the sooner they had children the better. "It is too bad that when you are both strong & fresh & impulsive," he told his future daughter-in-law, "you could not do as you like and let the little one come & be welcome at any time." To Bill, he wrote a short time later: "Keep in fine trim and let as many little ones come as you care to have." At the same time, he informed Bill of all the methods of birth control of which he was aware, including a womb veil, the introduction of cotton, syringing with the use of acids, condoms of two kinds, and coitus interruptus, but he suggested, rather, having "a baby come whenever it may come." The latter was the method chosen, for Christine likely became pregnant on the first night, or very nearly so. Less than two months after the wedding, Christine and Bill were in Europe and informed both sets of parents that she was pregnant. Christine's mother responded, noting how "excited and filled with delight" she was. Bill's father reacted in a different way toward Christine. "Oh those tantalizing underclothes that you showed me. I warned you of their danger I think. And yet on the other hand they simply made the tinder a little more inflammable." He noted to Bill: "This is altogether more serious than coaching a football team isn't it?"

Bill and Christine returned home from their European trip about three months before their first child was born and soon moved West. Bill had taken the position of assistant headmaster of his father's preparatory school in Belmont, California. If their letters were passionate before marriage, they became more so and much more explicit after they married. Separation occurred rather regularly because Christine felt the need to travel East to be with family and friends. She, however, would not return from California to her parent's home in Brookline for a year after their son, William III, was born. His name became "Patrick," because

INTRODUCTION

he was born early, on St. Patrick's Day, only 8 ½ months after they were married. In late spring 1904, Christine had returned for the first time to her parents with their one-year-old son. Bill stayed in California to help at his father's school. His letters were especially sensual. "You dear girl you," he wrote Christine, "I do love to get your letters so much. . . . Maybe I wouldn't have liked to 'celebrate' Dorothea's wedding night. My! but I'd make you wriggle with pleasure though. Oh, why can't we?" Bill asked. "Wouldn't you like to do the way we did one Sunday afternoon when we lay all wrapped up as we could and I gave you a corking 'offering.' . . ." Over a month later, Christine was still in the East, and Bill's expressions of longed-for love increased. "I'd do everything that love and passion could suggest," he told her. "The different sweet things that you said made me almost tremble with pleasure," he wrote. Anticipating her return, he suggested: "We could get partly undressed—so that we had only such clothes as would be delicious to hug & squeeze in & then you could sit in my lap & we'd kiss & hug & squeeze & cuddle each other until we couldn't stand it any longer. . . ." Then, he wrote, "We'd take off all our clothes, jump into bed and get just as closely wound up as we could and then lie there in absolute harmony & bliss." From her family's summer home in Cohasset, Christine wrote to Bill: "I cannot tell you how much I am looking to our first night together." She added that "when I get thinking of the delights in store I can hardly wait for the time to come." Yet she revealed what Bill already knew that there was a "terrible wrench leaving all the family again. . . . I wish I could have my husband and my family too."

The erotic Bill and the amorous Christine felt comfortable in expressing their sensual pleasures—something that was almost certainly less expressed in written form than experienced physically in the early twentieth century as the Victorian Era came to an end. That both Christine and Bill displayed little of their passion in public, but obviously displayed it in private, is similar to what Karen Lystra found in her study of Victorian love. Lystra in her *Searching the Heart* has indicated that "Victorian men were expected to hide their emotions in public and to loosen their expressive controls in private, communicating their hidden selves to the women they loved." As Lystra has stated: "Culturally speaking, head and heart were split within the masculine role." Reid conformed to this dual role. For instance, in his 440-page diary of the 1905 year of coaching at Harvard and meant for the use of future coaches, he noted "Mrs. Reid" only a few times, and never with any emotion or hint of passion. The closest Bill came to even suggesting that he ever stayed with Christine overnight was on his 27th birthday, when he added in his diary that "I went to Brookline with Mrs. Reid, had something of a birthday party at the Lincoln's and spent the night there." Both Bill's and Christine's personal letters, however, before and after 1905, were filled with explicit details of their love of the other. Lystra's study confirmed what other historians, such as Peter Gay, Ellen Rothman,

INTRODUCTION

and Carl Degler, have found that middle and upper class Victorians did not have a repressed sexuality. "Victorians did not denigrate sex," Lystra has stated, "they guarded it." What Lystra has suggested is that there may have been a Victorian public censorship or repression of physical love, but there was a strong private sexual expression of the educated and literate classes. She has noted:

> Forbidding sexual expression in public helped to create and also to explain a veritable explosion of private sexual expression whose pleasure was partially enhanced by the thought that speaking of sex was forbidden

But it was written, and it is here that we see the difference between public prudery and a private and candid correspondence. The correspondence between Bill and Christine is certainly on the outer edge of explicitly written sexuality. Their letters are more graphic than nearly all personal communications that have been published, and they continued in 1905 and after when Bill took the head coaching position for the second time at Harvard.

Christine had a difficult time adjusting to life in the West, especially with the intrusions of Bill's father and mother and a social life that was limited. She was much more comfortable living in the East with friends and family close by. Beginning in 1905, she had just that opportunity for two years. After the Yale football team shut out Harvard for the third straight year, Bill was invited by the Harvard captain to coach once more. He felt ready for the challenge, if the football situation was acceptable. Christine was delighted with the thought of living again in the East. By December 1904, they had their second child, Edith, just as Bill traveled to Boston to check out whether the condition of the football program was promising enough to return as head coach. To leave Christine, Patrick, and their newborn to check out the possibilities nearly tore him apart. "Leaving you was the about the hardest thing I've ever done," he wrote to Christine. "I feel like a deserter." Yet, he returned to Christine in about three weeks, agreeing to accept the head coaching position for two years at a yearly salary of $3,500 and an equal sum to be raised by the alumni. It was the highest coaching salary in America, and the $7,000 was far more than any full professor at Harvard was paid and nearly as much as President Charles Eliot, the head of Harvard since 1869. It was also considerably more than the $1,200 that he received for being assistant headmaster under his father. Within two months Bill returned to Harvard to begin spring practice and to see if he could keep Harvard athletes eligible in the quest to once again beat Yale. Christine would follow shortly thereafter, but not before a series of passionate letters were exchanged between them. By August 1905, Christine was pregnant with their third child, Christine, born in May 1906.

INTRODUCTION

The pressure of coaching the Harvard team in 1905 and 1906 was as trying to Bill as living in the West had been for Christine the two previous years. Early on, Bill spent extraordinary amounts of time on trying to be a successful football coach. He worked out a football schedule that he hoped would lead to victory over the only truly important institution, Yale; enlisted a number of volunteer coaches to help him; discussed football strategy with such luminary coaches as Glenn "Pop" Warner, Fielding H. Yost, and Amos Alonzo Stagg; developed practice schedules; spoke with alumni groups; recruited prep-school athletes; gained readmission of former Harvard athletes; discussed athletes' grades with professors; and hired tutors to attempt to keep athletes eligible. When the season began, the nervous streak that was in him, heightened to levels many people could not live under. At one point, he wrote that "I simply go around in the morning so nervous that I am unable to apply myself to anything." His loss of weight was noticeable, his lack of sleep was apparent, and his friend even added chemicals to his drinks so that he might get some rest. The two years of coaching, in which his team won all of its games but three, nevertheless convinced Bill that he did not possess the right personality to survive the rigors of Big-Time coaching. At the conclusion of his second season, he left a note for his wife, just before another loss to Yale. "I have never gone through such a trying athletic season before," he wrote, "and I never could have survived it if it weren't for your love. . . . I have been worried so, that I have been entirely unable to get my mind off of the work. . . . Tomorrow night," he emphasized, "I shall be free."

He was free to go West to again see if he could work effectively under his father's rather authoritarian rule over the Belmont School. Christine was again faced with the trial of moving to California and away from her parents, siblings, and Eastern friends. Christine actually stayed behind for two months so that she could be in her sister Agnes' wedding, while Bill returned to the Belmont School. Bill left a note for her just before he boarded the train for the West. At Belmont, "you are to have things as you want them," he wrote, "and if I can't get them, then we'll come East." After reading the note, Christine wrote telling Bill that he was "the best and dearest husband that ever was!" In her next letter, Christine suggested to Bill that their first night together they should take no precautions to prevent a fourth child—"I think we'll really have to take one chance, don't you?" To this, Bill responded: "The absolute freedom which you give me in helping myself to your charms is glorious beyond expression." And Bill looked forward to their reunion and almost immediately taking his "lovely bride to bed, and we'd both taste of the fruits of a perfect union." Christine agreed for she wanted Bill to take care of himself, "for I want you and 'tinker' to be in good shape when I get there. 'Tinker-bell' is feeling 'right pert.'"

No immediate children resulted once Christine re-joined Bill in California, but the tension of a socially elite Easterner confined by in-

INTRODUCTION

laws in a Western boys' school setting would soon reappear. The small irritations of married life were sometime magnified for Christine. In the spring of 1908, she took her three children for a vacation at the Lake Tahoe summer home of Bill's parents. When she got there, she wrote Bill that "we do love each other as much as people can, but we still jar and rub each other the wrong way, don't we?" But within a week she could write: "Oh! Piddie, do hurry up and come!" Christine had a jealous streak in her that played itself out more than a couple times in their marriage. Bill had written that he had given flowers to one of the women at the Belmont School and had stayed up one night talking with a Mrs. Jackson, and indeed swapping filthy stories with her. Christine became so infuriated with Bill that a crisis existed in their marriage for a short time. She finally admitted that "I've gone back to the days of our engagement or before and feel the same old thrills and pangs of jealousy as I used to then." Within two weeks the crisis was over, and Christine looked forward to Bill arriving for her 27th birthday and "our first night together! I have never felt so much like a bride, as I do now."

Living two more years in Belmont, Christine was ready to say goodbye to California and the Belmont School. Bill, Christine, and the three children vacationed with her parents in Cohasset in early summer 1909, and after a month, Bill returned to work at the school while his parents took off for Lake Tahoe. Christine, though, could not get over a statement that her father-in-law had made about Bill before they had left to vacation in the East. He had said, after a provocation, that Bill had been a "hindrance" at the Belmont School. "That," Christine said, "sticks in my crop" and was reason enough to clear out and return to the East. With children aged 6, 5, and 3, Christine was ready to abandon the West but not Bill. Her lengthy stays in the East prompted both Bill and Christine to glorify their sex lives when they would be together again. "I should hate it if we weren't both passionate," she told Bill after he had left Cohasset for three weeks or so, and "I love to give myself up to you so completely, and to feel that you love to have me do so!" Bill was ready to leave Belmont, except for one thing—his loyalty to his parents. "I feel the greatest sympathy for Papa & Mama," he wrote Christine, but it would "blast Papa's last days I am afraid, if this affair ends in my going, . . . it gnaws so at my heart." Staying in the West or leaving for the East was not solved for two years, and Bill told his wife while she remained with her parents: "I do and have appreciated all along your willingness to do what seems to me best in all this dilemma. I love you deeply for it." Christine and the children returned to Belmont for the Fall, but the discussions over moving East continued.

Early in 1910, Christine's father replied to Bill's inquiry about moving to the Boston area. He basically agreed that Christine could not "ever be truly happy in the school work & life at Belmont & especially while rearing her children." The year would became the decisive one as Bill came closer and closer to finally break from his father's school and

INTRODUCTION

move East. Yet, the decision was agonizingly slow. At the end of the summer, Christine had already made up her mind. She went East with her children to again be with her family. This time, however, she would remain there until Bill finally broke his ties to the Belmont School. When she did not return to California that fall, there was agony for both Bill and Christine. Never before were his letters as tormented, trying not to completely break with his parents and nevertheless promising that he would soon come to Christine. How could someone as conservative as Bill turn away from a position that was financially secure for a new job in some business in the East where he would have to start again at the bottom financially? Yet Christine had written that "if you love me don't discuss the question anymore," and Bill replied "I have got to a point where I don't care much what happens." But he did care, and wrote Christine a couple weeks later that he was "heart broken at what I have done and beg your forgiveness." This she did, and by mid-November, Christine sent a telegram to Bill stating that she was fully with him, and anticipated his arrival in the East by year's end. Awaiting him was a entry-level job selling bonds in the firm, William A. Read and Company, a company at which the husband of Christine's sister worked.

Beginning in early 1911, Bill was traveling in New England trying to sell bonds to banks and other financial institutions while living in a Brookline house owned by Christine's aunt. With some of the pathos of Willy Loman in Arthur Miller's play, "Death of a Salesman," Bill attempted to support his family like other Harvard graduates and Christine's friends' husbands were doing. It was difficult for both Bill and Christine, but the wish of Bill's father that Bill might again rejoin him at the Belmont School was not seriously entertained. Life would proceed for Bill and Christine, but generally not with the sexual intensity that had existed for most of the first decade of their married life. A fourth child, Charles Willard, was born in 1914, named after the husband of Bill's sister, Julia. The letters between Bill and Christine would never be the same, but there was evidence of their love for one another. The end of their saga is better told in the letters than recounted here. Christine died before Bill, who lived to be 97 years old and was still living in Brookline well after he concluded a successful career in the financial industry. When he died, some of the letters saved by Bill and Christine were nearly a century old—several were faded and lacked intensity, while numerous others remained bright and passionate well beyond their lifetimes.

Chapter 1

PREP SCHOOL - EARLY HARVARD: "REMEMBER LOVE IS FOR LIFE"

Wm. T. Reid, Sr., Pasadena, CA, to Bill Reid, Jr., Belmont, CA
2 January 1896

This letter is probably the first written advice that Bill Reid's father gave to Bill, age 17, about girls and life in general. It was during Bill's junior year at the Belmont School in California.

I am glad that you found Beatrice pleasant. I shall be glad to know her more. I cannot however help feeling that she is not at all likely to make of herself all that she is capable of becoming—or indeed to half—and she will not probably keep up with you. I shall not be at all surprised if a little later you will find someone, not more attractive as far as face and manners are concerned perhaps but with a truer culture and with higher aspiration. But I am glad to have you know her and I want you to know a number of other girls. And a little later I want you to go abroad and maybe on your way over or after you reach Europe you may meet someone who will prove to be a good deal to you. I hope so at any rate. It will come about some day but as this is a life matter you must go a little slow. That is looking a little ahead isn't it? Well it is wise in so important a matter to look ahead for the matter of a final attachment to some woman is the most serious thing in life & the finest if it is just as it should be. . . .

The highest pleasure consists in interest in the serious occupations of life. . . . I can never be content to think of you a follower. I must think of you as a leader. There must of course be workers in the ranks but there must be captains and adjutants and Colonels & Generals, and I expect you to be one of the generals. . . .

♥♥♥♥♥

Bill Reid, Jr., Belmont, CA, to Julia Reid, Paris, France
2 August 1896

Bill wrote to his mother who was touring Europe with her daughter Julia. He was playing baseball in a tournament with 272 teams from Oregon, California, and Nevada in Sausalito. He stayed with Herbert Martin during the tournament and discussed moral issues and relations with girls.

A Debutante's Passion—A Coach's Erotica

. . . He smokes a great deal but when I told him I did not, he never offered me any afterwards & treated me just the same. Another boy would probably have sneered a little. Then too I always refused punch, wine or anything of the sort at dances & on the first & hardest occasion he went without, himself. He swears too but almost every boy I meet does so that he is no worse than others. We went to a tamale shop one day & got some tamales & he & the rest, two other boys, took some beer. I did not take any but was quite disgusted with him, when he knew how I felt about it. Herbert began singing too & as it was at night I felt worse still. When we got outside one of the boys proposed going somewhere else & get something more. I immediately said, I hope you boys won't think I am inhospitable but I don't agree with you on this last proposition & am going home. Don't let me interfere with your plans. Herbert immediately said don't go home & I said allright I will wait for you on the tennis courts. One of the other boys immediately went with me & said that although his folks did not object to his taking beer he thought that I was right in doing as I had done. He neither swears nor smokes & I like him quite well. . . .

I have made up my mind firmer not to drink. . . .

I told the members of the team that I would not play on Sunday & so I am not playing today. . . .

The Harrison girl, Elsie's cousin who came down one day or rather was going to come down to luncheon, wanted me to stay a while at their house, but I called there one evening and the girl did not speak to me for the whole evening & so when I went away I made up my mind to get out of their way. She talked to some other boys who were there & did not pay any attention either to me or to Herbert Martin & so it was not accidental, as others noticed it too. I am not going to have anything more to do with her. After I had treated her as I had I think just for courtesy she should have tried to entertain me, especially since she knew I was in an entirely strange place. I also found out that she went to a reception at her aunt's and got a little tipsy and slid down the banister in that condition. I know that that is true & so I don't care to keep up her acquaintance. I tell you that although you don't seem to care much for Mabel Donaldsen, she would never do anything like that and has always treated me fairly & squarely & isn't what the boys call "fly." I like her better than before on top of my last experiences.

♥ ♥ ♥ ♥ ♥

Wm. T. Reid, Sr., Riverside, CA, to Bill Reid, Jr., Belmont, CA
25 December 1896

Bill Reid's father, in an extraordinarily long letter, chastised Bill, age 18, for his actions with his girlfriend, Emily Crissy, during his senior year at the preparatory school in Belmont.

PREP SCHOOL - EARLY HARVARD

My dear old boy,
I wish that this might be a happier Christmas for you than it is likely to be but I am glad that it is not to be a kind of an anniversary of a mistake that would throw a shadow over all Christmases to come. And this is not a possibility only but a probability or rather it would have been if you had gone ahead according to impulse. You have, even as it is, run the very serious risk of putting yourself in a most humiliating position. You have run a tremendous risk of having Emily's people say—"Well the fellow who at his age will make love to a child is so wanting in judgment and common sense that he is just the fellow to protect ourselves & our daughter against." Now that is what I should say if I were in their place & I should moreover absolutely forbid my daughter's continuing the acquaintance of a young man who at your age should so lose his head. And to have such a man as Mr. Crissy warranted in saying of a boy of mine that he has too little sense & too little judgment to be a fit acquaintance of his girl is not a very comfortable thing. . . . Love affairs or imaginary love affairs are the most common sources of fatal mistakes. . . .

I tell you I do not relish the idea of having the whole school saying, "Well Billy Reid, the adjutant, the great foot-ball captain—as we thought—the base-ball captain, the fellow who took nine hours for Harvard without flinching—the leader of the school—he gets down to a race with Sidney & Sacks—Sacks of all others—for a girl who has rather advertised the fact that she thought more at least of Sidney than of him. . . . If you were twenty-one, your letter to Emily would be ground enough for a suit for breach of promise if it were not followed by marriage. . . . Well, let this little turmoil of yours move you to a little thoughtfulness. Let things rest. No good can come of haste & infinite harm may. If the matter won't stand delay it is because there is no basis & if there is basis delay will not spoil it. It is all one sided now & certainly a boy of mine is not going to go about pleading. He must be sought after while he seeks, but he must not seek until he knows what he wants as you do not. . . . Face this pitiful little flame, get. . . the extinguishers & hurry it out.
               Papa
               ♥♥♥♥♥

Julia Reid, Riverside, CA, to Bill Reid, Jr., Belmont, CA
                                            ca. 28 December 1896

Bill's mother had a few words to say about Emily Crissy also.

. . . What you told Papa last summer about feeling that you would not dare become much interested in a girl without first getting his opinion was a very sound position. . . .

Emily. . . is not yet old enough to begin to think about boys & it is unfortunate for her that she came to Belmont & got such ideas put into her head. . . . Fortunately you are not of age & you have not promised anything, but you came perilously near it. . . . In California more than any other state people get fooled in their marriages. . . . It is because there are so many people in California of some questionable kind of past. . . .

♥ ♥ ♥ ♥ ♥

William T. Reid, Sr., Los Angeles, CA, to Bill Reid, Jr., Belmont, CA
4 January 1897

Bill's father continued to chide Bill for his actions with Emily and being lax in his ways.

. . . It is simply out of the question for anyone to hope to make a great success if he does not form careful & prompt business habits. . . . And now a word about Emily. I am a little afraid lest I may have left a wrong impression with you regarding my opinion of her. I like her & she is a likeable girl & I think a good girl and likely to make someone a good wife. All that I wanted to convey to you was that she is not likely to be the kind of wife that you will want & even if it should prove that she is, you don't know it now & you can't. She may be just as good as you are & may be better, but it isn't goodness alone but fitness, companionship & the capability of growth that you need. I don't care how sweet Emily is, the question is whether she is going to grow with your growth & develop with your development. If she doesn't her sweetness will appear to you to fade out & it will fade out because of want of basis. Now let me again say that I don't know that this will be the case & let me again say that you can't now know that it won't be & unless your affection will stand the trial of waiting for two or three years it won't stand the trial of wear for twenty & maybe fifty years, & that is to be the test. We went a few evenings ago to hear the University Glee Club & I then thought of you, & I was more than ever slightly impressed with the idea that you must not make up your mind now. The chances are so many that you will change & then if you did, think what a wrong you would have done to the dear little girl whose affections you had engaged only to find out too late that you were mistaken—And so too I may have left a wrong impression of my estimation of Emily's feelings for Gerald or Sidney, I think it very probable that she thinks much more of you than of either of them. I should feel mortified if she did not, but for a time there is no doubt that she thought more of Jones at any rate than of you. . . .

♥ ♥ ♥ ♥ ♥

Wm. T. Reid, Sr., Los Angeles, CA, to Bill Reid, Jr., Belmont, CA
8 January 1897

Bill's father had seen several girls in Los Angeles that he would have liked Bill to have met, and he wrote thinking of Emily Crissy and Bill's attachment to her.

PREP SCHOOL - EARLY HARVARD

. . . You are too young to do more than look around & begin to ask what your standards are. You don't know your own mind. You may indeed know your present mind but you cannot know your judgment—for your judgment is yet unformed. It is a good thing though for you to begin to accumulate material for a judgment. And so I do not know that I am sorry for your episode with Emily—provided she does not take the matter to heart, as I think she will not because she is so young & because she like you does not know her mind. She may know her present mind but what she thinks to-day she may not think six months from now. And you must remember that the question you are debating deals with all time. It is equivalent to a life & death question. If she were going to Wellesley or to Smith or to Radcliffe at Cambridge I should think it possible that she would keep pace with you, but I fear that without some such advantage she will not. It is true that the heart is greater than the intellect & it should be. . . . It is a touching thing to think of a sweet girl of fine disposition & fine instincts but with limited opportunities & limited abilities giving or wishing to give her affections to a young man of ability who has had or is going to have every opportunity & to whom therefore she can only be a companion in part. . . .

♥♥♥♥♥

Julia Reid, Belmont, CA, to Bill Reid, Jr., Harvard University
15 September 1897

Bill had graduated from the Belmont School and left to attend Harvard University. His mother, who inundated Bill with critical advice as a general rule, wanted Bill to be less sulky as he began his freshman year.

. . . Remember the feet, the cheeks, the lips, the eyes, cultivate a happy look or at least avoid falling into the habit of looking sulky when embarrassed. . . .

♥♥♥♥♥

Wm. T. Reid, Sr., Belmont, CA, to Bill Reid, Jr., Harvard University
17 September 1897

As Bill began his journey through Harvard, his father cautioned him about corresponding with girls.

. . . I am going to venture upon two cautions in this letter. First go slow about your correspondence. You must never lose sight of the fact that a girl's opportunities are pitifully limited and that it means a vast deal to her to correspond with a fine young fellow, and try as she may she cannot help raising the question whether there may not come out of it all the deepest kind of interest—love and engagement. And so you

A Debutante's Passion—A Coach's Erotica

are in the advantageous but dangerous position of being probably able to interest almost any girl that you would care to interest—dangerous because you may interest her more than you wish and so give her great sorrow and possibly yourself great trouble. So you will be wise and considerate, as well if you write, with caution and infrequently, at any rate for a time. And the temptation is going to be strong during your early college course. You are going to feel a little lonely, and in absence all the questionable qualities of people disappear and all the good ones come to the front and so one is in the greatest danger of idealizing those left behind wholly beyond their deserts. You will find yourself wondering I have no doubt whether Daisy for example or Elana is not just the finest girl living & the more you think of it the more will her attractive qualities come out until you will be in great danger of thinking that you are in love—and in the still greater danger of saying so—to find later may be that you are mistaken. Remember always that love is for life and is the most important thing in life. It means your own happiness & the happiness of the one you love—or the reverse—and probably means & I hope that it does—new lives for which you are responsible—for their morals their physical & mental welfare—Or to put it in a still better way, it means immortal beings for whom you will be responsible. So go slow & don't let impulse or sentiment get the better of you. And when the right girl comes along then I shall be very nearly as happy over it as you. . . .

♥♥♥♥♥

Julia Reid, Belmont, CA, to Bill Reid, Jr., Harvard University
17 September 1897

On the same day of the letter from Bill's father, Bill's mother gave Bill advice on friends, social position, and marriage.

. . . In selecting your friends look at worth and congeniality, ignoring wealth & position, unless they are accompanied by the other qualities. I can feel only contempt for a man who courts the friendship of wealth & position & neglects friends of worth who have not these. Papa has felt this quite keenly many times in his life. He felt no pleasure in being sought when he was president of Berkeley by people who had known him at the high school & never had paid him any attention. He believes in judging people by their character though he is not unaware of the advantages of birth & position. In thinking of marriage he feels the importance of antecedents, but even then personal worth if coupled with integrity & purity of life in one's parents & grandparents is all that one should demand. This is what I found in Papa & is what Julia [their daughter] has found in Charlie. Nothing can take the place of that kind of family in looking for a husband or wife. In friends, personal worth is sufficient, however desirable other things may be. . . .

♥♥♥♥♥

PREP SCHOOL - EARLY HARVARD

Wm. T. Reid, Sr., Belmont, CA, to Bill Reid, Jr., Harvard University
23 September 1897

Bill Reid's father admitted that he wanted to live his life again at Harvard, this time through his son.

. . . Your college life will probably be largely determined by what you do this year, and so I want you to throw off as many of the hindrances as you can at the beginning of the race and give the best that there is in you a fair field. Do you know my dear fellow, I am going, in you, to live my college life over again and through your enjoyment to enjoy anew my young life. It is hardly necessary I think for me to add that I shall be intensely interested in everything that interests you & that I wish for you every good thing. . . .

♥♥♥♥♥

Wm. T. Reid, Sr., Belmont, CA, to Bill Reid, Jr., Harvard University
26 September 1897

Bill Reid's father cautioned Bill about Daisy Cartwright, a Belmont girlfriend. The racist eugenics movement of the turn-of-the-century may have influenced his opposition to Daisy, but it was also likely that the elder Reid wanted Bill to meet an elite Boston girl.

. . . Miss Hamlin. . . got off on Daisy C. and the result was some information that is interesting and rather painful and I must tell you about it. It proves that Daisy's mother was a half-breed Hawaiian island girl with whom Daisy's father eloped. . . . This lady engaged a governess for the children and Daisy's father fell in love with her and made her his mistress doing the outrageous thing of building a room to their house and keeping the girl there to use her. This of course outraged the wife & she left him. . . . Unfortunately Daisy is his daughter and about one quarter Hawaiian. . . . Miss Hamlin says that she is wanting in stability and gives no promise of making a womanly woman. You don't know & could not know how dangerous the Hawaiian strain of blood is. It is simply a piece of good fortune if any one with much of that blood is his veins has any clear idea of uprightness of life. . . . I mean just this. She may have inherited from both her father and her mother a strong passionate nature, ill balanced or not balanced at all with a high moral sense and so she may be in great danger of marrying some one and then taking up with some other dashing fellow without principle and so wreck her home and the home of some one else. At any rate the danger is great it seems to me. . . . I am running the risk of having you think that I am interesting myself too deeply in your private affairs but my dear old fellow I am of the opinion that you can choose almost any girl that you wish and I want you to choose

A Debutante's Passion—A Coach's Erotica

deliberately and wisely and to put proper restraints upon your youthful fancies—remembering that there is nothing in life now more important than the choice the girl who is to share your life with you. . . .

♥♥♥♥♥

Wm. T. Reid, Sr., Belmont, CA, to Bill Reid, Jr., Harvard University
27 September 1897

Bill's father was happy that Bill went to see the Willards and begin his entry into the Boston society, something that Reid, Sr., promoted throughout Bill's tenure at Harvard.

. . . I am delighted more than I can well tell you at your reception by Mr. & Mrs. Willard & I am glad that you accepted their hospitality. Mrs. Willard is a daughter of Mr. Fairbanks—the manufacturer of Fairbanks's scale—a man of wealth and I believe of culture and influence—just the kind of people that I shall be glad to have you know. I am more surprised at your reception because Mr. Willard is thought to be very cold & reserved and so difficult of approach & it of course pleases me to have him open his house and his heart to you. I am told that Agnes, his wife, is a charmingly hospitable woman, and so I congratulate you upon your first introduction to a Boston home. Later I think that I may give you a letter to Dr. Shattuck. I should like very much to have you find an opening into some Boston society, but that will come later and there is no hurry about it. . . . I should like to have you go to Brookline and Jamaica Plain just to see the color of the maple trees. I should also like to have you see Brookline because we lived there for a couple of years & think it a beautiful place. We lived on Cypress Place, not very far from the station. . . .

♥♥♥♥♥

Wm. T. Reid, Sr., Belmont, CA, to Bill Reid, Jr., Harvard University
16 October 1897

A steady stream of advice came from Bill's father on becoming established into the Harvard social system during his important freshman year. The school newspaper and the proper eating club were two avenues to social success. Social success had eluded the elder Reid when he attended Harvard shortly after the Civil War.

. . . Make the best possible use of your athletic abilities in establishing you in the best social life at college. . . .

I wish you could get upon the Crimson. If you make full-back on your class team and do your work well you are very likely indeed to be able to make that the opening wedge to the societies you wish & so I shall not care for the varsity foot-ball or the crew if you can get on the

Crimson. In other words use all these things as a means to a greater end and do not let them be ends in themselves. . . .

If you make Freshman full-back and make a name you will have a chance for Varsity Capt. possibly, but don't set out for it. Get on the Crimson if you can. When do they begin to elect Freshmen to The Dickey? It is rather too bad that so much may depend on foot-ball ability. Oh well, one must simply learn to use whatever he finds available—& if foot-ball then foot-ball must be used. But it will be true, old fellow, if you make your team, get in with a fine club table and get a start in the societies. I tell you, you do not, I think, appreciate the start you are getting. . . .

♥♥♥♥♥

Wm. T. Reid, Sr., Belmont, CA, to Bill Reid, Jr., Harvard University
26 October 1897

Charlie Bull, a member of the Harvard varsity crew from California, had advised Bill's father on what he should tell Bill to advance his social status at Harvard, especially getting into a particular club, The Dickey. He also stressed the need to get into the best Boston society. Bill's father had his own social status and financial concerns, including a financially troubled ranch that he owned, and the desire to build a vacation house at Lake Tahoe. This summer home would become an important part of Bill's life and that of his future wife.

. . . I suppose that no one would ever question your accepting The Dickey. I would ask Bull. . . . Your success in foot-ball is very likely to get you into The Dickey in the first twenty, although you mustn't calculate on that. If you continue to be successful & get with a first class eating table you are all right. Indeed I think that you will be all right now if you can get at the right kind of a table. And so you see my reason now for wishing you to get settled with good fellows. . . . Bull's advice to go upon the Varsity base ball rather upon the Freshman crew is also good. . . .

It is perhaps just as well that you don't know just how hard it is to get through some of the Boston shell. When you once get inside it is delightful. And you will I feel sure make your way. . . .

You will I am sure join me in rejoicing because the ranch trouble is probably well settled and that too without my losing control of it. . . . Such dread had I of losing the ranch. . . . I am now thinking of building at Tahoe next summer. I hope to be able to do so. . . .

♥♥♥♥♥

Charles C. Bull, Harvard University, to Wm. T. Reid, Sr., Belmont, CA
27 October 1897

Charlie Bull, the Harvard crew star, gave a clue into young Bill Reid's personality, something that would cause him some grief in his future marriage and throughout his life.

A Debutante's Passion—A Coach's Erotica

. . . I have several talks with Billy giving him as good advice as I am able. His main fault now is in expressing his opinions too fully. One can't help admire this trait in any man, but when one is offending others and making enemies, it had better be held in check. You should write him and tell him to keep as mute as a clam. He is playing a very good game at full-back. . . .

♥ ♥ ♥ ♥ ♥

Wm. T. Reid, Sr., Belmont, CA, to Bill Reid, Jr., Harvard University
28 October 1897

Bill had just lost the freshman football captaincy to John Hallowell, a social elite from Massachusetts.

. . . I wish that you had congratulated Hallowell on his captaincy. You can't afford anything of the kind. It was a great compliment for you to be thought of for the place & to have so many votes. You can bide your time. I shall not be surprised if you ultimately come out capt. of something—provided you go along doing fine work and doing it with modesty. . . . Say as little about yourself as you can, as much in praise of others as you can. Continue your vigorous and dashing work and above all carry your praise with modesty. . . .

♥ ♥ ♥ ♥ ♥

Wm. T. Reid, Sr., Belmont, CA, to Bill Reid, Jr., Harvard University
7 November 1897

Bill's father cautioned Bill about athletics being an end rather than a means to a social end.

. . . Remember that your athletic abilities are to serve but two purposes—one to open up to you desirable college connections. The other to give you pleasure in the exercise of your physical powers. The moment you go beyond this and begin to think of athletics as an end in themselves, you begin to verge dangerously near the line of the sport of whom there is no more contemptible being in the world. . . .

♥ ♥ ♥ ♥ ♥

Wm. T. Reid, Sr., Belmont, CA, to Bill Reid, Jr., Harvard University
ca. 11 November 1897

Bill's father was not one to endear himself to others, and this included his son, who neglected his father by not writing as regularly as his father desired.

. . . I am disappointed. . . that your affections should not cause you to write, but in absence of that your sense of the proprieties of life should

PREP SCHOOL - EARLY HARVARD

have come to your relief. . . . Anything that loosens the obligations of life is bad but anything that crowds out the generous impulses—the impulses of the heart—the calls of affection—is infinitely worse. Nothing in your career could so disappoint me as what is called the Harvard indifference. It should be called Harvard snobbishness & is utterly contemptible. But I can hardly believe that you have so little bottom in you as to be capable of that development. . . .

Lovingly
Papa.
♥ ♥ ♥ ♥ ♥

Julia Reid, Belmont, CA, to Bill Reid, Jr., Harvard University
ca. 24 November 1897

As a warning to Bill, his mother wrote of her husband's sexual temptations when he was a young man in the Civil War.

. . . When Papa was only eighteen years old he was in the army as a volunteer & while at Alexandria near Washington he was on the street one day and saw a fellow from some other company speak to a young Negro girl & attempt to be familiar with her. Papa's blood boiled & he told him to let her alone or he would report him to the officers of his company. The fellow replied that he was not in his company (of which Papa was Sergeant) & that it was none of his business. Papa said he would make it his business then, and finally the fellow stopped annoying her by his attention.

That case was as contemptible as the case of Tess & Alex—and I don't wonder the ploy strengthened your determination not to go wrong, but temptations come often in a guise not so dastardly & outrageous as that that met Alex—or rather as that that he cultivated & welcomed. When Papa was only eighteen. . . he took a car load of cattle to New York. At Buffalo where not a soul knew him & where he had to wait some hours, while walking around the city a girl accosted him & invited him to her room. You see here the conditions were reversed. She was the tempter and he the unfallen & unspotted victim, but he did not fall a victim—though but for his firm determination never to yield how easily he might have done so.

Another time a young woman (older than he) said to him on the streets of S[an] F[rancisco] in passing him. I shall be in my room. . . alone at 3 this afternoon. It was in a respectable part of Van Ness Avenue. . . .

♥ ♥ ♥ ♥ ♥

Wm. T. Reid, Sr., Belmont, CA, to Bill Reid, Jr., Harvard University
27 November 1897

Bill's father wrote a long letter about Bill's athletic success that could lead, if Bill would take his advice, to social prominence and leadership at Harvard.

A Debutante's Passion—A Coach's Erotica

. . . I have read many accounts of your team's work besides those you sent me & I gather from rather careful sifting of the evidence that you are rather the best man on the team. . . .

. . . I had hoped that you would write more regarding your social life than about foot-ball. I shall enjoy immensely hearing of your friends & of the evenings you spend with them or the talks you have with them. And I shall also enjoy very much having you write about your visits here and there. These things are vastly more interesting to me than all your foot-ball success, but your foot-ball success makes all the rest possible. And now I am going to add a reason that will probably appeal to you more than anything. I have said, and you will at once recognize that what I say must be confidential. The door to the desirable societies is probably open to you, but if you do not cultivate a little the social side of college life, the door may gradually close. . . .

♥♥♥♥♥

Wm. T. Reid, Sr., Belmont, CA, to Bill Reid, Jr., Harvard University
30 November 1897

The dean of Harvard College, L. B. R.. Briggs, had just written to Bill's father about the poor grades that Bill had received in most of his classes thus far. The elder Reid responded to his son.

. . . I did not show it to Mamma because it would mortify and worry her, and it will mortify me if a like record is again returned. . . . Now get down to work just as you have been getting down to foot-ball. . . I think that you ought to know that I doubt if I should be willing to have you return to college if you were dropped. The mortification would be too great for me, but on the other hand it would be almost unbearable for you to have to return home—reputed unable to keep up with your class. . . . I am much afraid that you were not put on probation out of consideration for me. . . .

♥♥♥♥♥

Wm. T. Reid, Sr., Belmont, CA, to Bill Reid, Jr., Harvard University
1 December 1897

Bill was again offered some advice about his girl friend from the Belmont area, Daisy Cartwright. Later, Daisy would send Bill a letter of congratulations in July 1902, when he married debutante Christine Lincoln, a beautiful girl, well made and full of passion!

. . . I was delighted also with your invitation to Mrs. Gray's and with your having met some Radcliffe girls there. . . . You may be sure that [Miss Jackson] and Miss Lorrie are from nice families. You know enough I am sure to keep your eyes wide open as to the courtesies of the best society, and I am sure that you will readily add to your already good basis of good breeding and courtesy some of the graces of cultured Eastern society....

It is not always easy to keep the distinction between preaching and counseling clear, but it is my purpose to counsel and suggest rather than preach....

I feel a little uncomfortable about Daisy. Poor girl I dislike to think of standing in her way, but then I cannot let you take any risks regarding what may be the most important thing in your life. I feel quite certain that you will be level-headed & do the right thing by yourself—for that will be the right thing by her also. You are soon to be in a position to make comparisons and I feel certain that your better judgment will assert itself—although you may have a most uncomfortable struggle if you fall in with a beautiful, well made girl full of impulsiveness and passion—the finest kind of a girl, if sensible and well balanced but the worst kind if not....

♥♥♥♥♥

Wm. T. Reid, Sr., Belmont, CA, to Bill Reid, Jr., Harvard University
2 December 1897

Harvard and women of the East were compared by Bill's father to Stanford and California and Western women.

... Oh but the Harvard life is fine isn't it? How infinitely finer than Stanford or the University of Cal. Aside from the larger, broader and more generous life, there is that indescribable thing as Mrs. Fairchild says "tone" that no other college seems to have. There is a style and an air about Harvard men that other college men haven't. It is conspicuously absent from Yale men....

... [There] is likely to be the source of some disappointment that you are likely to feel with your young lady friends of Boston. Some of them at any rate are likely to be so hedged in by conventionalities and formalities as to conceal all heart, and this heartiness and this absence of conventionality is one of the charms of the Western girls. And it is one of the strange things in life that the very things that are loveliest are often most kept in the background. Still there is a reason for it. A girl is not safe to be impulsive and open and cordial—at least until she knows the young man through and through. And so the conventionalities of society are a necessary protection to young girls against the coarse and vulgar fellows....

Don't for a moment think that I am anxious to have you get into Boston society and to become acquainted with certain Boston families because they belong to Boston exclusive society. You will find among some of these best families some insufferable snobs, but on the other hand these fine families are based on merit & so entrance to these circles means entrance to the society of people who at least have had opportunities to know what is best. They have had the advantage that cultured wealth should bring, and all that you have to do is distinguish between the wheat and the chaff. Nothing would be more unfortunate than your admission to such circles if it should make anything of a snob of you. . . .

Get into the habit of asking always—what will she do for the home, will it be restful for the fellow who gets her to go home from his hard day's work, will she think more about her own comfort or about the comfort of her family. . . .

♥♥♥♥♥

Wm. T. Reid, Sr., Belmont, CA, to Bill Reid, Jr., Harvard University
4 December 1897

Fatherly advice was never lacking from William Reid, Sr., as he discussed a reception that he and his wife had recently attended, Harvard social life, leadership, and concluded on sexual morality.

. . . I am tremendously taken with that little niece of Dr. Willey—Miss Bullard—she seems to me one of the prettiest girls I ever saw, but Mamma doesn't like her at all because she says that she is so conscious and consequently so affected. Well that ruins any one of course. How unfortunate it is that a girl can't be pretty, or a boy a star foot-ball player, without running great risk of losing the charm of unaffectedness, genuineness, heartiness, enthusiasm. . . .

And now there is just one other thing that I have already spoken about and that I want to speak about again for that does give me concern and always will give me concern and it will cost you again & again the most serious struggle of your life, and it is no use to mince matters in talking about it. You are not going to make a fool of yourself in matters of dress, you are not going to feel the necessity of reckless & inconsiderate expenditures, you are not going to injure yourself by smoking, and you are not going to drink at all—but you are going to have all the moral force of your life, all of your intellectual convictions—everything that is best in you tested to the utmost by your sexual passions. I know what I am talking about. The fight will be a severe one and you will have to make it again and again, but it will be a great satisfaction to you to win. And it will be the harder because you will be running across respectable fellows every now and then—good fellows in every other way who have simply given up the fight and have come to think that indulgence is legitimate. Now the physical danger is frightful and unfortunately it is handed down to one's children—if indeed it does not send one diseased & rotting to his grave. But the moral loss is worse than the physical danger. Now your fine physique is at the bottom of it all and your affections contribute their share. And indeed the first characters I think find this temptation most severely, for the stronger it is the more it means physical vigor & life's best affections. And so old fellow buckle on your armor and wear it always. Say beforehand, and keep saying it all the time, so that you may never be taken by surprise and be swept from your feet by some whirlwind of passion—"I'll never get dangerously near the whirlpool of wine and women."

If you do, you will probably be drawn in. If you have ever seen the great whirlpool just below Niagara Falls you will understand the strength of the illustration. And now I will close by saying that I do not think the less of you for the temptations you are going to have to resist or rather the inclinations, and that I do not greatly fear your yielding, but I do know that you will need all the bracing that you can give, and all that I can add, and all that your ideal of the home that you are some day to make for yourself and some beautiful fine girl can bring—and now my boy all this with patience. The reasonableness of the caution will more and more appear to you, and God bless you in all your struggles and make you not only a self conqueror but a leader, strong and pure.

♥♥♥♥♥

Wm. T. Reid, Sr., Belmont, CA, to Bill Reid, Jr., Harvard University
10 December 1897

Bill Reid often confided in his father, though rarely in his mother. Here William, Sr., thought Bill's answer to an Eastern girl about the image of the West was appropriate.

. . . I very much enjoyed your ready reply to the young lady that you had left your revolver and bowie knife at home. . . .

♥♥♥♥♥

Wm. T. Reid, Sr., Belmont, CA, to Bill Reid, Jr., Harvard University
14 December 1897

Comparisons between the East and the West were always important to Bill and his father, whether it was about perceptions, women, or livability.

. . . Your remark about the greater beauty of California girls exactly agreed with my feelings when we first came to California. The California women seemed to me fresher looking, more attractive in feature, plumper in form and heartier in manner, but wanting sometimes in refinement or delicacy. But I must confess that I would choose a fresh, hearty impulsive girl a little wanting in the conventionalities of life over the girl who had smothered all of her heartiness, if indeed she ever had any, under conventionalities or reserve. . . .

I shall be very much interested in your final impressions of the girls you meet. You will have the advantage of me because you will in your first year—indeed you now know more girls than I did during my entire college course. . . .

♥♥♥♥♥

A Debutante's Passion—A Coach's Erotica

Wm. T. Reid, Sr., Belmont, CA, to Bill Reid, Jr., Harvard University
15 December 1897

Bill Reid's father wrote him about women he would meet at Harvard and in the Boston area, especially those of a lower class.

. . . I need not tell you to select your intimates with the utmost care. The right kind of companions will help you & you will help them & you will all get not only a finer but a keener enjoyment out of life than is possible for those fellows to get who are indulging their inclinations and their passions. I am a little surprised that you do not find a little more culture among the girls. I did not expect you to find them free from affectation. Indeed I thought that their affectation would probably disgust you. And I expected that they would take up certain current phrases which while slangy are yet expressive and sometimes forcible. Ah well it only shows how intensely human we all are. Of course the culture & the exactness of the Boston girl is drawn out to caricature in all the references to them in print and I thought it probable that you would find some ground for it possibly. You see I have had little chance to judge from personal observation for I knew very few girls. I am pleased, much pleased to have you find that your standard is rather higher than the standards you are meeting. As far as the standard of boys is concerned I am not surprised, only I am surprised at the proportions you mention.

My warnings and cautions before you went to college and my letter a week ago show how fully alive I was to the looseness of life you would find among young fellows who think that they are, and who are believed to be good, respectable and even clean fellows. These low theatres are abominations. There is not a redeeming feature in them. They exist because of their catering to low tastes and the more one goes to them the crasser his tastes become. And they are the shortest roads that are not direct to the bawdy house—for their chief attraction is the suggestiveness in dress and action of the girls who appear on the stage and the knowledge among all the young fellows that most of the girls are for sale simply or mainly because the poor things see no hope of a home and a family & yet have a craving for the affections of life that they cannot resist when a young fellow—a young college fellow—especially shows them attention. But the whole thing is bad thoroughly bad, and it is not made respectable by the fact that fellows, otherwise good, lose their balance and indulge.

Oh you will find what an enormous deal of chaff there is in the world in proportion to the wheat & that is why the wheat is at such a premium. And as I said in a letter or two ago, this my dear fellow is going to be where your battles are to be fought & so I like to see your evident surprise & disappointment at what you see. But the fact of the awareness of loose living & the rarity of fine leaders only makes it the more imperative that you should be a leader and set the upward pace just as some are setting the downward. . . .

♥ ♥ ♥ ♥ ♥

PREP SCHOOL - EARLY HARVARD

Wm. T. Reid, Sr., Pasadena, CA, to Bill Reid, Jr., Harvard University
18 December 1897

William Reid, Sr., likely an 1860's social outcast at Harvard, because of his Jacksonville, Illinois heritage, constantly urged his son to become part of Boston society. Only a couple months before, Reid, Sr., urged his son to "make the best possible use of your athletic abilities in establishing you in the best social life at college" and to create an "opening wedge to the society...." However as Bill had written his father that a large number of Harvard students frequented whore houses, he responded after discussing Bill's concerns with a friend.

... I am getting more pleasure out of your college life than I got out of my own and that I am enjoying it better than anything else just now....

[I told him] of your estimate of the proportion of fellows who visited houses of ill repute and he at once said, "I think Will is all wrong. I don't believe that there is anything like the proportion that he states. But whatever the facts may be I certainly hope that he won't under any consideration express such an opinion to others and especially that he will never say anything that will cast suspicion on any one" and he went on to say that there was great danger of one's doing another gross injustice and of himself becoming suspicious and cynical. Also that nothing could be more dangerous to friendships or the possibility of friendships as to have fellows afraid of another fellows remarks. . . .

♥♥♥♥♥

Julia Reid, San Francisco, CA, to Bill Reid, Jr., New York, NY
26 December 1897

Bill's mother criticized Bill in nearly every letter she wrote while regularly sending moral-religious sayings. Even the following back-handed compliment would have driven most any college freshman into near despair. One must wonder what he might have thought about her as a future wife's mother-in-law.

... Your letters are a great pleasure & comfort Billy boy dear. I can swallow down the bad spelling, bad grammar, bad writing almost without knowing it for the enjoyment of the subjects & sentiments of the letters. . . .

♥♥♥♥♥

Wm. T. Reid, Sr., Los Angeles, CA, to Bill Reid, Jr., Harvard University
31 December 1897

Reminders of the importance of society and society girls were offered constantly during Bill's freshman year at Harvard.

A Debutante's Passion—A Coach's Erotica

. . . Every one likes attention and girls are especially fond of it—and, if I may say so without the risk of an infusion of vanity, they are especially gratified to receive attentions from a full-back who is known more or less all over New England and who is known to be a fine specimen of —physical manhood— and I hope an erect broad square shouldered specimen, and who is believed to be a good specimen of moral manhood. It is I say a compliment to a girl to receive attentions from such a fellow. At any rate she thinks so [referring to a Miss Fairchild]. Besides you owed it to her after the attentions you have received at her house to show her attentions. . . .

♥♥♥♥♥

Julia Reid, Belmont, CA, to Bill Reid, Jr., Harvard University
7 January 1898

Bill's mother may have known better than others about the negative effect Bill's nervous system might have on his latter life. Her entire letter follows.

Oh Billy boy—such fun & enjoyment over your letters! Send them right along.
    Your nose troubles me. It may be a very serious thing. And the nervous tension you are under troubles me.
    I wish you could get away from the pressure of Varsity work. I fear, I fear, the nervous effects in after years.
    God bless & keep you.   Mamma

♥♥♥♥♥

Wm. T. Reid, Sr., Belmont, CA, to Bill Reid, Jr., Harvard University
11 January 1898

Bill Reid's father was never as concerned about Bill's academic education as he was about his son's marriage options.

. . . A word about your girl friends. I can't blame you for finding it hard to keep your head when you meet a bright eyed, bright minded & attractive faced girl. It is very unsettling but you must always exercise the most thoughtful judgment when alone before thinking seriously of love. Miss Sefton for example is a bright & an attractive girl & is going to inherit considerable property but her father is consumptive & has to live in San Diego to live at all or in some such climate. They are a most devoted family but there is great danger that the girl's children will inherit consumption.
    It is probable that even such serious objection will not stand in your way if you get taken off your feet by some affectionate, beautiful, graceful girl, but guard with all your might against such a danger, for I want you to give to the world such another boy as Mamma & I gave. And I must tell you that I was kept from thinking seriously of a beautiful girl who was very fond of me because of consumption in the family. She died of consumption some ten years ago and there is constant anxiety regarding one or two of her children.

PREP SCHOOL - EARLY HARVARD

There can be no objection to a girl of wealth & social advantages but a society girl is likely to be dangerous, unless she is a girl of sound sense and has some aspirations and wants a home and a family. The first test is that. The girl who doesn't want a home & a family is not the girl to marry. The affections of life, an interest in the ordinary affairs of life are all important and life and dash & all that are the outside that soon rubs off. The girl who likes little children is almost certain to be safe & the one who doesn't isn't likely to be safe. But your instinct and judgment will guide you, if you don't get swept away by a beautiful face and an attractive manner & a firm form. So guard yourself and exercise all the sober judgment you can & go slow. The girl who won't stand analysis and the test of time, the test of a year's trial won't stand the test of a life, and it is a terribly risky thing to neglect a sober consideration of all the pros and cons, whether a girl has good antecedents, not necessarily wealthy antecedents, but good home, like earnest, faithful parents.

And this is the question that you must in duty not only to her but to yourself raise regarding such a girl as Daisy. She is a girl, I suspect, who has. . . that unaccountable physical attraction which is good as far as it goes but thoroughly bad if that is all because it fades with age. The girl that attracts you because of her fine form and attracts you for reasons of passion is dangerous—unless with it there is nobility of character and a fondness for domestic life. Mabel strikes me as a girl who is likely to be wanting in refinement—not to ornament a home and to be able to meet such people as you are likely to have at your home. Emily I feel sorry for, for several reasons. She has no outlook, no good home surroundings & her tendency to sulks will probably be fatal to her ability to make a helpful companion. This depression that resulted in her attempting her life was a development that is almost certain to manifest itself again later in life and so to fill one with terror. And besides as I once said before, she is not going to have any chance. She cannot prepare herself for the proper companionship of an educated man, and so with many attractive qualities she yet cannot I think enter deep in your thoughts. I do not now recall the other girls that you know—Oh yes, the Robinson girl. Well I should fear her father's influence. But it isn't worthwhile for me to discuss the girls in detail. All that I can do is to put you on your guard. I have no disposition to long to decide for you or to guide you definitely in your decision.

I want however to say one thing more and to add a little personal experience that is very sad & that I want you to avoid. Of course it is confidential. I think that perhaps it would be better for you to destroy this entire sheet. I met a girl over 30 yrs. ago & liked her & she liked me. It proves that she devotedly loved me. I met her in Los Angeles the other day. Her hair is white & her youth is of course all gone. When she met me she said: "I knew that I should again see you before I died & I have so long, so long waited for this." She then told me that she promised that she ought not to talk with me as she wished but that it would be a great gratification to do so. She then said that I had been her ideal all these years. That whatever she did she did with the thought that it would please me, and that she had made her husband unhappy because he failed to meet the standard that I had set for her. She then said that if she could have been my wife she would have had no wish but mine, no thought but to make me happy & that although I had been her great & almost crushing sorrow yet I had been her constant inspiration. It was almost touching & most pitiful. I tell you it used me up. . . .

You owe a most serious duty to every girl with whom you correspond. You are very likely to be much flattered by silly girls because of your athletic abilities but I think that you are not in great danger of failing to see that they admire your strength and physical abilities and would as readily show their favor to another person as to you if he had your athletic ability. But I am not much afraid of your being finally flattered into serious attentions to a silly girl. I am just now concerned to guard you against running any risk of winning the affections of a sensitive, trusting girl such as perhaps Elana, if that is the way to spell her name, or a sensitive high-strung girl like Emily. The one might suffer all her life as has the girl I mentioned and the other might become overbalanced to the extent of going off at a tangent in suicide. And these two types of girls you should be considerate of.

And while I am on the subject I will just add this probably useless word—that the sensitive high strung girl is the one who is most likely to go off in pique in married life and to cause one to live in constant dread. I mention suicide in this connection because of the report in the papers that Emily attempted suicide for a far less serious matter than love & she and Elana seem rather good samples of two very different types both of whom might be very seriously affected by a love affair & show their trouble in very different ways. And so you owe it to the girls to be very considerate and especially in the matter of correspondence. You are not likely to get into a breach of promise suit but that is the way they come, which is another phase of the question. Now I did not intend to be drawn into this subject again soon and would not have been but for the sad interview in Los Angeles. Limit then your correspondence to girls whose correspondence you enjoy for its brightness & strength and open up just as few new ones as you can & open them up, if at all, only so far as to find them out & yourself out & shape them so that they may be dropped without a jar & don't write to a little girl who is likely to lean on you & depend upon you because she has no one else to lean on & depend on. I dare say that Georgia & the Lawrence girl are fine—on the ground that you think so but don't get involved so that you cannot honourably get out—until you are certain that you care to. It is bad enough for a man to love and not have it returned but it is deeper agony for a woman & it is the deepest wickedness for a man to let his vanity cause him to try to win the affections of a trusting girl, and it is doubly bad if the girl is young and without the advantages of a life of cultivating surroundings.

PREP SCHOOL - EARLY HARVARD

But this is quite enough on this subject. It may all be useless but you are a susceptible kind of fellow and so need I think to be put on your guard. It may be awfully nice to have half a dozen girls like you, but it is grossly wrong for you to lead them to love you. Mamma knows all about the Los Angeles affair. Now I wonder if there is danger in my writing you so freely of your not telling me things. . . .

I am not at all afraid of your making a mistake if you go in with your eyes wide open, but I had no one to help me to open my eyes. Write me a little what you think & write on a separate sheet of paper if you want to. . . .

♥ ♥ ♥ ♥ ♥

Julia Reid, Belmont, CA, to Bill Reid, Jr., Harvard University
13 January 1898

Bill's mother preached to Bill in every letter she wrote—about the need to write; on penmanship; on spelling; on being on time; on listening to his parents; on speaking correctly; on loving God; on going to church; on writing thank you notes; on gaining culture; and on attending lectures. This time she agreed with Bill relative to drinking and smoking, but she might just as well have criticized his letter-writing grammar as she once did by noting that one would prefer "keeping the passive voice right through & the series of clauses symmetrical instead of reversing half way through."

. . . I did not think you would touch beer or wine but I did not feel sure about the smoking. I am more glad than I can tell that you have not smoked. . . .

Your pet dissipation old fellow is athletics & the glory you get from them. I see ahead of you a terrific strain in football, . . . the strain in baseball. . . . I fear a nervous collapse. . . !

♥ ♥ ♥ ♥ ♥

Wm. T. Reid, Sr., Belmont, CA, to Bill Reid, Jr., Harvard University
17 January 1898

William Reid, Sr., was concerned about the potential of Bill going to Boston dances with "abandoned girls."

. . . Going to the dances you speak about in Boston is most questionable. If you will inquire you will find out, I think, that they are simply bawdy house dances and that the girls are abandoned girls. The chances are a hundred to one that before the evening is over you will be invited to their rooms. I know just what they are. You see you are likely to be a marked man—especially if you make varsity catcher in your Freshman year and you are bound to be quoted & copied after and it is certain that your movements will be known. Fellows who haven't your judgment will say "There is Reid—one of the best athletes in college and believed to be one of the staunchest fellows too—He goes to dance halls & if he goes it is all right." I don't like to write you fully but when you come home next summer I'll tell you. When you are twenty-one you may safely—possibly safely—look into some of the dark corners of life but I think you had better seek the clean & elevating highways. . . .

♥♥♥♥♥

Wm. T. Reid, Sr., Belmont, CA, to Bill Reid, Jr., Harvard University
26 January 1898

After receiving a very complimentary letter about Bill Reid from Prof. Hurlbut at Harvard, Bill's father decided to caution Bill about one of his faults.

. . . I think that I now have but one further caution to offer. You are in great danger if criticized of sulking as old Achilles did. Well you are a mighty big fellow and so maybe you may think that like Achilles you can afford now and then to sulk. I doubt it. At any rate guard against it & brace up even when things don't go right. Any one can sail a ship when there is a fair and steady wind. The great captain is the man who can carry his vessel through a storm or rally his company in the midst of a panic and carry them to victory. Napoleon once said to his generals "You say the day is lost, but it is now but 3 o'clock and there is time yet to win a victory. Order a charge & I will organize the retreating battalions & bring them to your support"— and he won the day. And this inclination to withdraw into yourself when others are around, is shown in your social life. You sometimes allow another fellow who is not your equal to take a pretty girl away from you simply because he has cheek. I don't want you to have cheek but I do want you to be on hand always and hold your own in the face of the cheeky fellow. . . .

♥♥♥♥♥

Wm. T. Reid, Sr., Belmont, CA, to Bill Reid, Jr., Harvard University
19 February 1898

Bill considered quitting Harvard during his freshman year. He was depressed, and his father tried to reassure him that this would dissipate over time.

Oh it will never, never do for you to allow yourself to get so down in the dumps as you were when you wrote your last letter. . . . I suspect that you have failed to keep up your social duties. . . . I am quite of the opinion that you have had something of a feeling of neglect and want of appreciation. . . . If you like to be appreciated take occasion to show appreciation, if there is a want at Harvard, supply it. . . .

And now let us not discuss Berkeley or Stanford. I should be in probably $500 a year if you were to go to Stanford or Berkeley but it would cause me extreme chagrin for you to give up Harvard, and you will be all over that idea by the time this reaches you, or if not by that time certainly within a month after you begin following my advice. . . .

♥ ♥ ♥ ♥ ♥

Julia Reid, Belmont, CA, to Bill Reid, Jr., Harvard University
24 February 1898

During the end of his first semester at Harvard, Bill wrote a negative letter about life at Harvard, to which his mother suggested the uplifting effect of a cola. If Kola's Phos was like Coke Cola at the time, it would have contained cocaine, a supposed psychological upper.

I hope you have not written anyone else as you did us about your feelings about Harvard. Please go right off & get your bottle of Kola's Phos & take two pellets before each meal & before bedtime. You poor Billy Boy. . . .

♥ ♥ ♥ ♥ ♥

Wm. T. Reid, Sr., Belmont, CA, to Bill Reid, Jr., Harvard University
8 March 1898

Bill had written his father that he was disenchanted with the Harvard baseball team because of favoritism for a position on the team. His dad responded by criticizing Bill's reactions.

. . . [There is a] strong tendency that you have always shown to sourness if you failed of the appreciation that you thought your due. . . . You will have a chance to make it right if you don't sit and sulk like Ulysses did at Troy. Don't, don't let it turn out after all that you have soured because you have not been put on a pedestal & had your class or the entire college standing round burning incense to you. . . . You owe it to yourself to throw it off and if you don't throw it off it will ruin your college prospects. You were right in line of the first ten of The Institute and may be in the first ten of the Dickey. . . . Too bad that you should throw away so much that was in your hand. You can yet recover most of it—not all—but enough if you will about face. . . . The prizes of life are to be won not by sulking & complaining but by enthusiastic and persistent work in the face of all sorts of difficulties. . . .

♥ ♥ ♥ ♥ ♥

Wm. T. Reid, Sr., Belmont, CA, to Bill Reid, Jr., Harvard University
20 March 1898

Bill was congratulated for being invited to a prestigious dancing club.

. . . I am very glad indeed of your invitation to the. . . dancing club. It is worth while for you to accept—well worth while. That promises to open

A Debutante's Passion—A Coach's Erotica

up a circle that is better than your Boston circle I think. Oh you are a fortunate old fellow. . . . I am much pleased with the tone of your late letters. Things are coming out all right with you as I felt certain they would. . . .

♥♥♥♥♥

Wm. T. Reid, Sr., Belmont, CA, to Bill Reid, Jr., Harvard University
28 March 1898

Bill's father advised Bill to drop baseball and spend more time connecting with the social groups at Harvard.

The more I think of it the more I incline to think that your going into baseball was a mistake. If you were to take half the time for social purposes with the boys that you give to base-ball you would I feel certain make more headway in forming pleasant associations and pleasant memories and besides put yourself in the way of desirable society connection than is likely to be the case through base-ball. Of course if you make Varsity catcher it will be a great triumph. . . .

♥♥♥♥♥

Julia Reid, Belmont CA, to Bill Reid, Jr., Harvard University
ca. 28 March 1898

Julia Reid had her own advice on girls for her son Bill. Julia, whose descendants could be traced to Governor Bradford of Plymouth Colony and William Brewster of the Massachusetts Bay Colony, was steeped in Latin and Greek and was a graduate of Elmira College.

. . . How many of the girls you have met have any reason to think you care anything for them? The finest natures among girls are very chary of letting their feelings toward young men be known until they receive some indication of partiality from the young men. When you realize that a girl can go only so far in showing attention without committing herself & that committing herself to a young man who does not respond is a thing which humiliates her not only in her own eyes but in his & in the eyes of all who know it, you cannot wonder that it is evidence of a nature wanting in fine feeling when a girl does it. If she has reason to think a young fellow is partial to her then a young girl ought & unless very shy or unless very contrary will show her liking in ways that are very delicate but unmistakable. Don't then expect too much advance from young ladies who have no reason to think you care more for them than for anybody else. "Cito fit, Cito perih" you know. No worse thing can be said of a young girl than that she is "forward. . . ."

Bide your time—those girls know nothing of your antecedents & the world is full of young folks with a dreadful inheritance of shame & weakness, who in the freshness of youth show no taint, but it is there.

This is why in older communities it is bred in the bone to be reserved at first. I don't mean by this that I think you ought to show more marked attention to girls than you do. I think you are probably doing enough. I think with a girl who responds readily, you are likely to do too much & give her reason to think you care for her more than you do. But don't expect too much on six month's acquaintance, covering a meeting of only three or four times perhaps. . . .

♥♥♥♥♥

Wm. T. Reid, Sr., Belmont, CA, to Bill Reid, Jr., Harvard University
19 April 1898

The continual concern for Bill to be voted into social societies at Harvard nearly consumed his father, who was living Bill's college life, something that had by-passed him three decades before.

. . . And be social. It will help you in your work to be in a good mood. In short use good sound common sense & do unto others, etc. When do Institute elections begin. . . ? How do you feel about your chances? You ought to be pretty certain to make all or almost all the desirable societies but don't set your heart in being in the first ten. You are not likely to be so fortunate. You might have a chance if you make catcher & are decent to people—especially since the Groton fellows [eating club] have taken you in. . . .

♥♥♥♥♥

Julia Reid, Belmont, CA, to Bill Reid, Jr., Harvard University
21 April 1898

Two days after the U.S. declared war on Spain over Cuba, Bill's mother wrote him about his baseball prospects and the impact of the war.

We thought of you many, many times yesterday & wondered how you could center your interest on baseball sufficiently at all well in the face of all that was transpiring at the Capitol. The excitement in S[an] F[rancisco] and vicinity is shown in the account of the departure of the regiment from the Presidio. . . .
    Oh but I am afraid of the balls that hit you. . . .

♥♥♥♥♥

Wm. T. Reid, Sr., Belmont, CA, to Bill Reid, Jr., Harvard University
8 May 1898

The advice of Bill's father might have been useful to Bill later in life, especially if he had listened and used it after he would marry.

A Debutante's Passion—A Coach's Erotica

Guard against the danger of letting little faults in a fellow outweigh his merits. . . . The fault you have inherited to some extent from me & it is a bad one & you should fight against it. It has been a disadvantage to me all my life. . . . But break up at any cost the tendency to pick flaws & try to cultivate a critical judgment of yourself & question whether you haven't characteristics that are likely to give as great annoyance as these that annoy you in others. . . .

♥♥♥♥♥

Wm. T. Reid, Sr., Belmont, CA, to Bill Reid, Jr., Harvard University
26 May 1898

Bill would not join in the Spanish-American War effort as many college students did, and as Theodore Roosevelt did as he led the Rough Riders in Cuba. His father, a Civil War veteran, was happy that he did not.

. . . I am glad that you haven't caught the war fever. It isn't worth the while. The war should not have been entered upon. The principle is worth maintaining but the people to be rescued are not worth rescuing at the cost of such lives as are to be sacrificed. . . .

♥♥♥♥♥

Wm. T. Reid, Sr., Belmont, CA, to Bill Reid, Jr., Harvard University
6 November 1898

Bill was now a sophomore at Harvard. In a long letter to Bill about his shortcomings at Harvard in relation to hurting his chances of becoming a future football captain and more importantly introduction into the social societies, Bill's father brought up a young lady that he thought Bill would be interested in.

I wish you could have seen Ethel Cooper. She was simply wild with enthusiasm. I declare if you had been here I think you would have lost your heart to her.

♥♥♥♥♥

Wm. T. Reid, Sr., Belmont, CA, to Bill Reid, Jr., Harvard University
8 November 1898

While Bill was winning a position as fullback on the Harvard football team, his father was continuing to push for his son's social esteem. The noted "fast set" were the wealthy, social elites, most of whom came from the Boston area and the elite prep schools of the East.

. . . It is discouraging to know that the fast set are first in the Institute, but it is generally the case—nine times out of ten and for the very simple reason that the fast fellows are the social fellows and so hang together and so I want you to be more social & so help to make a decent social set. . . .

♥♥♥♥♥

PREP SCHOOL - EARLY HARVARD

Wm. T. Reid, Sr., Belmont, CA, to Bill Reid, Jr., Harvard University
16 November 1898

As Bill's father had a great influence on Bill, it is not surprising with all his push for Bill's social prominence at Harvard that he would eventually marry into Boston society.

. . . One of the most serious problems of Harvard life seems to me to be the society problem. To go through Harvard and miss the societies, or the leading ones, is like a woman's going through life without marrying—the loss of the best part of life, and at Harvard this must be true of the greater part of the students. One may say that it is simply the survival of the fittest. . . .

Now the only man who can rectify that condition of things, or the only men who can are the athletes & the society men for other men have so little standing that they can get no following. . . .

♥♥♥♥♥

Wm. T. Reid, Sr., Belmont, CA, to Bill Reid, Jr., Harvard University
21 November 1898

Bill had just scored two touchdowns in a victory over Yale, and his father was overjoyed because this would push him into most societies at Harvard, including the prestigious D.K.E, the Institute, and Alpha Delta Phi. He was not sure that Bill should join the elites of the Procellian.

. . . [I am] delighted beyond measure with your success—more if anything with your social success. . . than with your athletic success. The one however is largely the result of the other. . . . I am going to advise you not to join the Procellian. I doubt if you will be invited but you can't afford to go there if it is anything as it used to be. . . .

Just think of you having it largely in your power to make clean living a badge of popularity instead of licentious living as it usually thought to be the price of popularity. . . .

♥♥♥♥♥

Aunt Hattie Reed, Belmont, CA, letter to Bill Reid, Jr., Harvard University
20 December 1898

The sister of Bill's mother congratulated Bill for his Harvard success and for being in a full-page football portrait in the Christmas issue of Harper's Weekly.

. . . The height of your ambition has been reached. Your prowess has been heralded through the land. Your self-denial and untiring work have received their merited reward. But better than all this, that which made

A Debutante's Passion—A Coach's Erotica

our hearts take a fresh bound were the words of Mrs. Hurlburt—"The boy is to be a power for good, and is going to set up a noble standard."

♥ ♥ ♥ ♥ ♥

Julia Reid, Belmont, CA, to Bill Reid, Jr., Harvard University
                                                            ca. January 1899

Almost as soon as the honors came to Bill for helping Harvard beat Yale in football, a rare occurrence, his mother pointed out what she considered his weaknesses.

. . . No one can work till 3 O'clock without loss somewhere. . . . You themes demand just as wholesome & healthy a body as your football. . . . One hour of work in a rested condition is worth three in a nervous, hurried, sleepy or artificially wakeful a condition. . . . Your nervous system is awry enough at best & you need to avoid wrenching it further. . . . The spiritual I regret to say is left out entirely. I don't suppose the majority of your acquaintances if asked would think of saying you were a Christian. . . . Deliver me from people who have no resources within themselves, but must always be in a crowd or in some excitement. Papa is afraid on the other hand you are in danger of courting popularity & are in danger of having too much. . . .

♥ ♥ ♥ ♥ ♥

Julia Reid, Belmont, CA, to Bill Reid, Jr., Harvard University
                                                            25 January 1899

Bill was warned by both his mother and father against sending a baseball shin-guard with his photo attached to Daisy Cartwright at Belmont.

Papa says he hopes you won't send the photo mounted on the shin guard as suggested. He says he would not send such a thing to any girl unless he was engaged to her. It is too marked. . . . Oh Billy boy—a girl can flatter you into thinking black is white. . . . Beware—beware. . . .

♥ ♥ ♥ ♥ ♥

Wm. T. Reid, Sr., Belmont, CA, to Bill Reid, Jr., Harvard University
                                                             22 March 1899

Bill's father told Bill for the first time of being forced out as president of the University of California in the 1880s, hoping that it would influence Bill in not sulking about leaving the Harvard baseball team because of a disagreement with the baseball captain. Then he commented on a new girl who Bill had recently met.

... My having to give up the presidency of the University was a bitter thing. I enjoyed the distinction & the opportunity & I hated to give them up, but I am working with earnestness & enthusiasm & I think with some success in the less conspicuous place with the hope and the belief that I shall do more good here & possibly leave a better name than I could have left at the University—& so I am rather contented & I am working without sulking—though not without a good many pangs which I have never before told to any one & I tell them to you now thinking that my struggles & successes and disappointments may help you. I am going to put forth every effort to make this school a force for good—for the best intellectual & moral influence on this Western Coast & I want you to look over and beyond yourself to what you have to do for your community which is greater than you. . . .

Miss L's . . . attractiveness might be physical. That is so subtle that one is very likely not to know it until too late. It is fine if combined with other qualities and if exclusive but abominable if it is paddled around to half a dozen other fellows. As Watt said, "It would be mighty hard to have to marry a girl about whom half a dozen fellows know as much as I do." I know, as I wrote from Mexico, what you are paying for self restraint but it is worth all that it costs. The only way for you is to keep clear & not dwell on the subject. Of course the sending to you of the garters was a tremendously trying thing. But don't be caught writing to any of those girls. If they get into a scrape they will show up letters in defense of their associations & of course if they can get a letter from a Harvard fellow they will pleasure themselves. . . . It is an awfully ticklish thing when a girl's chastity is in question & you have anything to do with it. . . .

♥♥♥♥♥

Wm. T. Reid, Sr., Belmont, CA, to Bill Reid, Jr., Harvard University
11 June 1899

Bill sent his father a copy of a letter from a girl he had recently met. Bill Sr., offered his advice.

. . . [A] girl will come across your path one of these days. I hope that you were not enticed into writing in answer to the letter you enclosed or copied. If it was written by a girl, she was either a fast girl, or a silly one or a poor creature who hoped that she might in some way win companionship. It is quite possible however that it was written by some college fellow with the hope of getting you into a foolish correspondence and then letting the thing out in you. You are however too shrewd I hope to be caught in any case. . . .

♥♥♥♥♥

A Debutante's Passion—A Coach's Erotica

Wm. T. Reid, Sr., Belmont, CA, to Bill Reid, Jr., Harvard University
21 November 1899

Bill was a junior at Harvard in the fall of 1899 when he decided not to play football, in part because he had been injured in a baseball accident, but more importantly because he was not in good graces with the football captain and coach. His father was happy that he had not played in the scoreless tie with Yale. In an important 12-page letter of many bits of advice from home, Reid, Sr., discussed girl friends, future wives, and his desire to know Bill's thinking.

. . . It will take only a year of married life to find out that you have either wheat or the lightest chaff. The butterflies of the race-course wealthy people with little purpose are well enough for an idle hour but when it comes to a companion for life to one who is to share your successes or your failures & who is to be the mother of your children then one wants—not the race goer's standards & want of serious purpose—but the girl to whom one instinctively turns in time of need. The hours of prosperity will take care of themselves, but even in those hours one wants a woman who will take a rational enjoyment in the use of wealth & who can call around your table people of culture & refinement, people whose talk shall not be mostly the lingo of the race track. . . .

When you can get time tell me about your girl-friends & whether any new & attractive ones have come in your way—and tell me especially about Miss MacKay. Miss Avery, by the way, is to me a most fascinating girl. She has a fine physique, a fine and appreciative mind and is handsome—just such a girl as I should like to have you fall in love with.

♥ ♥ ♥ ♥ ♥

Wm. T. Reid, Sr., Belmont, CA, to Bill Reid, Jr., Harvard University
25 December 1899

Bill's father did not know that in a couple months, Bill would meet the love of his life, when he reminded Bill two years before to stay at Harvard.

. . . I am sure that you will yet come to think that I would not have done you so ill a service as I would have done if I had allowed you to return to Cal[ifornia] during your Freshman year when you were so downhearted. Life, you will find, is full of ups and downs of great pleasures and great disappointments. . . .

♥ ♥ ♥ ♥ ♥

PREP SCHOOL - EARLY HARVARD

Wm. T. Reid, Sr., Mexico City, Mexico, to Bill Reid, Jr., Harvard University
29 December 1899

Bill wrote to his father that a young woman offered her affections to him. He was asking for advice. William, Sr., responded in a four-page letter to fight the sexual urge.

. . . I know all about it. You can't tell me a thing about your fight that will be new to me. It is simply terrific but you can win and it is worth winning. I won & you can although you have a harder fight in some ways than I had—harder because you are brought more into contact with temptations that are alluring. . . .

I want to caution you against another danger—the danger of becoming unwisely engaged as a foil. I wish almost as much as you do that you could meet the girl that would wholly satisfy you and become engaged to her. It would give you a fine anchorage. . . .

♥♥♥♥♥

By the way, if that vacancy in your team advertised "To let" isn't already filled (and from what I hear I am not so sure it isn't) I should like to buy it. Renting isn't satisfactory for the tenant may be turned out and I want to feel secure, I dislike getting ousted very much.

I am a pretty steady worker and no shirk. I also guarantee harmony and a freedom from stumbling which in a tight place counts. Should these credentials prove insufficient — I offer to serve "on trial" for any period.

Chapter 2

COURTSHIP:
"I AM HUNTING FOR A TEAM, YOU ARE TOO"

Wm. T. Reid, Sr., Belmont, CA, to Bill Reid, Jr., Harvard University
7 January 1900

Bill Reid's father told Bill about many things, including the debt of $75,000 on his ranch and $22,500 on the Belmont School "which came near swamping me," his desire to buy the Belmont School back from the Congregational Church, and having a $10,000 salary headmastership at the Belmont School, a position Bill could eventually move into if he would move back to Belmont after Harvard. And then there was also Bill's potential partner.

. . . Tell me more about Miss MacKay. . . .

♥♥♥♥♥

Wm. T. Reid, Sr., Belmont, CA, to Bill Reid, Jr., Harvard University
20 February 1900

Bill's father was still advising his son, 21-years old and a junior in college, about girls.

. . . I am afraid that you are too serious in your judgments. You must not expect maturity in a girl of seventeen or eighteen. Most of them haven't had as much guidance as you and so are not prepared for quite as severe views as you hold. Indeed I sometimes wonder if Mamma and I have not made a mistake in making known to you the strength of our views on many things in life. At any rate is it not probable that you are several years more advanced than most boys and girls and if so is it not unjust for you're to judge a symptom as a disease. A bright thoughtful girl has in her the material for an earnest thoughtful woman. The Venus of Milo was made out of a very ordinary looking piece of marble but it never could have been made out of it if there had not been in it some possibility. I would rather have a girl that sometimes came near the danger point but had sense enough never to go beyond it than to

A Debutante's Passion—A Coach's Erotica

have one so conservative and self contained as never to move beyond the pace of the mother with two or three children. . . .

It is simply certain that you are never to find a girl who will not do something or say something that you will not like [and] you will severely criticize. . . . You must not misunderstand me. I am in no hurry to have you become engaged. There is plenty of time yet, but I want you to come to a right and just basis for if you don't you are going to overlook some mighty fine girl. . . .

Aren't you going to send me Ruth's picture. . . ?

♥♥♥♥♥

Bill Reid, Jr., Harvard University, to Christine Lincoln, Brookline, MA
23 February 1900

The following appears to be the first letter preserved from the Bill Reid—Christine Lincoln correspondence, one of hundreds that filled their lives with both love and agony for the next two decades. Bill wrote from his Harvard dormitory room, 52 Thayer Hall, introducing the term "twasing."

Dear Miss Lincoln:

This is rather late in the day for "remarks" but I am going to make a few just the same. Judging from the letter and other "missive" which I received from you, after I had sent the pictures, I should say that you have a very comprehensive idea of twasing. In fact you seem to have grasped the salient features with wonderful alacrity for one so absolutely ignorant of all, a few weeks ago. I guess that you didn't realize at that time that twasing isn't confined to the banks of streams, or to horseback rides but may well take place in a hammock!!! (Rather a mean crack isn't it. — well I won't worry you with particulars.)

By the way, if that vacancy in your team [here is drawn an ox yoke with two openings one titled "taken" and the other "to let"] "To let" isn't already filled (and from what I hear I was not so sure it isn't) I should like to buy it. Renting isn't satisfactory, for the tenant may be turned out and I want to feel secure. I dislike getting ousted very much.

I am a pretty steady worker and no shirk; I also guarantee harmony and a freedom from stumbling which in a tight place counts. Should these credentials prove insufficient, I offer to serve "on trial" for any period.

Hoping that you may have this question thoroughly considered by Sunday afternoon when I hope to see you personally
    Believe me as
     Yours very Sincerely
      "Bill Reid"
♥♥♥♥♥

COURTSHIP

Bill Reid, Jr., Harvard University, to Christine Lincoln, Brookline, MA
1 March 1900

Bill soon wrote again to his eventual wife, Christine Williams Lincoln, the 19-year-old debutante from Brookline, a wealthy suburb near Boston.

Dear Miss Lincoln:

In looking over the list of young ladies to be invited to the "Hasty Pudding" dance, I came across a Miss Lincoln's name. If it is Miss Christine Lincoln that is referred to—and I shall find out as soon as I can—well and good. If not—I shall see to it that another Miss Lincoln appears on the list. It is rarely that I allow any one to get ahead of me on invitations when I have an equal chance with them. In this case I was handicapped however, for the list was quite large. . . .

If you can come—I want to ask the pleasure of your company at the supper. If you can't come I want you to know that I had a "thought" at any rate.

If you come I'll guarantee that the lamp won't go out and warn you that it is time to go—and no matter how well you look I will refrain from accusing you of "painting." Remember though that it is a two hour trip.

Hoping that you are not engaged (for supper I mean). Believe me as
     Yours Very Sincerely,
        W. T. Reid, Jr.

P.S. As captain of the nine the papers say I am hunting for a team. You advertise that you are too— - - -(pen broke).

♥♥♥♥♥

Wm. T. Reid, Sr., Belmont, CA, to Bill Reid, Jr., Harvard University
11 March 1900

This 18-page letter was mostly devoted to advising Bill on his future profession, with suggestions of business and executive work, law, university professor, and, of course, being headmaster of his Belmont School. Bill was just beginning to date Christine Lincoln, but his father continued giving him advice on dating.

. . . I am in some respects sorry but for many reasons I am glad that you have not yet found your girl. On the whole I am more glad than sorry for I feel quite certain that your mature judgment will be wiser and safer. And I feel quite confident too that one of these days she will cross your path & that when she does you will recognize her. You have now had fluctuations enough to be safely on your guard & so to be in some danger of making demands that you cannot yourself meet. But all these things will take care of themselves in due time. . . .

♥♥♥♥♥

A Debutante's Passion—A Coach's Erotica

Julia Reid, Belmont, CA, to Bill Reid, Jr., Harvard University
30 March 1900

Bill's mother could not know that Bill had already moved in the direction of choosing Christine Lincoln to be his potential wife when she wrote this letter.

. . . I am going to write you a bit of advice about judging girls. You know I was a girl once & not the most dignified sort of girl either, but underneath was a lot of real principle. I think you are a little hard on them. They are going through a kittenish age & many of them will lose all that flippancy in two or three years & be quite different, but a girl who shows no regard for church & no reverence for sacred things & no observance of Sunday to speak of is not so likely to settle down. I had a great deal of what you call "fly" about me but I was never absent from church or Bible class & was always engaged in some sort of mission work. So my conscience was kept pretty active & all these things I used to do naturally dropped off by the time I was twenty one & before. So look under all the nonsense without letting the girls know you are doing so. If they think you are trying to find out they will try to shock you perhaps. Just lie low & keep your eyes open & your ears too. . . .

♥♥♥♥♥

Julia Reid, Belmont, CA, to Bill Reid, Jr., Harvard University
24 April 1900

While Bill was dating Christine Lincoln rather steadily, his mother suggested another girl, Lucy Stebbins, who soon would be attending the Harvard Annex (Radcliffe).

. . . I tell you she [Lucy Stebbins] doesn't think of smoking & drinking. . . . Papa says she is the most wholesome, dignified girl he has seen for many a year. . . . If you ever dance with her—just dance & don't talk. She said she liked to dance with gentlemen. She knew well enough not to feel obliged to talk. She enjoyed the dancing itself so much. I hope you can & will pay her some attention as soon as she gets there & she said she hoped to see you. . . .

♥♥♥♥♥

Bill Reid, Jr., Harvard University, to Mrs. Albert L. Lincoln, Brookline, MA
8 May 1900

Bill wrote to his future mother-in-law after visiting Christine on a Sunday evening at the Lincoln's home in Brookline.

COURTSHIP

Dear Mrs. Lincoln:
In these few, tardy lines, I want to try and thank you for the thoroughly enjoyable evening I spent on Edge Hill Road last Sunday.

    I really can't remember when I have had such a very pleasant time before. Everything was entered into in such a genial way that the formalities, which limit good times so much now-a-days, disappeared entirely and I simply couldn't help feeling at home. I am only afraid that in feeling so at home, I rather over stayed. If such was the case the blame lies in your own household. I refuse to be responsible. Please tell Miss Christine that she is as much to blame as anyone and must answer for a good share of it. With kindest regards to all,
                Believe me as
                      Yours very Sincerely,
                            W. T. Reid, Jr.
♥ ♥ ♥ ♥ ♥

Bill Reid, Jr., Harvard University, to Christine Lincoln, Brookline, MA
9 May 1900

Christine captivated Bill almost from the beginning and certainly by May, three months after meeting the 19-year-old.

Dear Miss Lincoln:
I am very glad that you and your aunt enjoyed the "Pudding" play, and particularly glad that you enjoyed the "something" else—for I did too. I was with Walter Fitz, the pitcher of last year's nine and a great friend of mine. He did not realize why I was "out for the air" and of course I didn't tell him. I was finding mutual enjoyment with three in the party, a rare case.

    How you ever came to see me outside there, when you didn't see me when I wasn't more than six rows behind you during the entire first act is more than I can solve. There I was waiting for you to turn around and you wouldn't turn. . . . It was better for the wait, however.

    I am very much afraid that I shan't be able to come to the fancy dress party for we leave Cambridge for Philadelphia on the seventeenth and won't be back until the twentieth. I wish I might go, for I do care to go, in fact I should make a point of going if I were to be here. As for its not hurting me to go—I am not so sure of that—I remember the jibes you flung at me on that drive and think my chances of at least having my feelings hurt a pretty big one. My motto is—"Blame to whom blame belongs"—and you are to blame. What other occasion can you cite in which I have laid the blame on others? I don't seem to recollect any.

    I find on investigation that that umbrella belongs to Mr. Hoxie—mine is here in the room. Mr. Hoxie's address is 52 Thayer—it would please him immensely if you would write him and tell him where his umbrella is—it is a good chance to get him to call. (Hint — He will answer all

A Debutante's Passion—A Coach's Erotica

right). I know him pretty well—and I'll help you along all I can. I could—in a pinch call for that umbrella accidentally left there, but I'll sacrifice my wishes for yours.

By the way there were two features to that game I was telling you about which I forgot to mention—one is, that contrary to the custom of most card games, the two contestants (only two can play) occasionally hold each other's hands (card hands I mean of course). This is not common until the game is pretty well mastered, then it can be done without compunction.

The second point is, that besides the "suite of hearts" a stray card frequently is played. This is invariably the last card played—and it takes great judgment to play it well. The holder always consults the opposing enemy first. Now you know the main principles of the games. . . . Don't show the points to anyone because they are the secrets of the game.

True—my mails are overflowing—but your slight notes are so short that I can forgive you the wickedness of writing. Be real frank and wicked this time.

Very Sincerely,
Bill Reid

P.S. Let me in turn thank you heartily for that "corking" drive. I didn't half tell you how much I enjoyed it—unless you can read eyes.
W.T.R.
♥♥♥♥♥

Bill Reid, Jr., Harvard University, to Christine Lincoln, Brookline, MA
23 May 1900

The following are two letters composed by Bill after a bad evening with Christine, when, evidently, she criticized Bill more than he could take. The first letter is believed to be the one that was sent, and the second was apparently written but not sent. The letters may indicate why in the first decade of their married life, there were at times misunderstandings in the relationship.

Dear Miss Trustful:
I feel quite disgusted with myself for again overstaying my call and offer my apologies for so doing. It would seem from the repetitions of this discourtesy that I am accustomed to it—but I assure you, that is not so. I haven't been guilty before, since I came East to college. Each time I have called, I have made up my mind to look out for the time, and each evening I have ignominiously failed. It won't happen again so you won't have to tell me when to go.

I was rather blue last evening and perhaps a little peevish and I may have taken some of your comments a little harder than they were meant, but it seems to me you were a little unfair in some of your call downs.

COURTSHIP

I am afraid that I am over "frank"; I thought I could be so without being misunderstood—but you will not take things right and it makes it hard. You have played a splendid first card. I have played mine—. It's your move.

With many apologies, I am
>Yours very Sincerely,
>W. T. Reid, Jr.

♥♥♥♥♥

Dear Miss Trustful:

I feel quite disgusted with myself for again overstaying my call and offer my apologies for so doing. It would seem from the repetitions of this discourtesy that I am accustomed to it—but I assure you that is not so. I haven't been guilty before, since I came East to college. Each time I have called I have made up my mind to look out for the time, and each evening I have ignominiously failed. It won't happen again so you won't have to tell me when to go.

I was rather tired last evening and perhaps a little peevish and I may have take some of your comments a littler harder than they were meant, but it seems to me you were a little unfair in some of your "call downs" or criticism; if you can call it that.

It may be that I am playing "out of turn." Thus far you have played "one card" & that mighty well. I have played or at least tried to play several times without giving my whole hand away, but to no avail. I have played my first card and it is now your move. One side can't play the game for both.

♥♥♥♥♥

Bill Reid, Jr., card to Christine Lincoln

ca. June 1900

Bill wrote a card, probably enclosing flowers for Christine, and his calling card said: "Miss 'Chop Suey,' for Christine with love, 'Bill' [Mr. William T. Reid, Jr., was crossed out.]."

One rose from one boy to one girl.

♥♥♥♥♥

Bill Reid, Jr., Harvard University, to Christine Lincoln, Cohasset, MA

19 June 1900

Bill, returning from the summer house of Christine's family, finally felt comfortable with Christine, just as the most important baseball game of his captaincy was about to be played. The first of three Harvard-Yale games of 1900 was a disaster for Harvard, Yale winning 15-5. In that

A Debutante's Passion—A Coach's Erotica

game, Reid batted clean-up, got one hit in three appearances, but had an error, according to the box score. However, the official history of Harvard baseball states that "Reid played the entire season without an error, the first and only time that feat has been accomplished by a Harvard catcher." Harvard, did though, beat Yale in the next two games, 3-0 and 5-2. His athletic career as a player had been a great success.

Dear Christine:
An increase of four pounds in actual weight, a nature at peace with everyone, and a memory filled with pleasant recollections is what my visit to Cohasset did for me. I say "My visit to Cohasset"—my visit with you is really the way it should be put. I never enjoyed a visit so much in my life.

When the team saw me coming onto the field, I heard various remarks such as "Here's Bill just back from the seaside," "Yes" says one, "and from her side." They didn't realize quite how near they had come to it. Another voice popped up and said — "Hard work to break away wasn't it Bill," etc. I enjoyed it all quite as much as they did and didn't hide it either. "But then this is rather conceited." I based my conceit on certain confidences which you showed in me in those re-freshing woods. I have been sort of dreaming, ever since I came back—visions of Buggy, the Lighthouse, etc., keep bobbing up in my mind. It was simply corking———.

There is going to be a parade before the game tomorrow of the classes from '85 to 1900 so you must come early. I am going to look for you in the first base stands—and am going to find you too. To see everything I'd be on hand at about 2:15. Well, if I don't close now I shan't get this off "on time" so here goes.

_____. _____. _____. _____. _____ (this hasn't been explained yet.)

With much love,
"Bill"

If we win will hunt you up afterwards.

♥ ♥ ♥ ♥ ♥

Bill Reid, Jr., Newton Centre, MA, to Christine Lincoln, Cohasset, MA
25 June 1900

His junior year at Harvard completed, Bill took Christine to Class Day at Harvard, and was ready to leave for New Haven to play the second of a three-game baseball series with Yale. He was winning with Christine and would win over Yale.

Somehow or other I had a very peculiar feeling come over me as I closed the door of your carriage on Class Day night—It was a feeling of lonesomeness, in fact I began to feel so lonesome that I felt like following you home. I had had a splendid time myself—because I was selfish enough to keep you pretty much to myself where I could sort of gloat over you. Just how you felt I wasn't so sure. so when your note came answering my two questions I was very happy.

You say there were many things you wanted to tell me . . . but couldn't— well why are you afraid? I want you to speak right out when I am around, don't be afraid to say anything—I am not much of a friend if you won't express yourself to me. (This is not fatherly.)

As for my going to Gover's—you goose you don't suppose the reason I should go to see him would really be to see you? Of course it would. I look on his invitation as a chance to be near you. I'd come to your house allright don't fret about that.

We do take turns frequently—but somehow my turn always comes first. Now remember, I had my turn last on Class Day so its your first move next time.

Now about seeing you. We leave for New Haven on Monday afternoon & play Tuesday. If we win we shall go direct to New York & play again Saturday, returning Sunday morn. I shall be back in Cambridge on Wednesday morning. In either case—if you are to be at home—may I come to see you? Now please if you have plans, don't let this interfere. If you will drop me a line at my room in Camb[ridge], I'll get it allright. I want to know what you wanted to say on Class Day & to say something myself. . . .

With kindest regards to all & with best love for yourself also ——- ...
——-   I am
                Faithfully Yours
                    Bill.
♥♥♥♥♥

Wm. T. Reid, Sr., Boston, MA, letter to Bill Reid, Jr., Cohasset, MA
                                            ca. 1 July 1900

While Bill's father was in Boston and visiting his son, Bill was invited to stay with Christine Lincoln's parents for several days before returning to his California home.

. . . Of course you will be sensitive about wearing out a delightful welcome—but how absurd it is, isn't it, to talk to a man in your condition. Well it is not a bad saying that to the brave belong the fair. I know of course that you are booked for probably the most comfortable three or four days of your life. I hope that they may be as wisely as they will be happily spent & I believe they will be, however they end.

Tell Miss Lincoln that it would have pleased me if I could have had time enough with her to show her that I was not so much to be dreaded after all. . . .

♥♥♥♥♥

A Debutante's Passion—A Coach's Erotica

Bill Reid, Jr., on railroad to Belmont, CA, to Christine Lincoln, Cohasset, MA

ca. 20 July 1900

Bill's entire letter is included, written after leaving Christine in the East and traveling by rail through Canada on the way to his home in Belmont, while Christine was at her family's summer home in Cohasset.

Dear Christine:
Three long days have passed since I saw your white shirt waist disappearing around the corner of the Cohasset depot—and three mighty lonely days they've been too. I've had a great deal of time for thinking and I've used it all—most of it on one subject—you. I have made Rich very uncomfortable by making remarks like this to him. Doesn't the sun look beautiful setting behind that mountain. What a corking sight it must be in Cohasset. He at once says, "ok keep still Bill" it makes me envy you so and there is no help for it. Still I have kept on. I got off the train yesterday and gathered you a big bunch of wild flowers and then when you weren't in the car I threw them away because I dreaded to think of them, as for you & no you to give them to.

My, I do wish you were along—our car is almost empty & we could do about as we pleased. Rich would keep out of the way and we should be pretty much by ourselves. We passed through some mountains yesterday—rocky and rough ones with water falls, etc.—and I sat in my seat looking out & trying to imagine you as sitting beside me in my arms and looking too. It was easily imagined the reverie but also easily dispelled. Then too in the dining car I have thought what a nice thing it would be to have you eating there with me.

The above is an attempt at writing you on the train and a pretty mess it is too. You won't get this letter until I have been away from Cohasset for a full week and yet in reality I have only been away four days. You see every day I am away makes two days before you hear. Well—to go on. I got pretty nearly sick on the train & when I reached Banff where I now am, I had to go to bed. I stayed there an afternoon, & this morning I am feeling allright again. Now, I am going to go on where I left off before.

I spent the first two days on the train in sorting out a lot of clippings which I have brought along to put in a scrap book. It was quite amusing to read over the old accounts and look at the old pictures.

One can't go anywhere nowadays without running across Harvard men. When Rich & I entered our car in Boston, there sat one of our class mates Pap "Pettus" in the section next to ours. He went to Montreal with us. On the trip he said to me—"Say Bill tell me who C.W.L. is will you?" I asked him where he had seen the initials & he said—"Why on a dress suit case you were carrying through the yard." Then he went on to say—"How is Cohasset Bill and how is Christine Lincoln?"—whereat I gave him all the information he wanted.

COURTSHIP

Two mornings ago we reached a placed called Moose Jaw & while there I had quite a surprise. I was walking along the platform at the depot when whom should I see stepping out of the car ahead of ours—my mother & a little later—my father. They had been switched onto our train & were off for Banff where they expected to meet us. Of course all this was very pleasant.

As soon as Dad got a chance he said to me—"Well Bill, you're looking pretty well—you had a good rest at the seaside I take it." Then we had a good long talk at the end of which I showed him your pictures. He thinks the one you don't like is exquisite—you just ought to have heard him admire. All the way along he & Rich have been poking fun at me about you—just little remarks but with a point.

We are now up in the Selkirk Mountains with Sulphur Springs near at hand, and the rush & roar of a beautiful mountain stream ringing in our ears. The mountains are all snow capped and are perfectly magnificent. Rich has the same feeling about them that I have—the feeling of mere insignificance—the feeling that you are about as small as a speck in the earth as ever was. Everything mean one has done looks so indefinably small that one feels ashamed to think he has ever been guilty of such meanness. I believe it is a sort of communion with God. It is like a regular sermon of itself. I do so wish you were here—we could go off & sit by the river & watch it dashing along—we could think together and be together all of the time.

Another instance of how Harvard men are everywhere about came up right here in the hotel. I hadn't been here over ten minutes before Robert Williams & Edward Cary Williams popped in on me. They are on their way to San Francisco & are stopping off here. It was a very agreeable surprise. They immediately congratulated me on the baseball games & then asked me if I had started from Boston. "No" said I—"I started from Cohasset." "Oh I see"—said Rob—"How is Christine anyway?" Another pleasant little jab. I'm afraid people are getting onto us. What's the difference? I'm just as proud of it all as I can be. No one can say anything about it which doesn't please me.

Your picture stands on my bureau in my room where I can see it at all times. I only wish the original were here so that I might kiss her about ____ times. It's no fun at all—you make all together too big a hole in my life to allow of your absence without a void being left.

I shall be very anxious to hear how you feel & what you are doing—how Eben [Christine's recent boyfriend] strikes you & how the other fellows do now that I can't hold my end up. That's the true test after all.

I came very near telling you something in the carriage then just after you had kissed me good bye at the depot—for that kiss of yours was a very committal thing for you to do & I hadn't any business to ask you to do it without making a committal myself. Please don't ask what it was I wanted to say—I think it had better be said at another time.

Now, you little dear—just write to me perfectly frankly and tell me how you feel, what you are doing, etc. I will do the same & don't you fear

43

that anything you write won't be kept sacred because it will. You know me enough by this time to trust me or at least you ought to. I trust you implicitly—what you say goes. We have a fine chance now to know each other if we only take advantage of it—that is, if we each offer our inner most thoughts to the other. Remember what a lot depends on getting better acquainted & really knowing each other. We can have little talks this way as we had when we were together. Tell me in your answer if this is too long. I know you don't like long letters from some people at any rate & don't want to run the chance of over burdening you.

That picture gallery of mine is locked up at Cambridge—my "collection" now consists of but two pictures.

Do you remember the ride back from the Golf dance? That was the best ride I ever had—my but you did look "corking" & that fluffy gown and those arms. Well I'm getting homesick. Give my best regards to Miss Waldron.

There are a couple of corking looking girls here whom Pat wants me to meet with him. I tell him to go ahead, I'm not interested. I shall kiss no one—hold no one's hands & put my arm around no one until I see you again—my relatives excepted. It is now twelve here, therefore 2 o'clock at Cohasset—you are eating. I wish I was in my old seat.

Well good bye sweet one.
With lots of love.
"Bill" Reid

♥♥♥♥♥

Bill Reid, Jr., Mt. Shasta, OR, to Christine Lincoln, Cohasset, MA
25 July 1900

Bill described his trip through Canada, including Banff, glaciers, Vancouver, and Victoria, heading toward Belmont, California, after attempting to climb 14,440 foot Mt. Shasta. But often his thoughts were on Christine.

Two weeks are now almost gone and still I am not home. We have been loafing along, stopping where we pleased and as long as we pleased. The one thing that is missing to make the trip a complete success is you. The scenery has been grand, the traveling fairly comfortable, the company good but you're missing. In walking about here I frequently run across places—cozy little nooks—to which I have imagined bringing you. No mosquitoes, a cool breeze and no interruptions—perfectly corking nooks all of them. Then there are some of the most beautiful mountain springs and streams you ever saw—the water just bubbles right out of the side of mountains ice cold. . . .

I miss you like everything, you little witch you. I am afraid that stock of kisses I laid in is badly exhausted. I wish I could replenish my stock. Would you let me have all I want or are you sorry for those

COURTSHIP

you've already given? I am awaiting your first letter with considerable curiosity and with great impatience. I want to know how you feel. . . .

Lovingly Yours,
"Bill" Reid

P.S. Be sure to send me a Kodak of you in that sweater—sure now.

♥ ♥ ♥ ♥ ♥

Bill Reid, Jr., Belmont, CA, to Christine Lincoln, Cohasset, MA
30 July 1900

Bill was concerned that he would lose Christine following his return to California, possibly to Christine's previous boyfriend, Eben. His very long letter discussed a potential life with Christine, while he also boasted that he was the first of his group to climb Mt. Shasta, with his friend, Rich, coming in second. Most dropped out of the trek.

Dear Christine:
I wish you were here where I could get at you—I'd just about smother you in kisses for that sweet letter you wrote. You have no idea how pleased I was to get it and how delighted I was to find you so loyal. You see I was a little afraid when I left—not from anything you said or did—that your feelings for me might subside—so your letter was awfully reassuring. Tell me now—dear—"How long do you think they will last?" Honestly. Aren't you afraid they'll wear away? Speak right up now and tell me, what's in your heart? Remember that I shall do the same to anything you may ask. We have got to be absolutely sincere in what we say—to be honest with each other.

I figured that there might be a letter here for me when I got home so I immediately hunted up the mail. I looked over the file of fifteen and found what I thought was the one I was looking for. This I put aside for dessert. When I came to it & opened it I was awfully disappointed for there was a letter from someone else that I didn't care a cent about. One thing I did realize though was the fact that you remembered my address so I knew my second letter wouldn't have to reach you before you wrote. Pat noticed my disappointment and knew why at once. Well—While I was getting nice and blue, Papa came in and dropped your own dear letter in my lap—& then came the change. Oh, but I'd just like to hug you so. I fear for your ribs. Never mind I'll make up for lost time. Yet, if you only feel this way when I next see you, I can't somehow help feeling a little jealous with Eben hanging around. Well, however things turn—I want you to be happy in the end even if it makes me dissatisfied. Your happiness is what I want to see and I'd do anything for you.

Now I am going right through your letter so as to be sure and answer your questions. You cried when my letter came—I just wish I could have slipped in behind you and wiped those tears away. Do you really care that much. . . ?

A Debutante's Passion—A Coach's Erotica

So you thought I probably wasn't disappointed at the girl's letter which you forwarded? In other words you don't yet realize that I would rather have a letter from you than from any other girl I've ever met, or likely to meet or want to meet—that furthermore you are the only girl I am writing to or have written to in correspondence since I met you. That's true—every word of it, dear—now are you better satisfied?

Why are you fond of me? I am not man enough for you to be fond of—I wish I were. I think you have been mighty honest with Eben. Christine—it is fine and I admire it ever so much. You see I can find plenty to pride myself on in you.

Please be dead sure of your feelings before you discourage Eben—don't make a mistake. You see I feel rather guilty in stepping up as I did and I want you to think it out yourself. Thank you for not letting him kiss you, that makes me value those you give me ten times more. It is mighty fine to walk about here feeling that one girl three thousand miles away is saving her affection for you—& to have the pleasure of reciprocating. I haven't the faintest desire to kiss any girl—except you.

As for your letting him see you off, I think you are wise in refusing him that privilege. The more he sees of you—if he loves you, the harder it will be for him to make up his mind to give you up—then too it puts you in a false light to outsiders. Not on my account—but on Eben's. . . .

You can tell Eben all you want except you'd better not try to tell him how I feel towards you. You don't quite know that yet and I didn't want him to think that I don't care an awful lot for you, for I do—and a great deal more than you realize. You can tell him just about what you please as to my affection for you and you'll not make a mistake—use words of one syllable if you wish.

You ask me to suggest some book for you to read. That rather puts me in a box for I am not literary enough to have much of a stock. I am going to take up John Halifax and read that this summer and I should enjoy reading it with you. If you like, we can read it and occasionally comment on parts of it in our letters. We can learn to know each other better that way for the reading will suggest topics of conversation. Please now dear, don't do this unless it is agreeable. I would not have you do it if it is irksome for anything.

As to my mother's saying anything about your future—I did not mention that because you do not know her and because I seldom tell Ma anything. However, she has seen your picture & her words were—"Oh isn't she sweet." She doesn't know you as Papa does and I have not asked her for opinions at all. You needn't fear for Ma—she would be just as interested as could be if I would only confide in her, but I can't. She likes you very much from what she has heard. As I say I haven't given Mama a chance to talk with me about you. . . .

I expect to do all in my life that I can to make a better man of myself and to do all that I can to help my community along. This means

COURTSHIP

mighty hard work—harder work than most people do—& yet work that I shall be enjoyably wrapped up in. Do you think—honestly and after deliberation—that you would enjoy such a life. You have always been surrounded with plenty and with luxury—would the change to the life I speak of not be pretty hard for you? I do not mean that I do not expect to have plenty for I do—but I do mean that my life aim shall be a higher one than the ordinary. I want to find someone who wishes to work that way too—who will find not toleration in the work—but true enjoyment. I want someone who is not going to pine away under the charge. What do you think of such a life and how would such a life appeal to you. I'd like to know how you would feel under such circumstances. I wish you'd answer this pretty fully. . . .

Do you think you could ever care enough for anyone to feel perfectly happy & cheerful under any circumstances? Times of plenty and of fair sailing are not the true test—there are always bound to be storms and rough weather—the true test is whether one can withstand the storms and trials and still come out smiling.

What do you suppose I was thinking about during that climb of 13 hours? Your own sweet self. I thought out a great deal which I have put down on this paper—I had a little visit with you in a way. I must have a picture of you in that dainty pink gown you wear to breakfast & in that other one—then one in your sweater. Don't forget this please. . . .

Now little girl good bye—with lots of love for the dearest girl I know—and kindest wishes to the whole family.
              Believe me as
                Yours Lovingly,
                  "Bill" Reid

♥ ♥ ♥ ♥ ♥
Bill Reid, Jr., Belmont, CA, to Christine Lincoln, Cohasset, MA
                                                        1 August 1900

Christine's future happiness in California, something that would be tested after marriage, was early on the mind of Bill as he projected his future.

Dear One:
You, you that's all I think of nowadays and I am perfectly happy that it is so, for you mean a deal to me. I do wish you were here and yet I don't know whether you'd be happy here—and if you wouldn't be happy I should want you to stay where you are. You'd probably be homesick and lonely and I wouldn't have you unhappy for anything.

You are getting dearer and dearer to me as these summer days pass and I long to see you.

Here I wrote you just day before yesterday and yet I cannot wait a day longer before writing again. Christine dear, what is there on my side that I can do to please you—what faults can I attack for you?

47

A Debutante's Passion—A Coach's Erotica

What would you like to have me do? If you are going to seek out things to do because they will please me, I want to be doing for you. I want to be doing, whether you are doing or not.

People are saying to me—"Why Bill—why are you so quiet? You don't make half as much noise as you did last year. What are you thinking about?" I don't tell them, but I am thinking of you. I continually think what I'd do if you were here. It is a continual fight between my selfishness and my affection for you. My selfishness says, I wish she were here with me—my affection asks—Would she be happy? Five thousand miles from home and in a different life? I am afraid selfishness would win were not your happiness at stake. Affection says—I don't know whether she'd be happy or not. What do you think yourself dear?

I have ordered those pictures for you—I am so late that I may not get them, but I've written. Be awfully careful swimming won't you—I read where some girls were drowned in New Jersey, and if anything happened to you, I don't know what I'd do.

I want to tell you how pleased I was with a couple of things you did while I was at your house—which I didn't half thank you for.

First of all, you poured at a golf tea when you didn't want to—because I asked you to. Secondly, you dressed one night when you were all tired out—because I had come to see you.

I appreciate all that dear and want you to know how I appreciate it.

Now good-bye little girl
            With best love,
              "Bill"
           ♥♥♥♥♥

Bill Reid, Jr., Belmont, CA, to Christine Lincoln, Cohasset, MA
6 August 1900

Bill put his future life with Christine on the line in this letter. If Christine were to hesitate marrying Bill and moving West, it might logically come after receiving these thoughts from him.

Dear Little Girl:

I hope you will excuse me for writing so often, but I can't help it. . . .

I keep imagining you out here—and with varied feelings. When I look about and see how lacking in the refinements you are used to—many of the customs out here are—I can't help but wonder whether you would ever become reconciled to them. Affairs out here are largely in an unsettled state and are lacking in finish. How all this would affect you—were you willing to come—gives me a lot to think of. Indeed people at home are saying—"How much older Bill has grown this last year, he seems to be quieting down." I am no older but I am quieted down—I am thinking and it is serious thinking too. Further than that it concerns you I am wondering whether I am old enough and whether you are old enough to

COURTSHIP

know our own minds. Whether what we may think we feel is a seasoned thought or a temporary one. When such thoughts bear on the future for years to come it makes it pretty serious. I know what my future is to be; that part is not worrying me—it is your future I am thinking about.

Supposing what I have is a well seasoned thought on my part, were in a year or two to prove unseasoned, supposing during that time you are as true to me as you are now—supposing I were to respond as I am now to my feelings towards you—and after all were to find my feelings changed at the end of that year,—what have I done. I have not been fair to you—you have trusted me and been true and then I fail.

This is what is worrying me. I am ever so fond of you, dear, and up to this time I have told you almost all my thoughts. I hope they are seasoned—but I have no sure way of knowing. I seem to be growing fonder and fonder of you—but I am too fond of you to let me do you an injustice. It all comes down to this.

I like you mightily and you know it—I am not absolutely sure that both our minds are seasoned enough to remain as they are now indefinitely. If they don't, it is going to be hard for one of us. If it is you who changes—I shall stand the change with as good grace as I can—if it is I who change, how am I going ever to give you back all you have given me? Were I to change and you to remain steadfast I should feel like a criminal.

Now I don't see any possibility of such things happening, for as I have already said—you are drawing me nearer to you right along. But I want to provide you with a safeguard. If after this you would rather I didn't kiss you anymore until we are "dead" sure—I will gladly restrain myself, disappointed as I should be. If on the other hand you want me to keep on both with written and actual expressions of my affection—at the possible risk of a mistake—I will do so. I want simply to do the squarest possible thing by you, because, mistake or not I shall never forget you and shall always feel the fondest affection for you. In short—I want to do the honorable thing by you no matter what it is. I wouldn't any more take advantage of you—you dear, you—than I would kill my parents.

This is very poorly expressed but I want you to see things from every side and I want you to decide what you do decide—knowing all I can tell you, that may bear on your decision.

I don't want ever that there shall be a cloud on your sweet life and I am risking your misunderstanding me to protect you. If what I have said seems strange in any way—that is—if you read it wrong—ask me dear and I'll explain it.

I'll write you again in a day or two—when I shall be home. Please write me now what is best for you. With best wishes to the rest and with fondest affections for you dear

            I am
            Yours Lovingly
            "Bill"
           ♥ ♥ ♥ ♥ ♥

A Debutante's Passion—A Coach's Erotica

Bill Reid, Jr., Belmont, CA, to Christine Lincoln, Cohasset, MA
8 August 1900

Bill was testing out Christine on whether she would marry him, and, if so, would she feel comfortable living in California, so less refined than what she was accustomed to in the East. Other than the marriage question being soon answered, the rest was left for future experience.

Dear Christine:
. . . The place here looks just as natural as it ever looked and I feel just as much at home as ever. I often wonder how you would like it here. When I look about and see how lacking we are in this State in many of the refinements you are accustomed to, I can't help but wonder whether you would ever become reconciled to them. I can bury myself in work here and it won't matter to me—what you'd do or feel I don't know. I wouldn't have your sweet life clouded for the world, and once or twice I've offered a little prayer that I might be guided to do what is best for you. You seem to be growing nearer and nearer to me right along. When I think that some one else may get you—my judgment almost gets away with me. Well, if you feel that it would be hard out here and you'd rather be East in a different sort of life, just be so. We've got to consider possibilities to know each other. I don't believe in handling questions of such importance as these with gloved hands. They want to be taken up & examined carefully. When we know how we stand on these questions we have a working basis. But what we say must be as honest and as true as gold.
  Saturday morning Rich and I went to the city. . . . The comical was everywhere present. For instance the cutest little flaxen haired girl got caught by a wave and upset—getting completely soaked. Her mother took her over among some rocks & undressed her—wrapping her up in a heavy shawl. In this state the little thing sat until her clothes were again dry. To dress her again the mother had to exclude the glances of curious people—this she did by opening two umbrellas. One she put one the open side of the little retreat they were in and the other she held over head to keep those on the cliffs above from looking down. Fortified thus the dressing was quickly accomplished. . . . Saturday night we went to the theatre—The Red Lamp. It was very poor indeed and I hardly enjoyed it at all. As we were the guests of a former Harvard lad we had to seem to enjoy it very much. There was no plot to the play, the acting was only fair and the audience very ordinary. We couldn't expect much more at a 75 cents house though.
  Sunday we spent the morning on a sail, three of us boys. There was a nice breeze and I enjoyed it very much. Harold Howard, whom we were with, said at one time, "Is she going to be an Easterner or a Westerner, Bill?" I told him I wasn't sure yet but that I liked the Eastern style of girl mighty well. What are the chances of my getting an Eastern girl, do you know? Tell me, now little girl.

COURTSHIP

We spent the afternoon visiting the University of California. I saw my old home there; and am glad I did not go to college there. One reason is that I would have missed meeting you, or at any rate put it off a long time. Then there's no telling where Eben [Christine's recent boyfriend] would have come in—perhaps I wouldn't have come in at all. Lucky me, I say. . . .

Monday morning Rich and I put in running about "Chinatown." While there, I bought you one or two little things which I shall send right along. They are only trifles but they represent each of them a thought—of you. Monday afternoon we went calling. I took Rich to see several of my old girl friends. They were mighty cordial to us and I think Rich likes one of them pretty well. Two of them were beauties and he was quite enthusiastic over them. I talked away, all the time chuckling to myself with satisfaction over you. There are some awfully nice girls here but — — — — — you know how I feel.

In the evening Rich & I went through Chinatown. . . . We saw Chinese restaurants, josh houses, theatres, opium dens, gambling joints, etc. At the theatre we sat right up on the stage & then went behind the scenes and watched the actors "make up." Everything was very crude indeed, but quite interesting. We saw cheap women everywhere. At one house we saw some women who had on shoes that were not as wide as this paper. They could walk and run too. It was a very interesting experience even though I have seen it all before.

We came home on Tuesday and I found a couple of invitations awaiting me. "Platonic" [Daisy Cartwright] has written me very cordially. Here are a few of her lines. Remarking that she caught sight of me from a soda water shop she says—"My first impulse was to tear madly after you and grab you by the coat tails—then I reflected that it would be most unbecoming and unseemly." She goes on to say referring to a desire I once expressed that I might meet a girl whom I could love and do for & who loved & would do for me—that I was anxious to meet "her"—referring to these wishes she says—"and oh, Billie have you found 'the girl' yet? I'm so interested and anxious to know." She is my "platonic" I was telling you of. I am going to call soon and I'm going to tell her about you. If I knew one or two things I could tell her pretty nearly how I felt—these I shall take up in a minute, you alone can answer them.

Ordinarily I should kiss platonic when I call but this year "no." Furthermore, I shall tell her why. It is a comfort to hold off that way and feel that it is for you and your lips that I am saving my affection. I like Daisy very much but that is all. I am afraid she likes me more than that—but I can't help it. I have always been perfectly honest with her. I haven't even tried to make her think I cared more for her than I did. If she cares I can't help it. She is a very sweet girl and will make a fine wife for someone. I only hope she gets someone who is good enough for her. I've known her seven years and she has confided all her little affairs in me and I have done much the same with her. She has helped me much in my way of looking at some girls and has several times put me on my feet when I took fancies that I knew wouldn't last.

Now I have told you all about her and the way I feel. If you want to know anything more ask and I'll answer honestly.

Now for those two or three things I spoke of above, that I want to know. Before I get any more interested in you—that is before it is too late—I want to find out how much interested you are likely to get in me and furthermore how much of an interest you are going to feel or rather would feel in what I am to do in life. I ask this for my own sake as well as yours for it seems to me all important. If you don't know certainly clear, just be honest. Say just what you feel. Don't regard all this as mistrust—for it isn't. If I didn't think you'd be altogether honest about it I wouldn't tell you how much depends on it.

I do hope it will be all I wish, for I am really yearning for you. If it is all I wish and then you only care enough I shall be so happy. If you feel any doubts just ask away—I'll soon dispel them.

Now you little hearty you, good bye.

With best wishes to all & with love to you & lots of it.
I am Yours Faithfully
"Bill"
♥ ♥ ♥ ♥ ♥

Bill Reid, Jr., Belmont, CA, to Christine Lincoln, Cohasset, MA
8 August 1900

Included is another entire letter the same day from Bill to Christine enquiring whether she would be satisfied in spending her life with Bill.

Dear Little Girl:
I don't know how you feel, but I can't help sitting down every day or so and writing to you whether I have any letters of yours to answer or not.

It does seem so long since your first letter came. I am just hankering after another. I am just as anxious as I can be to hear what you feel about the things I have written you of—it means a lot to me—how you feel.

Right here at hand is a letter I wrote you while I was in the city the other day but which I decided not to send. I wrote it pretty carefully but even then what I wanted to say seemed extremely poorly expressed and I was afraid you might misunderstand me in places. If you were only here—dear—I'd just whisper it all in your ear.

I have been thinking an awful lot about you—indeed people about here are remarking that "Bill has matured very rapidly in the last year and is now doing a good deal of thinking." I am doing a great deal of thinking—that's true—and it has all concerned my future and yours—for I have come to relate you in a way with my future. How much more of a relation I may establish and how practicable the relation becomes depends a great deal on how you feel.

COURTSHIP

How do you feel towards me now, dear? The same as when I was at Cohasset or have you changed? Tell me now won't you, because I'd rather hear of the change now than later—I can stand it better.

How soon after my letters come do you answer and do you find it easy to put off writing? This sounds like a quiz but dear, I do so hate to have you—sweet one—way off there were other fellows may steal you away without my being able to raise a finger. You'll excuse me this anxiety won't you?

I want one no two or three or a dozen of those little snaps of Agnes' of you. One surely in your little pink gown, one in the little cart, one with sleeves rolled up, one with your sweater on, etc. Tell Ag. I'll pay for the films & give her a whole roll for every picture she takes.

Well dear, this is just a little note before I go to bed. I'll write a letter tomorrow. I simply had to write or I couldn't sleep.

You are simply doing me up. I don't half sleep "wondering," and I find it hard to really get interested in much that used to interest me, simply because my thoughts go to you.

This seems pretty plain doesn't it? Well I don't care if you do know how much I like you.

Good night and a hundred or so kisses.

Lovingly (I mean it)
"Bill"
♥♥♥♥♥

Bill Reid, Jr., Belmont, CA, to Christine Lincoln, Cohasset, MA
11 August 1900

Bill's entire letter reflects his bright outlook following a letter from Christine. The mention of a "Sunday Afternoon" talk would later arise in their correspondence.

Dear Little Girl:
For the last two days I have been just as "blue" as I could be and it was simply became I was longing for a letter from you and none came. Today I am all smiles—perhaps you can guess why. I don't believe you quite realize what an effect you have over me—how when you write I am cheerful, how when you don't I am gloomy. At any rate, that is just what happens. I hope you won't "control" yourself hereafter, for if you do letters will be heaping up as I expect they are doing now. I can't control myself—I've simply got to write.

I WISH I could just hug you, that's all I need, to make my summer a success—only of course you'd have to be here for me to do that. I should do so much kissing too, that I'd better just touch on that. As it is, my summer is not a success—true, everyone is very nice to me but then I just yearn for you. Just think, I went out hunting the other day and for an hour or more I didn't kill a thing although I kept scaring up rabbits

A Debutante's Passion—A Coach's Erotica

all over. The fact is that I was so absorbed in thinking of you that I didn't notice how I walked or where I went. When I "came to" I shot ten rabbits, five quail and a dove. Rich—his mind unoccupied as it was—killed nothing. That's the way you are affecting me. I really believe that I was about ready to sulk when your letter came—& I don't often indulge. In short your own clear self seems to be becoming interwoven in my own life. Now your letter.

I am real glad that at last you have acquired the power of reading eyes—what you saw that night has been there all the time—if you had only known it. They say more than my mouth can say but not more than my heart feels—there is a key for you.

You say "it looked as though I really cared for you." How funny, as if you didn't know I care for you—as if you didn't know I care more than I have dared tell you, as if every one around Cohasset didn't know or at least surmise. The Brett boy is here at school and when I can't keep still any longer I go and talk with him about his mother and what she has said of you. I enjoy and encourage all the joshing that I can because I like to show my loyalty to you. If any one were to say a mean thing about you, I'd knock him over so quick he wouldn't know what had struck him. You ask about Miss Bennett. Well, she is a girl I met at the Senior Spread in my Freshman year at Harvard. At that time I thought I was going to like her very much—but after a year's separation I found that she didn't suit me at all, and ever since then I have been trying to let our acquaintance—for that was all it was—wear off. She spent last winter in Dorchester and I went to see her twice. I kissed her both times—for she is quite pretty—and then felt that I wasn't doing the square thing by her. I think other fellows could kiss her if they had cheek enough to attempt it, and don't think she will ever amount to much. Only last night I wrote her a note in reply to three she has written me. I was simply dignified and cordial in what I said. I knew long ago that I could never love her—but I found it hard not to kiss her when I felt blue and in need of sympathy. She is the kind that lasts just about an evening. There—you have it all—if you feel uneasy, just ask, that's all. Remember that I knew her before Class Day & that I only invited one girl for that day. Furthermore I only thought of one & that is the one I am thinking of all the time—you.

Dear little girl, you know well enough how I feel. You say that I don't approve of you; well, I do and you ought to see it. Do you suppose I ever wrote seven letters to any other girl before getting an answer? Or do you suppose I ever spoke my heart quite so frankly to any other girl?—no—. What I feel, what I think, what I do—is all open to you & to you alone. You have the key to my heart, soul and all that belongs to me.

It is just as sweet of you as can be, for you to offer or intend to improve while abroad. You act as if you were trying to fulfill some qualifications which I have given you the impression you lack. That is not the way to look at it. I am the one to conform to what you want. If I only know

54

COURTSHIP

how far your affection for me would carry you—whether you'd be happy wherever I had to go or wherever I was—I could throw off my mask for with all my frankness I am still using a mask—& let you read all that is there behind it—which I have not let you read for your own sake.

I never intended to "cut" you that Sunday afternoon—there, I knew I was unjudicious—I was simply trying to draw you out into a serious talk. Forget all that, dear, I'm so sorry I ever said anything then.

I was so thankful when I read how fortunately you came out of your accident—that I offered up a little prayer of thanks. My, but I'm glad you are allright—that's just why I don't like horses—some one is always getting hurt. I wish that fool of a fellow had had his head banged against a pole. Speaking of being vexed at being late at the golf links—you may thank your stars that you got off as easily as you did.

Perhaps you'd like a mate to that but fine if you do—speak. How I should have roared to have seen your father holding you fainting in his arms.

How do I like to have you called my pal? Pretty well, but I'd rather have you called my _____, or be called your _____. At any rate something much stronger than pal.

What I came near saying at the station was not a scolding—far from it. It was three words—words I have never yet used to any girl. I _____ _____. There that's all, I'll tell more.

The pictures I took were all light struck so I didn't get a single one. Ag's [Christine's sister] camera must supply me. I am having the back of my watch fixed so that I can open it easier. I want to put a picture in it.

Tell your father that my blessing goes with his slumbers. He deserves a good rest, for I must have tried his patience tremendously. I always admire a certain kind of self control.

Dear, if the owner of those gloves was only with you now—you'd find him pretty much of an automatic kissing machine. Further you'd find a distinct response to whatever you chose to do.

Make a fool of yourself—when. I hate to have you feel that way, because you express what you feel, for it puts me in a pretty awkward light. Think how plainly I express myself. Please now, say all that you feel, I love to read it and you say it so well.

Your horrid disposition doesn't trouble me at all—it's your final disposition that's worrying me. If I knew what that is to be I'd be extremely happy—presuming it were to bring me a mortgage of course. There, now I have finished your letter. Now for a few words of my own suggestion.

Two days ago, two of the teachers who have been married during the last month & who accomplished their marriage so quietly that no one knew of it until it was done—came home. My mother provided Rich & me with rice and as they drove into the yard we showered it on them, much to their confusion. Further demonstrations were made in the house so they got quite enough "ceremony" after all.

My dear, I fully realize what a lot of questions I have asked of you & how often I have re-asked them. It may seem as though I doubted you,

55

but I don't. I simply shouldn't want you to decide the important question that I may sometime put to you—without your knowing just what all the conditions which bear on it—are. I shouldn't want you to decide and then find afterward that there were questions coming up which had never occurred to you. I shan't blame you one bit—dear girl—if you get out of patience with me for questioning so much—but remember that I am doing it to protect you against my selfish self.

While I was away a few days ago visiting, I had some very slim breakfasts—and I confess that many times I longed for your fresh eggs. Such a good time as I had at Cohasset—I'll never in my life forget it: The drives, the walks on the beach, the kisses, the talks all come back to me continually. I just set my watch back there three days ago. Up to that time it was Eastern time. I frequently figure where you are & what you are doing—& what I should be doing if I were there too.

I hope little Miss Chop Suey gets to you unbroken for I really think she is quite cute. I hope too that the belt fits. I wish I could put it on you. By the way, who buttons up the back of your dress now when you go bathing? I wish I could do that again, it was quite good fun, I thought.

The lavender I have been enclosing in my letters I pick out of the garden—we have lots of it. If you were here, I'd take you out & hug you under our lemon verbena bushes—they are as tall as I and offer good protection.

Here is a rather comical little squib I saw in some paper. "This modest head of lettuce, With blushes in confessing. How very much cut up she feels. To see the salad dressing."

Now you dear girl—good night. I wish I could plant a good night kiss right on you sweet little mouth and could give you a real loving hug—seeing I can't I'll have to get along with telling you of it.

With kindest remembrances to all the family and with fondest affection for you.

Believe me as
your lovingly
"Bill."
♥ ♥ ♥ ♥ ♥

Bill Reid, Jr., Belmont, CA, to Christine Lincoln, Cohasset, MA
14 August 1900

Bill had just received three loving letters from Christine in his first extended absence from her. This encouraged him to return early to the East to see her before she left on an extended trip to Europe and Egypt with her family. He wished to ask her an important question.

COURTSHIP

Dearest:

Your last letter—which lies open here before me and which I have just finished reading for the fifth time—made me so happy that I simply couldn't eat any supper. I sat there at the table, just as impatient to get away and reread it, as could be. Loved one (and I mean it), you don't know what a real blessing you are to me, and what an inspiration a letter like this one is to me. I feel now and have been feeling for some time that I am simply living for you—what I do and what I plan must be to make me more fit to associate with you—in whatever way you let me. I was never happier in my life.

I used to think that I could learn to love one of the girls out here, but I don't even feel the inclination now to "call" on her. I know, without calling, that I shan't ever think so again. I feel much as you do with Eben—You love him—but not with your whole heart and soul. I don't ever love this girl—I simply like her. The fact is that you have spoiled all for me and I am awfully pleased too. You see I am beginning to unmask a bit—I simply can't help it. I've got to or I fear my heart will be overworked caring for my affection which must bubble over somehow.

I shall start right in on John Halifax too—I am so glad you feel that you will enjoy reading it with me. It makes one more bond between us—for after all—in books, we seek mutual communion with men who have gone before us and with whom we still have a chance to become somewhat familiar. It gratifies me so much that you feel so responsive to it all.

It is just as sweet of you as it can be—for you to tell me not to feel jealous—If you were like other girls I know, you'd try to worry me—I love you all the more for it. Let me add that you need not worry (I am conceited enough to hope that perhaps were I to give you a chance you might). If you stay in Europe five years—when you come back you'll find me true. . . .

I feel as though I could smother two or three of you—I fear one of you wouldn't last long. You express my very thought so well in one of your sentences that I can do not better than quote it.—"The better I know you—the more I care for you—and if this keeps on, well" —I'm a goner. . . .

Dear Girl—I know you trust me—and I wouldn't anymore think of violating that trust than I would of cutting my own throat. How to be worthy of that trust has worried me much. I have prayed over that too. If in your letters you get run away with, then I get run away with, upset and well banged up into the bargain.

What do I think of beauty love? — just this. Beauty is a fine thing in one you love, but if it is the chief attraction it is not worth a copper cent. As Bacon so well puts it: "That is the best part of beauty which a picture cannot express," and "Virtue is certainly best in a body that is comely."

You are a perfect little beauty and I like just to look at you—but that is not why I like you. Your principles, your trust, your—oh your everything—is what I like. . . .

A Debutante's Passion—A Coach's Erotica

I agree with you in your definition of love absolutely. And you once told me that you thought you could sometime love me. If you only can feel that way—it makes me just thrill all over. If you should learn to love me—then you'd be willing to come out here wouldn't you? Dear me—were you here, I'm afraid I could not keep a judicious watch over my mouth—I fear it would speak. Please don't ask what it would say— remember I want to try and know you—and I am knowing you better— better all the time.

I don't see how Eben could possibly let money enter into his affections—here again I agree with you absolutely. This is a point over which I feel so strong that were I to get the idea that a girl loved me for money or position—I'd drop her as quick as a shot. That kind of a conception of love, is what creates devices, and I mean to see to it that my home shall be a harbor in which none of the storms of the ocean are to be dreaded.

To me your "theory" of married life is just ideal. . . .

I am going to tell you something which I can't keep away from you any longer. I am going to come East the latter part of this month, ostensibly to tend to my baseball affairs, but really to see you once more before you sail. Before I left Cohasset, I thought I might do it, but I didn't say anything about it to you because I thought that if I told you—and then in our correspondence we found that we were not fitted for one another—it would be hard to tell you I wasn't coming. I thought I'd let it depend on our correspondence—three of your letters is enough for me—and the last one—it's worth its weight in gold. I've had an awful hard time keeping this to myself. I wanted to tell you when on the way to the depot that last time but I thought it would be best—and surely wisest—to keep it until we knew better where we were. I thought of writing your mother on the sly and telling her, and I would have done that except that I was awfully afraid you'd get angry. That is, go visiting somewhere and I want you all the time. This last possibility decided me to tell you. What time will be convenient for you, and may I spend a few days at Cohasset? I don't usually ask myself around this way but in this case I don't see how I can help it. I shall want to utilize the moments, and I couldn't do that if I were to live in Boston. Don't tell your mother I asked this way but suggest it to her—dear—will you? She has been so kind to me and I over staid so long my invitation I hate to write myself. It seems to me that it would be wise to give the baseball reason to all except the family—the family you can tell anything to. Understand, I'm not ashamed to have it all known—"I'd take you in my arms and tell all Cohasset so" but to me it seems probably best to keep that to ourselves. There will be talk enough anyhow. Now perhaps you will realize why I haven't at any time expressed regret that I wasn't to see you again for over a year. I knew better. . . .

I may ask you a question I've never asked before—so just think up the possible questions. This one—"yes" or "no" simply will answer full and satisfactorily.

I am just aching to get into that little meadow brook with you—to kiss you and to show you how fond I am of you. I can hardly wait. . . .

Dear little girl—you've got an awful hold on me. Well—remembrance to all the family and all the love I am capable of to you.
    I am
      Yours Lovingly
       "Bill"

P.S., Do you spell that middle name of yours [Williams] with an apostrophe yet?

♥♥♥♥♥

Bill Reid, Jr., Belmont, CA, to Christine Lincoln, Cohasset, MA
18 August 1900

Bill wrote a letter basically to be writing a letter and to tell Christine that he is pleased that Eben is completely out of her life and that he likely won't being playing football for Harvard in the fall.

Dear Little Girl:
I don't believe I could have gone much longer without a letter from you—for somehow my happiness is pretty much dependent, first on your letters, and second on what you say in them. . . .

Dear little love, you I wish I could put my hand next to your heart, now—and kiss you. Never mind, it won't be long now, before I can, and I am awfully happy over it. There is something I want to find out about that heart, something I am impatient to learn—I'll ask you about it when I get back so be sure you know it through and through. . . .

I am very sorry about Eben and your disagreements, for Eben's sake, but almost glad, for my own. You see it means to me that you are just as true to me as steel—and it displeases Eben. I love you for it and with all the love I have.

I have made up my mind to give up football on account of my leg—and because you won't be here. I might play if I tried my hardest, but I don't believe my leg would last long & I want to save it for baseball. I do so wish you were going to be here this fall for I'd so love to take you to the games; I'd be so proud of you. Possibly, if the team is in a pinch, I will play—but not otherwise. I'll not play anyhow, if you'd rather I wouldn't. I am in your hands there.

I shall take up "Les Misereables" just as soon as I finish John Halifax. If I haven't leisure—I'll make it & if I didn't want to read it myself, I'd read it to please you. That's the way I feel about that. . . .

♥♥♥♥♥

A Debutante's Passion—A Coach's Erotica

Bill Reid, Jr., San Francisco, CA, letter to Christine Lincoln, Cohasset, MA
20 August 1900

Bill was anxious to be going East again to see Christine before she left for an extended trip to tour Europe. The entire letter follows.

Dear Little Girl:
Since your last "corking" letter came I have been so on the dead jump getting all my "calls," etc. in, that with the exception of the few minutes I snatched to write you yesterday, I haven't had a moment to myself. Rich and I have been spending the nights away from home where I had to be around to be decent. It is now 12:30 at night, but I am bound I'll get in at least a page or two. I am going to be awfully stupid I know for I haven't slept well for several days and am quite worn out. I am now going right through your letter.

I am very glad that the "presents" pleased you—they're rather unique, those Japanese curios. Chop Suey was patriotic because of a red & a blue one—chose the red.

When I get back, perhaps you may arrange it so that both my arm and the belt are around you—that will make it doubly satisfactory. Dear little girl—I wish you could thank me in your "better than words way." I refuse to accept the other thanks and expect you to thank me properly when I get to Cohasset.

I don't know what the watch charm is supposed to be—but I'll find out and tell you when I see you.

We certainly do know each other much better now, and I think I know myself, which is pretty important too. I'm afraid—dear—that you will never learn to love me. I haven't enough to me to win your love. And yet, how I should feel if you found you couldn't. Well—love like yours is the only kind to have and if I can't have that I won't have any. God bless you—anyhow—you honest little girl—You've treated me as squarely as it is possible to treat anyone. You know, you make me love you more and more—everything you say.

One thing—I am trustworthy and I'd sooner cut off my right hand than take advantage of you. Little girl, don't worry 'Platonic' or any of the others can't budge me one bit—if you want me I am yours or not, as you decide for yourself, and wholly yours.

Rich and I probably [will] start East on Monday—getting to Boston the first. When I find out when I am to arrive I'll telegraph you what train I'm coming to Cohasset on. You see I want you to meet me in the little meadow brook & take me into the woods where I can simply hug & kiss you. I know if I go up in the bus, you may be away & there the wait—& then I'll have to say hello to everyone & I can't stand it that long. If you can't come, I'll sooner see that you're not there & understand. I wish you'd wear that golf coat of yours, the one you met me in when I first went to Cohasset. I love you in that. This is awfully cheeky of me to plan all this, invite myself & all, but when I'm coming on only to see you, I can't afford to lose any time.

Darling, I'm not going to like any other girl, so don't think about that any more. I can hardly bear to think of you going away for a year almost without knowing you are all my very own and I—every drop, yours. But there, much as I should like you to decide before I get back, I shan't try to argue at all. Your future is at stake and you alone can decide it.

Music affects me in just the way it affects you, & I have become very fond of it lately too. Guess why? Think you a fool—because you like me enough to cry for me!!! You little beauty—no—of course I don't. I love you for it all. That little gingham dress—how I wish I could catch you wrapping my arms around you—perhaps I wouldn't stop your dear little sobs.

It's for you to decide whether you want me, awfully, awfully, enough to take me—that's all you have to do.

Dear old Conrad—he's a Digamma boy you know (that's the society I like best). I'll hear from him later on. I shall be very much interested to meet Ethel's sister—if she's as nice as Ethel I'll enjoy her very much. I am just through with John Halifax—I've marked all the passages I like & I'll show them to you when I get back. It will be more satisfactory than writing. It's a splendid book & I think the "home" in it is fine—except for a few things. That's what I want—a home.

I hardly agree about "love" as coming to us for what we should be than what we are. I think it's what we are that counts. Everyone should be better & yet you'd not love anybody.

I like the comparison between love & music—I always did like that. "Love is a great thing— — — — it hears with equal serenity" etc. is splendid. It bears on one of the questions I asked you about how a girl ought to meet reversals.

Nothing is sweeter than love—I like that, but it isn't so well expressed as some of the others—it's true allright.

Well—though I haven't said much it has taken me till 2:15 to get this far & I must close to get to bed. With the best of love to my little darling & the best of good wishes to all the family
     Believe me
      Yours Lovingly
       "Bill"
     ♥♥♥♥♥

Bill Reid, Jr., San Francisco, CA, to Christine Lincoln, Cohasett, MA
              22 August 1900

Bill hurried a note before leaving for the East to see Christine and ask her to marry him. It is their last letter prior to Christine boarding a ship to England for an eight-month trip with her family.

A Debutante's Passion—A Coach's Erotica

Dearest:
This is just a short little note of bubbling joy over your last letter. I have got to catch a train so it can't be long but it will be loving.

Sweetheart—I couldn't wait a minute—after reading your letter and seeing a little jealousy on your part—before writing and telling you that you need never feel any jealousy. I love you and you alone and God willing I'll show you that I do. You have kept growing and growing on me all through the summer until now I must have you. I don't know whether I can stand it to have you hold back until you return from Europe. I want to think of you—darling—as my very own—and know while you are away that you are mine and I, yours.

I have raised all the possible questions I know of and you—little dear—have answered as though I myself had dictated the answers—no as if God had.

I am coming East in a great hope—that hope lies all in you. How you act to me will determine whether my Senior Year at college is to be a grand success or a fitful failure. But there—I know that you will do what you think in your honest soul—is for the best and I shall abide by it whatever it is, no matter how hard. I love you too much to try and argue with you—I shan't try to persuade you at all. If you come—you shall do so of your own free will—and if you only will.

I have decided once & for all—it is all in your hands now—think little one what you are doing.

You have been wonderfully patient with me and all my questions—I shall try to be as patient, though it will be a hard wait.

You're telling me that you do not yet love me makes one love you all the more. I know you are honest from head to heel—and that is a fine quality.

So you feel that way I am in your heart that I am true. True—I guess I am. I haven't ever kissed my mother on the mouth but once—I am saving what little reserve there is for you. . . . .
"Bill"

♥ ♥ ♥ ♥ ♥

Chapter 3

ENGAGED, VOYAGE, AND STEAMER AFFAIR: "ARE YOU ENGAGED OR NOT?"

Christine Lincoln, Brookline, MA, to Bill Reid, Jr., probably Harvard University
ca. 11 September 1900

Just as Christine was about to leave on an eight-month journey to Europe with her parents, she wrote a note to Bill, telling of her love for him. It is likely that the previous night, Christine accepted Bill's proposal of marriage.

Dearest,
Thank you so much for that last message. It came at just the right time. You know that I love you, but I say it again because I know how much I like to hear you tell me so. Darling, take good care of my property for me, my dear, precious property. Oh! Billie, already I long to see you again! Those true gray eyes, I love them so. Dearest, there isn't much to be said. We love each other, and I know our love can stand the test of separation.
My one true love—
Yours
Christine
♥♥♥♥♥

Diary of Christine Williams Lincoln, 12 September 1900 - 6 April 1901
ca. 12 September 1900

Christine and Bill intended to get married, but there was no public announcement, nor were their families told, when she left with her family for an extended trip to Europe, including visits to England, France, Germany, Italy, Egypt, Monte Carlo, and Monaco. She kept a diary, and on the first day on the way to Liverpool, England from Boston, she met an artist, Henry Niorr, who had an immediate interest in Christine, and she in him. It would become the first major crisis between Bill and Christine. While Christine wrote numerous loving letters to Bill in the eight months, she never mentioned Bill directly in the Diary, but did alude to him.

. . . Met a very interesting fellow called Henry [Niorr], an artist. . . . I enjoyed the steamer very much, and was almost sorry to leave. . . .

A Debutante's Passion—A Coach's Erotica

[Later at the Russell Square Hotel in England] it was almost too much for me when the band played "Fair Harvard" while we were at dinner. . .

♥ ♥ ♥ ♥ ♥

Wm. T. Reid, Sr., Belmont, CA, to Bill Reid, Jr., Harvard University
13 September 1900

For two weeks, Bill's father was on a crusade to criticize Bill's shortcomings, one being his failure to write and tell him about his visit to Cohasset—this at a time Bill was nearly 22 years old and entering his senior year at Harvard.

Dear Will,
I find it difficult to keep from writing to you as if you were a boy of sixteen, for I am seriously alarmed at the tendency in you to defer and neglect important things to suit your whim or convenience. It has become so marked in you that I wonder whether you have inherited that fatal defect from Mamma's father. Characteristics often jump in that way and appear in the grand children or the great grand children. I say fatal defect because with a good knowledge of medicine and with the confidence of the community, he dawdled and dawdled along—doing what he was asked to do whenever it suited his convenience—always behind—knowing nothing about his business, almost never collecting bills and constantly annoyed by debts. He died with nothing in shape and lost even the old homestead in Jacksonville [Illinois]. Albert is worse than worthless. It would have been a great gain if he had never been born & it would be a tremendous relief if he would die. Now your never being ready at the time appointed, your never or almost never getting up to breakfast, your putting off things until they have to be done, your leaving vastly important things undone in order to attend to comparative trifles, your spending endless time dressing—taking an hour to do what you ought to do in ten minutes—all these things, these habits—that have already a firm hold on you, will swamp you in any business and will dead surely swamp you at Belmont. If you come here and succeed you will have to be on hand when you are due & not keep people waiting. You will have to attend to business as it comes up and not as is convenient, or you will fail.

Parents want and they have a right to expect that details regarding their boys and the school will be looked after promptly and painstakingly. The thing that brings all this up is the fact that you have not sent a line to me regarding a matter that is of more interest to me than any other single thing at the present time—and after I had shown my interest as strongly and in as material a way as I well could. It would seem almost a due, but I am sorry, very sorry if I am to get only what is due, and nothing from sympathy and impulse. However my present point is that common duty has been neglected. Now I don't want you to say that in my interest I exaggerate. I know a little more about business and the way people look at things, and about the qualities necessary to public confidence than you probably do, and though I feel seriously your want of consideration what might legitimately be called want of common courtesy, yet I pass that by in thinking of the serious bearing that all this kind of thing is going to have on your work here or your work anywhere. And it all bears such a frightful resemblance to Dr. Reed's characteristics, that brought absolute failure and almost disaster. No quality & no qualities are going to take the place of attention to the duties & obligations of life at the time that they ought to be attended to whether you feel like it or not. I presume that we shall have another week to wait before we can know a word about what may be the most important event in your life.

                    Papa

♥ ♥ ♥ ♥ ♥

Christine Lincoln, on Steamer to England, to Bill Reid, Jr., Harvard University
18 September 1900

Christine told Bill of the September 12th incident on the steamer to England in which she met an intriguing French artist, Henry Niorr.

. . . There are not many interesting people, but there are some. Do you remember a big fellow we met walking on the deck and you said "I'll bet he meets you!?" Well he has, and I like him ever so much. He has very interesting ideas and we have had some very nice talks together. We sit up on the hurricane deck in the evenings, and talk, and I shut my eyes and try to imagine that he is you. It is not very easy, though, because I know that if you were there we should be somewhat nearer together. He is a fine fellow, but he is not my boy, there is no getting round that. Already I long for a sight of your dear face. Do you know the first night I never slept a wink, but I was in a queer state. It seemed to me that you were there with your arms round me. I was sure of it.

♥ ♥ ♥ ♥ ♥

Christine Lincoln, London, England, to Bill Reid, Jr., Harvard University
20 September 1900

This letter and the above one led to a mild crisis towards the end of the eight-month journey through Europe and Egypt, when on March 30, 1901, Christine went into more details about the steamer incident with Henry Niorr. Christine enclosed a revealing letter, but it no longer exists.

I enclose a letter written on the steamer of which I am very much ashamed. . . . I had a queer fit on the steamer, sort of a reaction, I guess but it is all over now and I shall never have another. I am awfully homesick for you. . . .

♥ ♥ ♥ ♥ ♥

A Debutante's Passion—A Coach's Erotica

Wm. T. Reid, Sr., Belmont, CA, to Bill Reid, Jr., Harvard University
                                                    23 September 1900

Bill Reid's father was miffed for being left out of Bill's agenda when he had visited Cambridge at the end of the spring term at Harvard. He did not forget this over the summer. He also questioned Bill, who had lingering doubts about Christine.

... I came very near feeling that I was a convenience of which you were fast becoming ashamed—except as a convenience. I recalled your not introducing me to Christine after the Harvard game [with Yale], and one or two other matters that seemed to me to indicate that I was rather in your way while in Cambridge during the summer. ...

The possibility of your turning out after all to have such an exaggerated estimate of yourself as to wish to keep your parentage or origin obscured—all but infuriated me. ...

If you longer analyze, and doubt and question, the fault is in you and not in Christine. I believe in her through and through and you are not now, at any rate, worthy of what she is giving you. With all that you have seen of her, after you have tried her at every point to find her to ring true every time, I can't understand why you should let a doubt linger in her mind as to your ultimate devotion to her. ... Why don't you take counsel of your bilious moods? Why don't you take your clear hours—your sensible, level headed seasons and accept their convictions. Let me repeat, you don't deserve what Christine is giving you. She is in my opinion, from what you have told me, immeasurably superior to any girl of your acquaintance that I know anything about. And it pains me to have you leave any doubt in her mind as to your constancy or as to the certainty of your love. When she says "I know that if you meet another girl you'll tell me. But Bill you won't fall in love with any other will you"—there is implied a doubt. She isn't certain that you will be true because she feels that you are not certain of your own love. ...

♥ ♥ ♥ ♥ ♥

Christine Lincoln, London, England, to Bill Reid, Jr., Harvard University
                                                    23 September 1900

Meanwhile, Christine was in London visiting the Tower of London, St. Paul's Cathedral, Guild Hall, Hyde Park, Kensington Gardens, Parliament, Westminster Abbey, and Kew Gardens, while thinking of Bill.

It does seem so long since I last saw you, and I am longing so to see you again. At times I feel as though I should have to go straight home. The band here has a way of playing "Fair Harvard" while we are at dinner,

ENGAGED, VOYAGE, AND STEAMER AFFAIR

and, as you can imagine, that is nearly too much for me. . . . I miss you sadly. I keep thinking of the good times we could have if your were only here. . . .

I am anxious to hear whether you still feel the same towards me or not. Tell me how you like the picture of me. . . . I often think when looking at things "How Bill would enjoy this!" Well, dear, it's no use, I can't have you, now anyway. Your words, you know the ones I mean, are such a comfort. Not a day goes by without my repeating them myself.
     With all my heart
      Yours, Christine
♥ ♥ ♥ ♥ ♥

Wm. T. Reid, Sr., Belmont, CA, to Bill Reid, Jr., Harvard University
                   24 September 1900

Bill's father kept up his attack upon Bill, this time saying that Christine was a much better person than was Bill.

. . . I've just read your letter about Christine for the third time. I think I'd better not read it again for if I do I shall grow indignant at the thought of your questioning her or leaving her for another moment in suspense or in doubt. That fact is you don't deserve such a sweet, and confiding, and unselfish and devoted girl. Turn your microscope from her upon yourself and if you make a fair comparison of what you find you should turn away from yourself with utter impatience. There is nothing too good for the dear girl and you are not good enough for her. . . . I declare I almost wish that someone would come along and cause her to wonder whether you were after all the fellow or not. It would give you such an awakening as you never had before and would settle for you most effectively any doubts—if any can possibly remain—as to whether she is beyond question the girl for you. . . .

I have yet to find a want that she can't supply. If you feel like being quiet she snuggles quietly by you, if you are buoyant & full of happiness she is happy with you. If you attend a brilliant party among the most beautiful and attractive she is equal to the best, when you talk about the serious work of life she runs to you & puts her hand in yours and tells you that she wants to help you if she can and share your life with you. Dear me I should think you would be ashamed of yourself. . . .

What you should set out to do is to see if it is possible for you to fill Christine's life as full as she can make yours. . . .
♥ ♥ ♥ ♥ ♥

Wm. T. Reid, Sr., Belmont, CA, to Bill Reid, Jr., Harvard University
                   25 September 1900

Wm. Reid, Sr., filled most of 10 pages of contempt for Bill, for snubbing him, for not being democratic, and for emphasizing veneer over the real thing.

A Debutante's Passion—A Coach's Erotica

. . . It is time that you begin to strip the frills and . . . get at the pith and marrow of things. If any one has merit let that weigh, and outweigh the veneer of conventionalities. If I am not good enough to be introduced to Christine, then Belmont is not a good enough place for you to bring Christine to. . . .

♥♥♥♥♥

Christine Lincoln, London, England, to Bill Reid, Jr., Harvard University
25 September 1900

Christine and her family were staying at the Hotel Russell on Russell Square, London, when she replied to one of Bill's letters after spending the day at Windsor Castle.

Your "corking" letter came to-day, and oh! how glad I was to get it! Although it is only a day or two since I wrote you, I cannot resist the temptation to write you to-night. Darling, you could not have written me a better letter, only it did make me so homesick. That night when you walked over to our house, I was sitting out on deck with Ouisie [her sister] and I was talking about you as hard as I could talk. She was very nice about it, and I had a good time. . . .

   Many a time have I wished that I had [not] mailed that steamer letter, horrid as it was. . . .

♥♥♥♥♥

Wm T. Reid, Sr., Belmont, CA, to Bill Reid, Jr., Harvard University
29 September 1900

Bill had just told his parents that he was marrying Christine, and his father's advice was to go slowly in announcing it.

. . . My judgment would be to make the engagement final by getting the consent of parents. I should like exceedingly to write to her but I doubt if it would be just the thing until her people have consented. . . .

♥♥♥♥♥

Wm. T. Reid, Sr., Belmont, CA, letter to Christine Lincoln, Europe
ca. October 1900

Bill's father sent a copy of his letter to Christine, following announcement of her engagement to Bill. In it, he accurately outlined some future problems that Christine would face.

. . . As Will told me more and more about you & as it became plainer & plainer that he was growing very fond of you, I became greatly concerned for I could not help thinking that your life has been one freed wholly

ENGAGED, VOYAGE, AND STEAMER AFFAIR

from care & that your home has been one of luxury & ease & so I felt the seriousness of asking you to leave it & share with him the life that he has chosen to lead at Belmont—a life of activity, responsibility & in some ways, of self sacrifice & that too with a continent between you & the friends of your girlhood. And so when Will brought before you this severe test of your womanhood & affection you again rang out a sweet & clear assent. We could not then help, Christine dear, admitting you heartily to our affections & telling you how gladly we shall welcome you to our household. We cannot hope to make good to you all that you are to give up, but all that we have is yours & we shall be happy if we can bring something new into your life, if with it you can enjoy giving Belmont the helpful influence of your bright and delightful life. . . .

♥♥♥♥♥

Christine Lincoln, Paris, France, to Bill Reid, Jr., Harvard University
3 October 1900

Christine and family had crossed the channel to Paris, when Christine again noted the steamer affair. In addition, Christine's and her mother's comments about California foretold problems that could arise after Christine and Bill were married.

Your letter came last night as I was on my way to dinner, and I was so excited that I could hardly eat. Our room [for Agnes, Louise, and Christine] being the largest, is the rendezvous for the whole party, and I was bound I would not read it there where every one could watch me and make comments. Aunt Mary sympathized with me, and gave me the key to her room so I went there. . . .

Hardly a night goes by, but what I imagine myself as lying in your arms, with my head on your breast. If ever the time comes when I do, Oh! Bill, to quote you, "it makes me just thrill all over to think of it." If I did not trust you as I do, I don't know how I could stand being away so long. . . .

I entirely forgot to tell you how bully that sweater was on the steamer. I wore it almost all the time, and I assure you it made a great impression on board. One of the fellows there got up a newspaper and drew a picture of me with the sweater on for it. There were a few sly remarks about it in the paper too. Another letter has just come from you and still you have not received that beastly steamer letter I wrote. Dear, if you knew how I had worried over that horrid thing! I knew you would not be jealous of that fellow I spoke of, and yet if you had been I could never forgive myself. You need not worry that way, dearest, ever, as you know, I only wish I had not written you about him in such a way. You see I was all tired out, and it was where you did not feel quite sure of your feelings. There is no excuse for me, however, so why say any more. I am so sorry, though, I shall never see that fellow again, and it makes no difference to

69

me whether I do or not. I love you, and you alone, and that's all there is to that. . . .

Bill dear! aren't you awfully glad that we have never had the least quarrel or disagreement? I don't call that Sunday a quarrel, do you? I hope it will always be that way, and I mean to do my best to have it so, for I know that if we should quarrel it would be my fault. . . .

At the table the other night, Mamma said, "Well when I get home from this trip, I shall never travel again." So I said, joking, "Why Mamma of course you'll come out and see me in California, won't you?" She said, "No, you've got to do all the visiting. . . ."

Dear heart, do you really think I can make you happy. . . ? Bill, doesn't it make your heart beat faster at the thought? We two living together!

♥ ♥ ♥ ♥ ♥

Christine Lincoln, Paris, France, to Bill Reid, Jr., Harvard University
7 October 1900

Christine knew that Bill had been thinking of working on a master's degree at Oxford University, something his father had suggested. She did not think that being married at the time was workable.

. . . Dear, I guess it is better that you cannot get your A.M. abroad. Because I don't think we could have been married (it certainly does look queer!) next summer anyway, and I could not let you go off for a whole year alone. I know my family would not have liked it, and then we are pretty young. It would have been nice (rather a poor word) to come over here together, but I don't believe it could have been done. I should not want to marry you (yes, it does look and sound queer) while you were in college, and I'm pretty sure you would rather wait. . . .

♥ ♥ ♥ ♥ ♥

Wm. T. Reid, Sr., Belmont, CA, to Bill Reid, Jr., Harvard University
8 October 1900

By early October, Bill's father had calmed down about his son's shortcomings, especially after the engagement became known to him.

. . . Oh you are a fortunate fellow, a fortunate fellow to get a girl beautiful of face, comely of figure, accomplished in manners and attainments—and thoroughly appreciative and womanly. . . .

I think that that little girl of yours is going to be a democratic little queen. . . .

I like very much your wish for some sacrifice for the sake of a ring for Christine, but I don't want you & Mamma doesn't want you to go to the $4.00 table—unless indeed you can find a $4.00 that is excellent. Oh but that is impossible. We can't set such a table as we have for that.

ENGAGED, VOYAGE, AND STEAMER AFFAIR

And then besides I don't want you to cut yourself off from pleasant table comparisons. I should then be inclined to encourage you to go to a better table if by so doing you could have more agreeable company. . . .

♥ ♥ ♥ ♥ ♥

Wm. T. Reid, Belmont, CA, to Bill Reid, Jr., Harvard University
12 October 1900

Bill's father several times had asked Bill to quote as much as he could from Christine's European letters, and Bill responded.

. . . Oh I think she is fine, and the more she discloses herself the finer she seems. Someday you will understand the sound sense of her saying that she wouldn't give two shucks for a fellow without passion. It now takes your fancy. It was courageous in her to say it, & it was charming in her to feel it & . . . for her to want you to know it. . . . She evidently appreciates the strength and the firmness of refined passion & there is nothing, absolutely nothing that can promise so much happiness in married life. . . .

♥ ♥ ♥ ♥ ♥

Christine Lincoln, Geneva, Switzerland, to Bill Reid, Jr., Harvard University
12 October 1900

Christine wrote from the Grand Hotel Beau Rivage in Geneva, wishing Bill a happy 22nd birthday on October 15th. She had just told her parents about her plans to marry Bill, though her parents must have had a strong inclination of the possibility before this. She brought up the important personal trait, her temper.

. . . I do so wish I were there, I might give you a good big birth-day kiss, like the one you gave me. Dearest, I love you, I love you. . . !

Now to thank you for that "corking" letter, I never in my life had such a fine one. Dear, I do know now that you love me, and I am as happy, even although I am away. . . . I think it was perfectly splendid of your father to send me such a fine message. . . . But dear, it scares me too to have your father and mother have such a high opinion of me, I don't deserve it, indeed, I don't. They mustn't, do tell them what a nasty disposition and temper I have. Please do, dear, they will be so disappointed in me, if they find out afterwards. How can they say that about being afraid I might not like them. . . ! Of course I should love them if only because they were your parents. . . .

This morning I was fooling with Dad a little and I said, "Dad you must be nice to me, you'll only have me a year or two more." He said: "Are you really in earnest?" and I told him I was. Dear, I am afraid they both rather hurt, as I was afraid they would, that we had not told them anything

71

A Debutante's Passion—A Coach's Erotica

before; but I told them how near we had come to telling them that last night in Cohasset, and I think they won't mind after a while. . . ..

Dad says, "Tell him that I think a man who has managed two baseball teams ought to be able to manage a wife. . . ." I have just been talking with Mamma and Papa again & Dad says, "Tell him also that as long as he has succeeded in making a whole university happy, he ought to be able to make one woman happy and that's all I ask." Then I let him read what you wrote about being sorry that we had not told him before, and he said, "tell him that I guess perhaps it was just as well, for I was awfully tired then and it would only have added to my worries." So dear, you see, everything is all right, and we have nothing to worry about. Mamma says again, "Give my love to him and tell him he's a good boy." I know they are both very fond of you. . . .

♥♥♥♥♥

Christine Lincoln, Geneva, Switzerland, to Bill Reid, Jr., Harvard University
17 October 1900

Christine had waited for several weeks to get a reply to her steamer letter of September 12, and she was surprised by the answer from Bill. She also brought up her old boy friend, Eben, and made a comment about Bill's baseball playing at Harvard. She hoped he would not play on the football team during his senior year.

I have just received your letter in answer to that horrid thing I wrote you on the steamer, and oh! Bill, instead of the scolding which I almost expected and certainly deserved, I got the dearest, most loving words from the dearest and most loving fellow in the world. . . .

I have more time than you do, so just write me once in a while and I shall understand it is not because you don't want to. . . .

I wonder if you have happened to run across Eben anywhere! I guess not or you would have told me. I am rather curious to know how you two would strike each other. I know, of course, that he could not help liking you, no one could. . . .

It is splendid, perfectly bully that you did not get one error [in baseball] that whole year. . . ! I do so hope you won't play foot-ball . . . .

♥♥♥♥♥

Wm. T. Reid, Sr., Belmont, CA, to Bill Reid, Jr., Harvard University
21 October 1900

Bill's father was overjoyed with the informal engagement of Bill and Christine, and he wrote possibly the most upbeat letter in his life, mostly about how terrific he thought Christine was, now that she had agreed to live at the Belmont School, and where he would build a 2,600 square foot house for the two of them.

ENGAGED, VOYAGE, AND STEAMER AFFAIR

. . . I doubt if I hoped for all that has come to you in Christine. I believe that she is the finest girl I ever knew. . . .

Oh she's a jewel if there ever was one. . . . Dear girl, I hope she will like us all. . . .

♥ ♥ ♥ ♥ ♥

Christine Lincoln, Vevey, Switzerland, to Bill Reid, Jr., Harvard University

25 October 1900

Christine was swept up with the beauty of Switzerland, but in her 15-page letter she again warned Bill of her unseemly temper, while wishing him a happy 22nd birthday. She did not know that Billl's family was Republican, nor that Bill's father had been forced out as president of the Univeristy of California by a Democratic legislature.

To-day is your birth-day, and you don't know how much I wish I were where I could give you a good big kiss and a hug. . . .

I wish I could tell you that I am improving, but I'm afraid I can't. I do truly try, Bill, to control my beastly temper and conquer my faults, but I don't succeed as well as I ought to. I wish I were more worthy of your love, and I shall keep on trying to be better no matter how discouraged I get. I am afraid you will have a hard life of it with me, Billie dear, but remember I have warned you. . . .

I suppose of course that you are a Republican like most sensible people. I never thought of asking you before. All California, so I read, is Republican, isn't it. . . ?

I never go to bed at night without thinking that perhaps sometime when I crawl (elegantly put) in I shall feel your dear arms around me. . . .

♥ ♥ ♥ ♥ ♥

Wm. T. Reid, Sr., Belmont, CA, to Bill Reid, Jr., Harvard University

28 October 1900

Always the advisor, Bill's father opined on Bill and Christine's wedding date, suggesting that it not occur until Bill received his master's degree from Harvard.

. . . Christine is wholly right in thinking that it is not wise for you to be married next year. It would be altogether a mistake. Don't think of marrying until you have your A.M. & are ready after a four or a six months trip to get down to work. I am delighted to be able to make things easy for you but you are going to have the opportunities of a millionaire's son and you must not run the risk of appreciating in a large way what you are going to enjoy. . . .

♥ ♥ ♥ ♥ ♥

A Debutante's Passion—A Coach's Erotica

Christine Lincoln, Berne, Switzerland, to Wm. T. Reid, Sr., Belmont, CA
29 October 1900

Christine responded to Wm. Reid, Sr.'s letter to her, after the engagement to Bill was made official, but not announced to the world. In it, Christine noted a couple problems, her temper and being away from her parents—two difficulties that would later plague their marriage.

Dear Mr. Reid:
I cannot tell you how touched and pleased I was when I received your letter yesterday. I must admit that it scared me a little too. You have set a very high standard before me, & I thank you very much, and shall do my best to live up to it, but I may fail. Then how disappointed you will be in me. I cannot bear to think of it. If I do fail it will not be through lack of trying though. I almost wish that you did not have such a high opinion of me. I don't see why you do. I have told Bill often that he must tell you what a bad temper and disagreeable disposition I have, but I fear that he has not done so. You see the trouble is that no one could be cross with Bill, and so he has never seen the worst side of me. I do try to control my temper, but it flies out before I know it. It is true I have led an easy and useless life, with few, if any, responsibilities but I have thought pretty seriously. I am not a bit afraid of work only afraid of not being able to do it well & I will do the very best I can to be worthy of your good opinion & Bill's love. I love him with all my heart & that being so I ought not to go far wrong. I used to try to tease him a little by saying that I was as much in love with you as with him, & indeed I am very fond of you. I should be proud & happy if I could win your affection & trust. I think the way you and Mrs. Reid have treated me is too splendid for anything, and I am more grateful than I can say. As Bill has already written you, my father & mother now know all about it. They are much pleased as they are very fond of Bill, but they do not like the idea of my going so far away. It is a great relief to me to have told them, for it seemed only right that they should know, and I trust that Bill will feel the same way. . . .

♥♥♥♥♥

Christine Lincoln, Munich, Germany, to Bill Reid, Jr., Harvard University
10 November 1900

The time away from Bill was already wearing on Christine as she wrote a lengthy letter from Munich. She noted: "Can I stand it over here seven months more?"

You don't know what perfect torture I have been in for the last few days! In the first place I had not heard from you for over a week. That was bad enough but I should not have thought so very much about it if I had not got a letter from Ethel saying, "I must tell you what happened to Bill Reid!" Then she told me that you had gotten off a car on the wrong side and that another car came along just as you were in the track. She went on to say that you had presence of mind enough to jump on the fender, or whatever it is, and then said, "Wasn't it a narrow escape?" Not a word as to whether you were hurt or not, and so worried and anxious as I have been the last three or four days. . . . All the enjoyment went out of everything, and I could neither eat nor sleep. . . .

You say you hope I will like your plan of going to Europe on our honeymoon. I do, it's perfectly "corking." What glorious fun it will be, perfect bliss! To be always together. . . ! To be with you night and day, Oh! Bill, it makes my heart pound at the very thought of it. What it will do when the reality comes, I don't know. Then it will beat against you, think of it. . . !

♥♥♥♥♥

Christine Lincoln, Stuttgart, Germany, to Bill Reid, Jr., Harvard University
11 November 1900

Christine's love grew stronger in absentia, or so it seemed.

. . . It is sweeter to be caressed by the hand that could kill, than by the one that at its worst and strongest could only scratch. . . . I think that that is true, at least I know I feel that way. I am so glad that you are so big and strong. I like to think that you could kill me if you wanted to. There is a certain fascination about it, I suppose. Still another is, "Where does friendship end and love begin?" You know I can't at all remember when I began to care for you in this way. It must have been ever so long ago, before we said anything—because when we did, it seemed quite natural, you know. And it always grows. It goes on growing like a thing that's planted in good earth & has lots of life in it and is going to last forever. But it really does grow. I know that I'm ever so much more glad to see you when we meet now that I was a month ago. If it goes on like this I don't know where it's going to end. . . .

♥♥♥♥♥

Wm. T. Reid, Sr., Belmont, CA, to Bill Reid, Jr., Harvard University
14 November 1900

The engagement ring was not only on the mind of Bill but of his father, who would pay for it.

. . . I looked over a tray of [engagement rings] and selected one that I thought about Christine's quality and asked the price. I was taken aback when he told me $250. It was brilliant but not at all ostentatious—a ring that I should be perfectly willing to have you give her. . . . Well, Christine is a little luxury and nothing is too good for her and within the limits of good taste. You want the best or nothing. . . .

♥♥♥♥♥

Christine Lincoln, Munich, Germany, to Bill Reid, Jr., Harvard University
17 November 1900

Christine told Bill of her love, fantasizing about married life. But she also again warned him of her temper.

. . . Oh! Billie, what fun we will have if we do come abroad together! I am looking forward to it already, the being with you night and day. I cannot imagine anything more absolutely blissful than to lie in your arms all night. To feel those dear strong arms around me and your dear face against mine! It makes me thrill all over to think of it. Does it you? Oh! Billie, there isn't a single night that I don't think of it! Do you consider it immodest of me to say such things? Tell me, dear, won't you. . . ?

About my temper, Bill you must take my word for it, for, as I wrote your father, it is impossible for any to be cross with you and so you have never seen the worst side of me. You did catch a glimpse of it that day on the links, but I assure you I can be a good deal nastier than that even. I am really glad, in a way, that I was so horrid that time, because I want you to know that I have got that in me. In spite of my numerous faults, though, I don't honestly think you will have a hard life of it with me, because I love you too much, and that will keep me from very great mistakes. If I thought so, I would try not to marry you. . . .

♥♥♥♥♥

Christine Lincoln, Munich, Germany, to Bill Reid, Jr., Harvard University
ca. 20 November 1900

The Lincolns were to have an extended stay in Munich, residing in a pension, and Christine was taking German lessons. She told of observing a grand military ball and a Jewish wedding.

. . . The next day there was a Jewish wedding celebration in the same hall, and that was ever more fun to see than the ball. It began at one P.M. and lasted until 4 A.M. I don't think we'd better have that kind, do you? Well, for the first four or five hours they did nothing except eat, drink healths, and make speeches. The bride was very pretty and attractive. . . , the groom was very devoted. . . . They were so excited and happy that I loved to watch them, and I kept wondering how we would act and feel in their place. I also wondered if they weren't thinking that the best was yet to come that night. . . .

♥♥♥♥♥

ENGAGED, VOYAGE, AND STEAMER AFFAIR

Christine Lincoln, Munich, Germany, to Bill Reid, Jr., Harvard University
24 November 1900

Christine replied to Bill's letter and the clippings about Harvard football, while she awaited the results of the Yale game in which Bill would not take part. But her heart was elsewhere.

. . . We are having such dreary cold days here that it makes one feel very "blue." I don't care much for cold weather anyway. Do you have cold weather in California. . . ?

The sweater is lying on the trunk side of me, I like to see it. If you were here, I would put it on and then you could "stick your mouth inside and get at the choice spots" all you wanted to. My own dear love! I wish you were here, I'd just kiss you to pieces. . . .

♥♥♥♥♥

Wm. T. Reid, Sr., Belmont, CA, to Bill Reid, Jr., Harvard University
26 November 1900

The elder Reid looked forward to Bill taking over his Belmont School after his marriage to Christine. He also looked forward to Bill and Christine's children.

. . . Your engagement too has given me a new motive for wanting to live. I am almost afraid to have you know how almost my whole life now consists in anticipating the babies that I hope will come to you and Christine. There is nothing that can come into my life that would so fill it out with happiness and so I can settle for life except for what you children can bring into it, and I want to leave things so that your life shall not be filled with the fury and the grind that has filled me. . . .

♥♥♥♥♥

Christine Lincoln, Munich, Germany, to Bill Reid, Jr., Harvard University
28 November 1900

All of Christine's letters contained versions of her love for Bill, but she only rarely brought up something that was on her mind, the steamer incident and her previous letter to Bill.

. . . Now I am going over your letter—I read them all over yesterday beginning with the Steamer letter, and I do love them so! You write the very best, and dearest ones I ever knew or could ever imagine, just full of love and it is such a pleasure to read them over and over. . . !

♥♥♥♥♥

A Debutante's Passion—A Coach's Erotica

Christine Lincoln, Munich, Germany, to Bill Reid, Jr., Harvard University
29 November 1900

The "blues" of Christine may have been symptomatic of an underlining personality behavior or just because she missed Bill and knew that she would not see him for over a half-year.

Although I wrote to you yesterday, I feel so much like writing to you to-night that I cannot resist the temptation. I have spend most of my Thanksgiving Day in bed, and I have been thinking of you so steadily all day that you seem very close to me to-night. If only you were physically so! What wouldn't I give to see you if only for a few minutes! I had an awful "blue" fit this afternoon, and it seemed as if I should go wild with the longing to see you. . . .

♥♥♥♥♥

Jacob P. Palmer, Tiffany Diamonds, New York City, to Wm. T. Reid, Sr., Belmont, CA
3 December 1900

Jacob Palmer of Tiffany Diamonds and Bill's father had known each other since college days at Harvard. The senior Reid wanted the best for Bill and Christine.

. . . I only wish that you and your son were here, so that I could show the goods as an object-lesson . . . In the first place strictly fine quality diamonds have been increasingly scarce for the past few years. Their scarcity has been increased by the Boer War. Prices therefore for very fine goods are higher than they were a year ago. . . . As to size, Tiffany & Co. can give you for $100 a pure white diamond, weighing say 1/32 less than ¾ Kt. and set in a lady's 18 Kt. ring. For $160 the same weighing 1 Karat. For $200 the same weighing 1 3/16 Karat. For $250 the same weighing 1 3/8 1/32 Karat. These prices are for perfect diamonds, first quality in every respect. And as a rule this is the quality for engagement rings. . . .

♥♥♥♥♥

Christine Lincoln, Munich, Germany, to Bill Reid, Jr., Harvard University
6 December 1900

Christine's twelve-page letter discussed her future engagement ring, her former boy friend, and closed with a pledge of love.

My own dearest Love,
   . . . Dearest, you did not really think that I could want to get it [the engagement ring] over here did you? Don't you realize that half the pleasure of having it would be having you choose it and put it on my

finger . . . ? I wish almost that you had not asked me what kind of a "ring" I would rather have because I want you to give me whatever you want to. . . . As long as you did ask me though, I suppose I must tell you that to me a "solitaire" seems more like an engagement ring. Please, though, give me just whatever you want to. I shall like that the best. . . .

I don't wonder Corrine laughed when someone asked her about Eben and me! It makes me laugh to think that I could every have fancied for a moment that I "loved" him. When I compared the "love" that I have for you and the feeling that I had for him, it seems too ridiculous for anything. He wrote in his last letter, after sending his love to all the family, "I send it to you too if you will accept it." Lest he should by any possible chance make a mistake about the way I feel towards him. I wrote, "Remember that I am your friend as much as ever if you will accept my friendship. . . .

We sang some college songs, among them "Fair Harvard" and you can imagine where my mind was then! I thought of last Class Day on the stairs of Beck Hall! We must go up there next Class Day for Auld Lang Syne's sake, don't you think so? Dearest good-night. I love you every minute with my whole heart and soul. Take good care of your dear old self for me.

With all the love I am capable of and kisses and hugs. I am
Yours lovingly,
Christine William's Reid
♥♥♥♥♥

Christine Lincoln, Munich, Germany, to Bill Reid, Jr., Harvard University
8 December 1900

Christine noted the 1898 Harvard-Yale football game in which Bill, as a sophomore, starred by scoring two touchdowns (no one had ever done that before against Yale), and getting a full-page picture in Harper's Weekly. She also wanted to comfort Bill after he had recently told her that the Harvard elite had snubbed him.

. . . I shall never forget that game either for it was one of the best times I ever had. Little did I think then, though, that I was going to marry the famous Harvard full back. . . .

It made me simply want to go home and see you. I felt as if I must go and kiss you and try to comfort you a little, and yet I knew how hopeless it was to feel that way, for I could not go. I don't know how many times I have really seriously considered going home to you! It has been very, very often, for my longing for you is almost unbearable at times, and my heart aches so that it is absolute pain. I begin to think of the reasons why it is better that I should be away, and I manage to stifle down my longing for that time. I suppose Billie, it is better for us to be apart, isn't it? I cannot always think so, but I guess it must be. Your mother said it

A Debutante's Passion—A Coach's Erotica

was, and I think her reason is a good one, though it does seem as if we know a great deal about each other now. . . .

When I come home, to pay you up, I shall have a big fire in the fireplace and make you sit there with me in your lap for a whole hour, perhaps two! Now will you be good? You darling. . . ! "Just take me in your arms and fondle (I like that word, it expresses so much and you do it as well!) and kiss me." And may I kiss you too. . . ?

♥♥♥♥♥

Bill Reid, Jr., Harvard University, to Christine Lincoln, Munich, Germany
12 December 1900

Certainly one of the highest honors at Harvard was to be named to a Marshalship during the senior year. Bill told Christine of the politics and social class rancor behind the selections. Particularly galling to Bill was the "fast set," a group of rich Harvard men, perhaps one in twenty at Harvard, who set themselves apart, many living in the luxurious private dorms called the "Gold Coast." They also dominated the Hasty Pudding Club, first formed in 1795 as a social club. It was an honor to be elected to the Pudding, something Bill attained because of his athletic prominence.

My own, darling, little girl:
You loving sweetheart—you—if it hadn't been for your blessed love—I don't know what I should have done these last few days. You see, the question of my nomination, by the Pudding, for a Marshalship has been before me all the time. I knew that the Sears, Fairchild, Lyman crowd was working hard as it could to keep my name out of it—and I also knew that the Chas. Rotch, Chas. Jaynes, Loud, Harold Clark crowd—the steady, thinking crowd, was working for me. I knew it would be close—and couldn't help feeling very much wrought up. I felt that an attempt was being made—by the fast set—to down me and that possibility worried me more than anything else. I felt that they had a right to vote against my election, but that they had no right to decline to allow me to be nominated—when a strong sentiment in the class as a whole, demanded it. That is, I felt that a strong injustice was being done me in allowing that set of fellows to decide whether I should be allowed to run. You see—with a slate—if I wasn't on the slate, I should have to refuse outside nominations, was to help the slate men along. Well—that batch—the fast set—wanted to keep me off the slate & thus from having anything. Had it been the sober set opposed to me, I should have had nothing to say, but to feel that the fast set was trying to run me out, made me extremely anxious not to get run out. Well, the meeting to decide the question was held last night—and after a good hard fight in which the best men in the Pudding got right up & talked, I won out. That is to say, I shall be nominated by the Pudding slate as a Marshal—Lawrence, Daly & Hallowell to be also up. I am now satisfied. . . !!! I'm heartily

sick of this mean, underhanded system and the wire pulling crowd that is trying to operate it. I reiterate, I am satisfied, just to have beaten that crowd.

What my chances are before the class, I don't know & what is more I'm not deeply interested. If the class finds out what has been going on, and stands by me, I shall of course be very much gratified—if they don't, I shall feel that in a semi-fair competition I lost by the will of the class, and shall be satisfied. If the class doesn't choose to confer an honor on me—well & good that's allright—I'd rather not have it.

This sounds rather "sour grapes" in writing, but it is not the way I feel in the least. My contention is for fair-play—that assured—I'm satisfied.

It would have done you good to have been at the meeting and seen how the "right" cropped out in spite of the threats and expostulations of the "wrong." I'll give you a little account of what was said:

When the question of running four men for the Marshal positions was raised—Harry Lyman, Ellis Postlethwaite and Eddie Sears got up and demanded in substance—"Why four men should be run anymore than eight—and why, when it had been voted to have a slate—we shouldn't have a slate—or why—if four men were to be put up for the Marshalship—several men should not be put up for the other positions."

Harold Clark then got up & said—"The questions of running an extra man for a Marshalship and an extra man for any other position—are two absolutely different ones—there isn't a fellow here who, whether he acknowledges it or not—does not know & feel—that Jim Lawrence, Dan Daly, Jack Hallowell & Bill Reid have done the most for this class and, as far as honors are concerned, are in a class by themselves. You all know that the class as a whole wishes the four men to be put up and if the Pudding leaves any one out, there is no telling what measures will be taken by the class at large to defeat the whole slate."

I then got up—and said—"That if I was to be run for a Marshalship I wanted it understood that the other three men should be run too—or I would refuse to run. That whatever satisfaction & honor was to be gotten out of a Marshalship was to be gotten out of the feeling that the Marshalship came as a gift bestowed by the class—when every other possible candidate was up before the class—and not as a gift by a club vote whereby a worthy rival was to be denied a chance." I went on to say —"that rather than take a Marshalship by default, as such a procedure would accomplish, I'd much prefer to be left out of everything."

A little murmur of justification followed my little "speech" & when Jim Lawrence got up and vehemently declared that he would refuse to run unless all four were up, the case was practically won. Those of the fellows who had been on the "fence" came over to our side and the Lyman, Sears crowd skulked off in one corner. In the "standing" vote that was taken the "right" won. Lyman, Fairchild, Sears etc.—were simply wild—they were almost foaming at the mouth. The rest of us watched them with great satisfaction.

A Debutante's Passion—A Coach's Erotica

Then, the question of who should be chairman of the Class Com.—that is, permanent President of the class, came up, and it was suggested that the defeated Marshal have the place. I then got up again & said: "The Chairman of the Class Committee is the permanent President of the Class—and should be on hand, on succeeding Class Days, for reunions, etc. I live in California and if I were to be elected I should feel that I was not the best man—as I could not hope to 'come on' every year. Therefore I wish to state that whether I get elected or not I shall refuse to serve. . . ."

The next row occurred over the selection of orator. The fast set wished to elect Lyman, but the rest of us rebelled. I was not tongue tied as in the case where my own fate was to be decided and so I got up and spoke out. I said: "In deciding to have a slate this year, we decided that it was almost necessary to make sure that the best men in the class got a fair show. Therefore by taking things into our own hands we have assumed a sacred responsibility. If we put up a man from our number for orator merely because he's a Pudding man we disregard our mission and the slate becomes a thoroughly bad influence."

Eddie Coolidge—of the [baseball] nine—got up & said—"There's no use talking, we haven't a speaker of any sort in the Pudding and there is no use trying to say there is. The best speakers are the debaters and one of the men who helped beat Yale last week is a 1901 man. I move that we put him on the slate."

This was finally done, and so the matter was ended. The other positions go to men you don't know, so I shan't say anything more about it. We downed the vicious crowd—that's the main point. When the election is to take place hasn't yet been decided—it may not "come off" till after Christmas. I don't care when, Christine dear, you little know what a comfort your love has been. With apparently the "fast" set of the Pudding against me & therefore only a small chance of fair play, I naturally felt quite worried. But through it all, I have said to myself, "Well, whatever happens, that darling, true, loving little girl loves me, and that's worth everything else in this world to me." I wished oh, so many times, that you were where I could go and "love" you—where I could take you in my arms and show you what you are to me & how I love you. With the feeling that whatever else happened—you still loved me—I faced the whole situation with an absolutely calm face—with a calmness and dignity which the fellows wondered at. They saw I was not scrambling for a place—they saw I meant to receive any treatment without a whimper of any kind and they wondered. Why, you blessing you, do you suppose I felt & acted that way? Because as long as I know you love me, nothing—absolutely nothing—can discourage or disconcert me. Oh—I am so, so fond of you—so, so proud of you and so, so wrapped up in your love—that I don't know what to do.

When all was over last night I went to my room and kneeled down and thanked God for you, and I prayed that I might be worthy of you. . . .

♥ ♥ ♥ ♥ ♥

ENGAGED, VOYAGE, AND STEAMER AFFAIR

Wm. T. Reid, Sr., Belmont, CA, to Bill Reid, Jr., Harvard University
13 December 1900

Several weeks before, Harvard was defeated by Yale 28-0 in a game in which Yale gained 555 yards to only 153 for Harvard. Bill Reid had not played football his senior year, in part because he did not like either the 1900 coach, Ben Dibblee, or the captain, Charlie Daly. Almost immediately after the defeat by Yale, Bill was asked to coach the Harvard football team for 1901, a distinct honor for Reid.

It is mighty fine to have you called upon to repair the fortunes of Harvard football. Nothing has come to you in your athletics that is such a recognition and such a triumph. . . . Of course I should like immensely to have you snow Dibblee & Daly under by turning out a winning team. . . . I heartily consent. But let me anticipate a little and say that I would not be willing to have you coach for pay after getting out of College for any consideration. That would be a distinct step down. . . .

♥♥♥♥♥

Christine Lincoln, Munich, Germany, to Bill Reid, Jr., Harvard University
ca. 15 December 1900

Christine had just been to Nuremberg with its churches and city wall, but there were no letters forwarded to her. She returned to Munich, where the most important item, a letter, awaited.

. . .You say I am "the finest person to fondle, caress and squeeze," well! you are certainly the very finest person to do the fondling, caressing, and squeezing, and I do love to be squeezed, as much, and I guess a little more than you like to squeeze me. Do you remember those nights, where after coming home from a dance or something, we would be in the sofa together? You would take your collar off and there I could put my bare arm around your neck! Oh! I did love it so, did you? Those were dear old days, weren't they, Bill. . .?
 Good-bye my own dear love—God bless you—
 Lovingly
 Christine

X O X O X O X O X O X O
——— X O

♥♥♥♥♥

A Debutante's Passion—A Coach's Erotica

Bill Reid, Jr., Harvard University, to Christine Lincoln, Venice, Italy
16 December 1900

Bill again wrote Christine of the undergraduate politics at Harvard, especially in choosing the class Marshals that was dominated by the Hasty Pudding Club. While he had no love for the Harvard elites, his love for Christine was as strong as ever. In addition, Bill discussed some aspects of the football coaching position he had been offered at Harvard, and he offered some comments about his place at Harvard.

I guess it's a good thing for you, that you have been so far out of my reach these last few days—for I'm afraid if you had been here and I had gotten hold of you I'd have made short work of you. I have been just ravenous for you——. Last night, when I got into bed, I just snuggled up in the bed clothes—stretched out my arms, as if to wrap you up in them, and tried to imagine how it would feel to have you actually there—where I could draw you close to me and kiss and hug you. It was regular "torture." How I have yearned for you, those lips, those eyes, those cheeks!!! If you were only here now—I'd put my arm around you and walk you over to the fire—into my lap—put my arms around you—draw you close—and put in an hour or two, fondling, hugging and kissing you. You'd slip one of your dear little hands into my breast, and we'd be absolutely happy wouldn't we? I know we would but—tell me so—won't you. . . ?

. . . I was planning to try and break up the whole [election] affair by getting one of the other candidates for a marshalship, as well as one or two of the candidates for other positions to withdraw with me & thus leave vacancies, so that new nominations and a new election would have to be arranged for. I hoped in the meantime to get one or two of the clubs to withdraw from the slate all together thus make the election a public as well as a representative one.

[The election of class Marshal] is in the hands of the class—if they want me they'll have me—if not they won't The whole affair is to be regretted. . . .

[When the Boston *Herald* reported that I was chosen head football coach] of course I had a rush of reporters to my room at once. When they came, I expressed surprise at the article, denied that I had been appointed, that Dibblee & Daly had kept me off [the 1900] team, and then refused absolutely to discuss the question further. I told them I was baseball captain—that if they wanted foot-ball facts they'd have to go to the foot-ball captain & so turned them off on Campbell; then before they could get to him, I telephoned him & told him to simply state that no appointment had yet been made & that there was nothing further to say—and then to say absolutely nothing else. He did this and nothing appeared in today's papers. . . .

ENGAGED, VOYAGE, AND STEAMER AFFAIR

In the spring of 1902 following the foot-ball season I am likely to be asked to help coach the nine. That is to say, in a year & a half, I will have been Capt. of the nine, head coach of the Eleven and assistant coach of the nine. Now that's more than any man has ever had offered him, during the entire history of Harvard. It's a big proposition, you see. . . .

♥♥♥♥♥

Bill Reid, Jr., Harvard University, to Christine Lincoln, Venice, Italy
ca. 17-18 December 1900

In one of the few letters in which pages were missing (the first four), Bill showed that Christine was not the only thing on his mind. Beating Yale in baseball was high on the list. Yet, in this 22-page letter, Christine was certainly not left out.

. . . It is quite true that we are not going to play Princeton this season—it is unfortunate but true. I mean in base-ball of course. It's just this way;— When we started to arrange games with Princeton they astonished us by issuing an ultimatum declaring that if we played at all we should play 3 games. Now I don't intend to allow any college to dictate to Harvard. If they decide that they want to play three games or none allright—that's their affair, but for them to tell us that it will be 3 or none is a mistake. What they ought to have done was to try to arrange three games— & failing of that to say that they could not then afford to play at all. That would be dignified and yet firm. But for them to notify us—before a single arrangement had been made—that it has to be 3 or more was too much. . . .

Harvard has not made it her policy to engage in a duel contest or rivalry with any other college than Yale; Yale is our goal— & all else is merely a preparation to reach the goal. . . . Harvard is out to beat Yale— not the universe—she is out to beat Yale & not for the championship, for none exists. . . .

I did not decide all this on my own responsibility—but on that of Prof. Hollis, Coach Nichols and the Athletic Committee. . . .

I rather guess I do remember the time we were caught in the rain. I just wanted to hug you in the worst way—you might to have seen that in my eyes. I was afraid of them myself that day, because they were such easy reading. I didn't want you to read it all—just then. If you only had—hugged me—you'd have found a willing & responsive (demonstrative) subject. You did look so cute standing all wrapped up on that porch—I am afraid I loved you right then. Anyhow—what does it matter—you had me from the very time I first met you—on. I made a little struggle—but found the web so strong—yet as gentle, loving & delightful—that I wouldn't have escaped for the whole world. . . .

♥♥♥♥♥

A Debutante's Passion—A Coach's Erotica

Bill Reid, Jr., Harvard University, to Christine Lincoln, Venice, Italy
18 December 1900

Bill wrote a steady stream of letters to Christine, who replied to Bill in letters as long as 36 pages in length.

. . .I love your dainty figure—your soft red cheeks, your beautiful lips, your eyes, your neck, oh, just all of you. . . .
    I just wish I could be with you on Christmas, to slip on your dainty little finger—a solitaire, if that's what you would rather have, anyway a ring. I wish I might kiss it on, and solemnly pledge my whole life to you, nothing could make me happier. . . .
    To think of meeting and overcoming life's battles, with you at my side—oh—I just long to begin. To think of waking at night and feeling you next to me, to think of waking in the morning and seeing you still asleep, beautiful and sweet, to think of you as a mother—the most sacred and blessed of all womanly attributes, just makes me thrill with purpose, with joy and with thankfulness. . . .

♥♥♥♥♥

Bill Reid, Jr., Harvard University, card to Christine Reid, Venice, Italy
19 December 1900

One of the few cards exchanged between Bill and Christine follows.

Christine
For the dearest, sweetest—most loving little girl—that ever was. May the New Year bring with it the fulfillment of all your hopes and desires—and may it bring you safely back to one who loves you more than words can tell—& who is waiting with wide open arms to receive you.
    Love a million times over—
              "Bill"

♥♥♥♥♥

Bill Reid, Jr., Harvard University, to Christine Reid, Venice, Italy
ca. 19 December 1900

Bill pledged fidelity to his fiancée, and at the same time proudly told her that he had been elected a class Marshal. Jim Lawrence had received 350 votes, Reid 346, Charlie Daly 263, and John Hallowell 252. In addition, Bill had also been offered the head coaching position in football, which he had not accepted at this point.

. . . It is a big comfort to be decent after all—even if it does take a struggle. You girls don't realize just what a fellow has to fight against. . . .

ENGAGED, VOYAGE, AND STEAMER AFFAIR

After such a lot of pettiness as has entered into this election against me—I feel deeply gratified at having the class stand by me so loyally. I got the place in the face of the biggest odds that could be worked against me, and I think I can rightly take considerable satisfaction in it. This is the first time in the last ten or twelve years when a base-ball captain has even gotten a marshalship. This too makes it a satisfaction. . . .

I am very sorry for Hallowell—I wish he'd beaten Daly, for I think that Daly is really small. . . .

♥♥♥♥♥

Christine Lincoln, Munich, Germany, to Bill Reid, Jr., Harvard University
19 December 1900

Christine's extremely long letters tell of her experiences in Europe, of common friends back home, but mostly of her desire to be with Bill.

Your letters are the very dearest, sweetest I ever knew or ever dreamed of! I simply adore them, every one, and I can't tell you how much I appreciate your writing so faithfully. That is one of the ways to my heart, and I love you Oh! so much for taking so much time and trouble. When you are so awfully busy too! Oh! I am such a lucky girl, I realize it more and more every day. Dearest, you are the very first man in the world! Now for that letter, it makes me just tingle all over whenever I read it. Needless to say, I tingle rather often. His heart is the most comfortable pillow imaginable and his eyes the dearest and most loving in the world. There are none like them, and when I think that they are all mine now, well—I am blissfully happy. — — — . . .

"Will I let your hand snuggle up to me when we are married?" Billie dear, you know I will. That idea, strange and incomprehensible as it may appear, has entered my head too! I can quite believe that it is a pleasant, to put it mildly, feeling, and I am quite anxious to know for myself just how it feels. You have never experienced one of the finest feelings that I have had, and I am rather afraid you never will. That is to have the person you love best in the whole world take you right up in his arms and hold you tight against his breast. Then think how delicious it must be to put your arms round his neck and cuddle up to him! Have him whisper "little girl" in your ear and give you a kiss and a tight squeeze! Think of that ! Now don't you envy me. . . ?

That Scituate Beach drive was indeed a fine one, and I liked the talk too. We seemed to get closer together that night somehow. Mentally, I mean, we seemed to get always pretty close physically. It's so queer, but I do love to feel you near me. . . !

It was a very flimsy pretext that of my being out to mail a letter that evening last spring. I wonder I dared give such a one. I "met you half way" that time all right anyway. My heart gave a bound too when I saw you coming up the hill. I can see you now as you looked then, you dear

A Debutante's Passion—A Coach's Erotica

old fellow. As to my being able to have most any one, it's perfect rot, that's all there is to say about that. . . .

The maid just came in and, having asked and found that I was alone, asked if I did not find the time pass slowly. She does not realize that I am along only outwardly, you see. Poor little thing! The way the servants have to work over here is terrible! I believe she gets something like a mark (25 cents) a week too. Of course that means more over here than it would in America, but it's little enough. . . .

Billie, I am just crazy for a kiss this very minute! Oh! if you were only here, how I would kiss you and hug you and love you! I do long for you so, I don't know what to do. I lie awake for hours after I go to bed, and just think, think, think of you. . . .

♥ ♥ ♥ ♥ ♥

Bill Reid, Jr., Harvard University, to Christine Lincoln, Venice, Italy
22 December 1900

Bill's very long letter discussed the likelihood of accepting the head coaching position in football "unless you don't wish it," as well as activities at Harvard, including the death of an undergraduate acquaintance. But, he began his letter with a salute to Christine.

My own darling, little wife:
If I only had you here now, what a time I should have. To begin with, I'd just walk up to you and simply pick you up in my arms and hug you—then I'd give you a good long kiss—at the same time looking straight into your beautiful eyes. I could look straight into your eyes—unflinchingly too—because there is absolutely nothing happening in my life that you don't know about—no double life to conceal—no disloyalty to hide. I love you—you alone and with all my heart. After that kiss and that look—(I just love to think of it) I'd take both your hands in mine—hold you off a moment (I couldn't stand it any longer) and glory in you and then I'd draw you to me again, and just cover you with kisses. I'd do this until I made you "croon"—for I love to hear you—and then I'd put an arm around your lovely little waist and guide you to my chair before the fire. There, I'd sit down and draw you gently to me. I'd see to it that that beautiful, sweet face of yours lay next to mine and that your mouth was close to mine. Then I'd close my eyes and fondle and caress you. I'd "love" you—oh so tenderly. Perhaps!!! Your little hand might stray in on my breast—I know it would. If such were only the case now, who could be happier than I. . . . I love to hold you so close that I can feel your chest heave—for it gives me a feeling of "protection," and a feeling of "nearness" to you. . . .

Oh, but you are such a beauty, such a dear, and such a comfort!!!—You, darling bride, you, my own little girl, I love you.

ENGAGED, VOYAGE, AND STEAMER AFFAIR

This is a clear, mild, sunny day, just the day for a drive. Ah—dearie—wouldn't it be just bliss itself to go off together this afternoon? What a picture you would be—dressed in my favorite dress—beautiful, loving, sweet—and how proud I'd be to be seen with you and to have people say—"I guess they're engaged" or better still—"I guess they are in love." My eyes and my attitude towards you (it couldn't be helped) would give the whole thing away. . . .

♥♥♥♥♥

Bill Reid, Jr., Harvard University, to Christine Lincoln, Venice, Italy
ca. 24 December 1900

Although engaged albeit without a ring and formal announcement to Christine, Bill was always aware that Christine's old friends might still get between the two of them.

. . . I think your reply to Eben was a very wise one—you don't want to give him any hopes—and you answered him in such a way as to bring that point out. . . .

As for the ring—I hoped dearest—that you would want to wait, but I wanted you to have the ring over there if you'd enjoy it more. How I shall enjoy putting it on your dear little finger. When I do it—I'll have you with me alone—where I can fondle and kiss you all I want and where I can give myself and my life with the ring. . . .

I'm so glad too, that you would rather have a "solitaire"—I like them much better than anything else. But I wanted you to have what would please you most. It will be a "solitaire" then—so don't worry for fear it will be something else. . . . Is there anything we don't absolutely agree on. . . ?

Isn't it dandy that we are so demonstrative—it's so much nicer than being half cold to each other. I can't imagine such a thing with us, can you? I just want to have my arms around you all the time—to kiss you and to hug you. At night I want you to lie in my arms and in the morning I want you where I can just turn over and kiss you "good morning."

Just wait until we do sleep together—& then I will show you just how I imagined kissing and hugging you—& you can show me how you did it. Won't it be fun. — Yes, bliss, I shall hold you to your threat of building a fire and sitting in my lap before it—for about ten hours—instead of one or two. I'll undergo threats like that—anytime.

"Christine William's Reid,"—at last you acknowledge the apostrophe in there don't you? I love it—& I love your new name. . . .

♥♥♥♥♥

Christine Lincoln, Munich, Germany, to Bill Reid, Jr., Harvard University
27 December 1900

Christine responded to Bill being invited to be Harvard's coach in 1901 and the controversy within the Hasty Pudding over the Marshalships.

A Debutante's Passion—A Coach's Erotica

. . . Dearest love, I do indeed think it's perfectly splendid about your being asked to be Head Coach of the football team next year. I am glad to know that the teams and all have so much sense, for I was beginning to think, judging by those Pudding men, that something else must be the trouble with Harvard and fellows.

I would just love to kiss you and hug you, and show you how I appreciate your sweetness. Billie, I love you. . . .

Well, sweetheart, I must say good-night now. . . . I wish I could give you a good-night kiss as I used to at Cohasset. . . .

♥ ♥ ♥ ♥ ♥

Christine Lincoln, Venice, Italy, to Bill Reid, Jr., Harvard University
31 December 1900

Christine, touring Venice but feeling rather blue from her lengthy travels through Europe, expressed concerns about her future father-in-law's expectations. The concerns would be realized during her two extended stays in California in that decade.

. . . I had a long letter from your father to-day. Oh! Such a nice one. But it scares me. Billie dear, it really does, when I think how much he expects of me. All I can promise is to love you with my whole heart and soul and to do the very best I can to be a good wife to you. . . .

♥ ♥ ♥ ♥ ♥

Christine Lincoln, Venice, Italy, to Bill Reid, Jr., Harvard University
2 January 1901

Even in January, Venice was a city that Christine wished she could share with Bill.

Billie dearest,

Although I wrote you only a day ago, I cannot resist the temptation to write you to-night. Oh! How I wish you were here! Venice is really the most fascinating place you can imagine, and if we do come abroad together, we must come here, for I know you would love it. . . .

There is a very loving couple in the palazzo opposite us. They come out on their little balcony all the time and kiss and "love" each other. Agnes and Albert [sister and uncle] watched them through opera glasses most of the after-noon. It is rather too tantalizing a sight for me. Venice is certainly a romantic spot, but the romance in one sense of the word, anyway, is lacking for me. Billie, sweetheart, I do want you so. . . !

♥ ♥ ♥ ♥ ♥

Christine Lincoln, Venice, Italy, to Bill Reid, Jr., Harvard University
3 January 1901

ENGAGED, VOYAGE, AND STEAMER AFFAIR

In a letter about love, football head coaching, and Reid's strength related to Hercules, Christine understood why Bill, as baseball captain, refused to play Princeton in a 3-game series, when Princeton would only play a 3-game series or none at all. And there were other homeruns to discuss.

. . . I am rather sorry that you are not going to play Princeton this year, because I should like to have you give them a good thrashing. I shall never forget the game last year when you made one of your homeruns.

Dearie, I am sure I don't know what more to say about your being head-coach of the football team! . . . So I am not going to influence you either way. . . .

We saw a statue of Hercules to-day and I looked at him but thought of you all the time. He had nice big shoulders and strong arms like yours, and so I liked to look at him. I love your strength, Bill, do you know it? There is a fascination in being picked up and hugged by a big, strong man which you, how sorry I am for you, will never know. Oh! it is delicious! I am so glad that you are so nice and strong, though I should love you just the same if you weren't. . . .

I suppose "we girls" don't quite realize just what fellows have to fight against, but then neither do you fellows realize what hard times girls have, though not in the same way, of course. I think we have much the worst of it, but you probably disagree, with me this time, for once. I can't tell you how awfully thankful I am that you are "decent," as you say, and I do appreciate that, sweetheart, and I love you and respect you for it.

Billie, it seems as if I really could not wait until next June, I am just hungry for you. — — — I love to think that you long to sleep with me in your arms, for I long to sleep there very, very much. How perfectly delicious it will be!

♥ ♥ ♥ ♥ ♥

Bill Reid, Jr., Harvard University, to Christine Lincoln, Cairo, Egypt
6 January 1901

The new year opened with Bill pledging his love to Christine in somewhat stronger terms than before.

. . . "I Love you." I "love" you with all the love I have and I love you alone. I love your beautiful dark eyes—I love your soft white neck—your red cheeks—your dainty little mouth and your little wee hands. Then, if I were to allow you to get far enough from me to see it—I love your whole, sweet figure— — Oh—I just love all of you. . . .

Dearest—I've longed and longed for you—and I've thought & thought of you.—You little darling you—why can't I have you!! I just worship you—You're my religion now—Did you know it?

♥ ♥ ♥ ♥ ♥

A Debutante's Passion—A Coach's Erotica

Christine Lincoln, Venice, Italy, to Bill Reid, Jr., Harvard University
6 January 1901

On the same day that Bill wrote Christine in a loving way, Christine offered her imperfect self to Bill, while also commenting upon Bill's question of smoking.

Do you realize that I have written to you every day this week except yesterday. . . ?

"Just wait until we do sleep together;" yes dear, I am trying to wait patiently, but I warned you before that impatience was one of my faults. It will indeed be fun showing each other how we imagined hugging and kissing each other. I suspect that we may agree as to the nicest ways too. . . .

Dear, it was sweet, awfully sweet of you to say I should make a perfect wife, but I am afraid I shall be very far from that. I shall have a perfect husband, however, and it would not do to have too much perfection in the family. . . .

To offer to give up smoking just because I might not want you to! I didn't mean it that way a bit when I asked you, I just wondered well—I'll tell you when I see you. Of course you can smoke if you like, I know you would never overdo it or get so that you could not stop. I am awfully glad that you are not going to begin until you get through college, I think that is splendid. . . .

♥♥♥♥♥

Bill Reid, Jr., Harvard University, to Christine Lincoln, Cairo, Egypt
9 January 1901

Bill answered many of the questions in a 41-page letter about love, about love if children arrive, and whether Christine would hold second place behind their children.

. . . Tiny dear—it's the same old story over and over and yet I never tire—instead—my feelings seem to gather strength as time passes, and I am glad.

I am saturated (not a very good word) with you and your ways and doings that every single thing I see, think or do, is connected with you. For instance today is a soft, balmy day, that makes me think of you, in a blue dress, out driving with me—it recalls the kisses and hand squeezes of those drives—it starts a train of thought in my mind which brings back to me those dear old drives in a hundred different ways.

Do you remember the first time I tried to take your hand and you wouldn't let me? You said you thought I'd think less of you.

ENGAGED, VOYAGE, AND STEAMER AFFAIR

I remember I sobered down very much and became reflective, and begged your pardon. You told me you weren't "mad" I remember and that made me happier. It was awfully mean of you to refuse me. I never exercised such self restraint in my life before. It was positively "awful."

Then I remember the day when you did let me hold your hand. It was during a drive up that "short cut" near the station. You had on gloves. First I took glove and all. I could not stand that, even though I knew you might not let me hold at all if I tried to take off the glove. Then I took off the glove & how good it did feel. I remember slipping my fingers between yours and squeezing. At first there was no response, then, after a while, a little and then a really good squeeze. It just sent thrills all over me. I'll never forget it. Then to make it easier for you to squeeze back, I invented the "telegraphic system." That settled matters well.

Another time I remember we were sitting in the hammock on the porch. It was dark and I couldn't help trying to take your hand. I did so, but you drew yours away. This I asked you if you didn't trust me. You didn't say anything but stuck your little hand in mine an instant and then, before I could squeeze it, drew it out again. I knew you trusted and it made me awfully happy. I thought and thought of that that night and concluded that I needn't despair, that sooner or later I could hold your hand. I don't know whether you surmised then that I was some day to ask for your hand—I thought of it as a possibility. I just love to recall all those little advances. They seem so funny now that I can take you in my arms, can kiss & hug you & "love" you all I want. Our "approach" was a delightfully gradual one wasn't it. . . !

I think that I noticed a little attempt on your part to resist me when I first was trying to win you. When I learned definitely that you weren't engaged, I made up my mind that I'd not let you deny me. I guess you realized at about the same time that I was pretty well smitten. It didn't take you long to "suite" me thoroughly either. Each time I called I knew I was harder & harder gripped and I liked it. . . .

So you are going to study to be a wife worthy of me are you—well, you won't have to study long. — "and worthy to be the mother of your children." —Oh, Tiny, you are darling. You don't know how that made me feel. I can't describe it. To have you want to be the mother of my children!! It's just sublime. Little girl, such a blessing as you are, is seldom bestowed on any man. I realize it and simply worship you & that's not enough. I am proud, oh so proud of you, and when we have had a little one I'll be almost beside myself, I know. Your wanting to have children is the key to a married life for us. . . . Baby dear, I should be awfully fond of our baby, that's true, but I should worship its mother. . . . You will never hold second place in my love. . . .

♥♥♥♥♥

A Debutante's Passion—A Coach's Erotica

Bill Reid, Jr., Harvard University, to Christine Lincoln, Munich, Germany
10 January 1901

Christine had asked what Bill was wearing when he wrote his letters. He replied.

. . . This afternoon I had on leisure shoes, a pair of socks with figures somewhat resembling Maltese Crosses on them, a heavy suit of brownish Scotch tweed with a very—almost imperceptible red check—a white shirt, a turn down collar—and a necktie, four-in-hand of Turkish design. . . . I am writing now (2:30 a.m.) in my night-gown. . . .

I too, am just longing for the time when we can kiss "good-night." This of course includes going to bed together too. I often wonder whether you'll be embarrassed at having a fellow in the room while you are getting to bed— & then having him get into bed with you and snuggle up to you. How about that? I suppose I could in a pinch wait until you got into bed before coming into the room—or we might turn out all the lights. But I'd hate to. . . .

♥ ♥ ♥ ♥ ♥

Christine Lincoln, Naples, Italy, to Bill Reid, Jr., Harvard University
11 January 1901

Maybe it was the Italian setting that brought out Christine's desire for Bill.

. . . Dearest, I just love to think ahead of "us two" living together, of children and everything. Perfect bliss it will be, won't it? I love to think of the good talks we shall have together when I come home too, I just long for one. You are splendid, and I am not afraid to tell you anything now. Oh! Billie, I just adore you! I had a big "surge" there. . . !

"Slip into the same bed with me every night," Oh! Bill, Bill! What bliss it will be to be in your arms at night! Sweetheart! Don't you think it seems hard to wait sometimes? I wonder if you do. . . !

♥ ♥ ♥ ♥ ♥

Wm. T. Reid, Sr., Belmont, CA, to Bill Reid, Jr., Harvard University
11 January 1901

Christine had written Bill's father about future family plans. He was delighted that she wanted children and told Bill so.

. . . [Christine] expected to have some different chickens to care for in Cal. . . . She makes it clear enough all the time that she isn't going to have any of the fool ideas of no children that so many society girls have. . . . There is nothing so fine as for a girl to want children and to say to her fellow that she wants to be the mother of his children. . . .

♥ ♥ ♥ ♥ ♥

ENGAGED, VOYAGE, AND STEAMER AFFAIR

Christine Lincoln, Naples, Italy, to Bill Reid, Jr., Harvard University
13 January 1901

Christine thought about Bill's parents and going to see them in California that summer.

. . . It is too bad that your father and mother are not coming on for Class Day [at Harvard], after all. It must be a great disappointment to you, and we are as sorry for we hoped to have them with us at Cohasset. I am glad that I shall be there in the summer, anyway, I should feel terrible if I did not expect to. Then your mother will have a chance to see if she can stand having me for a daughter-in-law. Oh! I do hope that she will like me, it is pretty "scary" for me. . . .

♥♥♥♥♥

Bill Reid, Jr., Harvard University, to Christine Lincoln, Cairo, Egypt
16 January 1901

This lengthy 26-page letter covered many of Bill's activities at Harvard, giving insight into the reason for Bill joining the Y.M.C.A., why he attended his Thayer Hall dormitory dance, and what he thought of the low-cut dresses of the women attending.

. . . I ushered at Chapel on Sunday again and after service I was invited to join the Harvard Y.M.C.A. You remember—I told you when I first wrote of ushering—that I did so not, because it amounted to so much in itself—but because it might lead to other things. The first step has come pretty quickly. I joined the Y.M.C.A. I told them that I couldn't be expected to do much, that I was too busy. Well—they wanted my support & the use of my name. The coming in touch with that movement in college will do me good & anything that will improve me is going to have full sway. You see—my darling wife—I mean ultimately to try and make of my self, a fit husband for you. I want you—some time, & as soon as possible, in life to realize & know what manhood is. I know, but I can't do yet. . . .

Now I must tell you about the Thayer's dance at Paul Revere Hall. It was quite a "grand" affair I suppose but I must say that I didn't enter into the spirit of it, one bit. Everything was done in a lavish scale—as the clippings I enclose will show. It was a real good society function, & disgusted me about as much as those I've attended before did.

All the "fast crowd" of the [Hasty] Pudding were there—most of them in a very bemuddled condition, a function however, seemed to be regarded by many of the girls with considerable satisfaction. I am glad to say that I saw no girl offenders, the one thing that did make me tired was the lowness of the cut of many of the dresses in front, particularly with the middle aged women was this true. Some of them were so low cut that their general appearance suggested a "pipe rack" to me

A Debutante's Passion—A Coach's Erotica

& that's no exaggeration. I don't know of anything hardly that grates on me so much as to see a woman immodestly exposing her breasts to public view. I heard many comments on the part of the fellows. . . .

♥♥♥♥♥

Christine Lincoln, Naples, Italy, to Bill Reid, Jr., Harvard University
17 January 1901

Christine fantasized about Bill while touring through Europe.

. . . I love those great long kisses we have too, and it was just "bully" the way you described them. They do indeed seem to "draw your whole soul to mine," and the feeling is luscious to say the least. "Love me till you're a nuisance" will you? You have a long and difficult task before you, poor boy, you little know what you are undertaking. I am so glad that you want to "love" me. . . .

Do you ever think, sweetheart, of the first night that we shall sleep together? I do very often. To lie in your dear arms all night, Oh! Bill, it makes me breathe hard at the very thought of it. How delicious it will be and all the other nights too! It does seem like a dream, but such a "pleasant" one that I never want to wake up. . . .

♥♥♥♥♥

Christine Lincoln, on board ship in the Mediterranean, to Bill Reid, Jr., Harvard University
20 January 1901

After offering observations about the Egyptians and those on board the "Furst Bismarck" in the Mediterranean, Christine provided her own observations about loving and being loved.

. . . "It is chiefly the men who wish to be loved—women wish to love some one." Well, I don't know, I know of one girl anyway who wants to be "loved" very much indeed, quite as much as to "love. . . ."

♥♥♥♥♥

Bill Reid, Jr., Harvard University, to Christine Reid, Cairo, Egypt
20 January 2001

Bill brought up the steamer letter again, this time noting a discussion that had occurred between Bill and Christine's cousin Ethel Williams. These are excerpts from a 36-page letter.

You are just a perfect darling—that's what you are—for writing me such a load of letters in one week. Here I've had six, and everyone of them just as sweet as it could be. . . .

ENGAGED, VOYAGE, AND STEAMER AFFAIR

I had supper with Ethel and I finally told her that I'd read the steamer letter. I feel that she knew me well enough not to be greatly disturbed and I knew that I could prove to her that I'd not considered her as "cheap" (as she feared) by telling her that I knew that it was only a letter between girls and hadn't been written for a fellow to see; that in seeing it I considered it as a piece of good natured fun from a lively relative. She wasn't in the least embarrassed and the matter dropped. She asked if I minded as she told you in her next letter—of course I said "no I shouldn't mind"—that I meant to tell you myself anyhow. She then apologized & said—"I ought to have known better than say that—of course you'd tell her." She little respects, though, I guess that I tell you absolutely everything I think & do—I'd like to see myself concealing anything from my "tweety" wife—I guess not. You're "carte blanche" in regard to everything I think, do, feel, act or see. You can just rummage about all you want to and it will all be old—because its all been told you once. What's more you'll find the more you rummage—the oftener you'll come across items labeled "love."

Ethel then told me that you'd said in your last letter that—you had something to tell her—but that you couldn't write it & then added—"I'll bet that's it—allright" (referring to our engagement of course). I disappointed her awfully, by suggesting that probably you meant to tell her that I had read the steamer letter. I said—"of course she doesn't want you to know it while you can see me & get embarrassed & so she's probably waiting for you to come over." She got quite downcast. I hated to put her off the track so, but I want you to have the pleasure of telling her—yourself, and the more doubtful I can make her—the better it will be. . . .

I had the one consolation in knowing that I was dancing with "her" [Christine's] best friend [Dorrie]. The Blue Danube was played four times—and every time, I danced in a sort of dreamy way—longing & longing for you. I've got so I almost dread that waltz because it's hard to stand hearing it. . . .

Why do you suppose—you loving, loyal beauty, you—that all this brings you to my mind? It's because—dearest—you have many times shown exactly the spirit of the Western girl. If you've forgotten the times, I'll remind you of a few. In recent letters, you "almost wished sometimes that I had no honor" so that you can show me that it was me you loved. . . .

♥♥♥♥♥

Christine Lincoln, Cairo, Egypt, to Bill Reid, Jr., Harvard University

23 January 1901

Christine's Uncle Albert told a story to her sister Agnes, that said much about Christine and Bill's love life.

A Debutante's Passion—A Coach's Erotica

. . . Albert said a very amusing thing to Agnes. She told it to me afterward, and although it may not be quite "proper," I am going to tell it to you, it is so funny. He was telling her that he was going to play some tricks on us next summer, and he said "When Bill and Christine are sleeping together next summer, I am going to come down the chimney and pretend I am Santa Claus and scare them." "But," said Agnes, "they won't be sleeping together next summer, Albert." "Why yes, they will," said Albert. "Oh! no, people don't sleep together until they are married," replied Ag. "Why not?" "Well because they don't," said Ag. "Well, I bet Bill and Christine will anyway," said Albert, and that seemed to settle it. Did you ever? What do you suppose put such an idea into his head. . . ?

You don't really mind because I did not go to college, do you? Would you love me more if I had? Tell me, dear, honestly now! That is one of the few subjects on which we do really disagree for I think only a few girls get any good out of college. To my mind, it spoils the others. Well, I don't know much about it. . . so, if you want me to go, don't hesitate to say so, darling. I would do anything, even that, to please you, my beloved. . . .

♥♥♥♥♥

Wm. T. Reid, Sr., Belmont, CA, to Bill Reid, Jr., Harvard University
25 January 1901

Bill was advised by his father to concentrate on beating Yale in baseball in the spring and not spend all his time with Christine, who would be returning from her European trip.

. . . When do the Lincolns expect to reach Boston? You won't be worth much after their return, I am afraid, but you mustn't let Christine interfere with your first game with Yale. That at any rate you must try to win out this year & I want you to win the first two & so close up your athletic career triumphantly. . . .

♥♥♥♥♥

Christine Lincoln, Cairo, Egypt, to Bill Reid, Jr., Harvard University
26 January 1901

Only briefly mentioning the pyramids, a sphinx, the tomb of Ramses II, and a trip on the Nile River, Christine's sad letter of 14 pages bemoaned her trip away from Bill.

. . . Why, oh! why, can't I be with you! I want to come home and be loved, loved as only you can love. I hate it over here. I might have known I never could stand being away from you when I love you so! Four months more! Oh Bill, Bill! The thought of it drives me mad! What a fool, idiot I was to come. It gets worse and worse all the time. . . .

ENGAGED, VOYAGE, AND STEAMER AFFAIR

I wish we two were alone together far away from every one else, where we wouldn't see a single soul but each other. I want to be just "loved" from morning until night and all night too to make up for all this suffering. Would you like to be alone with me, Bill, just me, you know, no one else? Tell me, dear, would you . . . ?

♥ ♥ ♥ ♥ ♥

Christine Lincoln, Cairo, Egypt, to Bill Reid, Jr., Harvard University
29 January 1901

Christine dreamed about the perceived bliss of married life.

. . . You will be a perfect, absolutely perfect husband and, Bill darling, I can't tell you how I look forward to living my life with you. Bliss, that is what it will be. We won't have any of those horrid little disagreements and petty quarrels that most married people have, will we dear. . . ?

♥ ♥ ♥ ♥ ♥

Christine Lincoln, Cairo, Egypt, to Bill Reid, Jr., Harvard University
1 February 1901

Christine had recovered from her blue days in Cairo as she traveled the Nile River.

Here we really are on our way up the Nile and it is perfectly great. The only drawback to my pleasure being the fact that you, my love, are not with me. . . .
   That is one of the worst things over here to see the poor people. It takes away a lot of the pleasure. . . .
   It is so lovely now. I have to keep stopping to look up. Stretches of golden sand, palm trees, the blue, blue sky, and the water. . . .

♥ ♥ ♥ ♥ ♥

Bill Reid, Jr., Harvard University, card to Christine Lincoln, Cairo, Egypt
ca. 1 February 1901

Bill remembered Valentine's Day.

To the dearest Valentine God ever created—with loads of love.
   To the little girl who has so come into my life as to completely overshadow and dwarf every other living creature.
             Lovingly — "Hubbie"

♥ ♥ ♥ ♥ ♥

Wm. T. Reid, Sr., Belmont, CA, to Bill Reid, Jr., Harvard University
3 February 1901

A Debutante's Passion—A Coach's Erotica

Bill Reid's father cautioned Bill about the intensity of the love between Bill and Christine.

. . . It is a mighty hard strain on a string to keep it tuned to such a high pitch. . . . I am not going to do much cautioning but you and Christine are living at an extreme tension. . . . You can't know of one another's little failings, and if you are not careful you will come to think—fiddlesticks you already think, that she hasn't any, and she—well she seems to be just about as badly off. Now go it a little more slowly if you can, but how absurd for me to be offering grave counsel to two such warm blooded creatures. But let me tell you that the only objection to California climate is that it is too evenly beautiful—there isn't variety enough to give spice to it & so if you & Christine should have clear skies occasionally clouded you must be ready for it. . . .

♥♥♥♥♥

Christine Lincoln, Cairo, Egypt (on boat), letter to Bill Reid, Jr., Harvard University
4 February 1901

Christine noted that as of February 4, 1900, the two of them had not even met.

. . . Are you really going to marry me, Bill? How unreal and yet real it all seems. A year ago I had not even met you, and now you are clearer to me than all the rest of the world put together. It's a strange world, isn't it. . . ?
"A good mutual snuggle" when we go to bed together! Oh! Billie dear, how delicious that does sound! Won't it be great? Yes, blissful! I do so love to think of cuddling up to your dear breast, held tight in those loving arms. Then I will put my arms around your neck and kiss you and "love" you, and you will "love" me too. Oh! Bill, Bill! Then my hand will slip in on your breast as we like to have it, and it will "love" you. Dear, I do look forward to it so, don't you. . . ?

♥♥♥♥♥

Christine Lincoln, near Cairo, Egypt to Bill Reid, Jr., Harvard University
5 February 1901

Christine continued showing her love for Bill, and at the same time revealed empathy toward poor children she observed in Egypt.

Last night a big, bright full moon, and I all alone! How I did long and long for you, darling. . . .
  It is no exaggeration to say that at least every twentieth person, down to little toddling children of three and four years of age, is blind of an eye. Nothing in Egypt is as painful to witness as the neglected conditions of

very young children. . . . It is hard to believe that the parents of these unfortunate babies err, not from cruelty, but through sheer ignorance and superstition. To wash young children is injurious to health; therefore the mothers suffer them to fall into a state of uncleanliness that is alone enough to engender disease. . . . I have seen children with the surface of their eyes eaten away. . . .

♥ ♥ ♥ ♥ ♥

Christine Lincoln, Cairo, Egypt, to Bill Reid, Jr., Harvard University
ca. 9 February 1901

In her lengthy letter from Cairo, Christine responded to Bill's talk of marriage and answered the bedroom question he had earlier posed.

. . . Since you ask me, dear, I think that very probably I shall be very embarrassed at having a fellow in the room at night with me, but it will be a pleasant kind of embarrassment. The kind you'd rather have than not, don't you know? As long as the fellow is you, I think that I shall rather enjoy having him in the room, and as for having him get into bed with me and snuggle (I do love that word) up to me—well—you know already how I feel about that, but I shall tell you just the same, knowing how much I like to have you tell me things like that, that I know I shall just love to have you slip into the same bed with me and let me cuddle up to you and "love" you all I like and have you "love" me and hold me tight against your heart in your loving arms. Won't it be simply blissful darling loving each other, sleeping together and all? Somehow I seem to look forward to lying in your arms all night more than to anything ever before! It is a delight to think of it ever, and I do very, very often. You can't complain of my not being "frank" any more beloved, can you. . . ?

♥ ♥ ♥ ♥ ♥

Christine Lincoln, on board S.S. Puritan, to Bill Reid, Jr., Harvard University
10 February 1901

That a daughter of a prominent American family went to Europe during her engagement was not unusual, for it was one test of a future marriage. Christine came to despise her time away from Bill, nevertheless.

. . . I do miss and long for you so! Why can't I have you here to enjoy it all with me, then it would be some fun! Your mother told me that your sister was engaged when she was abroad too, so I guess we have one bond of sympathy between us anyway. . . .

♥ ♥ ♥ ♥ ♥

Christine Lincoln, on board S.S. Puritan, to Bill Reid, Jr., Harvard University
15 February 1901

A Debutante's Passion—A Coach's Erotica

The Lincoln family was touring the Mediterranean Sea on board the "Puritan" when Christine criticized a young German couple just engaged, who were overly demonstrative in public. She also likely revealed her naiveté when invited to a circus by a touring Englishman.

. . . Last night, an Englishman, who is a "corker" by the way, invited me to go to a circus with him. Of course I was wild to go, not having had any such dissipations for a long time. But the doctor said I'd better not, as I might catch some disease from the natives, so I have to give it up, much to my sorrow. The gentleman is forty at least, so don't worry, if you ever thought of such a thing. . . !

♥♥♥♥♥

Christine Lincoln, on board S.S. Puritan, to Bill Reid, Jr., Harvard University
18 February 1901

Still touring the Mediterranean, Christine admitted to a passenger that she was engaged, something that she said she would not reveal to others than family.

. . . I did a really awfully foolish thing yesterday and it just shows how lucky it is that I'm not at home. I hope you forgive me, but it was a silly thing to do. I was sitting on the lower deck in as secluded a nook as I could find reading your dear letter and just gloating over your love and longing for you, when the German girl came along and said in a most significant tone, "You get letters all the time, don't you?" I said "Why yes, I get a good many," and then tried to sort of turn it off by asking her if she had received any that day, but she wouldn't turn. She said, "I guess you're engaged, aren't you now?" Well, I twisted and turned as best I could but I blushed so that it was no use and I finally "owned up" to it. . . . Do you mind, dear. . . ? The trouble was she caught me unawares when I was so happy over your letter and the loving things you had said. . . .

Everything I do with you just makes me tingle all over in an exquisitely delightful feeling of absolute contentment." I know well how that "tingling" feels and I just long for it again. It's delicious, and more than that. . . .

♥♥♥♥♥

Christine Lincoln, Cairo, Egypt, to Bill Reid, Jr., Harvard University
ca. 20 February 1901

Christine joked about a prince being on their Mediterranean ship, while noting that Egyptian women often marry at very early ages. She also described visiting an Arab's modest home.

. . . In return for your speech about practicing hugging on Reba Thomas, let me tell you that there is a Prince on board and that on moonlight nights the dark corners of the deck are very attractive. He is a stunning fellow too, and these steamer chairs hold two so comfortably—well—perhaps the less said the better, I intend to break it to you gently. . . ! To be serious again. . . .

My donkey boy the other day asked me if I was married, and when he heard that I was twenty and not married yet, he seemed quite shocked. (They are married when they are ten or twelve over here and are considered out of it at twenty.) Finally I told him that I should be married after I went home. He asked all about "my husband" whether he was nice or not & so on. You may be sure I set his mind at rest on that point. They are just like children these Arabs! I like them, most of them. . . . I had an interesting experience. Aunt Mary's donkey boy asked her to come and see his wife and children so she & I went. (He was only rich enough to have one wife, I guess. . . .) Well, he came to the boat for us and we followed him along through narrow winding streets till we came to his little mud house. Inside was his wife with the youngest baby in her arms. She looked about fifteen years old and was a perfect little beauty. She was all dressed up for the occasion and had on a red and yellow dress, huge earrings and necklaces and bracelets and rings in profusion. Her eyes were blackened underneath and her nails reddened. The baby was very amusing, a fat little monkey, and we sat and played with it until her husband came back and brought us some coffee. I don't know what we should have done if we had not had the baby to play with, for she could not speak any English nor we any Arabic. So there we sat and stared at each other and all the neighbors collected in the door way and "rubbered" too. There was a donkey tied inside the house and the hens lived there too. The floor and walls were of mud and there was ceiling only over a small part of it. They were just as cordial and nice to us as could be and tried to make us eat fruit and everything. . . .

With heaps and loads of love and kisses and hugs, I am
Ever your lovingly
Mrs. Bill Reid
♥ ♥ ♥ ♥ ♥

Christine Lincoln, Cairo, Egypt, to Bill Reid, Jr., Harvard University
23 February 1901

Christine was miserable in Cairo, away from Bill since September, while the return in May seemed so far away.

I have been so desperately "homesick" for the last few days that really I hardly knew what I was doing. My body was here in Cairo, but all my heart and thoughts were far away. I was perfectly miserable with longing for you. . . . The orchestra played some of the dear old waltzes while we were at dinner one night and I was ready to cry. I nearly disgraced myself for the tears would come to my eyes. It was all I could do to control myself and force down that awful lump which would come in my throat.... Three months more! Oh dear...! If I ever do get folded in your dear arms again... I am afraid I shall cling to you so that you will have hard work to get rid of me. I can never get "loving" enough to make up for the long wait....

Dear, I hope you won't be disappointed in me, but I have any amount of faults, awful ones too, you know. You will realize that, won't you, love, and help me with them...?

♥♥♥♥♥

Christine Lincoln, Cairo, Egypt, to Bill Reid, Jr., Harvard University
ca. 24 February 1901

At one point in her letter, Christine replied to Bill about giving up smoking as well as going out West with him later in the summer. The Englishman she had met on the Mediterranean cruise was noted. She also commented on one of Bill's baseball team members and star freshman pitcher, Walter Clarkson, who would later play for the New York team in the American League.

.... Dear, about smoking! I said I would do just as you like about it, that is give it up entirely, whether I approved of it or not, because you did not think it was right "even if, at the bottom of my heart I did not agree with you." Meaning that I did agree with you absolutely, don't you see? You read it the other way, and I don't wonder, for I did not put it very plainly. That's what I meant, though, lovey dear. I quite agree with you, only, don't you know I told you that I did not always live up to my principles? However, I will live up to yours, dearest. . . .

You might think it funny that I don't enthuse more over going out West with you next summer. The fact is I simply cannot realize it all yet, it's impossible. From Egypt to California is a pretty big step. . . . What time we shall have together, . . . it seems like a dream. . . .

Last night, Mr. Lowell, the Englishman on board the "Puritan" whom I mentioned before, took Ag, Ouicie, and me to the Circus here. I really think he has an idea that I am daft on the subject of circuses, for he invited me once before. . . . The circus did not amount to much, but we had a very jolly time. He is really an awfully nice man, and we expect to see him again next spring. He was asking me our plans and when I told him that we were to be in London in May, he said we must let him be our guide and show us round. It will be fine having someone there that we know, I think much pleasanter. He's going to take me to the races and that will be bull fun, I guess . . . .

I do hope that Clarkson will get through [academically] all right. How horrid of him to bother you and give you so much trouble. Tell me how he does, won't you. . . ?

♥♥♥♥♥

ENGAGED, VOYAGE, AND STEAMER AFFAIR

Wm. T. Reid, Sr., Belmont, CA, to Bill Reid, Jr., Harvard University
25 February 1901

Bill's father gave his "hearty consent" for a wedding trip to Europe, wanting his son and daughter-in-law to go first class, but not extravagantly. And he was concerned, unnecessarily as it turned out, that it might delay child bearing.

You are most fortunate in having such a girl as Christine. . . . I also fully appreciate the fact that Christine has always been used to the very best and without question. . . . I am afraid that I see in your trip a putting off of the baby question. If you begin by putting it off I am afraid that you may hesitate too long both for Christine's good & for the good of your children, for you know that child bearing while sometimes very serious is almost always very healthful. And besides children are about all there is to life after all. And I am looking forward to your & Christine's children—well I can't tell you with what anticipation. It is true that I am anticipating them as I never anticipated anything in life. It will make me as happy as it will make you I suspect. . . . I don't want to step out of this life until I have that supreme happiness—of seeing a grandchild. . . .
 Hadn't you better destroy this entire letter. . . ?

♥ ♥ ♥ ♥ ♥

Christine Lincoln, Naples, Italy, to Bill Reid, Jr., Harvard University
1 March 1901

Christine reminded Bill of a golfing incident the previous summer.

Indeed I do remember your "lost" ball on the "rock tee" and as you say, your losing "control of your lips and arms!" I am afraid I may have wished sometimes that you did not have so much self control! Terrible confession, isn't it? Oh! there are lots of awful things for you to find out about me still; but I suspect may have guessed that one. . . . How loath I used to be to pay up when you drove over the bunkers! How well I remember the dread with which I used to anticipate it. (Truth being that I could scarcely wait for the time to come.). . .
 You say it is "bliss to feel me right up close to you," well—it's bliss to be there, I tell you. I love to feel you breathing against me, your chest moving, it's delicious. . . !

♥ ♥ ♥ ♥ ♥

Christine Lincoln, Naples, Italy, to Bill Reid, Jr., Harvard University
4 March 1901

Christine recalled her depressed letter from Egypt, wanting to be less blue in the future.

A Debutante's Passion—A Coach's Erotica

It is only a day or two since I last wrote but my heart is so overflowing with love that I feel as if I simply must write. . . . I read over old letters and thought and thought of you and only! how I did long for you. I am perfectly oblivious to everything around me when I am absorbed in thought of you. . . .

I am sorry I sent that second "Egyptian" letter if it made you "feel awfully." I was "feeling awfully" at the time, but I wouldn't have sent it if I had known. Well, never mind, my love, in three months we shall be together and can then be as "blue" as we like together! It will be rather good fun being "blue" then, won't it?

I cannot understand why when you are all the time seeing scores of girls a hundred times more attractive and better than I am, you should still cling to me! But oh! dearest, I can't tell you how thankful and happy I am that it is so. . . .

Well in a year from this June we will be alone and on our way to Europe—then you'll have me all night too & I'll love you to your heart's content. . . .

♥♥♥♥♥

Christine Lincoln, Rome, Italy, to Bill Reid, Jr., Harvard University
12 March 1901

Christine thought of Bill's desire to be as close as possible to her and responded in a way possibly unusual in the late Victorian era. And this came from a society girl—at least a debutante.

. . .I loved your saying this—"I long to get right next to you—as it is—I feel as though there was too much in the way." I can't help agreeing with you, Bill, really I can't. You are quite right as usual. I had a most delicious thrill when I read that. I guess there won't be a great deal of "sleep" for the first few nights! I shan't mind, though, shall you?

Dearie, I see that I shall have to make a most dreadful confession. You remember my saying that I wanted to "love" you in that red dressing gown of yours? Well, you said that I needn't wait until we are married but that you would put it on some night next summer and then I could "love away only there will be more than a nightgown under it." Well, you see, dear (I'm afraid perhaps I ought not to tell you this) partly the reason that I wanted so much to "love" you in it was because there would be "only a nightgown under it!" You see I'd like to get near to you too. Do you think it is horrid or indecent of me to tell you that? You see I do tell you things that most girls would not tell a fellow, as you say, but I don't think it does any harm. Please tell me if you'd rather I didn't. It is an awful fascination to talk about sleeping together and all that, and sometimes I can't resist it. . . .

Your father says awfully nice things about me, and in one respect that he speaks of, I'll not disappoint him. It's quite true that I don't care a snap of my fingers for society, and another thing that's true is that when I have you I shall not care a snap whether I ever see another fellow or not. (In fact I really don't now.) My husband is all the world to me, and I mean that. If I didn't I wouldn't marry you. I don't believe in the way these society people marry and then each goes his or her own way. If they can't both go one way, then they'd better stay single. It's not true marriage, do you think so. . . ?

♥♥♥♥♥

Christine Lincoln, Rome, Italy, to Bill Reid, Jr., Harvard University
16 March 1901

Christine loved Rome, but she was ready to return home and be with Bill. The fact that her teeth ached, and would soon go to see an Italian dentist, did not help with her blues.

When Dad brought in the last two volumes of your letter, I was stretched at full length under my bed, and it was all I could do to keep from reaching out and grabbing them. Perhaps you may wonder what I was under the bed for! Well, I was playing a most thrilling game of hide-and-go-seek with [Uncle] Albert and a friend of his. In fact a wild game is going on at the very minute, and it's all I can do to write. You dear, dear, boy I do love you so! That has nothing to do with hide-and-go-seek, but it came over me just that minute how very much I did care for you. . . .

I am feeling more "blue" than usual these last few days as I am having and have had a good deal of trouble with my teeth. . . . Life seems to be made up of disappointments. . . .

. . . Well, only about ten weeks more before I shall see you! Think of it! Dad wrote to-day to engage our passage. . . for the 23rd of May. That's not so very, very far off now, is it, dear? I hope you won't mind my coming home so soon, but I do want to so much. Bill, Bill! I really believe I shall die of joy when I see you. How I shall just revel in "loving" and fondling you. . . !

♥♥♥♥♥

Julia Reid, Belmont, CA, to Bill Reid, Jr., Harvard University
18 March 1901

Bill's mother gave keen insight into one of the flaws of their family—one that could produce problems after Christine and Bill were married.

. . . [Your sister] has lived with an atmosphere of criticism around her just as you have & you both are quick to pick flaws & throw friends overboard to an extent that grieves me very much. . . .

♥♥♥♥♥

A Debutante's Passion—A Coach's Erotica

Wm. T. Reid, Sr., Belmont, CA, to Bill Reid, Jr., Harvard University
21 March 1901

Social status was always important to Bill's father, and he was particularly aware of it when Bill became engaged to a debutante in an elite Boston family. In almost a premonition of relations between Bill and Christine, Reid, Sr., gave advice about idealizing Christine too much.

. . . I am to drive at the University Club to-morrow night with Pres. Hadley [of Yale] and others and on the fourth of April to attend a dinner given by Prof. Howison to D. O. Mills, Whitelaw Reid & several other distinguished people. And here again I am enjoying these activities largely because I want Christine to feel that she is coming into a circle that is probably not more obscure than the one she has been used to. . . .

Let me inject first a little word of caution. It is not at all likely that your present feelings are going to continue at such a white-heat. Absence minimizes failures & magnifies excellences & so you are likely to find that you have idealized too much. I am not intending to cast a shadow of doubt over your affections, but to say that if a little feeling of disappointment comes over you after you have had her for a while you need not feel alarmed. On the contrary, if it doesn't come you may be surprised & grateful. I have no reference to anything that is permanent for I think that you are probably right in believing that she is sun & solid gold, but even gold dims. . . . And besides I am preparing you for your seasons of biliousness, when you are likely to be unreasonable & so put her patience to the test. . . .

♥ ♥ ♥ ♥ ♥

Christine Lincoln, Rome, Italy, to Bill Reid, Jr., Harvard University
22 March 1901

Christine and Bill considered their future time in bed, and raised a strange question about Bill being able to hurt Christine physically after they are married.

. . .Dearie, you don't know how I loved your saying "I don't see how I am to make myself get up if I once get into bed with you." I want always to be a help to you, but I fear I may prove a hindrance in this case. I very much fear I shall act somewhat the way I did the night of the first Yale Game. Do you remember how I kept saying, "Bill, you really ought to go, you know," and then I put my arms around your neck, kissed you, and clung to you all the closer? It did not seem to act as a spur exactly but I can't remember feeling so very sorry that it didn't. Well, I have warned you, you at least know what to expect. I suppose we might settle matters by my getting up first. But no, I guess that would be rather too "scary" and anyhow I doubt if I should have any more desire to than you. I expect that we are very naughty to talk so much on this subject, but it is so fascinating that I can't seem to stop. Even to think of it is a delight, what the reality will be is beyond words to express. . . .

Someday I suppose I'll say in a trembling voice that I take you for better, for worse. Then you will be really and truly mine and oh! how blissful. Me to our. Yes, how funny and how nice it sounds. Then I shall belong absolutely and entirely to you. You will have a right to beat me if you choose. Did you know about that privilege? Funny that I am not more scared, isn't it? The fact is I would love even to be beaten by you! If I could see you now I'd gladly take a beating. . . .

♥♥♥♥♥

Christine Lincoln, Rome, Italy, to Bill Reid, Jr., Harvard University
23 March 1901

Christine, just back from the dentist and experiencing pain, explained why she believed women give up more for marriage and why, from a traditional standpoint, they should do so.

Here I am back again from the dentist's but my head is nearly splitting in the tooth-ache, and I am tired out with it, so forgive me if this letter is terribly stupid. My longing for you is about unbearable to-day. If you were only here to hold me in your lap, and tell me that you love me, I should forget all about the pains and be perfectly happy. . . .

. . . I agree with you that the man has quite as much to do with making it a happy one as the woman. What is true is that it certainly means a lot more to a woman than to a man. It is her whole life, or ought to be, while he has his work and outside interests. It is just as it should be, of course, yet I think perhaps a woman gives up more when she marries than a man does, don't you? I doubt very much if you would give up your work if I asked you to, would you? The truth is I should not love you as much if you did. Yes, I should, though I'd love you whatever you did. But you see what I mean, don't you? I have no interest except in you, but you have your work, at present baseball, etc. . . .

♥♥♥♥♥

Christine Lincoln, Florence, Italy, to Bill Reid, Jr., Harvard University
28 March 1901

Christine told of her long-time friend, Ronald Lyman, who was possibly looking for more than friendship with Christine. She asked Bill for advice on how to deal with him.

A Debutante's Passion—A Coach's Erotica

... I want to ask your advice. You remember meeting a fellow called Ronald Lyman one day at our house last summer? Well, I am a tiny bit worried about him. He has been awfully nice to me for three or four years, always coming to see me once a week or once in ten days, etc. Then he comes and visits for two weeks near us in Cohasset, having just found out when I am to be there. I have given him two photographs, one, you remember, last summer, and I write to him. I hear from him about once a week, but I answer once in two or three. There has never been the least atom of sentiment between us, we have always been just good friends, nothing more. . . . But lately he has taken to signing his name "Always yours" or "Always your Ronald," and I don't care for that, as he's not mine and I don't want him. . . . Tell me what you think, dear. . . !

♥♥♥♥♥

Christine Lincoln, Florence, Italy, to Bill Reid, Jr., Harvard University
30 March 1901

Only two days after writing about her friend Ronald Lyman, Christine, in an eight-page letter, brought up the more important steamer incident of 12 September 1900. It would be the cause of much anguish for Bill after he received this letter from Christine, over a half-a-year following the brief steamer episode.

After much thought, I have made up my mind to tell you something I had meant to wait until I got home so that I could tell you instead of writing. It is so hard to write it and then harder still to have to wait such a long time before hearing from you, but I am going to do it just the same. It happened on the steamer coming over to England. As long ago as that, and yet I have not told you before, not because I intended to conceal it from you, but because, as I said, I wanted to wait until I was with you. Well, you will remember my speaking in the letter I wrote you on the steamer that there was a fellow on board of whom I saw a good deal. One evening he said "I know I have no right to ask this, but will you tell me whether you are engaged or not? I asked him why he asked and he replied that he thought I was engaged. I did not see why I should tell a person I scarcely knew a thing like that merely to satisfy his curiosity so I replied that I wasn't. Oh! How in any time since then have I wished that I had told him then and there that I was! He said nothing more then but the next evening he told me he loved me, had fallen in love with me the first moment that he saw me, wanted me to marry him, etc. Of course I stopped him as soon as I could and told him that I loved some one else and was all but engaged. He asked me whom I loved and I told him. Then he said "Do you think he would mind if I kissed your hand?" Then, fool that I was, I let him because I was so sorry for him. I feel dreadfully about it Bill, it has worried and weighed on my conscience ever since, but until now I couldn't write it to you because I did so want to be with you when I told you so that I could put my arms around your neck, kiss you, and tell you that I loved you and no one else. . . .

I detest myself! Why did that fellow have to go and fall in love with me? At least that was not my fault. . . . I wonder how you will feel when you have read this . . .! I shall never come back to America unless you forgive me and love me still. . .! Once more, forgive me. . . .

♥♥♥♥♥

Agnes Lincoln, Cannes, France, to Bill Reid, Jr., Harvard University
6 April 1901

Christine's younger sister, one who smoked to the consternation of Bill, wrote from Europe that she was happy that Bill would be her brother-in-law. Bill had sent money to Agnes to buy flowers for Christine. The end of Agnes' four-page letter follows.

. . . Oh, I am so glad you are going to be my brother. There is not another fellow in the world who I would like to marry Tiny, but you are so well suited that although I hate to have her leave us, yet I am glad. You understand my feelings, don't you, brother "Bill. . . ?"

♥♥♥♥♥

Bill Reid, Jr., Harvard University, letter not likely sent to Christine Lincoln
14 April 1901

Bill was stunned by Christine's March 30th elaboration of the September 12th steamer letter. Bill replied, while on Harvard's spring baseball trip to the South, in an eight-page letter, but it was evidently never sent it, for it was uncompleted along with another partially written response, and the usual envelope was not attached. However, he must have sent some type of reply similar to that found below.

My own true, little girl:

Here I am way down in the South, with its balmy soft, warm air, its green grass and its lazy inhabitants—happy as a king. Happy because I love you, dear and because I found two letters from my darling waiting for me at the hotel. All of my happiness now-a-days has its source in you, you know, you are the center of my very life, and I love you, dote on you and idolize you. If you were only here tonight I'd take you out on the piazza which is just outside my window, and draw you down into my lap and "love" you and kiss you and hug you. I'd put my arms around you and hold you tight against me and you'd slip your hand in on my breast and make me feel so good—Oh! Why aren't you here?

A Debutante's Passion—A Coach's Erotica

Now, darling, I am going to take up your letters in reverse order, because you told me something in the second one, which I must discuss, before I can take up the first. I am referring to your relations with that fellow on the steamer.

Little girl—it cut pretty deep and I was about half stunned all the morning—all of my life, interest, ambition, and spirit left me———not that I was angry—but because I love you so that I couldn't bear to think of any other fellow as having any privileges with you. I am so glad you didn't say anything to me about it at the time, for if you had, I don't see how I could have borne it; I should simply have given up. I don't believe you ever realized just how much it hurt me to learn that you had kissed Eben [Christine's previous boyfriend] and that you had allowed Roger Scarfe to squeeze your hand. I was disappointed as could be—because all of the time I was away—in fact ever since I first met you—I have reserved every right, to my affections, love and person, for you, and you wrote me at Belmont that you would do the same. . . . I never gave such a possibility another thought until you told me about Eben and then later on told me about Roger. I tried to conceal my disappointment when you showed a reluctance at speaking to Roger about it—and a disappointment which I couldn't help but feel I was justified in—seeing that I had given up a month's vacation at home to "come on" and be as "fair" in my treatment of you as I could be. And then little one, to have had you let an absolute stranger kiss your hand—a week after you had promised yourself to me—makes me almost choke.

You say that, "I have wished many times since then that I had told him then & there that I was engaged." Your saying that, was hard too, because it seems as though you couldn't resist him when he didn't know, while you'd have gotten along all-right if he had known because then you'd not have had the chance. I love you so, that I don't care how, when or where a girl meets me—she can't lay a finger on any bit of me—nor can she receive a response of any kind from me. I want to be just yours—and if you won't have me I'll try to live alone. I wouldn't ever marry any other girl—I couldn't. . . . You little know what a fearful jealousy a fellow, as deep in love as I am with you, can generate when any other fellow takes the slightest liberty with his sweetheart.

You will remember my telling you, as we faced the deck together that September day and passed that fellow, that he'd meet you. I knew he would, but I felt safe & so I said no more. When your steamer letter came, I knew you'd had a reaction and I knew that that fellow had had to do with it, how much, I little suspected. You say that the fellow "loved you & was sure of it." My little darling, what is love, founded on a week's acquaintance, worth? How much consideration of your happiness does a fellow exhibit who is willing to marry you on a week's acquaintance? It hurt to have you say that "he loved you & was sure of it" and accept his statement. . . . Were you quite fair in saying that he was "sure". . . ?

ENGAGED, VOYAGE, AND STEAMER AFFAIR

I'd like to have people know that you are mine & I'm yours & that no one can take the slightest liberty with either of us. That is the "one thing" that a man must have in his home—an absolute monopoly of his wife. It's "hands off" to every one else. You let your pity get the better of you. When "Platonic," last summer, wanted to kiss me & I wouldn't let her (I pitied her) but you came first and so I was absolutely firm. If she'd tried to kiss me, she'd have found my arms out at full length forbidding it and if she'd persisted I'd have left. Friendships, pity, nothing can come between you & my love.

Forgive you? Of course I'll forgive you, but dearest, you will reserve it all for me, after this, won't you? If anything else like that happens, it'll break my heart. . . .   I want you all to myself. . . . Give me what I have won—and you'll never have cause to regret it, for love like mine—a true fearless, devoted, everlasting love—will furnish you with everything that a man can provide for a woman—and will provide it for you—and you alone.

♥♥♥♥♥

**Wm. T. Reid, Sr., Belmont, CA, to Bill Reid, Jr., Harvard University
30 April 1901**

Bill confided in many things with his father, though not his mother. He had obviously written to his father about the steamer incident, and his father responded.

I don't wonder that you were disappointed with the steamer episode. It wasn't up to her usual high standard & was too near a compromising position. I don't wonder either that she dreaded to tell you, but I am glad that she was strong enough and fond enough of you to tell you. I guess that will be her last. If the confession came before the experience you had with the girl in Boston, I can readily understand your severity to her. Oh every one of us has an inexcusable amount of vanity & girls have rather more of it than men have. They like attention and will often shade their conduct for the sake of attention. . . .

♥♥♥♥♥

**Wm. T. Reid, Sr., Belmont, CA, to Bill Reid, Jr., Harvard University
18 May 1901**

Bill's father made additional comments about the steamer incident, only shortly before Christine returned from her lengthy stay across the Atlantic Ocean.

It often takes a crisis to develop strength as well as weakness. It looks as if Christine's crisis did that and it looks too as if it brought out a weakness that she had hardly before been conscious of. Your letter evidently cut her to pieces and yet it appears to have been considerate. At any rate it awakened her fully to the seriousness of anything of the kind if it should become a habit. Well I am heartily glad of the awakening even though it was an unpleasant one all around. Her references to it were certainly sweetly penitent. I shall be greatly interested knowing her more thoroughly and guessing at the reason. . . .

♥ ♥ ♥ ♥ ♥

Chapter 4

RETURN, MARRIAGE, AND HONEYMOON: "A DOUBLE BED AND YOU"

Susie, Mattapoisett, MA, to Christine Lincoln, Cohasset, MA
                                                    3 June 1901

After Christine returned from her voyage, one of her friends congratulated Christine on hearing of her engagement. The answer to her comment would be determined in the next decade.

. . . I hope you aren't going to spend the rest of your life, after you are married, in California. . . .

♥♥♥♥♥

Christine Lincoln, Boston, MA, to Bill Reid, Jr., Harvard University
                                                    23 June 1901

Bill and Christine were together rather continuous for a month when Christine was gone for a short time.

I am sorry I am going away to-day, for if I weren't I should see you to-night. It will be my turn to be jealous if you go to Glover's and don't come to our house. We take turns quite frequently, don't we. . . ?

♥♥♥♥♥

Christine Lincoln, Banff, Alberta, to Agnes Lincoln, Cohasset, MA
                                                    19 July 1901

Later in the Summer, Christine traveled to California with Bill, as Christine's Aunt Mary chaperoned, taking the northern route through the Canadian prairie and mountains. Christine wrote to her sister about Canada and the West.

. . . All the next day we went through prairie and they are exactly like the desert, only grass instead of sand. There are little bits of towns now and then, awfully deserted-looking places, and houses scattered round. There isn't a tree to be seen anywhere, and it must be a dreary place to live. When I get my ranch I shall stipulate for a tree now and then. . . .

A Debutante's Passion—A Coach's Erotica

It was just what you imagine a Western town to be like. About one decent street, one hotel, one bakery, etc. . . .

Aunt M[ary] & I went for a walk on the other side of the track. I tell you we were kept busy. When in my life did I see such swarms of mosquitoes, and all hungry. Gee whiz! We walked in a regular cloud. We just hurried along and stood on the edge of the prairie just so that we could say we had been on one, and then hustled back to the station as fast we could go. I had other reasons for hustling too, for the heat, being tired and all made me diarrhetic. . . . To-day I have been living on . . . boiled milk, brandy, and soda mints. I expect I shall be down to the brandy and soda mints to-morrow. It does make me simply furious, for it's spoiling all our fun. I made Bill go off and leave me, so he went fishing and has not returned yet. He wanted me to go rowing, but as I could not possibly go without the W.C. [water closet] and was afraid the manager would object to my moving it, I had to decline. . . .

In spite of it all I am having a bully time, and "Willie" is the biggest brick that ever was. . . .

♥♥♥♥♥

Newspaper Clipping
ca. 3 September 1901

Bill and Christine were engaged, unofficially, the previous fall, just before Christine went on her eight-month trip overseas. The September 1901 engagement was officially announced in the newspapers at the time Christine was spending two weeks at Bill's parents in California.

Miss Lincoln is a brunette, with a great fondness for athletics and out-of-door sports. She goes in for golf, is adept at horseback riding and swimming. She made her debut in society two winters ago. She spent last year abroad studying the languages. She is from one of the oldest New England families.

Reid is one of the best athletes ever at Harvard, baseball 4 years, 2 years captain, 2 years in football. Reid belongs to Hasty Pudding, Dickey Club, is President of the California Club, and is in the Memorial Society. He is a Class Day Marshal. He has been appointed head coach for football for 1901. He returns to Harvard for post graduate work and then plans to go to Oxford.

♥♥♥♥♥

Wm. T. Reid, Sr., Belmont, CA, to Bill Reid, Jr., Harvard University
16 September 1901

The Steamer Affairs of the previous September was still on the minds of Bill and his father, even after the formal announcement of the engagement.

RETURN, MARRIAGE, AND HONEYMOON

Dear Will,

I enclose a check for $250—which should clear your docket & leave you enough over to carry you. . . .

I am anxious to know how things are going with you & Christine. The whole matter ought to be set at rest as soon as possible and then should not be left behind any unsettled scores—or any unhealed sores.

I will write her a carefully prepared review of the whole matter if you wish & the way in which I should act & what I should expect if I were in your place. I expect things to come out all right—but at any rate they must be clear. They must either come out as you wish them—that is to say with the atmosphere clear—or the whole matter must be reversed at whatever cost for you can't afford to marry with an open sore before you. And the only way is to say with absolute frankness what conditions are necessary to set things at rest & if they can't be met, then the unwelcome slip of reconsidering the engagement must of course follow. I don't anticipate anything of this kind. The matter has given me extreme concern for I do so want it to be settled so that you shall feel easy & happy over it. Write me something at once—Give my love to Christine and tell her that I miss her—we all miss her mightily. Tell her also to write to me with the utmost frankness if she so wishes.

Lovingly,
Papa

♥♥♥♥♥

Christine Lincoln, Bear Island, ME, to Bill Reid, Jr., Harvard University
24 September 1901

While Bill was leading the Harvard football team in preseason practice, Christine was spending time with her friend, Dorrie, at Bear Island, Maine. She concluded her letter with some love numbers that are not clearly defined.

The fact is I am spoiled, terribly spoiled, and it's all your fault. Yesterday was the first time I have traveled without you since I came home from abroad, and I missed you awfully. . . .

I imagine you making the poor men rush round on the football field (and rushing round yourself I'm afraid). . . .

There is no other house on the island, except the light house, so I doubt if I shall get much social life here. Dorrie and I went for a short row this p.m., but I haven't rowed for such a long time that I got quite tired. It's good exercise though, and the only kind I shall get here, I guess. The island is small, you see. Never mind, I'll get some golf & horseback when I get back. . . .

I wish I could kiss you. . . .! I love you; "painfully evident," isn't it? 1, 4, 3, & 1, 7, 3.

♥♥♥♥♥

A Debutante's Passion—A Coach's Erotica

Christine Lincoln, Bear Island, ME, to Bill Reid, Jr., Harvard University
27 September 1901

Christine, who was subject to deep depression in her life, gave an indication of this while visiting her friend Dorrie on Bear Island, Maine.

It is almost a temptation to stay here longer, if by so doing I could get more letters like the one that came yesterday. Truly, Sweetness, you do write the dearest letters, and I felt a year younger and ten percent better every time I read it. You were a dear to write when you are so busy and I appreciate it.

I am so glad that the football prospects look brighter. . . .

We go to bed between eight and half past and the nurse gives me a good rubbing each night. I sleep like a log and we don't get up until about eight. Then I take a cold bath, delicious! After breakfast Dorrie and I take rugs and pillows, find some sheltered spot and lie there and talk. Yesterday, we took our lunch and sailed all day. There was a good stiff breeze and we had a fine sail. I steered a good part of the time, and as the boat pulled hard, I got plenty of exercise. I am feeling much more rested and my back is steadily improving. My eyes are all right now. The nurse says she thinks I got tired and it just went to my back, and I agree. . . .

I suppose it is being so tired that has made me depressed, but I have been feeling that I am not half what I ought to be to you. You mean so awfully much to me just everything in fact, and it doesn't seem as if I could ever begin to be all that to you. But your letter was so sweet and loving, that it cheered me up like everything, and I felt that if could care for me like that why perhaps I wasn't so rotten after all. . . .

Dorrie wants me to stay here a week more awfully, for she thinks it would do me lots of good. But, I must get back, as long as there is a chance of seeing you. . . . I shall see you to-morrow night. . . .

♥♥♥♥♥

Wm. T. Reid, Sr., Belmont, CA, to Christine Lincoln, Cohasset, MA
3 October 1901

Bill must have felt comfortable having his father write a letter to Christine about the Steamer Affair that occurred over a year before. Here is the entire letter from Christine's future father-in-law to Christine.

Well there is certainly one thing that Bill can do to perfection—and that is neglect whatever he doesn't feel interested in. But that isn't what makes the finest success. The finest character is he who does what he ought to do whether he likes it or not. That's what gives us a well rounded man. Any one can work faithfully & enthusiastically at what he enjoys—But if I say anything more I shall talk to unwilling ears I am sure, and that I don't wish to do. Well the point of it all is this that Will has written but one petty postal of about a dozen words since he left Belmont, and I began to think that you had joined with him and so we began to feel as if we were abandoned.

But you naughty, naughty girl. Why in the world didn't you write me in detail about your visit with Dorothy and Mrs. Lyman? I should have enjoyed it immensely. And besides that sort of thing is just what you need as I think. You are naturally reticent and so when you have anything to say you don't say it. Now sit down when you next see either and write me all about it, or write me all about your last interview. You know me well enough by this time I hope to believe that I am sympathetically interested in whatever interests you. I have hoped too that you believed enough in me and trusted me enough to wish to talk to me or write to me on any subject that interests you and with entire freedom. I am delighted to have had you go to Mrs. Lyman and delighted too that you found that after all there was some reason for my thinking well of her. She can tell you many, many things that you should know and that no one else is likely to tell you so well & so wisely. And her spirit about life and work is so fine. She believes in that stimulating and enjoyable mixture of work and play—society and duty that lies at the foundation of that which is best in life. I suspect that you think of me as a man with but one moving impulse—with but one enjoyment in life—hard, unrelenting work. In that you are wrong. I believe thoroughly in the social side of life but he who has nothing but the social side lives a trifling unworthy life. And Mrs. Lyman I should expect to combine the two in excellent proportion. Anyhow she has some mighty good ideas and she has a fine appreciation of the best there is in life. Why won't you sit down one of these days & tell me all about your talk with her. You have nothing to do except give a simple and full account of it.

I am delighted to know that you enjoy thinking over our talks. I have many, many times wished that I could talk with you again—not in the way of lecture for you don't need lecturing. You only need showing the way for as soon as you know what you ought to do you do it & do it without sparing yourself. You have the strongest of all of qualities—conscience, but you have so little thinking to do that it is not to be wondered at that you have not thought some things out—some things that you will have to think out. Your frankness to me, dear, was delightful. I am glad to know that Bill seems happier. It will not be difficult for you to make him supremely happy—provided you love him enough and tell him about it, and show it to him, and don't get jealous and sulk. You are too big to let jealousy take complete possession of you and get the better of your love—that is presuming that you do love Bill devotedly.

And let me say just one word more about the old affair in connection with this point of telling of and showing one's love. It is preeminently called for in the present case for it is my opinion, dear, that if Bill had known of that affair before your engagement he would have broken off his attentions to you long before it came to an engagement. At any rate that would have made an engagement impossible with probably nineteen men out of twenty, and that being the case you can readily understand that the foundation could be very easily knocked out of Bill's love for you if you left him in doubt of your love for him—and he would have just ground for questioning it according to my view if you did not assure him of it again and again and show it to him again & again. Of course nothing could be more wrong than for you to be demonstrative in word or act if you didn't feel it, but if you do feel it—if you are devoted and satisfied & happy in his love it would be a serious wrong in you not to show it. You ought not for example to wait for him to hold his arms out for you. You should on the contrary go to him many, many times and ask him to open them for you—that is to say if you love him with your whole heart, for there was an ugly sore that ought to be healed and that can only be healed by your making it perfectly, unquestionably clear to him that he can't regret the matter more than you do, and that there is nothing that you would not gladly do to atone for it all. And the only possible atonement is a knowledge that the matter is your greatest sorrow and atoning for it your greatest, even if it must be a sorrowing pleasure. Remember all the time that you must never leave in his mind for a moment longer than is possible the question—if there ever was the question—whether you value less dearly than he does—than all men do—that which is a woman's most sacred possession, & that all that you have and are, are sacred to him.

All that, he believes, but when one is as sore as he was when the blow first came he needs, oh you don't know how he needs your often repeated expression of devoted satisfied love—repeated in words and in actions. If you haven't that devotion and if you can't make Bill feel it—if you can't heal over the old sore by your devotion then the engagement should come to an end. It troubled me most seriously. Nothing ever more troubled me than to see how utterly depressed Bill was. I dreaded to have you return—oh nobody knows how I dreaded it for I wanted to see it all fought out to a finish before you left. As I have heard nothing from Bill since he left I of course know nothing about how he is feeling. And you too have left us in the dark.

Now dear child you won't misunderstand me in any way will you. Don't for example begin by wondering whether I should like to have the engagement broken. It would be a sad thing indeed to me to have anything of the kind happen. I have great faith in you and I expect to love you as dearly as I love my own daughter, and if the engagement were to be broken I should still think of you with affection—provided it were broken from the conviction that a mistake had been made and not from recrimination. And now we will talk no more about that affair—provided only that you love Will wholly & devotedly & trustfully & that you go to him as often with your expressions of love and confidence as you like to have him come to you. A love falls a good deal short of its best if it waits to know who gave the last kiss or who has given the greater number—unless indeed each feels that he wants to get into the other's debt in expressions of love and confidence. There is no danger of you expressing too little, but on the other hand there should never be more expressions than there is feeling. And selfishness and pique that stands in the way of love only proves, to me at any rate, that the great essential of love is absent. No one loves as he ought to love unless he thinks more of the loved one's comfort and happiness than he does of his own. There now you have enough of a lecture haven't you. Well it is full of love anyhow and full of confidence that both of you have the genuine article and that you have besides strength enough of mind and character to deserve each the best that the other can give.

Lovingly Papa Reid

♥♥♥♥♥

Bill Reid, Harvard University, to Christine Lincoln, Cohasset, MA
9 October 1901

After defeating Williams, Bowdoin, and Bates, the Harvard football coach was pining for Christine following Harvard's victory over Amherst College.

My own Little Darling:

God bless you, how I wish I could be with you tonight to love you, fondle you and hold you in my arms. I am simply crazy for you, little girl and it's all I can do to keep from speeding down to Cohasset to see you. Tonight, after the game, at supper, [assistant coach, William H.] Lewis said to me—"Come back Bill, come back, Cohasset will look out for itself." He hit it right. I was down at Cohasset, heart and soul, with you.

You are an awful comfort to me dearest in all this worry and responsibility. No matter how dark the outlook seems, or how blue I am, it is always sweetly comforting to know that you love me. . . .

During the game today, I constantly thought of you and wondered whether you were in the stands or not. I felt as though I should be able to get along somehow or other 'till Saturday if only I could once see your dear face. . . .

At last there appeared in the team that "fight" which I have been trying to instill in the men ever since the season began. With the score 0 to 0 at the end of the first half, they went to it . . . the second half and in twelve minutes scored twice and almost a third time. . . .

♥♥♥♥♥

Christine Lincoln, Cohasset, MA, to Bill Reid, Jr., Harvard University
ca. 11 October 1901

Christine knew what would cheer up her fiancé while he coached the Harvard team.

121

A Debutante's Passion—A Coach's Erotica

Missed seeing you. . . ! Still Saturday's certainly getting nearer, and then hurrah! You see I do love you, in fact it's stronger than that, I worship you. I do really. Will you kiss me a lot when you come? I want you to just awfully. If you don't, I warn you I shall turn aggressor and unsex you. Ain't I naughty. . . ?

♥♥♥♥♥

Christine Lincoln, Cohasset, MA, to Bill Reid, Jr., Harvard University
ca. 14 October 1901

Likely in response to William Reid, Sr.'s October 3rd letter to Christine, Christine told Bill that she had written to Bill's father.

I wrote a long letter to your father this morning, and I will keep the first edition for you to see.
    Sweetheart I am so happy, I am just bubbling over. I think we are closer together somehow that we ever were before, and I love it so. . . . .
    You dear you, I am crazy to see you again! You are just everything to me, you know. . . .

♥♥♥♥♥

Bill Reid, Jr., Harvard University, to Christine Lincoln, Cohasset, MA
22 October 1901

By late October, the Harvard football team had won seven straight including West Point in the last game. Bill missed Christine greatly.

I love you so that I don't know what to do; you are my whole life, my everything, my all. I think of you, as I go to bed, when I get up, and all day long—with a loving, faithful heart and a devoted and fond affection. . . . Loved one if there had only been an earlier train to Cohasset on Sunday night, than the eight forty three, I'd have come back to you that day. . . .
    I'm coming down Saturday night. . . .
    The [football] men are fighting like mad & feel greatly encouraged. I shall await with great interest the outcome of the Carlisle [Indian School] game as I think we are likely to beat them quite handily, even with some substitute backs. I think the game will be a "fierce" one as our team's blood is up.
    Now little darling, a good, long, sweet kiss, a fond tight hug and all the love that's in me—to you 'till I once more hold your precious self in my embrace.

♥♥♥♥♥

Bill Reid, Jr., Harvard University, to Christine Lincoln, Brookline, MA
10 November 1901

Bill, highly wrought up about the outcome of the upcoming game with Pennsylvania, wrote Christine the night before the contest.

RETURN, MARRIAGE, AND HONEYMOON

I am greatly worried with all the excitement, responsibility, and distraction that this game tomorrow is bringing with it. I feel nervous, blue and incapable—and it's not fun, I can tell you. My comfort, hope and inspiration is you—you darling you. You've been so very kind, thoughtful, and loving to me—and oh, but it has done me worlds of good. I've thoroughly realized how glum I have been, how peevish and irritable—and how sweet, cheerful & comforting you have been. . . . I wish you were here in Philadelphia tonight so that I could love you, kiss you, and hug you—that would ease the strain tremendously. I certainly am in poor physical condition—and the grueling that I am undergoing in worry, thought, and suspense isn't going to leave much of me behind, when it's all over. . . .

I thought of you all the way down [on the boat] last night & almost wrote to you—if I hadn't felt so completely done up I'd have done so. As it was I went to bed at 9:30 & had a good sleep. I awoke feeling much refreshed & expect to get a good rest tonight. Really, you have no idea what a load this is to carry. I had the bridal chamber on the boat—& the fellows jollied me a good deal. . . .

♥♥♥♥♥

Wm. T. Reid, Sr., Belmont, CA, to Bill Reid, Jr., Cambridge, MA
11 March 1902

Bill's father wrote about some unknown concern for Christine in a letter discussin hiring a Harvard man, the grandson of Horace Mann, for the Belmont School.

Dear me, what an exciting and rather frightful time you had of it! I don't wonder that you were in consternation about Christine. I don't know but that she better sometime try the experiment of jumping out of a fifth story window and see if that will have any effect. Nothing else seems to faze her. . . .

Tell Christine that if I had been on hand I should have made my kissing a little bit less bloody than you did yours. Give her very strong expressions of our affections and confidence.

♥♥♥♥♥

Wm. T. Reid, Sr., Belmont, CA, to Bill Reid, Jr., Harvard University
9 April 1902

Three months before the wedding, Bill Reid's father counseled Bill on the high expense of a European honeymoon, something for which he had promised to pay. To cut expenses, he had Bill inquire about a transport ship, or delay the trip for a few months so as not to be in the busy season.

. . . As it is, neither of you will care a continental who is on board, and although you would doubtless take great pride in parading the deck

A Debutante's Passion—A Coach's Erotica

with Christine on your arm, yet it would be just as well to restrain your vanity if it is going to be so exceedingly expensive.

This is your outing and not mine, and I am not even going to give anything in the way of positive advice except about getting your passage. Don't calculate too much upon the sale of the ranch. . . .

♥ ♥ ♥ ♥ ♥

Christine Lincoln, Brookline, MA, to Bill Reid, Jr., Annapolis, MD
15 April 1902

Bill was assisting the Harvard baseball team and was on a baseball trip with the Harvard team to Annapolis, when Christine wrote.

. . . I want to "love" you just awfully much. I feel very "lovey" to-night, and I wish you were here. You would get a good kissing and hugging if you were, so look out for yourself. . . .

Agnes and I went down to Cohasset to-day on the 8:42 train to play golf. It was a most gorgeous day, and we had a dandy time. We had one rather "scary" adventure for, when we were walking along the loneliest piece of the road on the way to the links, we met two most unattractive men. However, it was all right, but still it might not have been and I felt relieved when they were out of sight. Ag thought it a great joke because I said I would have hit them with a golf club if they had attacked us, but I would have had a try at it anyway. . . .

♥ ♥ ♥ ♥ ♥

Bill Reid, Jr., Annapolis, MD, to Christine Lincoln, Brookline, MA
15 April 1902

On a trip South with the baseball team, the team visited the nation's capitol and then on to Annapolis. Bill missed Christine, and he told of the racial incident concerning William Matthews, a black freshman star infielder playing in the "Jim Crow," segregated South.

I feel awfully "huggy" this morning and am just about crazy to get you in my arms again—it seems as though I hadn't seen you for a month and yet this is only the fourth day away. . . .

You beauty you—it makes me thrill all over to think of loving with you for the rest of my life—just to think of your soft white cheek, your bully arms and breasts and your nice warm nether limbs—and your love and affection. . . .

Sunday afternoon I went up to the Capitol in Washington & climbed to the top of the dome. Of course we had to have special permission, but we got it. The view from there is simply magnificent—miles & miles on every side. Washington is certainly a beautiful city—and a clean one. . . .

RETURN, MARRIAGE, AND HONEYMOON

We arrived at Annapolis at about 7 o'clock & had supper, then sang & then went to bed. My bed would be fine if only you were in at with me. . . , how delicious you would look lying there in your dainty pink & white "nighty" and your irresistibly tantalizing ways.

Matthews has created quite a stir down here. The papers commenting on him about like this: "It certainly is an eye-opener to the Southerners to see a colored man on a team from aristocratic Harvard," etc. The Annapolis team has got four thoroughly Southern men on it & they are red-hot over the prospect of Matthews playing against them. If he were to play they'd try to kill him if possible. That's the main reason why we've put [Edward] Collidge on second. You see shortstop does not come in contact with so many men as the 2nd baseman does & so if Matthews plays on shortstop he's in the most protected spot on the infield. We went to Commander Wainwright of the post & talked the situation over with him & he said this—"We have invited the Harvard team down here irrespective of the make up of the team—and you are to play any man you choose. If any cadet refuses to play, then that cadet will not be allowed to play on the Annapolis team again—and we'll keep order here in this government school if we have to order out the entire 'military' of the post"—and he meant it. Now we're put in a very curious predicament. Annapolis is the best place we've struck yet for our Southern trip—and the only place where a colored fella will be so much as tolerated in a hotel. Matthews is to be with us four years & we have got to provide a Southern trip for that length of time. If we play Matthews here in a game, we won't be asked here again & we've no good place to go. If we don't play him we will not make the disciplining of the Cadets necessary, will keep good feeling between Harvard & Annapolis & have a place to bring Matthews to for three years more. They let him practice, eat & sleep with us here but draw the line at his playing. We want him to play very much but don't wish to get in a squabble with the U. S. Naval Academy & we wish to come again—so on the whole we have decided not to play him today. If the baseball men here had not promised to ask us here next year if Mathews did not play, we'd play him anyhow. Even in Washington he had to eat in his room as the hotel people said that they could not allow him in the dining room—owing to their Southern patronage. It is a hard question. . . . We have to go on the basis of "In England, do as the English do. . . ." Mathews is acting superbly & the fellows are all with him. There has been no insult of any kind offered him because the Johnnie Rebs fear the "Yanks." All the games here are regarded by Southerners as contests between North & South. . . .

The Matthews question has been taken up by the women of the town & the post & they feel almost insulted if he were to play. No woman or girl goes out alone here without a pistol, & they can all shoot. Such precautions are necessary for protection against the Negroes who are ready to assault white women at every turn. The women feel that the

A Debutante's Passion—A Coach's Erotica

recognition of a colored fellow on our team will make the colored people here very proud & the women fear more frequent attacks. . . .

♥♥♥♥♥

Bill Reid, Jr., Annapolis, MD, to Christine Lincoln, Brookline, MA
17 April 1902

After a week in the Annapolis area, the baseball team was about ready to turn North and play Army at West Point before returning home. Bill's thoughts were not always on baseball, but also on his honeymoon with Christine.

I am crazy to see you, to love you, to hug you, to squeeze and kiss you and to sleep with you. It seems as though every single sense was on edge, and every fondness aroused. . . .

I wish I'd been on hand to pull that corset bone out—I feel quite expert at it now. I shall have to see whether any others need tending to, when I get back. . . .

I feel so strongly about keeping the Captain's room that I doubt if I should favor a change under any circumstances now. I want that we should have a good time on that trip & particularly on the ninth of July—& space and bed accommodations, with privacy—will add much. I am anticipating the close quarters of a steamship berth very much. Gee, but you are a deliciously soft, warm, beautiful thing to snuggle up to. . . .

♥♥♥♥♥

Wm. T. Reid, Sr., Belmont, CA, to Christine Lincoln, Brookline, MA
17 April 1902

Bill's father, always the advisor and often meddler in his son's affairs, wrote to his prospective daughter-in-law, suggesting that she have a child early and that birth control methods would be dangerous to her health.

. . . There is absolutely nothing in life that I now look forward to with the satisfaction that I feel when I think of you with a baby. . . .

You cannot afford to take any chances in the matter of miscarriages and you certainly cannot afford to use drugs or acids—and it is of course utterly out of the question for you to think of living apart. . . .

It is too bad that when you are both strong & fresh & impulsive you could not do as you like and let the little one come & be welcome at any time. . . .

♥♥♥♥♥

Christine Lincoln, Brookline, MA, to Bill Reid, Harvard University
ca. 29 April 1902

RETURN, MARRIAGE, AND HONEYMOON

In a quick note, Christine asked if he could come to dinner.

Try to arrange, if possible, to be over here to a seven o'clock dinner tomorrow night. . . . I am anxious to hear about the steamer. Don't answer this unless you feel like telephoning. . . .

♥♥♥♥♥

Wm. T. Reid, Sr., Belmont, CA, to Bill Reid, Jr., Harvard University
10 May 1902

Bill's father had received a letter from Christine about the approaching marriage and possible children. His advice turned out to be true.

. . . I should be happy, very happy if it should after all sense-wise to let nature have her way as Christine is inclined to. . . .

♥♥♥♥♥

Wm. T. Reid, Sr., Belmont, CA, to Bill Reid, Jr., Harvard University
18 May 1902

In a very long letter, Bill's father appreciated Bill's comments on the California ranch and his coming to work at the Belmont School. Then he had to tell Bill of the methods of birth control, none of which, he believed, were as good as having children.

. . . I enjoyed one thing that you said in your last letter more, I think, than anything you ever wrote me. It was that you hoped that I would sell the ranch for whatever I could get for it if keeping it was likely to give me further worry, for one of the greatest pleasures that you anticipated in coming to Belmont was that of working with me. . . .

I have so long been an autocrat and have come to rule in such an autocratic way that I suspect that you will sometimes chafe under it for it is almost impossible for one who has long exercised power to give it up. . . .

There are two or three ways—legitimate—I think to put off pregnancy, but the orthodox, the fine way is to do as most of the English do—as young Wheeler a most successful young lawyer of San Francisco is doing & as Phil Brown is doing—Keep in fine trim and let as many little ones come as you care to have. Wheeler has five and he & his wife are as proud of them as they can be. The number is rather large for they are both young yet & if they continue they will have from three to five more. That is wholly for you & Christine to decide & no one has any right to do more than lay before you facts or facts and probabilities. . . . There are methods—1st what is called a womb veil—a rubber appliance for the woman to introduce. It covers the mouth of the womb but it is very liable to give serious trouble & if it is not carefully put in and taken

A Debutante's Passion—A Coach's Erotica

out & kept very clean it is most likely to cause serious & sometimes incurable or almost incurable disease. It ought not to be thought of. 2nd the introduction of cotton to be withdrawn in a day or two—less objectionable by far than the womb veil—pretty effective and. . . unobjectionable. 3rd syringing—never safe if acids are used and never good even with pun water for it washes out the secretions that keep the parts lubricated and healthy. 4th the wearing of condoms on your part. Condoms are of two kinds—gold beaters skin—very thin but very liable to break. They are inoffensive—if they don't break, but they take a good deal of the edge of the enjoyment away from both. The other kinds are of rubber—safe and very little dangerous, but they about halve the pleasure. 5th withdrawal just before the climax. This calls for an immense exercise of will & self restraint and is likely to leave the wife just short of a climax & so to be unsatisfactory to the husband & wholly selfish as far as it goes. That is about the round of conditions. Carenzza [Italian for sexual caressing] is theoretically good but I don't believe in it. God or nature meant that intercourse should be intercourse and not a lolling on the edge of it.

It is none of my business nor none of Mamma's business what you do so long as you do not endanger health, but both of us will be delighted if you & Christine conclude that you are willing to have a baby come whenever it may come. . . .

♥♥♥♥♥

Christine Lincoln, Cohasset, MA, to Bill Reid, Jr., Harvard University
7 June 1902

Bill was studying for his masters degree exams, while Christine was at her family summer home, visiting with a best friend, Tede Tileston, but thinking of her future with Bill.

You've no idea of how I am looking forward to our trip abroad, especially because, for one I shall have you all to myself. How great it will be! Day and night! I cannot imagine anything more absolutely blissful! I am so anxious to get as close to you as I can (in both ways). . . .

Tede and I took a bathing cap and a towel apiece and went off for a walk. We found a lovely little cove, sheltered from the wind, and more important still, from the vulgar gaze. Well—it was delicious! The sun and wind do feel so good that we lay and basked for quite a while before we went in. The water was just cold enough to be perfect, and altogether, we had a most enjoyable time. Don't mind if I tell you that I kept thinking of you and wishing you were there in spite of my costume, or rather my lack of such a thing. . . .

I was in bed before nine o'clock, and had a fine sleep. My bed is a double one, but unfortunately I am single. . . .

RETURN, MARRIAGE, AND HONEYMOON

How are the rotten exams? Gracious! But I too shall be thankful when they are a thing of the past. . . .

♥♥♥♥♥

Bill Reid, Jr., Harvard University, to Christine Lincoln, Cataumet, MA
8 June 1902

Bill studied while Christine played—and he thought of Christine.

Today didn't open with much of a prospect in the way of comfort for me—no hugs, no kisses, no loving as I have usually had—nothing but books, notes and study. And then came the next best thing to being with you—hearing from you. . . .

I keep saying to myself—its less than a month now & then I'll have her. The thought of a double bed & you just makes me feel "ecstatical. . . ." No one looks to July 2 with more delight, glee & satisfaction than I (you included). . . .

I wish I could have seen you bathing — yi !!!!! Well, I will one of these days—mm—it makes my mouth water.

♥♥♥♥♥

Christine Lincoln, Cataumet, MA, to Bill Reid, Jr., Harvard University
ca. 9 June 1902

Christine wrote from her beach-front location, enjoying water sports with her friend, Tede Tileston, while Bill continued to study for his exams.

I am leading such a healthy life here that I feel more husky than usual, and consequently more "lovey. . . ."

Yesterday we had a very energetic day, in spite of it being Sunday. . . . Tede & I went out in a canoe for a little while, but it wasn't much fun. . . . We went out sailing. . . quite exciting at times and got back just in time for dinner. . . . After dinner, it being dead low tide, Tede and I set out in quest of clams. . . and we got a good lot. It was pretty stiff work & the ends of our fingers are all hurt & sore. . . . Tede and I came back, got on bathing caps and towels and walked. . . for about a mile and a quarter to another beach. This one was not sheltered at all from the wind, and the surf was great. We took a Kodak with us—but I don't like to tell the rest. We had about the most glorious bath I have ever had. Before going in we raced up and down the beach. The water was delicious and the waves dashed us around. . . . It was blowing so that when we ran along the beach, the sand came up and pelted us, and you've no idea how it hurt. . . .

Tede says for me to tell you that she will take good care of me, but that she finds it impossible to restrain my immodesty. Between you

A Debutante's Passion—A Coach's Erotica

and me though, we're two of a kind. You just ought to see the color of my — er — er— face, of course. . . .

♥ ♥ ♥ ♥ ♥

Bill Reid, Jr., Harvard University, to Christine Lincoln, Cataumet, MA
10 June 1902

Bill was not only completing his master's degree, but he was also coaching the Harvard baseball team less than a month before he married Christine. He was exhausted.

Little one, you dear:

I only wish I could get to you and could get you in my arms—if you wouldn't get a corking hugging, kissing and squeezing, then my name isn't Bill. I'm simply frantic for you—my only consolation is the fact that I know that you are having a good rest as well as a good time. I love to have you say that you feel "husky"—you'll be that way when we get married won't you. You see I am going to pick up fast now and if we can both feel tip top—oh joy, bliss, thrills and quivers!!! What a time we'll have. I'm crazy for you even if I am pretty well done up. You are such a delicious lusciousness to look at, kiss, hug, squeeze & love that everything else that I can do with you seems like a hazy dream of unparalleled bliss. [drawing of four-poster bed] Ain't I naughty.

Your second letter came just before I went into History 2, and under the stimulus which the nectar in it furnished me, I simply knocked the paper into a cocked hat. I wrote the entire period & didn't then quite finish. Prof. Wright—good old soul—promised to look over my paper this afternoon in order to relieve the suspense. He did so & told me just now that he hadn't quite made up his mind as to whether my mark was A or only B+. In consequence I am feeling pretty nicely, though exceedingly run down. I weighed yesterday and tipped the scales at 157—a loss of 8 lbs. since I saw you, due entirely to the ceaseless work I've done. Really I never gulped down so much in such a time before. I never dreamt that I could do it. My stomach almost "threw up" too but by eating little I kept it quiet. I am so lame from sitting down that it's a pleasure to stand up as to lie down. I practically did the work of two courses from Feb. to June in those four days. I was almost ready to give up, but your love & confidence in me made me simply "fierce" & I did do it. My Latin 10, I think I did well in too—though I couldn't finish the paper. I feel quite pleased with the outcome, and I am now done. God bless you, but you've been so much to me all this time—so dear & loving & kindly—it was just what I needed.

The team has left for Princeton. . . , and I am going down by the midnight. I shan't sleep much because I am too unstrung, but I couldn't sleep anywhere else either. . . . I am going to the theatre tonight to see if we can't get a bit relaxed. We may go to "The Prince of Pilsen"—that's better than "The Defenders" at the Columbia. I don't like the name at all, but I couldn't stand a serious play as I feel now, so please don't scold me too much.

You asked about the Bowdoin game—it rained & so the game was cancelled. Thank heavens it has been cool here, or I could never have studied as I did. The cold air braced me up greatly.

I wish I could have surprised you Saturday night with a letter, but I was so, so busy & worried that I could not have written any sort of a one & I never like to hurry when I am writing to you. I like to go slow and love you all the way.

I wish this lobster could get such a "dose" as you said you'd like to give him—he's crazy for it.

You and Tede certainly must be having a fine old time swimming, clamming & going walking with a towel & a cap. If I could only see you that way, it would be simply divine—& so would you—for you are you know. You must let me see those Kodaks sometime "for exchange is no robbery."

You tell all about these things in such a fascinating way that it makes me feel great to read, over & over what you say.

I am looking forward so much to seeing you on Thursday. It will be such a joy to be with you & not have to think of those exams, etc. I can love you peacefully, which is simply inexpressibly fine.

You haven't got many more days of single life left & I am so glad. I want to "double up" dreadful much.

Mama gets here on Saturday, so Miss Watson tells me, that's awfully nice isn't it. Because my work is done & I can ease up now.

Well you darling you, take good care of yourself and know that I am loving you hard all this time and that I am so glad you're soon to be back.

I don't know how the Princeton game will come out—it's a toss up. We may put it out by a run or so. With best wishes to Tede, I am as always & for ever
Your "Bill"
♥♥♥♥♥

Profile House, NH, telegram to Bill Reid, Jr., Cambridge, MA
28 June 1902

Bill made arrangements for their second night after marriage, staying at the Profile House in New Hampshire, a short trip before going abroad for their honeymoon. It was here, or possibly the first night in Boston's Hotel Lennox, that Christine became pregnant. Three years later Bill would remember the first night: "Let's see, four times was it? It makes my mouth water & makes me squirm about in my chair a bit."

Will reserve nice room for you July third.
♥♥♥♥♥

A Debutante's Passion—A Coach's Erotica

Ch. H. Greenleaf, Franconia Notch, NH, to Bill Reid, Jr., Brookline, MA
1 July 1902

The Profile House at Franconia Notch, New Hampshire, was in the White Mountains. It would host Bill and Christine Reid on their second night of marriage. The room rented would be either $5 or $6, part of the Flume Hotels Company, a location between two lakes, with a steamlaunch on one and rowing on both. Numerous walks and climbs were available as were fishing on Profile Lake and riding horses and buggy rides.

♥♥♥♥♥

Daisy Cartwright, San Francisco, CA, telegram to Bill Reid, Jr., Cambridge, MA
2 July 1902

One of Bill's old girlfriends, sometimes known as "Platonic," telegraphed Bill on his marriage to Christine.

Congratulations and best wishes for the happiest of futures.

♥♥♥♥♥

Tede Tilewton, Peterboro, NH, to Christine Lincoln Reid, Cohasset, MA
10 July 1902

One of Christine Lincoln's best friends wrote soon after the wedding.

Everyone who was at the wedding has been misguided enough to inform me that you were the most beautiful bride they ever saw, and I had to agree with them!
    You left a good sized blank in our hearts when you went off . . . . I did not need to hear from your mother that you were in the seventh heaven.

♥♥♥♥♥

Bess, Hyannis, MA, to Christine Lincoln Reid, Cohasset, MA
13 July 1902

A friend of Christine wrote shortly after the wedding.

Really Christine I never went to a lovelier wedding than yours and it must be great for you to look back upon it. At the church when the wedding march struck up, my heart went thump, thump for you and I gave Ralph [her fiancée] a terrific nudge in the ribs. I actually felt that I was being married myself for I had chills and fevers throughout the ceremony. You looked perfectly lovely Christine and seemed as calm as a clock. Your house and grounds did look so lovely and everybody seemed so enthusiastic and merry.

♥♥♥♥♥

RETURN, MARRIAGE, AND HONEYMOON

Albert Lincoln, Brookline, MA, to Christine Lincoln Reid, Glasgow, Scotland
26 July 1902

Christine Reid's father ended his 4-page letter to Christine Reid with precious comments, as she and Bill journeyed on their honeymoon. Mr. Lincoln had just shipped 1820 pounds of Christine's materials to Belmont, California including 10 barrels and 17 boxes of presents.

. . . Love to you both, and many kisses for you. Bill, I've no doubt, gets all he wants or ought to have. . . .

♥♥♥♥♥

Francis C. Ware, Villars sur Ollou, Switzerland, to Christine Lincoln Reid, Brookline, MA
8 August 1902

Francis Ware, Bill's classmate and chemical engineer, had met Christine first at the Harvard Senior Dance when Gordon Allen had prematurely congratulated Christine on her engagement to Bill. This letter was a congratulation of marriage, which he could not attend, and to tell Christine about the high esteem Bill was held by Harvard men.

I write to you instead of to Bill, as that arrangement makes it possible for me to tell you how high a place he has won in the hearts of his classmates, and the subject is as pleasant as I am sure you most heartily agree.

In spite of the fact that you appreciate and admire him more than any of us, if that is possible, I am sure you are glad to learn as often as possible how his career and character have affected the college and set a standard of manliness for all to imitate.

He came to Harvard, a stranger to the surroundings the customs and the people, but with Harvard's motto and spirit in his heart, and if I am not mistaken was chilled and discouraged during his Freshman year by "eastern exclusiveness" or "Harvard indifference," it matters little what that intangible atmosphere of aloofness is called, one name is as false as another.

But in spite of this drawback he was known and respected to such a degree by the end of his sophomore year that he was chosen captain of the next year's baseball team and had exhibited so fine a spirit that the game was half won in which he played. His earnestness and determination were inspiring, and resulted in team play supported by a college enthusiasm which has been sadly lacking Harvard.

By the end of his Junior year he was undoubtedly the most popular man in college and an immense influence for purity in athletics. In fact, he is a Harvard man in the best sense of the word.

A Debutante's Passion—A Coach's Erotica

I hope he is going to remain in the East for a few years at least; and if that is impossible, that he will come back for the Triennial Reunion on Commencement day, 1904.

Of course all this is no news to you, but unprejudiced t e s t i m o n y aids in proving a story; and I so heartily wish you all happiness in the future that it is a pleasure to tell you so.

Please remember me to Bill, and give him my congratulations on his fine work with the football team. He and Dave Campbell are a strong combination and I wish they could work together once more. We should have another victory to celebrate.

With kindest wishes and regrets—for the long delay.
                Sincerely
                Francis C. Ware

♥♥♥♥♥

Agnes Lincoln, Cohasset, MA, to Christine Lincoln Reid, Edinburgh, Scotland

11 August 1902

Christine's 19-year-old sister, Agnes, conjectured in a letter to the honeymooning couple that she would be an aunt in 1903, and probed her sister about any possible pregnancy.

Wasn't it kind of the King [Edward] to be crowned on my birthday. . . ? I hate being nineteen. I feel so awfully old. . . .

I get so excited when I think of . . . the first child. . . . Have you been sick, Tiny? Please don't think it is cruel of me to ask, but I am so interested. However, don't tell me if you don't want to. Just tell me to shut up, and I'll know I have no right to ask.

♥♥♥♥♥

Mrs. Albert Lincoln, Cohasset, MA, to Christine Lincoln Reid, London, England

14 August 1902

Christine's mother, in a rather depressed mood and recovering from an illness, wrote to her daughter, far away in England.

My darling, darling, darling Christine,

I cannot tell you how much I enjoyed your letter from [Bettwsycore] telling us of your exciting ride with the drunken coachman. What an experience for you and Will. I have missed you so dearlie that I have avoided mentioning your name at times, fearing I might break down should I do so. I should not write you this if you had not written us that you and Will had also missed us too. Well, you dear ones, you are always in my thoughts, and I have had a great deal of time for thinking as I have

RETURN, MARRIAGE, AND HONEYMOON

been able to do very little else for about five weeks now. My strength comes back very slowly. . . .

Well, you darling, I send you heaps of hugs and kisses, and some to dear Will also.

Fondly,
Your Mama

♥ ♥ ♥ ♥ ♥

Mrs. Albert Lincoln, Brookline, MA, to Christine Lincoln Reid, Baden-Baden, Germany

7 September 1902

Christine had just written to her mother that she was pregnant, and her mother gave her advice about her pregnancy. The baby was conceived almost immediately after the July wedding.

It is all for the best, but I wish that you might have had your European trip without any thoughts of self, for nausea is a very strong reminder, but I think will bother you only a short time. Now dearie, instead of the two months, as I spoke of in my last letter, I shall want you and Will with me until after the baby comes. We are planning for Agnes and Louise to go to California with you whenever you want them to do so. You spoke in your last letter of the magnetism in the future, which would surely draw me to you in California, but I need no more powerful a one than your beloved self. We do miss you so, and each day more than ever.

I am going back now to the days before you were born. I was very happy I remember, did about as usual only tried not to get over tired. Under the circumstances, you will come home by Christmas if not before. You will then be about five months along, a safe time to come across the ocean. I would not wait later. You write such enjoyable letters, and are so good about writing. I don't know as I have any more advice to give you for you are, and always were a very intelligent child. Should anything come to my mind to guard you against, I will certainly do so. You will get along all right just like your Mama and think how excited and filed with delight we shall all be. Give much love to Will and tell him we are hurrying up his father about the plan of your house.

♥ ♥ ♥ ♥ ♥

Albert Lincoln, Brookline, MA, letter to Christine Lincoln Reid, Baden-Baden, Germany

10 September 1902

Christine knew in August that she was pregnant and told both her parents and her in-laws in California. Her father wrote to her in Germany.

135

A Debutante's Passion—A Coach's Erotica

Ma has told me all & I have read your "private" letter! Well my dear little girl I'm glad you accept your fate so philosophically. Of course it was to be expected but I had hoped with Ma that your trip abroad might be unencumbered & free from this anxiety, for of course there is more or less anxiety in your situation although it ought to be a merely natural one. I feel as if I ought to write Mr. Reid Senior at once to alter the plan of that house very materially, put in more rooms & make them small, provide a sunny nursery which can be quickly heated in cold weather, with rooms for nurses, place for baby carriage, etc. with a room for William Jr., . . . undisturbed by the cries of William III. . . .

♥♥♥♥♥

Wm. T. Reid, Sr., Belmont, CA, to Christine Lincoln Reid, Interlaken, Switzerland
14 September 1902

It was only natural for William Reid, Sr., to feel the need to give advice to Christine after being informed that she was pregnant.

I wish that you could know how brimful of happiness your letter filled me. I wish for your own & Bill's convenience that there might have been a delay until your trip abroad was over, but it means a good deal to me and to Mamma that you and Bill mean to take life in all seriousness and are quite ready to begin seriously. No little one ever came that will receive a more hearty welcome than your little one when it comes. I am already counting the time when we may expect it. Tell us as exactly as you can. Oh those tantalizing underclothes that you showed me. I warned you of their danger I think. And yet on the other hand they simply made the tinder a little more inflammable. Well dear, fight against the tendency to depression and all sorts of unreasonableness and if you find it getting hold of you sit right down and tell me about it all—how horrid Bill is—how negligent, how little he loves you, & how he sometimes pretends to love you when he really doesn't but only pities you and all that.

What does Bill say and how does he feel. This is altogether more serious than coaching a football team isn't it?

♥♥♥♥♥

Albert L. Lincoln, Brookline, MA, to Christine Lincoln Reid, London, England
14 November 1902

As Christine and Bill returned to England, prior to returning to America, Christine's father ended his letter to her with a curious note about a "procrastinated article," likely one that Bill had been asked to write about Harvard athletics for a major periodical.

RETURN, MARRIAGE, AND HONEYMOON

. . . If you don't bring that much procrastinated article to a close soon I shall expect my grandchild to have a base-ball head and a foot-ball body.

♥ ♥ ♥ ♥ ♥

Wm. T. Reid, Sr., Belmont, CA, to Christine Lincoln Reid, London, England
24 November 1902

Bill's father often told Bill about his financial concerns including new ventures that he was considering, the debt on the ranch and on the Belmont School, and later the cost of the boat and building a house at Lake Tahoe. Here he was rather upbeat, for once, to Christine.

Tell Bill that I have just sold our wheat for $1.37 ½ . . . which is 38 cents . . . more than I got last year. Indeed wheat has not been so high for a dozen years I think. We shall net a little more than 5% on a valuation of $150,000. It will all go into improvement and stock however. But I am feeling mighty good at the outlook. I am now negotiating a new loan at 5%. If I accomplish it & I think I shall it will make a great difference with us. It is pretty fine to be reducing our debts by about $12000 a year and our interest account about or a little over $500 a year. Two more years besides this will clear up everything on the school and then we shall have clear sailing for we can run the ranch debt off rapidly. So you see I am feeling pretty good. I am looking forward, too, to your house building. . . .

Well, dear child, I love you & long to have you come. You are going to bring much into my life.

     Lovingly Papa

♥ ♥ ♥ ♥ ♥

Julia Reid, Belmont, CA, to Bill Reid, Jr., probably Brookline, MA
20 December 1902

Bill's mother awaited their first grandchild, not realizing that it would arrive well before the due date, for the baby, William III (Patrick) was born in March on St. Patrick's Day.

We are so anxious to hear about your ocean trip & so eager to see you both. Everybody is delighted at the thoughts of the April arrival. . . .

♥ ♥ ♥ ♥ ♥

Cohasset –
June 28, '04 –

My sweetest, most precious husband,

Two of the dearest letters that ever were written are before me ready to be answered. Oh! they are so delicious, and I have just feasted on all the love and passion they express. You can't say enough to satisfy me and the more I get the more I want. I cannot tell you how much I am looking forward to our first night don't, it was a dog license!" Isn't that rich?

Chapter 5

LOVE AND CHILDREN: "IF YOU WERE HERE NOW WE'D BE IN BED"

Bill Reid, Jr., note to Christine Reid

9 January 1903

Bill and Christine had returned from their honeymoon to Europe and were living briefly with the Lincolns in Brookline. Bill wrote Christine a note of appreciation, probably just before he left for California. There he would live with his parents, for Bill was beginning his career as assistant headmaster at the Belmont School. Shortly thereafter, Christine would join him in their life in the West.

For the little girl, whose dainty figure, beautiful eyes and loving ways make me the happiest fellow on earth; with all the love, devotion and admiration which God has given me. I love you absolutely dear one—& I am all yours.

♥ ♥ ♥ ♥ ♥

Albert Lincoln, Brookline, MA, to Christine Reid, Belmont, CA

21 February 1903

Christine Reid had left her parents' home sometime earlier in February to begin life with Bill in California at the Belmont School. She was 7 months pregnant with her first child, William III, to be called Patrick or Pattakin (Patakin, Pattikins). Her father had just sent 10 more suitcases to Christine.

... We miss you terribly but we are not going to make ourselves unhappy so long as we know you are happy with Bill in Belmont. ...

♥ ♥ ♥ ♥ ♥

Albert Lincoln, Boston, MA, to Christine Reid, Belmont, CA

15 July 1903

On Christine's 22nd birthday, and one year after marrying Bill, she had written a depressed letter about her unhappiness as their 4-month old,

A Debutante's Passion—A Coach's Erotica

Patrick, was nursing. Her father commented about her unhappiness, and, because their income was not large, he offered to buy Pat's food. He would eventually help to pay for most of Bill and Christine's new house that would cost about $10,000.

My poor dear girl,
What a terrible letter to write on your birth-day! It came last evening & we are all very sorry that you are so unhappy & we so powerless to help you. I have no doubt you will try to cheer up & take things philosophically, but you must keep on trying & not let yourself get into such a frame of mind as the last page of your letter indicates. Suppose you must wean "Pat" dear boy? He must be weaned sometime & when you consider that Ma hardly nursed any of her children except you, you must consider yourself fortunate you have been able to nurse your baby so long. I had to have a wet-nurse & old Dr. Bigelow told my mother that very few American mothers were able to nurse children & that they ought not to. . . .
 You have enough to do to get along with $1200, without this extra expense, so as soon as "Pat" begins to have his food bought, let me pay for it. . . .

♥♥♥♥♥

Albert Lincoln, Cohasset, MA, to Christine Reid, Belmont, CA
5 October 1903

In a long letter to Christine from her father, he questioned the amount of peace and contentment for Christine in Belmont as well as her homesickness for the East. The Lincolns were to celebrate their 24th wedding anniversary the next Friday.

What you write about that dear baby makes me wild to see him again, & I certainly can't blame Mr. R[eid, Sr.] for running in 5 or 6 times a day to see him. How can you? He must be pretty satisfied with Bill's management, if he can run off as he has & leaves everything to B. But Bill's letter really made me anxious & I fear he is doing altogether too much. Comfort him all you can. It is very evident from the dear boy's letter that he is terribly afraid you are not as happy as he thinks you ought to be, but he ought to read your last letter to Louise & then he might believe that however much you miss us all & however you may long at times for Cohasset & the East, yet you can be very happy when you have cast your lot & once in your own house you will be. As someone, I think it was Mr. Buffirm said to me the other day, no house is big enough for two families—as a permanent thing. Am delighted that work has begun in earnest but how such a big house can be put up & finished in 3 or 4 mos, I can't understand. . . .

♥♥♥♥♥

LOVE AND CHILDREN

Albert Lincoln, Boston, MA, to Christine Reid, Belmont, CA
17 November 1903

Christine had complained to her father that her mother-in-law, Julia Reid, was interfering in child rearing and coming in too often to see her grandson, Pat. Her depression about living in California continued. Her father tried to soothe over Christine's anxiety.

. . .I don't believe, however, he [Pat] has advanced far enough to know the meaning of a "slap" & I'm glad you don't propose to be one of the slapping kind. It's all nonsense to suppose a baby can't be corrected without physical punishment & slapping them is the last thing you or I would think of unless under an impulse which we certainly ought not. . . . If Mrs. Reid believes in this method of training a child she is of course entitled to her belief & I suppose she so trained her children & they certainly don't seem any the worse for it, but Patsy is your child & you & you & Bill alone are responsible for his bringing up—so you must do what you think best & of course any advice you get which you don't like you needn't follow—nor do I see why you should openly resent it. It's a grandma's privilege to give advice, and we old people expect to advise those younger than we are, but if she is anything like me she can't expect her advice to be followed unless it's agreeable.

I am afraid, my dear little girl, that you are a little impatient with what seems to you like interference but which Mr. & Mrs. R. probably intend merely as a show of proper interest in their grandchild, for he is their grandchild you know as much as he is mine & mother's & you must make the same allowance for their faults as such grandparents that you make for us. . . .

I want you to continue to try to make the best of things, to look on the bright side & not on the dark, & to make a sturdy fight against depression and worry, but think how much you have to be thankful for. If Bill had done something else, like Ginn's business for example, you might have been stranded alone in Chicago while he was traveling on the road somewhere & you couldn't begin to look forward to the freedom which he will enjoy in the long school vacations nor to the resources which he will soon enjoy.

I do think it too bad you cannot have your meals together & don't now understand why you can't. If he is in another building why don't you go there. . . ?

♥ ♥ ♥ ♥ ♥

Albert Lincoln, Brookline, MA, to Christine Reid, Belmont, CA
3 December 1903

Sympathetic to Christine's depression in California, her father tried to be upbeat in his letter to her.

141

A Debutante's Passion—A Coach's Erotica

. . . We don't like to write too strongly to you from fear of making you more homesick. So I try to think of you enjoying the glorious sunshine in Belmont with your two precious boys & keeping them both happy with your deep affection. Fathers & mothers cannot, ought not & must not think of keeping their children to themselves, & we must be thankful if they are where we can get a good letter from them once a week. . . .

♥ ♥ ♥ ♥ ♥

Albert Lincoln, Brookline, MA, to Christine Reid, Belmont, CA
12 December 1903

Christine's father said that this would be the first year Christine would be away at Christmas time, and he sent her some extra money that came from her mother who had inherited some property.

. . . All you can do is to make the best fight possible against homesickness & to fight the feeling by doing for others. . . .

♥ ♥ ♥ ♥ ♥

Agnes Lincoln, Brookline, MA, to Christine Reid, Belmont, CA
ca. 19 December 1903

Christine's nineteen-year-old sister likely did not help Christine's homesickness when she wrote to her just before Christmas.

. . . We all dread Christmas without you. Wouldn't it be fun if girls even when they married lived with their families. . . ?
    By jove I wish I could fall in love. I am getting tired of dances and want a baby. I'd like to start right in and have one now. . . .

♥ ♥ ♥ ♥ ♥

Daniel J. Hurley, Harvard University, to Bill Reid, Jr., Belmont, CA
4 January 1904

The 1904 football captain asked Bill if he would return to Harvard to again coach the team. As late as the early 1900s, the captains still appointed football coaches at Harvard and elsewhere. However, Bill would not consider coaching Harvard unless he were "given final authority with the captain in deciding disputed points of policy."

Will you accept the position of Head Coach of next year's foot-ball team. If so, I want you.
    Kindly let me know at once, as I wish to make the appointment.

♥ ♥ ♥ ♥ ♥

LOVE AND CHILDREN

Ira N. Hollis, Harvard University, to Bill Reid, Jr., Belmont, CA
8 January 1904

What might otherwise be considered an insignificant letter was important, for the just retired Chairman of the Harvard Athletic Committee, Prof. Hollis, and other Harvard men hoped that Bill might return to the East and help the football team beat Yale. The Harvard Athletic Committee, without Hollis, voted "no" on the request of the Harvard Football Graduate Association to offer Bill $3,000 to coach the 1904 team. The Committee would change its mind in another year.

Thank you very much for your very pleasant Christmas greeting. I have wished you were here in Cambridge a great many times during the past few months. We needed all our friends last fall. I have never felt worse over a defeat. The football team needed a celestial fire of some kind. . . .
    I hope you may cross the continent sometime. . . .

♥♥♥♥♥

Albert Lincoln, Boston, MA, to Christine Reid, Belmont, CA
ca. 23 January 1904

Christine and Bill had been promised to have their house completed on the Belmont School grounds several months before, but it was still not finished, and they were still living with Bill's parents. The Lake Tahoe summer house being built by Bill's parents appeared to be going up more quickly. Living with the elder Reids almost assuredly put stress on Christine.

. . . I was very glad to see the photos of the Tahoe cottage. It looks mighty attractive & I should think Mr. R[eid] would be tickled enough to have it all built. But when is that other house likely to be finished? The builder's all right isn't he. . . ?"

♥♥♥♥♥

Bill Reid, Jr., Belmont, CA, to Christine Reid, Brookline, MA
19 May 1904

Christine, in the first trimester of her second pregnancy, took the train East with one-year-old "Patrick" to visit family and friends for two months while Bill stayed in Belmont working at the Belmont School. Within days, he missed Christine a great deal.

You don't know what a void you have left behind you, a hugging void, a kissing void and a cuddling void. I have missed you every minute and my thoughts have flown so often to you that I have been unable to accomplish anything. I wish I could get hold of you now & kiss you & love you, it would be so good and at night how good it would feel to lie

143

A Debutante's Passion—A Coach's Erotica

with you and squeeze you and especially when we are both stripped. I tell you it's a delicious feeling. I don't believe that you like it as much as you used to, but I do. You are so soft and warm and delicious. It is most tantalizing to sleep in the big bed, to feel as I do, & to know that for the present there is no remedy.

Poor little girl, I'm afraid you've had a pretty hard trip of it. I believe I've felt every jolt and bump that you've had, so deeply have I sympathized. I am feeling greatly relieved to think that by now you are well settled in your state-room. How I wish I could be with you to do for you; the only thing that will make me feel easy, without being able to look after you myself, is to know that you are having everything you have desired for your comfort & happiness. You must get plenty of sleep—and if you can't get it in any other way, I want you to get a nurse to sleep in the room with the baby—thus leaving you to rest in peace. You owe it to sister to do this. It was awfully hard to leave you. God bless you, but I felt that you were going to have a pleasant change and a restful visit. Here's a kiss, a hug, a squeeze & cuddle, and a _____ (guess) all in one. . . .

♥♥♥♥♥

Bill Reid, Jr., Belmont, CA, letter to Christine Reid, Brookline, MA
22 May 1904

Bill's long letter was in part a reply to Christine's letter mailed from Chicago on the train ride East. Bill wrote protectively of her and to tell her that his salary was raised from $1200 to $1500 for the next year.

How I do wish you were here; how I should like to take you in my lap—there to fondle you and kiss you and hug you and in every way show you how much you meant to me, and how wrong you are in the suppositions which you made in your Chicago letter. You don't know how sad and self reproaching I felt as I read over your timid though eager appeal for a little display of the love which you have so richly earned. To think that I have acted in such a way as to cause you, you dear old girl, to wonder whether I wasn't losing my fondness for you, is pretty hard. God bless you, sweetheart, I love you dreadfully. No one has admired the "stuff" you have shown in putting up with things here, or appreciated it more than I and no one has been prouder of you as a dear little mother, than I. . . .

This is Sunday afternoon and the bed looks so comfortable! Would you if you could. . . ? Do you think that tonight you would feel like lying with me without a thing on, mouth to mouth in a good juicy kiss, breast to breast, with "him" in his natural warm, blissful cubby hole, and our legs wrapped with one another? I tell you I would—again and again. This summer weather—it's fierce!! By the time you get back I suppose you'll feel embarrassed with me again & I, I guess I shall feel like a groom on the first night, though probably a little more effective. This isn't exactly a description to read before the family circle & perhaps I shouldn't write so, if you feel that way tell me. . . .

I want you to promise me that you won't do any heavy work this summer. Get some one else to lift him [Patrick] for you & to carry the water for you—You must not run any risks. Let well enough alone & restrain your ambitions whenever you get a chance. Don't take any chances in automobiles & all that—remember that an accident to you might end very seriously & possibly worse than that. An automobile ride with a fool boy of a chauffeur isn't worth the risk. I do feel so solicitous of your health & well being. Remember you owe it to me to take extra precautions at this time, even if it only be to satisfy my whim. . . .

Mama told me a day or so ago that my salary next year would be $1500 so I guess Papa hasn't forgotten. . . .

♥♥♥♥♥

Bill Reid, Jr., Belmont, CA, to Christine Reid, Brookline, MA
26 May 1904

Bill replied to Christine's letter, noting that it had not been the kind of loving letter he desired.

What wouldn't I give to have you here in my arms this minute! How I would hug you and squeeze you and kiss you—take you on my lap and fondle you. I'd like to lie all day with you on the bed—touching you at every possible point with our lips pressed close together, and our legs wrapped together in the snuggest possible way. Wouldn't it be bliss itself though? I can't imagine anything more delicious, can you? I suppose I ought not to write all this but it simply goes to show how frantic I am for you.

And yet, you precious little girlie, you ask me in the letter that has just come whether I love you as I used to. . . . You are the dearest, sweetest, prettiest girl that every happened and you've got me body, heart, soul, mind, and senses—a willing captive. It seems as though I must get to you & then to think of over two whole months—it's pretty hard. . . .

♥♥♥♥♥

Bill Reid, Jr., Belmont, CA, to Christine Reid, Brookline, MA
29 May 1904

In a long letter of love and news of their house being close to completion, Bill asked about their 14-month old child, William III, or Patrick as he was called. He was also concerned that Christine might wish to stay in the East, where her social life was to her liking.

A Debutante's Passion—A Coach's Erotica

. . . Oh, I could eat you up. Aren't you glad now that you aren't here—think what you are escaping. . . .

I see from your last letter that "you" are about ready to throw California over—& to live in the East. . . .

The baby certainly has behaved finely & I am very thankful, for your sake. Do take care that people don't tire him out & don't let them monkey with him. We're both nervous enough to have given the baby a slice of it & I am very anxious that his little nerves shan't be taxed. I'm afraid of all the girls—it's fun to play with him & they'll do it to the limit if they get a chance. . . .

♥ ♥ ♥ ♥ ♥

Bill Reid, Jr., Belmont, CA, to Christine Reid, probably Brookline, MA
ca. late Spring 1904

Bill longed to be with Christine and their young toddler, while Christine was visiting her parents and friends in the East

. . . I dread awfully going back to that great empty room, it will seem so vacant and desolate without you & the baby. At night I shall miss the cuddles dreadfully & my good night kiss—and I'm afraid I'll confess to missing the little cries that have emanated so regularly from the crib. Dear little fellow—he's the best ever. Just what I am going to do without you both, I don't know, but I shall try to be patient in the thought that you are having such a good time, for I know you will. I shall work steadily along so as to see if I can't take more of a place here next year & really begin to be a part of the executive head—instead of a non entity. I shall keep after them on the house and will have it ready by the time you get back.

And now, Wifie dear, remember through all the summer that my love and my heart is always with you—and I shall offer up a prayer for you every night. I have sometimes indicated to you that I didn't take much stock in prayers—well, when I'm in trouble or when I feel that I am powerless, then I do feel like prayer. And when you are away where I can't be with you I shall ask the good Lord to watch you for me & I know you'll be in good hands. If anything should happen to you I don't know what I should do—it would kill me. You have grown to be so much a part of me that I cannot bear to think of a separation. I want you to feel my love every minute—to feel my sympathy in any circumstance and my satisfaction in every joy. Have just the best old time you know how and I will have the possible time I can in that thought.

God bless & keep you dearest,
   with love
    Hubbie * * * * * * *
      * * * * - - - - -. - - - - -, - - - - -, - - - - -, - - - - -,
- - - -, - - - - -, - - -.- - , - - - - -, - - - - -, - - - -, - - - - - * *

♥ ♥ ♥ ♥ ♥

LOVE AND CHILDREN

Bill Reid, Jr., Belmont, CA, to Christine Reid, Brookline, MA
1 June 1904

Christine's letters could make Bill immediately sad or happy. Her last one proved happy. Adding weight to 175 pounds was happy for Bill, who often lost considerable weight when stressed or depressed.

. . . Your last letter was a dear one & I've read it over & over. . . . If you were here now we'd be getting to bed. Yi!!! wouldn't I like to have it so. . . .

I find myself constantly reminiscing old times with you as I think of you in your old haunts. One of the sweetest memories I have of Brookline was the night I caught you looking for me on Edge Hill Road. I'll never forget how thrilled I was when I had put two & two together & realized that you really cared for me. . . .

I got weighed yesterday & found that I weighed 175 with my clothes on & that is a considerable gain for me. . . . I'm not a "tuber" yet however. . . .

♥♥♥♥♥

Bill Reid, Jr., Belmont, CA, to Christine Reid, Brookline, MA
5 June 1904

Bill and Christine sometimes used the word "guess" early in their married life for the sex act. The fantasy for Bill of living and loving Christine seemed almost better than the life he lived when they were together. This letter gives us some indication of the paradox of loving when they were separated and loving when they were together.

. . . Wouldn't it be just perfect if we could get into bed without a thing on & lie all night long in each other's arms. Think of the joy of pressing close together in the ecstasy of a good long guess. The thought of your deliciously soft arms, breasts, your hot plump cheeks, and your delicious legs—drives me nearly wild. . . . To think of getting into bed with you and having you join me in all the ravishing delights which two passionate & demonstrative lovers can devise—makes me inexpressibly anxious to get to you. Really, I feel just about as anxious—as I did the first night.

Your dear letter found me anxiously on hand—and was so sweet. I've read it over & over particularly one particular part which runs like this—"I should like nothing better at this moment, than a good _____." I love to have you tell me you want it. . . . Bless you, you're so precious. I really believe I am worse gone on you than I was when we were engaged, if such a thing is possible. . . .

I came across the accounts of our wedding today. . . . The cab ride into town—the dear blue dress you wore—it was so temptingly thin & light too, & you did feel so good. The undressing you in the hotel—um!!! Getting into bed with you & then being so tantalizingly helpless. Wasn't it simply inexpressibly great though. . . .

147

A Debutante's Passion—A Coach's Erotica

I agree with you, that on the whole this separation is going to be a good thing for both of us. I think we've just missed having a perfect life of it. . . . I am expecting things to go on much more smoothly when we are once more together. Having the "home" is going to give me an opportunity that I have always cherished, of really living with you alone. And if you'll just meet me at the door when I come & give me a "loving"—I tell you, you won't ever wonder whether we aren't drifting apart. You used to meet me that way at Cohasset & in Brookline & I did love it so. . . . When you get back, we'll have to have a good talk & see if we can't clean up everything & henceforth live ideally together. Goodness knows, if I can't get along with the dearest girl that ever was—I'd better clear out. It was dear of you to say that you aren't going to leave me again in a hurry—& you can bet I won't agree to it again—in a hurry either. Oh, I'm so glad I've got you. . . .

♥ ♥ ♥ ♥ ♥

Bill Reid, Jr., Belmont, CA, to Christine Reid, Brookline, MA
7 June 1904

Bill's letters were frequent and repetitious about what he was often thinking.

. . . I do love to get your letters so much, they,—they are so dear. Maybe I wouldn't have liked to "celebrate" Dorothea's wedding night—my! but I'd make you wriggle with pleasure though. Oh, why can't we? Wouldn't you like to do the way we did one Sunday afternoon when we lay all wrapped up in each other—when we got just as far up as we could and I gave you a corking "offering"; when we went to sleep with "him" in, and then woke up and did it "again;" Um—What wouldn't I give. I can feel your hot cheeks against mine now, and I remember with a thrill how nice and passionate you were and how deliciously easy he slipped in. And this is the way in which I keep a resolution which I made—that I would try & not be quite so sensual the next time I wrote. . . . I just love to have you tell me how much you want it, how often, and how much you like to think of what I so delight to leave in you. . . & know that you're delighted in taking it from me & like to feel it & know it's there. . . . Well, let's go to bed. Leave off your nightie won't you dearest & let's get right into each other's bareness in every possible manner, Um . . . !

I am glad to hear that you went to the theatre—I wish you'd make it a point to go a lot. There aren't many good plays out here & those that are—usually have a patched up cast. Besides it's pretty awkward getting up to the city. . . .

♥ ♥ ♥ ♥ ♥

LOVE AND CHILDREN

Bill Reid, Jr., Belmont, CA, to Christine Reid, Cohasset, MA
11 June 1904

Among other issues discussed, Christine had told Bill of the marriage of her close friend, Dorrie, and Bill noted progress on building their new house in Belmont.

My darling little girl:
It did me a lot of good to have you tell me how anxious you are to get back to me and how much you think of me. Everything of that kind goes to make me fonder & fonder of you, & more loving. If you were here now, we'd be in bed & all rolled up together in a forsaken "loving"—how I wish it were only true. I'm getting more & more anxious to kiss & squeeze you, every day,—and I'm crazy to have you in my lap.

I can very well understand how "lonely" you felt after Dorrie had gone off. I guess, if I'd been there, you'd have found some one to keep you pretty close company, particularly that night; and then perhaps you'd not have felt quite so forsaken. We'll certainly have to take a wedding trip one of these days, as you suggest, & make it as realistic as possible. I shall be greatly interested in hearing Dorrie's experiences—a bride can tell some awfully interesting things if she wants to, particularly if the husband is inexperienced. . . .

I have been very busy during the past few days & really feel as though I were doing something. I have been twice to the city on errands, have helped box up some of the Tahoe stuff, have gotten almost all the repairs in Hopkin's Hall done, & have been to Palo Alto to hustle Lammeister up [to finish their new house]. . . . I find out now that it will cost 25% more to have our curtains with one color on the outside & another on the inside. . . . I expect that next week will see quite a bit done at the house. . . .

Well, you darling girl—I wish I could have you with me just now. I feel just like squeezing, kissing, loving and "guessing" you. Do you think you could stand it all? This summer is uncommonly long, seems to me. . . .

♥♥♥♥♥

Bill Reid, Jr., Belmont, CA, to Christine Reid, Brookline, MA
15 June 1904

Bill's long letter told of his weight going back down to his usual 165 pounds, of receiving pictures of his child, Pat, of the need for Christine to spend money on her clothes, of going to San Francisco to get furnishings for their new house, and trying the new boat at his parents' summer home on Lake Tahoe. Yet, he dwelt upon his love life with Christine.

. . . You could sit in my lap & we'd kiss & hug & squeeze & cuddle each other until we couldn't stand it any longer—& then we'd take off all of our clothes, jump into bed and get just as closely wound up as we

149

A Debutante's Passion—A Coach's Erotica

could and then lie there in absolute harmony & bliss, and when the climax came, wouldn't we simply be in heaven. . . . I tell you, you can't appreciate what a joy it is to have a stunning girl get into bed with you, press you against her soft warm, delicious breasts & body—struggle to get in you as far as possible and then squirm and wriggle with delight and sympathy when the inexpressibly blissful moment arrives. I'd give anything to change places with you once—to let you know the bliss of it all. It's simply glorious. I suppose I came pretty often last year, but it's your own fault. If you will be so pretty & bewitching & you'll have to stand the punishment—because it's no use—no fellow who loves you & is as passionate as I could ever resist your charms. Yi!! I'm all shaky now. . . .

Dear little son—I was thinking today—how I love & miss him. He certainly is the greatest ever. . . . Pat's growing so fast—he'll be a big boy too soon. Goodness—think what we've accomplished in these two years. . . .

I'm afraid you're trying to "skimp" all you can. Otherwise I don't see how you can have gotten along without cashing that first check. Now please don't—I want you to go in and have the best possible time in your power. Go to the theatre, concerts, entertainments, etc., and get a good taste of them because your opportunities here are so few. . . .

And now I come to the ravishing part of your letter where you speak of wishing I were going to call. . . and that we might have a "loving" on the lounge & later a ____ (corker) upstairs. Wouldn't I just like to be following you up those stairs to bed though. . . ! I'm beginning now to feel, the way a fellow who is very thirsty feels, —when he wonders why he didn't simply gorge himself with water when he had the chance.

♥♥♥♥♥

Bill Reid, Jr., Belmont, CA, to Christine Reid, Cohasset, MA
19 June 1904

Bill was looking forward to seeing Christine when she returned, first to the Reid summer house at Lake Tahoe and then in their own new house in Belmont.

It is a beautiful, cool Sunday night here, and I am all "on edge" from having read and reread your last dear expressive letter. . . .

. . . Perhaps I will be a little embarrassed the first night—but I shall be so anxious to get into bed with you that it'll be pretty hard to think of anything else. I think I can arrange it so that we can sleep the first night in the new house—that is the first night in Belmont; I expect to have you first at Tahoe where we'll christen the cottage or rather where I'll "Christine" it. When we first sleep in our house we ought to make a grand occasion of it—suppose we agree to let each other do whatever we want that night? Are you game. . . ?

♥♥♥♥♥

LOVE AND CHILDREN

Bill Reid, Jr., Belmont, CA, to Christine Reid, Cohasset, MA
22 June 1904

Christine had been gone from Belmont for over a month, and the sexual abstinence was wearing on Bill.

Your last letter came a day ahead of the usual schedule and therefore a welcome surprise. And it was a bully old letter too. I am awfully glad, sweetheart, that you like to have me sensual because I am so fond of you that I feel that way most of the time. I love you so that I could almost eat you up expressing it—and I feel as though just kissing, squeezing and hugging you wasn't doing enough to you. And I know it isn't doing enough to you—when I am conscious of the ravishing delight that I have experienced in sleeping with you. Kissing is really such a small part when compared to the pleasure of lying together stripped, passionate and free to satisfy our cravings and longings that when I talk of kissing you it doesn't seem half expressive enough.

The time or moment rather when I feel as though I come the nearest to absolutely perfect harmony & love for you is when, after we have lain breast to breast, mouth to mouth and with legs deliciously & dangerously interwoven, for as long a time as we dare————————-I come over on top of you or you on top of me and you reach down and take hold of me (it makes the thrills run all over me) and stick me in, in, in,—until there is nothing left to show I'm a boy;—when I slip in and out so smoothly and can feel you "hugging" me, warm and hot, inside; when you put your arms around me & squeeze me and wriggle about until I'm almost beside myself with delirious joy; and when at last with mouth to mouth in a long juicy kiss, a tight embrace and a liquid expression of blissful content in our eyes—the supreme moment comes when I give the best of me to you and you joyfully accept it————just then I feel as though I were about as near to you as I can get and as I were approaching an expression of what I feel. That's a long sentence, but it had to be long to tell the story. And the lying there still in afterwards is always delicious for you are always so nice down there.

There, perhaps now you know how I love you & yearn for you. It's such a delight to do it to you because you are so beautiful, so passionate and so responsive & because I know that no one else can do it. As I think of it I don't see how I can stand wearing things again. You used to think I liked it but I tell you I didn't—what's to compare with the nice, soft, warm, inviting "charm" of a girl and the feeling of it by a man? Absolutely nothing, it is simply incomparable.

Little girl—I'd give you just such a time as that described above—tonight—now—if you were only here. Well, we'll go at it good & plenty when you get here—& won't it be "scrumptious" though.

Loved one—you need have no fear of a lack of heartiness in my welcome to you when you return. It seems to me as though I won't be able to hug, kiss or squeeze you as I long to do, without just about crushing you to pieces. Welcome!!! Well I just guess. You dear girl—I wish I could give you a little welcome right now.

When I said I'd meet you at Tahoe—of course I meant Truckee because I wouldn't give you the chance to get in my neighborhood without laying hands on you. If you will set any day after the twenty first for your start I will plan my work accordingly. I would set the date earlier except that it is not of my choosing—I have to make it conform to Papa's plans for coming down to take my place. Bless you, I'd like to have you starting now—but I will try to be patient, comforting myself with the thought that you are having a rest and a good time. . . . .

Indeed I do wish you could meet me at the station at Cohasset, and how I wish we could go over some of our old drives together. I saw a picture of Nantucket beach a day or two ago & a feeling of great homesickness came over me. In the picture I could see the hotel where the ball nine stopped one day just before the Yale Class Day game & I could see where we drove into the sand there one night. And then I thought of North Scituate & that moonlight night when we drove out on the beach & I took you in my lap & squeezed & kissed & hugged you & felt way up those soft delicious legs. My!!! how I did thrill all over & how crazy I was to do it to you. And the. . . naughty hammock. . . . Wasn't it snug & wriggly in that hammock though—with your dresses way up & your legs all wrapped up in mine. And buttoning up your dress in the bath house and lying with you in the down stairs lounge. Wasn't it bully time though? Oh, dear!!! . . . .

Give my love to all the family & keep a passionate kissing, hugging squeezing and _____ing for yourself.

♥♥♥♥♥

Bill Reid, Jr., Belmont, CA, to Christine Reid, Cohasset, MA
26 June 1904

In a letter that would presage future correspondence, when Bill was separated from Christine for periods of time, Bill would continue to fantasize about his love life. Bill's attitude about Darwinism and marriage probably reflected the times when "survival of the fittest" was strongly in vogue, as he criticized Ellery Clark, who won two Olympic gold medals, the high jump and long jump, in the 1896 Olympics in Athens. His attitude toward marriage and children reflected his conservative nature that would continue throughout his lifetime.

My own darling girl:
  Your last letter written from Cohasset, was a corker and I have read it again and again. To recall all of the good times we had there is hard enough, but to have you anxious to go out with me at night and lie with me in bliss—is almost unbearable. Oh, deary why can't we be together?

LOVE AND CHILDREN

How I would like to accept your invitation—I am just crazy to do it to you, —and under those circumstances it would be unusually delicious. I'd like to make up for that time when we rolled about on the sand and I ached to lift up your dresses and stick him in. I'd have given a kingdom to have done it that night. And to think now, that if I were there I could do it over and over again—is simply torture. My!! How glorious it would be to lie out in one of those "burrows" with him clear in and still trying to get in farther—with our lips pressed passionately together—how delicious it would be to lie this way, wriggling, twisting and rolling about in delight until absolutely as one we expressed for each other our most devoted affection. I, by giving you a bully good bit of the boy in me and you by accepting it with delicious expressions of satisfied joy & pleasure. Yi!!! But the thought of you lying in bed—in your tempting way—without a thing on—and encouraging me to pitch in and help myself to you—drives me almost to distraction. You bet—we'll go at it at Tahoe. Will you give me all I want? I shall want it every five minutes I'm afraid. . . . .

I agree with you that we have everything to be thankful for—home, baby, and each other. You dear girl—you alone are enough to make anyone happy. I'd like to squeeze & kiss you all to pieces. I just love you to death. I wish you were here now in that pink dress I love so, without corsets & with light under clothes on—it would be so delicious to press you to me and half feel your delicious soft self through it. It's such fun lying with you in those thin dresses—I can feel your warmth through them and it makes a delicious anticipation of the delights to follow. I am going to kiss you all over, legs, arms, breasts, and again and again in the one dear spot where I simply cannot leave you alone. You'll let me now, won't you. Oh, to lie with you on those cool summer days—all cozy and snug and looking into your dear, loving eyes—would be absolutely inexpressibly delicious. . . . .

And now I come to the place where you say "tell him" I am looking forward to holding "him" & helping "him in." Dearest, that makes me feel so delicious down there, you don't know—I am crazy to have you & do so love to feel your hand there—it's so thrilly. And you know how to make it feel so good. I love to feel you & have you feel me—preliminary to enjoying ourselves—it is such a delight to know that we are taking liberties that no one else can—& that we have a right to. I'm looking forward so, to the thousand and one pleasures we shall have when we get together, and an enjoying getting ready for them. Shall we need—a little oil do you think, or will you furnish a delicious substitute? I love to have you so smooth down there—it shows you're anxious for me. . . .

To me Ellery Clark's action on his wedding day was disgusting. To think of his giving his bride only one hour of his time on her wedding day—seems too unnatural to believe. I agree with you that people like that should not marry & especially when one has an hereditary disease. The Lord made man so that the strongest and manliest men should be attracted to the womanliest & prettiest girls & vise versa—this to

153

perpetuate the "best" in the race. And here is a strong fellow disregarding this provision & marrying a girl afflicted with a loathsome disease. I call it entirely unnatural. . . .

. . . Ted Little's remark about Pat seems to me a good illustration of what I term the decadence of married life. He and Catharine have used prevention so much that the natural affection for children which they would have felt had they had one, has gradually disappeared to be substituted by a feeling that children are a nuisance & therefore undesirable. It crops out in all couples who simply love to have a good time. See if you don't find it so. . . ?

Well, dearest, good bye—love to all, and affection unlimited to you—you darling. I love you with, body, heart & soul.
Lovingly & admiringly,
"Bill."
I see Harvard won—I thought they would—we've got a system that is hard to beat.

♥♥♥♥♥

Christine Reid, Cohasset, MA, to Bill Reid, Jr., Belmont, CA
28 June 1904

Christine warmed to Bill and his letters, replying to his suggestions.

My sweetest, most precious husband,

Two of the dearest letters that ever were written are before me ready to be answered. Oh! They are so delicious, and I have just feasted on all the love and passion they express. You can't say enough to satisfy me and the more I get the more I want. I cannot tell you how much I am looking to our first night together! I find myself thinking of it all the time and sort of making plans. What nightgown I shall wear, . . . for a few minutes. . . . There's no use talking I shall be terribly embarrassed, but it will be a most enjoyable kind of embarrassment, I tell you. When I get thinking of the delights in store I can hardly wait for the time to come. . . .

The moon these nights is enough to drive you crazy. I hardly dare to look at it, it makes me so anxious for you, and it recalls so many delicious memories. Remember the night we stayed down on the beach until three o'clock in the morning? Wasn't it scrumptious?

Your "dare" as to the first night in our new house, is accepted. Come on now, do your worst, I'm not afraid. Don't you wish you could? — You ask me what I'd like to do to you and what I'd like to have you do to me. Well, I say we repeat our wedding night as nearly as possible with a few variations. I want to have the fun of undressing you, and I shall be terribly disappointed if you don't want to undress me. Then I want to hold "him" in my hand and "love him" a little, for I do, you know, awfully much. When I go to bed at night, my hand feels so empty, and I keep wishing I had only to reach it out to find "him."

"She" is such a dear one, and "he" does feel so good! especially when he's where he belongs! Then I'd like just to lie on you with nothing on, and roll around on your soft, warm body. Gracious! Merely writing it sets me "on edge," as you say. Then, we'd turn over, I would show "him" the way, and well—you know the rest, and wouldn't it be bliss? Do you think my "movement" is perfect? I hope so. . . .

I will order the extra pictures of the baby as soon as I go to Boston again. . . .

♥♥♥♥♥

Bill Reid, Jr., Belmont, CA, to Christine Reid, Cohasset, MA
29 June 1904

The heat of the letters between Bill and Christine continued at a boiling point.

My onliest little love:

In just about a month now, I'll have you back and maybe I won't be glad. You dear, you, I've missed you awfully and have constantly found myself providing for you in my plans, only to realize immediately that you couldn't possibly take part.

I guess if I'd been in bed with you when you had those dreams you'd not have called them "idle," for I'd have kept you good & busy & would have given you your heart's desire of fun. I love to have you want me so that you dream about me—and only hope that you will continue to want me after you get back and have had one or two good nights of it. I'm crazy to do it to you & then to go to sleep with you with him in. I think we can arrange it somehow—at any rate let's try. It will be cozy and nice and so deliciously satisfactory. I can just imagine the pleasure of dozing off—knowing that we're just as mixed up in each other as we can be—that you love it, and that we are expressing affection even while we sleep.

I ran across a pamphlet today on "Sex Relations" & read it through. There is one sentence which I'd like to know your opinion about. "Treat thy wife as a lover, save only when thou woulds't have her to be a mother." What do you think of it? It seems to me all very well as a theory but I'd like to see the boy & girl who are passionate—& fond of each other—who could be persuaded to do it only when they had children in mind. I think we're entitled to our good times & I don't consider them as wrong either. The full article went on to say that to bring this idea about the couple should sleep in separate beds, eat vegetables largely, exercise, etc., etc.—& satisfy the passions by kissing & personal contact—but without the only real contact. Did you ever! Do you want me and hold you against me for satisfaction? The fellow wrote that article had probably never "been there" & didn't know wholesaled delight that one feels while "at it."

A Debutante's Passion—A Coach's Erotica

I tell you when a fellow gets a beauty like you in bed with him and has her anxious to have him just help himself to her ravishing delights—I'd like to see the fellow who'd stop to eat vegetables or put off the bliss until baby time came. Jingoes, I'd have him "clear up and still wiggling" in about half a jiffy. And the kissing would come in too. . . .

Well, dearest, I'd like to get my arms around you now and kiss & squeeze you hard—& perhaps even _____ you. . . .

♥ ♥ ♥ ♥ ♥

Bill Reid, Jr., Belmont, CA, to Christine Reid, Cohasset, MA
1 July 1904

Bill would not always remember Christine's birthday, nor the wedding anniversary, but her twenty-third birthday was much on his mind in 1904.

My own little dear:

It is hard enough to be away from you at all—but especially hard to be away on such an occasion as this, your birthday. How I wish I could be with you today and tonight that we might hold a sort of communion together and that I might tell you how I love and cherish you. I'd like to sit with you in my lap, before the fire, and hug & kiss and squeeze you and tell you how much you mean to me in every way.

My lover, my wife, my little son's mother, my all. You are all there is for me in the world and it is my ambition and hope to do for you. You are in all my plans, thoughts and hopes—the only girl I ever loved, the only one I care a rap about and the dearest, prettiest, sweetest one that ever was born.

Two birthdays ago, not counting this one—we were just married—for over two years you have lived and shared with me. May the future bring with it a fit reward. God bless you, for all that you have brought into my life, may I be given a long life to do for you and may I grow fitter and fitter each year to be worthy of your dear self, is the devoted wish of

                Your fond and affectionate
                Husband.

♥ ♥ ♥ ♥ ♥

Christine Reid, Cohasset, MA, to Bill Reid, Jr., Belmont, CA
3 July 1904

Christine was in no mood to write this letter. Writing a day after their second wedding anniversary, contemplating leaving the East and her family, and possibly not being in their new house in California, was tearing at her heart.

LOVE AND CHILDREN

My darling boy,

Yesterday was our second anniversary, and I fully intended to write to you then, but I didn't have a chance. It certainly was too bad that we couldn't celebrate it together, but never mind, we'll try to make up for it somehow or other. I got a letter from you yesterday, but you didn't mention our anniversary, for which I was thankful, as I had not realized it in time to write you a special letter. . . .

Well, dearie, perhaps it will interest you to know that our tickets are engaged for the twenty-third. Also, you will be interested to hear that Auntie . . . has decided not to go with us. So there will probably be just Aunt Mary, Pat, and yours truly. I cannot help feeling that it is better that Auntie B has decided as she has, although in many ways I should have liked to have her and she would have been a great help but now I shall get a nurse instead, and I am sure that will be better all round. . . .

I believe we are due in Francisco on Wednesday morning, the 27th, so I shall see you in less than three weeks after you get this. It is going to be a terrible wrench leaving all the family again, and I do wish I could ever go anywhere without having to say good-bye to someone that I love so dearly. It certainly is pretty hard lines. Don't think by my saying that sweetheart, that I shall not be awfully glad to get back to you—but I am sure I don't need to tell you that. It's only that I wish I could have my husband and my family too. I judge by what you wrote that your mother, and perhaps your father, will be at Tahoe while we are there. Is that so? Won't it be too many? And how about Julia and Charlie? [Bill's older sister and husband] Aren't they going up sometime? You haven't said a word about their house! Did they decide not to build this year after all. . .?

Ouisie [Christine's youngest sister Louise] went out with Gerry last night, and had a fine time. Ag thinks that's a "go," but I have my doubts. I don't know him well enough to say whether I hope it is or not. . . .

Probably you have been wondering where under the sun those pictures of the baby are! Aren't they slow in finishing them? I haven't received them yet, and next time I go to Boston, I shall drop in and give them a piece of my mind.

Do you think the house is ever going to be done? Give your honest opinion. You can tell Lanceister that I shall never forgive him if it isn't ready for me when I get there. I shall be terribly disappointed, and discouraged.

I will tell Dad what you said about getting the tickets straight to Belmont, but he is so busy that I hate to bother him. He says he will not actually buy the tickets, until I hear that the date is O.K. for you and your father.

As yet I have not bought you any shirts, but will try to if I can get over to Cambridge. Possibly I shall risk getting them somewhere else, because if I don't, you will have to get them in S.F. anyhow. I am going to get some like the ones father had, with the soft cuffs. I am sure they will stand the Belmont laundry better, and will do just as well for you to "charge" round in.

A Debutante's Passion—A Coach's Erotica

"Sister" [Agnes] is well, and sends her love. She gives me very little trouble, except that I am terribly crabby and irritable at times (Well, that's nothing new, I can hear you say). . . .

I believe I have got to go to a tea . . . this P.M. Oh Dear! I can't stand any of them, and it will only make me crosser than ever.

Well, I guess I had better stop. I am in no mood for writing. I love you, though, and am always
>   Lovingly
>   Wifie-

*

O X - O O O X - O   (guess?)
♥ ♥ ♥ ♥ ♥

Bill Reid, Jr., Belmont, CA, to Christine Reid, Cohasset, MA
5 July 1904

Bill responded with 12 pages to Christine's loving letter of June 28th, one of the sexiest that Christine had ever written.

The letter that I've just got is absolutely the finest, most delicious one I've every read and it leaves me all a quiver every time I read it. It makes me ache down there with passion but it's a delicious ache, and I love it. Every time you speak of wishing you had him in your dear hand to hold him and love him—I simply get weak in the knees and a delicious something comes over me down near my stomach. Oh, the sensations I feel when you tell me things you'd like to do to me—simply beggar description. Do tell me some more.

If you are looking forward to our first night I am well nigh crazy about it. I'm just full of it and when your hand goes down and takes hold of me you'll find the plumpest, fullest, most delicious handful you ever felt. Oh, how your hand will feel. I'll just give it to you over & over again that first night and you'll know its coming each time too—there'll be bigger doses than ever. Oh, dear, it's beautiful to sit here in this same room where we've enjoyed ourselves so—and to feel my breath coming quicker & my cheeks getting hot— & to know that the only climax will be their cooking down.

If you could only come in now!! I'd take you in my lap & hug & kiss you oh, so passionately and put my hands up your soft, tempting legs and feel the wonderful delights of your body & legs—and you'd be feeling me. Then I'd undress you—rolling about with you on the bed a few minutes, after I'd get everything but your shirt & fascinating pants off—and how your dear cheeks would burn & your eyes shine. Then I'd strip you absolutely naked and lay you on the bed, and you'd be there in a perfectly irresistibly voluptuous way with your legs well apart & and your arms over your head & tacitly invite me. And then I'd put my head right in between your legs & give you a good long, passionate kissing. Then you take hold of me and um!!! how entrancing it would feel as you showed me in. And then with arms about each other, kissing & hugging we'd wiggle & roll about until absolutely together we let loose all our passion & did everything to make the climax supreme. I'd come out & go in clear up; you'd wriggle & murmur your delight & I'd double up my face in absolute bliss. And when it was over we'd lie there hot & passionate & absolutely happy & contented until we were a little rested and then we'd do it again.

You little witch you, you irresistible beauty I'd go to the ends of the earth to sleep with you. You simply can't know what a delight your beauty, your soft legs, your delicious breasts that I so love to rub against; your huggy waist or your heavenly lips & cheeks—are to me. If you had a mind to you could simply lure me to any place or to any end you wanted. I love to have you planning what nightgown you'll wear & all those details—I've been doing the same. You bet, I'll want to undress you—um!!! The delight of it!!! Remember now there's no backing out that first night—we can do just whatever we want & the other has got to let it go on as long the one wants. Oh, I'll just kiss you all over— & I'm looking forward to it so. It's simply heaven up between your legs and I'll want lots of it. And your embarrassment—it will be as good as sleeping with you the first night again,—oh, joy!!!!

The stories you wrote are corkers especially the one about the "lobster" being on the girl's stomach all night. That appeals to me—just now most effectively. And the one about the girl with the perfect movement. Oh, I know what that means, sometimes you get going I feel as though I wanted to pour my whole body into you—it's so blissful and your little after movements are so expressive and the squeezes you give him, way in. Oh, but you are delicious—I'll bet no other girl in the country knows how to give the good times you do.

I love the picture you sent—I just love them all & you I simply adore. When I look at your pictures in the black paris dress I want to put you on the bed, pull your dresses up & give it to you. You feel so warm when we're criss-crossed between each other that I always like to lie with a tempting layer of your underclothes between us until we can't risk it any longer. Yi!!! It does hurt so to think of it. I wish I had that picture of you stripped on the beach, you can just see & you can't quite—& it's simply irresistible. Let me tell you right here—You'll never get away from me like this again.

Does Catharine like it?

159

A Debutante's Passion—A Coach's Erotica

"That night down on the beach" I guess I do remember it—I had your dresses way up & your dress open & we rolled around in rapture. Gee!!! But that was a treat. The only thing I'd like to do that we haven't done is to go out in a canoe & lie in & together under the trees along the river at Riverside. I remember our lying together in the train two or three times—up at Freed on the Canadian—& sleeping that way—& the delicious times you used to give me out driving. You'd hold me & squeeze me & play with me till I came & then you'd do still more & simply drive me wild with pleasure. Down at North Scituate on the beach, when I first felt your legs way up—on the lounge at Cohasset—oh, what delights we had—& I don't regret a single one. Remember getting into bed with me mornings & how delicious it felt through our night gowns? Oh, dear, I have got it bad—& I am glad, oh so glad of it—because you respond & that's all the fun.

Won't we just "cut loose" the first night in the house though I'm going to do everything to you that I know how & I hope you'll do the same to me—it will be heavenly won't it. If only you could reach out tonight & hold him & go to sleep holding him—I'd love it so, and I'd give anything if you could lie on me stripped & roll about on me—Oh! The feeling of shoving him up & into you—particularly when you are hot & he goes in slick and easily—is indescribable. How I'd like to have you "show him the way" this minute, & then give me your inimitable movement.

To have you say—"it's a struggle for me even to be respectably cordial to other fellows" make me so happy. I don't deserve such love as that but I do feel so happy over it—and I will try to be more worthy hereafter. If you'll just love me I can accomplish anything—if you don't I'll simply get nowhere.

While I was in the city today I kept wishing you were with me so I could help you across the streets & thus touch you, how I'd liked to have had you on the train where we could have gotten our legs entwined & our hands together. I thought of it all day, & the way I thought of you dearest was the tenderest I think I've ever felt. I think you'll find my eyes full of love for you when you get here and . . . itching to get you close to me. . . .

Well, good bye—you darling I'd like to hug you so—I don't know what to do. Three weeks about, & by gracious I will!!!! Give my love to the family and don't let the Patakin forget me. God bless you both.
        Lovingly
         'Bill'

* * *   _____ . _____ . _____ X _____

P.S. Be sure to keep these letters out of the way—they'd be too interesting reading for people.
♥ ♥ ♥ ♥ ♥

LOVE AND CHILDREN

Christine Reid, Cohasset, MA, to Bill Reid, Jr., Belmont, CA
10 July 1904

Christine thanked Bill for her birthday gift of candy, and awaited being able to give him the gift he wanted soon when she returned to Belmont.

...You were awfully good to give me the candy. I am enjoying it so much. I will try and thank you for it properly when I see you. Just think! It is only a little over two weeks now before I shall, and then—I thrill all over at the thought. I am looking forward to our visit at Tahoe every so much (excuse the expression!) especially because it will be such a fine rest and change for you. And you need to get away, you dear thing, I know you do. Please don't think I am horrid, but I am sort of hoping that your family won't be there all the time we are. I want you to myself a lot. This is to be a sort of second honeymoon and I must have you. In one way I suppose it will be better if they are there because then we can leave Aunt Mary and the Pattikin with them and go off by ourselves. I expect we'll do that some anyhow, however. . . .

When I heard that I could get very cheap rates out about the middle of August, I wondered if you would rather have me wait until them and take advantage of them. It's too late now, and I hope you won't mind (?) It's queer, but I didn't exactly want to stay until then.

Now I must tell you about my birthday presents. Mother gave me a very pretty belt buckle, father five dollars, and Bunny [likely brother Albert III], Ag, & Ouise a dandy edition of "Les Miserables." They knew I was crazy about it, and now I shall insist on our reading it together next winter. I do want you to have it as I do, or at least appreciate the beauty of Victor Hugo's style. . . . Pat celebrated my birthday by having the first really bad night he has had. It is teeth, of course, same old story, and I have been expecting it before this. . . .

Oh! Biddy darling, haven't we got lots of fun before us? Do you know I feel in a way as if our married life was only just beginning! That sounds improper when you think of Pat, but you understand what I mean, don't you. . . ?

The thought of lying in your arms again so soon is almost too much for me. You dear old thing! I love you to pieces.

♥♥♥♥♥

Bill Reid, Jr., Belmont, CA, to Christine Reid, Cohasset, MA
10 July 1904

Bill remembered Christine's birthday, but at the same time he had forgotten their second wedding anniversary. He tried to reassure her that their new home in Belmont would soon be ready.

161

A Debutante's Passion—A Coach's Erotica

. . . It's so nice to go to sleep and know that you're right there, snuggled close. And tonight I'm just ready for a good long loving bee, in bed. Would you like to be stung? I think I could sting you in a pretty delicious way.

Our wedding anniversary passed without my thinking of it so concentrated was I upon your birthday. I hope I planned my letter right—it ought to have gotten to you on the morning of the eighth. . . .

I am awfully glad to hear that you've set the date for your return because now I can feel that every day is bringing you nearer. Less than three weeks now, just think of it. . . .

Dear little girl—it will be hard for you to leave home I know, but you must remember that I've been alone all summer and want you back. I hope your people haven't weaned you from me—would you want to stay longer. . . ?

Of course the house is going to be finished—it's practically done now. The front porch ceiling, steps, etc. is all faulted & done, as is all the exterior painting in fact. The bath tub, seat & wash stand are up in the general bathroom; the basins are in all the rooms, the basin & seat is in our bathroom & by Wednesday night the plumbing will be all completed. The hardware is practically all in (even in the attic), the attic floor is oiled, & the library, hall, living room & dinning room have had a coat of wax on the floor.

The mantel men are to come tomorrow & I will see that they do. . . . I gave them a piece of my mind last week. . . .

The screen door is on the screen porch, the little doors are on the closets in the front guest room (under the attic stair landing) & under the front hall stairs, the door to the back hall stairs is in, the pipes on the roof which leaked so, have been repaired, we have about a half a ton of coal in the basement, & from three to five men have been at work every day for the past week. When the mantels are in—there'll only be tag ends left. . . .

♥♥♥♥♥

Bill Reid, Jr., Belmont, CA, to Christine Reid, Cohasset, MA
13 July 1904

Bill's letters to Christine intensified as Christine's return to California came closer. Toward the end of the letter he noted his continued interest in football at Harvard. In less than a year; he would be appointed head coach for the 1905 season.

As the 27th draws nearer and nearer, I can feel my heart beating faster and faster with the exhilaration of anticipation. To think that in less than two weeks now, I shall have you, you darling, in my arms seems almost too good to be true. How good the first hug and kiss will feel and how delicious the first cuddle. And the little Pattakin—I shall hardly know him I expect.

LOVE AND CHILDREN

Shall you "want" me the night of the day you get to Tahoe—I'd kind of like to know ahead so as to make up my mind one way or the other. If you won't want me it'll be much easier for me—if I don't anticipate. I'm not trying to fish at all—I simply thought you might be too tired. My! but I've got a nice little supply to expend on you—I'll bet you'll agree that you've never felt anything like it. I can just feel the thrills running all over me as we lie, all wrapped up in each other, and with passionate hugs & kisses, let loose everything in us expressive of affection and delight. Nothing that ever has been, will ever touch it. After this long, hard wait it will seem like heaven indeed to feel you lying up-up—& wriggling deliciously about to make me give you more. We'll have the time of our lives. . . .

I expect to move our freight into the attic next week as well as to get our beds in, bed I mean. Just think of it—we can do anything we wish to each other unmolested—what a hot time it will be!!!! I'm only afraid you'll back out. . . .

I had a letter yesterday from Wrightington the football coach—telling me of the new rules etc.—besides the new plays he hopes to use this year. He wants my opinion—It's mighty nice, I think & I shall write him with great care. . . .

♥♥♥♥♥

Bill Reid, Jr., Belmont, CA, to Christine Reid, Cohasset, MA
15 July 1904

Less than two weeks before Christine arrived, Bill could think of little other than the first night with her.

Your last dear letter came yesterday and I can't tell you how happy it made me feel. You dear girl, you I'd just like to kiss you to pieces, and if I had you here tonight, I guess I'd do considerably more than kiss you. I'd do everything that love and passion could suggest. The different sweet things that you said made me almost atremble with pleasure—and absolutely crazy to get hold of you. And everything appeals doubly to me tonight, because it is very chilly, and the fire, almost embers now, seems so inviting. We could get partly undressed—so that we had only such clothes as would be delicious to hug & squeeze in & then you could set in my lap & we'd kiss & hug & squeeze in & cuddle each other until we couldn't stand it any longer—& then we'd take off all our clothes, jump into bed and get just as closely wound up as we could and then lie there in absolute harmony & bliss. And when the climax came, wouldn't we swiftly be in heaven. Oh, but it's tantalizing to think that the distance between us is all that prevents. I tell you, you can't appreciate what a joy it is to have a stunning girl get into bed with you, press you against here soft, warm, delicious breasts & body—struggle to get you as far in as possible and then squirm and wiggle with delight and sympathy

163

A Debutante's Passion—A Coach's Erotica

when the inexpressibly blissful moment arrives. I'd give anything to change places with you once—to let you know the bliss of it all. It's simply glorious. I suppose I came pretty often last year but it's your own fault; if you will be so pretty & bewitching & you'll have to stand the punishment—because it is no use—no fellow who loves you & is as passionate as I, could ever resist your charms. Yi!! I'm all shaky—now.

If you are glad I'm lonely in the same way, I am glad you ache for me. There's no need of your describing how you feel because I know from experience. Heartache!! Yes that's it all right—& plenty of it. If it weren't for my tutoring & my other work—I simply couldn't stand it. As it is, my greatest comfort is that you are having a good time of it. . . .

I'm afraid my weight gaining was a false alarm as I weigh my usual 165 now—again. Still I'm feeling & looking well & am not disposed to grumble. . . .

And now I come to the ravishing part of your letter where you speak of wishing . . . that we might have a "loving" on the lounge & a —— (corker) upstairs. Wouldn't I just like to be following you up those stairs to bed though. Dearest wife, to think of you're volunteering to come home just to ease me up—that was so darling of you. I gloated over that sentence & the devotion it shows—even if I should never be willing to put you to the test. If you'll just give me pretty nearly all I want when you get back—it will be so satisfying. I'm beginning now to feel the way a fellow who is very thirsty feels,—when he wonders why he didn't simply gorge himself with water when he had the chance. This is I am wondering why I didn't simply lie with you for a week before you left enjoying your lusciousness to the limit. Poor wifie, aren't you afraid to come back? And won't you be embarrassed—first time. . . ?

♥♥♥♥♥

Bill Reid, Jr., Belmont, CA, to Christine Reid, Chicago, IL
17 July 1904

Bill wanted Christine to receive several letters on the railroad, and thus sent the letters to Chicago. He wanted Christine to know that their new house would be ready when she returned.

. . . I'm so full of boy that it seems as though I must overflow before you get to me—but I'm exercising a good deal so I shall certainly keep it for you. My—You will never have felt anything like it when I let loose. Oh, but it does seem too good to be true to think that you will be here so soon now, & our self denials at an end. I can just feel you, delicious & warm & smooth, as I go in. That feeling is simply too delicious for words. I know I'm about to do something to you which no other fellow can—that you are not only willing for me to do it, but are crazy for it—and that I have a bully old supply of the real thing to give you. My!! but your soft body against mine, with me in & our arms around each other & a delicious look of passionate abandon in your eyes is a condition that makes me

LOVE AND CHILDREN

almost beside myself with delight. And after it's all over, it's a great feeling to know that I've left a good, warm, passionate remembrance way up in you, that you can feel it & that you love it.

As to the family at Tahoe, I feel just as you do—but I don't think we shall be troubled much. Papa expects to come down the day after you get there & as Julia & Charlie will have left—there will only be Mama, Howard, & Sukagawa still there. We can & will go off together a lot & perhaps—if we find a green cool nook sometime, perhaps our eyes may blur a little with the delicious feeling that comes only when a demonstrative, passionate, healthy boy & girl get together & do to each other everything possible to have a good time. Are you there. . . ?

If you had waited till the middle of August before starting [to California], I don't know what I'd have done—goodness would you want to torture me? These next ten days are going to crawl & I shall find it all I can do to stand it—but the middle of August—!!!!!

Your birthday presents were fine & I shall enjoy reading "Les Miserables" with you more than I can tell. . . .

I am awfully anxious to see the Pattakin—he must be too wonderful for anything. To think of actually walking seems almost too astonishing to be true. My!! but what a "socker" he must be. . . .

The mantels are, at last, all done—including the putting in of the extra tiles in the library. They look finely too—particularly the olive & white tiles. Ours & the red ones are handsome. . . . The front door lock is now on, . . . the side steps finished & even so many other minor details have been done up. The water tank on the hill has had its first coat & I expect to move our boxes, barrels, etc. into the attic, within the next day or so. Before I leave for Tahoe, I shall get our room ready for occupancy on our return. We'll have to do without hot water—'till you can buy our stove. There are so many different kinds that I thought you'd better get just what you want.

. . . Please now don't try even to carry baby—let Aunt Mary do it—& have a porter take your bags, etc. Don't let yourself truck a thing even if there's a big hurry. A strain isn't worth a million missed trains or cars. If anything happens, I shall simply go crazy—so please, do exactly what I ask. . . . Be sure you bring all the letters!!!

♥♥♥♥♥

Bill Reid, Jr., Belmont, CA, to Christine Reid, Chicago, IL
18 July 1904

Bill had just received Christine's letter of July 10th and felt the urge to write immediately. At one point Bill made reference to the war between Japan and Russia, which was concluded in 1905 with a treaty brokered by President Theodore Roosevelt. The letter is ended with the largest five-pointed star that he ever used with 9 "X's" and 1 "O" in the middle of the star.

A Debutante's Passion—A Coach's Erotica

My very own precious wife:

It was only yesterday afternoon that I last wrote you, but I can't wait any longer before answering the sweet letter I found awaiting me when I returned from the city this evening. It was so artistically suggestive that it kind of makes me feel pretty "lovey" down there & very anxious for one of the little squeezings you give "him" when he's way in. That way of yours is simply corking and I love to lie with you & feel you fondling me. That little, entrancing touch of inward passion—almost draws every drop of "joy" out of me—and I've sometimes wished I could be drawn inside out—the feeling is so blissful. Well, by the time you get this you'll only be three days off- - - - - - & then how we will go it—those plump, hot cheeks, that mouth—those legs—that heaven!!! Yi—but it seems too good to be true.

I'm not making any allowances for your appearances, because you never need any. Wait till I get you in my arms and in bed & you'll see!!!! My! but what a kissing, hugging, squeezing, loving and ____ing you'll get. Um!!! To think that you've turned your dear self over to me to do with what I want, just sends thrills up my back & all over. I'll be like Pattakin on the beach. I won't know where to go first.

I'm very much afraid though that if I feel as I do now, we'll have to give it to each other without much delay—(the first time)— because otherwise you'd be likely to lose the biggest present you've ever had, & that would be a dire shame.

When I go to kiss you, this time or rather whenever I do, because I'm going to a lot, you'll have to give me all I want without pushing me away. I want to stay down there & love you- - - - - -remember, you've promised. Your embarrassment will add fifty per cent to the fun. Oh, it's going to be heavenly beyond words. I hope we shan't have to sit around much before going to bed—for if we do I shall be like I was the first night—so anxious & achy as to make it positively uncomfortable. If we went to bed when I want to—it would be positively indecent, there'd only be one guess & every body would guess it. Won't it be fun next morning when people look at us & wonder & we look sheepish. It will be a wedding night over again & no mistake. We must try to sleep with him in—it will be so cozy & we can know we're losing no time all night. I know that when your train rolls into Truckee, I am going to hear my heart beat—just as I did when I was approaching—King's Station—when I first saw you after your return from abroad.

Don't think a moment more about the clothing you got me—of course I'll like it. It is funny I bought four shirts in S. F. today—but I guess they'll all come in handy. You haven't told me what you've bought yourself. I hope you did get things just as you wanted them.

Before I go any further I want to reiterate to you what I said yesterday—namely please don't try to lift or carry anything—get a porter, carriages & whatever you need & if you have to miss a train to go slowly & safely, please do. You're my all & if you have anything happen to you—it'll simply ruin my life. That's strong, but I mean it & I'll never forgive you if you don't respect my wishes in this—even though you feel differently yourself.

Little of interest has happened lately except that one of the Japs was trying to learn how to ride a bicycle & losing control ran straight for the most objectionable thing in sight—in this case the thorny English holly shrub on the front lawn. The Jap came off with only a few pricks—but Langstroth, who saw it all, said that from the expression on the Jap's face one might have supposed he was about to attack the Russians.

Well, sweetest this is only intended to be a word of cheer & welcome to you—& I must get to bed. Tell Aunt Mary how glad we all are that she is coming and tell her that she can have the best there is—if she brings you both to me, safe & sound. Don't fail to telegraph a day ahead, because as I say there are many arrangements to be made which are wholly dependent upon your arrival.

Three & a half days—& we'll be together—isn't it a joyful thing to look forward to—how lucky we are. Kisses, all over, hugs & squeezes all day & night to you.

      Lovingly & longingly,
      "Bill"

*

♥ ♥ ♥ ♥ ♥

Brookline Mass.
Jan. 3. 1905.

You precious little girl you! — I've thought and thought of you since I got here and the feelings of love and affection which haven't gone out to you from my brimful heart aren't worth while thinking of. I love you mentally, morally & physically and I've loved you here in each of these ways as best I could. How I wish I could kiss & hug all this into you & perhaps put something else in into the bargain, instead of having to imagine it all. Really, I think we're just getting into the real stride of our married life — and its great. I only wish that in going to bed tonight I could look forward to a delicious taste of it all — instead of to a lonely cold, double bed. Never mind tho' I

Chapter 6

THE CALL TO HARVARD:
"ANXIOUS TO HAVE ALL YOU CAN GIVE"

Bill Reid, Jr., note to Christine Reid
                                                    ca. **27 December 1904**

Bill and Christine had been together since August. Now, he left for the East to check out the possibility of a football coaching position at Harvard, leaving Christine with her two children William III (Patrick), nearly two, and Edith (Didie), less than one month old, in California. Reid's father delivered Bill's note to Christine.

Dear little girl:
 I love you so. I do feel awfully to be leaving you. A dozen times I've been on the point of turning back. What I am going to do even if it is only three weeks I don't know. We are so near one another now that it seems as though life weren't worth living without you. . . .
 Now God bless you—you dear girl—I love you with all my heart & you alone. Kiss little sister for me & . . . keep Miss Dean till I come back without fail, promise. Have Dr. Norris up whenever you feel the least bit nervous. Remember it would just about kill me if anything happened to my little family. When you go out put on rubbers & wrap up—the pain of a trip to you if you got sick while I am away would be unbearable. Please for my sake go to bed early & have a nap every afternoon, even if you have to refuse callers. I will take just as good care of myself as I know how. . . .
 Cheered up, girlie, I'll soon be back. . . .
 Drop me just a postal every day till Pat gets well. Go easy on your dear self.
                    Lovingly Bill.
                    ♥♥♥♥♥

Bill Reid, Jr., on train past Reno, Nevada, to Christine Reid, Belmont, CA
                                                    27 December 1904

Less than one day gone, Bill felt terrible leaving Christine and the two young children.

A Debutante's Passion—A Coach's Erotica

I don't want soon again to go through my experience of this morning—leaving you was about the hardest thing I've ever done. Bidding you goodbye when you went abroad didn't compare with the wrench this gave me. I feel like a deserter, leaving you with the two babies, and as I wrote, in my vest in the Strand which I gave to Papa to give to you, I simply had to force my feet down to keep from flying back to you. . . .

♥♥♥♥♥

Bill Reid, Jr., on railroad East to Boston, MA, to Christine Reid, Belmont, CA

28 December 1904

Bill had not yet reached Chicago on his trip to check out the football climate at Harvard.

. . . Cheer up little one—only three weeks and I'll be back. Remember that I love you and you alone & that you will always be in my thoughts. I shall offer up a little prayer for you every night—& will count the days before I have you in my arms again. Dear little girl, I do love you so. You are just everything to me. God bless you & keep you, the little Pattakin & sister.

♥♥♥♥♥

Bill Reid, Jr., on railroad East to Boston, MA, to Christine Reid, Belmont, CA

30 December 1904

Bill had arrived in Chicago, stayed several days to talk with alumni, and was on his way East to visit Harvard before accepting the head football position at his alma mater.

Wifie dearest:
 . . . I'd like to spend tonight there [Chicago] with you in the same old room. I guess we wouldn't have a royal time. When I arrive I am planning to run out to Brookline in order to keep my animal spirits in check. They're giving me a good tussle cooped up here for 5 days, but I'm bound I'll win. It seemed to me that every fellow in Chicago had a girl & it was quite uncomfortable to think that I didn't have mine. Well never mind—I'll be soon back— & he who laughs last, etc. . . .
 I shall hate to go into the Brookline home & not find you there. It will seem most unnatural. And I suppose I shall have your old room which will be worse yet. If you were only along it would all be great. We could go about our business all day & snuggle at night. It's too bad that it isn't to be so.
 I get dreamy at times & think of our house & I go in & up the stairs & surprise you & have a good kissing & hugging & then I see sister &

THE CALL TO HARVARD

Pattakin—how I wish I could. I hope Pattakin is well now & that you are rested. If so I shall be as content as I can be without you.

Well, I love you dearest—most to pieces—Wish I could hug & kiss you this moment. Wish I could sleep with you & we could blend ourselves together in every delicious way. . . .

♥♥♥♥♥

Aunt Hattie Reed, Belmont, CA, to Bill Reid, Jr., Brookline, MA
31 December 1904

The sister of Bill's mother and an important individual in running the preparatory school gave Bill advice shortly after he left the Belmont School to determine whether or not he would accept being coach of the Harvard football team.

This is the close of a year that has brought you great joy as well as great anxiety. The year in the school has been of great value to you I am sure, for you have made a record not to be ashamed of. You labor under some disadvantages for the fact that your father is one in ten-thousand, and while you are "a chip from the old block" you have yet your spurs to win. This it seems to me you are doing.

You entered upon the work here totally inexperienced in many of the difficult problems for solution, while he had worked through similar ones long ago. . . . You may make mistakes, but out of these you may gather wisdom as he as done. I know of no one whom I think can in any measure, keep, and promote the growth of the school your father has built up, except yourself. If the task seems too irksome then you are right in looking to other fields of activities. If you assume the responsibilities you will succeed in an eminent degree, ascending the ladder as each rung is placed underfoot. . . . When you spoke of owing a debt to Harvard, if I had been apt in my reply, I would have said, it may be that debt would be more fully met from this field than from the athletic ground.

With your beautiful and lovely family & the pleasant home on the hillside with its fine outlook, there seems little for me to wish for you in the glad year of 1905, except a peace of mind. . . .

♥♥♥♥♥

Bill Reid, Jr., Brookline, MA, to Christine Reid, Belmont, CA
3 January 1905

Bill's 25-page letter in clear penmanship shows his concern for being away from Christine and their young family. His business at Harvard took him to dozens of Harvard football men, including football captain Dan Hurley and William H. Lewis, a Walter Camp all-American in the early 1890s and first black player to be so honored. Lewis would become a key coach when Bill took the position. The Harvard stadium noted is the first

171

A Debutante's Passion—A Coach's Erotica

reinforced concrete stadium ever built, one constructed in 1903 with Greek columns adorning it. Bill was extremely busy, but he remembered his first night with Christine at Boston's Hotel Lennox.

I've thought and thought of you since I got here and the feelings of love and appreciation which haven't gone out to you from my brimful heart aren't worth while thinking of. I love you mentally, morally & physically and I've loved you here in each of these ways as best I could. How I wish I could kiss & hug all this into you & perhaps put something else in into the bargain, instead of having to imagine it all. Really, I think we're just getting into the real stride of our married life—and it's great. I only wish that in going to bed tonight I could look forward to a delicious taste of it all. . . .

I lay awake over half the night thinking about you & my leaving—& you'd have found me wide awake & ready for you. I have already answered your questions of us being closer together than ever before—I certainly feel so—& I think we'll get even much closer—particularly if you will only let me love and fondle you all I want whenever I want. I have sometimes felt when I wanted to love you or kiss you—up your dear legs—that you didn't want me to because you didn't think it nice for me—while I meanwhile am crazy to & love it so. Please let me love you all I want in any way—'cause its so delicious. Let me judge whether its "nice" for me or not. You're nice all over, I know it & insist in every privilege with you. . . .

After supper I went to the Dr's [Nichols] & met Hurley & we three talked the New Year in & then Dan & I walked out to Brookline. I had a good rest & he came for me with a carriage next day & we drove to Cambridge. On the way we stopped at the Stadium & it's a great sight—stirring even when vacant. . . .

We went over and saw Lewis & had luncheon there & talked steadily for three hours. He was most loyal and enthusiastic in every way & among other things thinks that the prospects for a team next year are very bright. I saw Lewis' three babies—great big eyed youngsters with little curly heads—just the kind of a baby you'd like to have "brown & bootiful"—but not so "bootiful as Pattakin or Edith. . . ."

It is reported that Dean [LeBaron] Briggs is enthusiastic for my coming & is busy trying to arrange for a college position for me, to lend dignity to the position of coach. This is hearsay, so don't take it for too much. A New York Harvard man said . . . "if the getting of Reid is a question of money—let me know. . . ." Everyone has said—"Bill, you're the only man who can pull us out of this hole & by God—you've got to do it. . . ." Jack Hallowell said—"I think Bill is the man & I shall do all I can to get him on & to help him, though I don't like him personally." Good for Hallowell—that makes me feel better already—it's the first really genuine thing I've ever heard him say & it's too bad he didn't say it six years ago. . . .

The proposition is a fierce one & I shall be greatly interested in the opinion of Dean Briggs, Pres. Eliot & others. There is the chance of a

THE CALL TO HARVARD

lifetime here with Dr. Nichols, to put football on a sound & lasting basis, in two years. [Walter] Camp is head coach of Yale baseball, showing Yale's attempt to solve her problem, while we are trying to throw our baseball strength into our football. . . .

As I came out in the car this aft, I passed Hotel Lennox & I looked up at the window of the room in which we had so much fun that first night. Let's see—four times was it? It makes my mouth water & makes me squirm about in my chair a bit. Gee! but that was great. I'll never forget the blue dress you wore that night or how deliciously thin it was & how good you felt through it—what fun it was taking it off— — and oh joy—what absolute bliss it was a little later when we lay stripped in that soft bed. Yi—!!! It makes my breath come fast. Don't read this aloud to Aunt Mary. . . !!!

♥ ♥ ♥ ♥ ♥

Bill Reid, Jr., Brookline, MA, to Christine Reid, Belmont, CA
6 January 1905

This very long, 36-page letter is included in its entirety because it sets the tone for Bill coming to Harvard to coach for the next two years and defines much in his life with Christine.

My onliest little darling:

You are a corking little wife that's what you are, and I love, l-o-v-e you no end. A letter every day and such dear ones—oh, I wish I could just get you in my arms and hug you all to pieces. And my how I'd like to sleep with you, only I'm afraid there would be little sleep for either of us. I feel so fond of you that I feel as though I'd like to do just every thing to you that a boy can do—to show that he has absolutely and entirely given himself up to you, to be in the same bed, with absolutely nothing on and with every freedom to one another—wouldn't it be simply luscious. To get all we want of that which each wants & loves, would be bliss itself. My, but I am anticipating my return like everything. I know that I am dwelling a lot on this fascinating side of things and yet I can't help myself. When you give "it" to me you join in so deliciously that it is simply ideal and I can no more help anticipating it & lingering in the thought than I can help flying. You are a peachy girl, that's all there is to it. It's fun to do it to a pretty girl, but to do it to a beauty & have her love it & you & want more is heaven. Yum, it's hard to think of it & stand it!!

Really though wife, I think we are beginning to really live a married life & it's bringing full measure of joy to me. I love to hold you in my lap & to kiss and fondly you & to have your dear face against mine. Oh, dear, you're the whole show, that's all there is to it. I love you dearly & from the bottom of my heart & steadily. I have been feeling and am coming more & more to feel a devotion & affection for you that passes all understanding. It's been growing gradually during the past ten months,

A Debutante's Passion—A Coach's Erotica

& still continues to grow in a way which I never believed it was in my nature to do. And I'm supremely happy about it, simply overjoyed. I could write on and on out of my heart this way, but if I am to get in anything else I must force an end to it all. Confound it all, I love you awful much. And let me add mighty little of it is due to my delightfully passionate longing for you. It's deeper than that & goes right down to bed rock.

I have had a most busy time here and have not sat still for a moment. First of all I am going to tell you a story on Stephens. It seems that last fall he took a girl to the theatre. Wishing to do the thing up brown he sent her a box of candy & a dozen of roses etc., etc. After the theatre he took her to supper & then ordered a cab to take her home. Well, they started off when it occurred to Stephens that he'd look & see what he had left in his purse. He found he had but 35 cents. So he determined to see the girl home & then to fix it up best he could with "cabby." He left the girl & told cabby to drive him to Harvard Square. On the way out it occurred to Stephens to jump out of the cab & escape. So he opened the door cautiously & stepped out, without for the moment, attracting the cabby's attention. As luck would have it he slipped & hit his shins a sharp crack on the curbing. Much angered he began cursing, which caused the disappearing cabby to look around. Recognizing his passenger he stopped his horse, jumped down, & started in pursuit. The course lay up commonwealth Ave & Stephens took to the path which runs through the little park in the middle, & seemed to be gaining when all of a sudden he ran into one of the benches & dropped in a heap. Cabby, catching up, pitched into Tom & beat him about the face most vigorously. After cabby had satisfied his anger, Stephens got up & took a car for Cambridge, where he told Overson that he had an ulcerated tooth. Overson believed it & so Tom carried on his part. Next day Stephens played in his class team & got still further touched up, with now a legitimate excuse for everything. Isn't that just like Stephens though.

I saw Stephens & Overson a day or two ago & had a good talk with them. Stephens gets his degree, though he was dropped the year after I left him & has improved very much. His mother & father however are divorced, his father having turned into a regular drunkard. His poor incapable mother is trying to do what she can for him & last summer, for his sake, prevented—by diversion—Tom's homecoming. Mighty sad, the whole thing isn't it.

Besides Overson & Stephens I have met Ned Sampson, Palmer, Page Wheelwright, Peter Higginson, Chas. Schweppe, Stickney, Cathin, Morris, Matthews, Mr. Leantl of Leantl & Pierce, & dozens of others whose names I can't recall but whose faces are familiar. It was mighty pleasant & every single one was as hearty as could be & all expressed the hope that I would come, though all recognize with me, that it's a hard question to settle. I met one of my old friends "Marvin," now a teacher at Groton & after talking of the football situation he said, "Gee Bill, I'm awful sorry you didn't go out for the crew instead of for the eleven, we need you to reorganize the crew." I thought that mighty nice of him, he being a crew man.

Dr. Lyon called last night & inquired most interestedly after you. He said he was very sorry to have missed the chance of Christening the baby, whereupon I said we'd bring the whole fifteen along sometime, which seemed to fluster him somewhat!!!!

I had a delightful call on Dorrie & found both her and Roger in. We chatted an hour & I think them a splendid couple & their relations to each other just about perfect. Both of them are just as happy as can be & just as devoted to each other as it is possible for them to be. Dorrie had on a very dainty apron & looked "honey" & "wifie" like. I want that we shall strive for their standard as it "radiates" happiness. I was greatly impressed & can now join with you in giving Dorrie "full measure." Their house which is just about opposite President Eliot's is a nice cozy one, beautifully & tastefully furnished & just right for two. I liked it better than any of the other young couple houses I've seen. I really had a delightful time there. Roger & Dorrie are both for my coming, Roger declaring that he would have his own boy do it under similar conditions. As I left I "congratulated" Dorrie, who was much pleased, while poor Roger got red up to his ear top. Said Dorrie, "We're both awfully happy, Bill."

I called on Catherine Williams & think she too is nice, but not in the same class with Dorrie. She complains a great deal, about the lack of double windows in the house, about Harold's small salary, comparing it to what some other fellows she knew are getting etc., etc., making it very, very hard for Harold. He's doing well & giving her all he's got & it seems pretty hard to have her so self-centered as to consider only her own wants, giving no attention to Harold or his career. I don't think they can ever get to Dorrie's condition on the present basis of living. Withal, however Catherine is very nice. Her baby had a hard time of it a day or two ago—at night—& she sent over here for brandy for it—did you ever!!! I just saw the baby this afternoon & was greatly disappointed in him. I saw some very flattering snapshots of him in his carriage & was greatly taken aback, when I finally saw him in person. But then it isn't every wife that produces corkers like Pat & sister.

Agnes and I took dinner with Ted & Catherine Little tonight & we had a most enjoyable time of it. I ate like a hog, three helpings of roast beef, potatoes, beans, & jelly, four big portions of salted peanuts, two helpings of dessert, a helping of salad (I'd have taken two had I been asked) & soup, bread & butter & cake. It was informal, the whole thing & most enjoyable. We talked over everything, Di Gamma & all. Ted & Jaynes feel just as I do about the club they neither of them have paid out more than I, & have fought the new house with me. Ted & Catherine took Ag & I all over their house which is cozy and fine, more suitable I think than Harold & Catherine's though all of them are nice enough.

A Debutante's Passion—A Coach's Erotica

Ted & Cath. sleep in separate beds, side by side. Pretty hard conditions to stand it seems to me, or perhaps they occupy one bed till sleeping time. However, I like to feel you there all night, either by feeling your soft warm back against mine or by sticking out a foot. The only trouble I find with a double bed or with any of them for that matter is the fact that I can't sleep on, in & around you at the same time. I can't get next to you enough. Bless you, dearie, Allie Morse has consumption, isn't that fierce. Poor old fellow, I'm awfully, awfully sorry. Catherine said for you to be sure & come on next summer, she said she'd had great times with you. Ted piped in with—"Yes, & she told you a lot of pretty gay stories." I was a little afraid of that. Ted is likely to tell some of them over your name—he has no sense whatever.

Mr. Whitney & Mrs. are divorced or rather are living apart. It seems that Eleanor married a fellow whom the fool mother didn't want, but whom the father (sensible fellow) felt was O.K. The fellow was poor & not up to Mrs. Whitney's society ideas, though he has made Eleanor supremely happy. I think it's Eleanor Whitney's people, at any rate Rex wasn't the fellow. Ted & Catherine both expressed a hearty wish that we should come on.

I met Rex on the street a day or two ago. He has given up law & has bought a $24,000 seat on the Stock Exchange. The why's and wherefore's I don't know. It seems to me risky & foolish, but I may be wrong. People wonder where the "price" came from.

I went shopping today & like a dutiful "hubbie" bought three suits of winter underwear. Balbriggan $3 a suit at Noyes'—marked down from $5. Louise has gotten Aunt Mary's shoes & I shall get her clothes when I get a chance. Met one of the Barker girls on the street & she inquired after you most interestedly & was most delighted with the picture of Pat I showed her.

I must now tell you of a couple of joshes that are floating around town. It has been proposed by some Yale men that our crew & their nine—play an intercollegiate game of Parcheesi. They claim that since neither team knows anything about its own game, a simple game like Parcheesi, would be much more interesting & altogether more effectively played.

Again, the Ivy orator last year, said of the crew, it's like Ivory Soap, "It Floats." That's a awful crack at the crew, but is true.

Now for the football situation. I have seen any number of men since I last wrote & they feel about as follows.

Jack Hallowell is strong for me. He thinks I alone can save the situation & told me frankly that where as he hadn't believed in my ability before, that now he felt absolute & entire confidence in me. He agrees that Dr. Nichols can take it after I leave but that he would be lost as matters stand now, since he knows no football. I had my little squabble out with him as I said I was going to & we are now on a new basis. I am relieved too & I know he is behind me. I sent Marian Ladd 1 1/2 dozen of pinks & it pleased them both immensely. They knew that I had stretched a point to do a hearty thing. If I come, I could not have made a more politic move, though it was not all politics.

Matthews says I must come & says that the undergraduate feeling for me is high & strong. I told him that I considered the undergrads most unstable whereupon he said, that they were not so on this question anyhow.

Al Eyre told me that his employer said that he'd give me $5000 himself if I'd come into his office. That is gratifying if it isn't a possibility.

John Dunlop. One of the most prominent of the staunch coaches said, "Bill there's no two ways about it—you're the only fellow who can do this & save the situation & you've got to that's all." He said he'd back me to the limit as did the other two & would come out every day if I want him to. He is a fine fellow, clean cut & I know you'd like him.

Norman Cabot says "I'm the man to do it & he hopes to God I will." His opinion doesn't figure much but his support is loyal anyhow.

Peter Higginson. Coach & captain of the crews that have beaten Yale. "I hope the devil you can come—you've a great chance—it's merely a question as to whether you can stand the sacrifice."

J.J. Storrow of the Athletic Committee, one of Major Higginson's head men & coach of the crew. "If you plan to come on merely for the sake of trying to turn out winning teams for the next two years alone—no. It is a bigger question than that. If I come to form a system & above all to leave Camb[ridge]. itself with a good moral reputation—Yes—heartily so. If I can see my way to it."

And now comes a bunch of opinions that Papa will especially value. Pres. Eliot, Dean Briggs, Dean Hurlbut.

Pres. Eliot. He has had "grippe" [the flu] but told his Sec. he'd be glad to see me so I was ushered up to his bed room where I found him sitting in a chair by the fire. He started off with a no. of questions. How Papa was, how Mama, how you, how many children, how old Papa, how large the school, what my part in it, how Papa's hold on the school maintains itself—that is whether he is loosening his hold. Whether the school property is saleable in case it were to fail as an institution, whether we own other property, etc., etc., etc. I answered every question & when he had the situation pretty well in hand he said. "Well, Mr. Reid frankly, I don't see that there's anything to discuss at all, your part is clear. You have gained all you can from athletics & if you lose now you may be worse off." Then he asked Papa's own view, asked how such a move would be accepted by the community, how long I thought I should have to be away, etc. Then added, now my view of football isn't the same as my colleague Mr. Briggs holds. I do not believe in the modern game & cannot see that it has either improved or shows any signs of doing so. My criticism will appear in my forthcoming report, etc. In other words the President said that "if it were a question of what the University wants me to do, that it wanted me to build up & keep up Belmont School—the

A Debutante's Passion—A Coach's Erotica

accomplishing of which would be a service to all the colleges indeed of America. As I left I told the President that he had made the stroke of his life time from my mother's standpoint & that I knew that she would always give him absolute support hereafter in anything he tried to do. We really had a very jovial time of it & even the President smiled & laughed occasionally.

Dean Briggs said that he expected Pres. Eliot to take just that stand, that he had once criticized my catching as tricky because I had feined with a throw to first base & had then deliberately (horrible thought) thrown the ball to third. Dean Briggs said to me—"I sometimes wonder if the President ever remembers that he was once a boy." Dean Briggs is strongly for my coming & for at least two years. He said in brief—"I have changed from my opinion of last year because the situation is no longer one of athletics & football, but one that is eating out the vitals of college life & society here. Distrust, enmity, etc. are rife & owing to the football failures." It seems that Cochrane "Dug" drank a great deal in the Porcellian & while under the influence of liquor said some most unfortunate things which got to the players through one or two Porcellian players who overheard. These sayings which were quite truthfully reported did not really represent the sober Cochrane, but were so accepted. As a result, distrust of Cochrane arose & great trouble followed. He was hissed by the crowd etc., etc. I mention this as indicative of what the Dean refers to. Said the Dean further. I want you on, not for the winning of the games, but for your moral influence. I want you for the morale of the whole thing. I want you to set the tone to things. It is well worth it & it needs to be done. It's a great task, but will bring you in contact with an immense body of young men who need your steadying influence. The one year scheme says he is neither fair to me, to the college, or to Dr. Nichols, though it is hard on Papa. He says, you can't do it in 1 year & if you failed to win or get the system founded you'd lose half the effect which I know your well established policy would have. Dean Briggs then told me of two "brief masterpieces" (isn't that well said) of Pres. Eliot's. Said he—"Harvard athletics are a good illustration of intelligence applied in an unintelligent way." Capital!! I think & again—"Harvard athletics are unintelligent & therefore unsuccessful." Splendid again.

Dean Briggs does not agree with Pres. Eliot & I think his opinion is worth more here—because he's more in touch with college life & is a believer in athletics. I had luncheon with the Dean & asked him to write me out a telegram to send to Papa. He wrote as follows: "Work here, well worth doing. Needs two years—will write." As he is to write I shan't buttin' any further. I haven't yet sent the telegram & aren't sure I shall. I may though. Dean Briggs does not believe that I will lose caste, — he thinks if I do the work as I can, I shall be a distinct gainer.

Dean Hurlbut is strong for it. He took me into his office by a big fire & said—"I want you to know that I believe that you have the finest

THE CALL TO HARVARD

head on your shoulders of any young fellow who has ever attended this place. I believe you can do this job. I believe you could general an army & I've said so. I consider you a fellow of rare ability in this line & Harvard has produced almost none—like you." Wasn't that handsome of him though—& yet I feel mighty funny through it all. He said also that if I went into politics he didn't know what I wouldn't do. Well, he is in favor of three years. He wrote me out a brief statement as follows: "For every interest of Harvard College I want you to come. I prefer three years to two, for three years would put your system into a whole college generation, but I should take thankfully whatever you can give. The only question I raise is whether you can afford it. If you possibly can come, I want you to." I tell you I call that mighty nice.

Lest Papa should feel that he has been left out of the consideration I will add this which is what he said. "You ought to have time to show your system—& you can afford 2 or 3 years if your father is well." I disagree there. I think 2 years is absolutely the limit, the outside, outside limit. Dean Hurlbut will also write so I shall stop with this inkling of his position. I am giving in this letter just the kernel of each man's position. The consideration of the question was not so brief as my memory jottings might lead one to believe. One hour & a half was the least time I was with any one man.

I have tried to get hold of Mr. Ginn, but have thus far failed. Dr. Merrill, I called in, & he was delighted, sent his best to you & no matter "how I decide wishes me the best of success."

I did, however, have a long talk with Major Higginson & it was a good one too. His position was as follows. "I'll tell you Reid (in his snappy way) the situation in football is at present one of different, fresh & diverse ideas. Now the way to cross that street is on your own two legs & on no one's else. The work of organizing the work is worthwhile said he well worth it, but remember you've got to do it & also pay the bill." (Shrewd) Said he, that work is a great one & you'll have to manage men—let me tell you here, in that connection two things that have been said which mean the same thing. First, Carnegie's rule. "He knew how to get better men than he to do his own work, Second, never do what you can get anyone else to do." Both valuable proverbs, which he slung in as he went along & which stuck in my memory.

Then, said he, & here is the best of his thoughts & they are fine— "Nothing is so much worth while as helping other people." This football help is well worthwhile if you, your father & your respective wives are willing to pay the price. In the giving of the world, said he, you are young & it is a question of how much you can afford to subscribe. If it were money you were called upon to give, it would be easily settled. Drawing out a hand full of coins he said, here, I can give that money away—that doesn't amount to anything, for I can replace that, it is not a loss, but if I give time that is a real gift & cannot be replaced. If you give a year or two to this work you cannot get it back—it is gone, it is a sacrifice. And

A Debutante's Passion—A Coach's Erotica

yet, "You can't get anything that is worthwhile in the world without a sacrifice." Then said he, what is to be your remuneration? I told him that I had been offered most anything in reason, but rather felt inclined to accept simply enough to cover my lost salary & my expenses. Telling him of Wheelan's suggestion to Papa I asked Maj. Higginson his opinion. Well said he, "That's something that I would like to mull over a bit. When I was first in employ of the city, said he, I did a big job when I needed some money badly & then refused my pay & turned it back to the city treasury. Just why I did it, said he, I don't know. I earned it. But I do know this much, I always feel warm near my heart when I think of it. I'll mull it over a day or so & let you know later." While I was talking someone came up about the Symphony Orchestra's future. I am, said Maj., for anything up to a million & went right on talking, a living illustration of his own theory that a money gift is easy, time a harder one. You see he leaves the question unsolved & says "up to us" to decide.

So much for these opinions. I tell you it's hard to see what to do & yet getting these views is mighty interesting. Summing up the entire situation it is something like as follows. The football situation was never more in need of a reorganization & never was there a better chance to bring such reorganization about. I have the backing that no one else here has, and the only man considered, & think I can do it up brown in two years—leaving Dr. Nichols in splendid & permanent shape. One year will be pretty brief & will hardly be fair try for me, for the college or for Dr. Nichols. If I lose the first year & leave, Dr. Nichols would build on my good system & win & then he would get the credit for making & securing the situation & I would go down in general history as a final failure. I believe then that while I feel that I cannot only form the system but can also make a good stab at winning in one year, I am nevertheless taking big chances of failure if things do not work out quite so well as the promise. And I should want to do this work so that it was an unquestioned success which I can do in two years, with Dr. Nichols. It is a one year risk & a two year's certainty—that is what it amounts to.

Only one man says don't come, every one else says it's a good work, needs doing, you can do it & we hope you will. We recognize that it is a flat footed sacrifice—but hope you can see your way to it.

Everyone agrees that I can make no mistake if I stay where I am, that I risk something by the change, though they think the risk well worth all that it costs.

In a nutshell, three years is out of the question. The conditions are just to my liking. I can do my trick in two years. I run a risk in trying it for one alone. Is it worth it? It's a "pecan" to crack, there's no doubt about it.

I have about seen everybody who can throw light on the situation & my remaining calls are for policy's sake in case I accept. If I omit certain fellows they're likely to feel slighted & if I asked for their help they might feel a little touchy.

I am investigating the matter of the schedule. Dartmouth, Penn & Yale & getting at some interesting facts to which I will tell you later. I am following up the poor students of the football situation through Hurley, to see that they are at their work. In short I am starting some things which are for the general good even if I don't come. They are vital & would fall to my lot if I took the job & since I hold it at an option I feel as though I should look after them as a sort of trustee. Hurley is a "brick" & has put himself absolutely at my disposal. He rings me up every night & asks for orders or if there is anything he can do. He's a corker.

I called on Aunt Belle & Mrs. Gray day before yesterday. Mrs. Gray wasn't well & I couldn't see her but Aunt Belle was most cordial & inquired for you & the babies most interestedly. Aunt Belle says Mrs. Gray won't live much longer & that she, Aunt Belle, is in constant dread of death for Mrs. Gray. Pathetic, but Mrs. Gray is ready & happy to go. She prays that she may go before she loses her faculties & becomes a burden on others. She is a grand old lady—of the salt of the earth.

I coached Albert [Christine's brother] in Algebra to 10 last night. He came home much elated over it. I think he is marked too high, at any rate he's not up to that mark from my standpoint.

In talking with Dean Briggs we took up the subject of Al Eyre. It seems that what Eyre told me about Pomfret School is true. Eyre went there to teach & was given the Physics class. He had never taught Physics in his life & said so, but was told to go ahead. He did so & not a boy failed his Harvard exams, while several even got honors. He has great ability & is bright. His faults are that he talks a great deal & has absolute confidence in his own ability. He thinks that he has solved every difficult athletic question that ever came up here. He is the Moses who led the children of Harvard out of every difficulty. The Dean agrees that he is a smart fellow & that he has more energy & push than any other fellow about College, a queer combination, isn't he.

I was delighted to get the details of how much better Pattakin is & of what a peach sister is—it's very cheering. Dear little children, they're bully both of 'em. And I'm awfully glad to hear that you are resting so well. It does me good to hear that you are doing so nicely. God bless you. I wish I could play with Pattakin now & see sister looking around—it would be great.

I rather hope to start home next Wednesday, Jan. 11th, but I can't be absolutely sure. I want, while I am here, to get the situation by the throat. I am doing no loafing, being on the go from morning till night.

Will you as before, please show the readable portions of this to Papa, as I cannot write it over. It has taken me six hours as it is at a steady sitting.

A Debutante's Passion—A Coach's Erotica

I got a wonderful New Year's letter from Aunt Hattie, almost a benediction. I will bring it back with me. Your father & mother were perfectly delighted with it.

By the way I think your father favors the 2 year plan, also a good substantial salary well above my present one. We have not yet talked the thing over finally because the evidence is not all in.

Papa has raised my salary to $1500 did you know that? Mama writes as follows—"Papa says, tell Will I neglected to tell him that Edith's salary will be a hundred dollars making the total revenue of the household on the hill $1500 if they tend to their business." That's mighty nice isn't it. I guess you'll have to do the immediate honors till I come. Don't let it slip a minute as Papa will greatly enjoy our attitude in it all. If you can give him a good kiss I think he'd be delighted & if you'll have him up to tea for this letter he'll be immensely pleased I think. Good old Dad he's the most generous fellow that ever lived & in many ways one of the most noble. What I suggest may not appeal to you. I merely suggest it, that's all.

Well, my precious, I've written long & all, but I trust it will be worth looking over even if it is merely a question of its bearing on this momentous question. I myself am unsettled & will be wholly ready to accept Papa's judgment in this matter.

Be careful of your dear old selfie—don't get too tired or try to do too much. Remember you're mine. Get plenty of sleep, rest & look well & happy & it will be the greatest satisfaction to me when I get back. I am eagerly looking forward to the day when I shall start back & I yearn for the moment when I shall have you in my arms—hugged close & kissed. Also not a little for the first wedded night after my long fast.

I pray for you all every night & think of you & us frequently, and always with a warm, loving and devoted heart.

God bless you & the chicks—love to all— & to your own dear self your husband's all—heart, body, soul & mind.

Devotedly & fondly,
"Bill"

[On top of letter, he jotted in]
Snow, rain, sleet & slush. 10 degrees above & stormier growing.

♥♥♥♥♥

Bill Reid, Jr., Brookline, MA, to Christine Reid, Belmont, CA
11 January 1905

Bill did not forget Christine, as he was close to accepting the position of head football coach. He revealed additional feelings toward him by those associated with Harvard football.

It was only last night that I sent you my heart's love and yet tonight I find it brimming over again. I do love you so you dear little girlie—never so

THE CALL TO HARVARD

much as now—just with all there is in me and absolutely. If you were only here now I think I could say that I have never been so happy before. Just what it is I don't know but I am wildly in love with you as I have never been before. I know of course, that I'd dearly love to get into bed with you and with absolutely nothing on, just give myself up to the blissful enjoyment of your delicious self—but this feeling reaches way beyond that—oh, its bully. I haven't felt entirely satisfied with my love heretofore, not that I've ever doubted it—but I have felt that it wasn't as serene and satisfying as it ought to be. I've been hungry for something else—and at last I think it's come. You, darling, I think you'll see the difference—You'll find me more sympathetic, more fond, more loving, more everything. Don't feel uneasy—I'm in my right mind—only I do feel so elated. . . . I am awfully anxious to watch you undress, that's something I never shall tire of. . . . My being on here has awakened every dormant sense in me and I see lovely possibilities in life at every turn. . . .

Major Higginson after three days of thinking put himself on record as hoping I can come & think the work worthwhile. . . . Prof. Hollis says he hopes I can come but also says that he thinks that Dr. Nichols will be very foolish to accept the responsibility after me, since Dr. Nichols promises to be the greatest surgeon this country has ever seen. . . . [Captain] Hurley told me that he would resign if I don't come— & [Trainer] McMasters said—"Bill, if you don't come, I don't care whether I have anything to do with the teams or not. . . ." I had an offer of $5,000 at an office in town—the one Eyre is in. I don't know what the work is but there is the offer. . . . They've conducted a regular campaign here for me until my stock has run up way above par. As an inducement for me they have worked out this scheme. If I come in I am to be a trustee of the Lowell Estate, a Trustee of the Institute of Technology—Secretary of some big mill— & at the same time, receiving a salary in the position of Athletic Director—an office to be created for me especially. . . . I know that I can do it—I know that at present Dr. Nichols is the only other man who can—& he needs a chance to learn the game. It's hard when the cry is pitiful, not to listen. . . . Of course all of this enthusiasm means great hopes & great disappointments in case the hopes are not fulfilled. . . . The opportunity of stepping in & doing the whole show a good turn is the greatest athletic opportunity that has ever presented itself in the United States. . . .

Your father suggests a one year plan with an option of two—thus leaving me a chance to get out if I do more in one year than just now seems probable. I think the suggestion a very wise one. . . .

♥♥♥♥♥

Bill Reid, Jr., note to Christine Reid

undated, likely 1905

This is one of the rare notes between Bill and Christine.

183

A Debutante's Passion—A Coach's Erotica

Dear little girl,
   I love you with all my heart—besides giving me your own dear self, you've given me two of the dearest babies that ever were.
                           Lovingly, Bill
                        ♥♥♥♥♥

Christine Reid, Belmont, CA, to Bill Reid, Jr., probably Belmont, CA
ca. 8 March 1905

Bill had returned home from his fact-finding trip East in late December and early January, had accepted the football coaching position, and was again on his way to Harvard to take control of the faltering Harvard football team. It is most likely that Christine placed this letter in Bill's suitcase.

It is hard to think that when you read this you will be far away from me, and it makes my heart ache pretty hard. My love for you is so great that it's a pain as well as a pleasure, but I would not have it otherwise. (You came in just now and wondered, I guess, to see me get up and go out, but I want to finish this. . . .) There is such a tumult surging inside of me, but every beat of my heart is for you, and I love you as much as one person can love another, I guess.
   I am restless and miserable without you. I wish that I could be as much to you as you are to me, but I don't think I shall ever be able to. I get pretty discouraged sometimes and I know I am pretty poor stuff. Please don't think I am saying that hoping you will contradict it, (perhaps I am!) but it's true too. . . .
   God bless you, sweetheart, you are the best and dearest husband a girl ever had. I am ashamed whenever I think how I have fussed about things—forgive me and I will try to do better. Well, I've said it all, and yet I feel like saying three words over and over and over. Can you guess them? Yet even they seem weak. — I love you.
                           Wifie.
                        ♥♥♥♥♥

Bill Reid, Jr., probably Belmont, CA, to Christine Reid, Belmont, CA
8 March 1905

Bill likely left this letter for Christine as he went to the train for Boston.

Dear little girlie:
   You haven't been out of my thoughts a moment during the last two weeks. I have loved you silently again and again and frequently had you only been near, I would have taken you in my arms and hugged you, oh so hard.

THE CALL TO HARVARD

We certainly are on the smooth track now and really we have little to complain of in this separation of a month. Just think fine weather, health at home & friends & then reunion. I wish I could take little sister for you nights and do such poor services as I have done—all this while but that is one of the incidents of the greater joy we shall feel when we once more get together. I realize now in a degree how old Hector felt when he left his wife and child—for the field.

Dear wifie, dear Pattakin, dear Edith—dearer to me, all of you, than anything in the world. God watch over you all & protect you for me.

One month—girlie—& you, I & your family will all be together again. Just think of it, I shall try to get everything ready for you & the chicks & therein will be my greatest comfort.

I want you to have what you want to eat, to see the doctor whenever you feel uneasy & in every way to ease your work up. Dear girl, such a mother never was before.

Well, I'm not going to let this note "blue" up, for we are really mighty lucky in that it's only a month. Just remember that my love & sympathy is with you wherever you go & that I am thinking of and hugging you constantly.

God bless you & keep you—
   With the deepest love & affection to you dear—
    "Bill"
♥ ♥ ♥ ♥ ♥

Bill Reid, Sparks, NV, to Christine Reid, Belmont, CA
                   9 March 1905

Bill was beginning his trip East to take over Harvard's football program. Christine and the children would join him soon for the next two years.

. . . How I wish you were here. I know you'd enjoy it, spring is in the air & one cannot help feeling it. A good morning kiss to you & my heart's love. Bless you, girlie, I feel awfully happy even if I do feel lonesome. We have come into such a happy life with each other that it is a delicious memory & my mind dwells on it at every turn. Everything beautiful that I see, the mountain torrents, the snow capped mountains, the beautiful pines, the blue sky, the air, the sunshine, all of them seem so in keeping with the peace of my innermost thoughts. And, darling, my harmony with the universe. Oh, I'm so glad I'm married & that it's you—the whole thing is so wonderful . . . .
♥ ♥ ♥ ♥ ♥

Bill Reid, Jr., Ogden, UT, postcard to Christine Reid, Belmont, CA
                  10 March 1905

Bill made sure that Chirstine would get a short communication.

A Debutante's Passion—A Coach's Erotica

Dear Wife:
I suppose that you will get my last letter—at the same time that you get this. Although I wrote the letter 12 hours ago, I tried to mail it but we didn't come to a single "on time" & the weather is fine—no snow & the traveling comfortable. Your dear note, is my morning cheer. I love it & you. Love to Aunt M. Take good care of yourself & God bless you.
Affectionately, "Bill"
♥ ♥ ♥ ♥ ♥

Christine Reid, Belmont, CA, to Bill Reid, Jr., Brookline, MA
10 March 1905

Christine wrote her first letter to Bill, who was on his way to Cambridge, Massachusetts.

Piddy dear,
It seems impossible that it was only the day before yesterday that you left me. It really seems like ages, and it frightens me to see how awfully much I miss you. I always know I am going to but never fully realize how much until you have gone. The house seems so empty, and I feel like a ship that has lost its rudder. It's no use I'm simply head over heels in love with you.

Your note from Sacramento came last night, and you were an old dear to invite me so soon. My heart was nearly bursting it was so full of love for you, and I lay awake a long time (for me!) thinking of you and having the only kind of a cuddle that I could. You don't know how big and cold, and lonely that bed is now, and no matter how often I reach out I can never seem to touch anything soft and warm as I am used to. It is horrid!

Sister [Edith] had a very good night. She was asleep at seven, waked at twelve, then at four. Slept again until half past five and was awake then until quarter of seven when I took her into bed with me and fed her. Then we both snoozed a little before I got up. To-day she has been very restive and colicky and I haven't been able to do a thing. I began this letter this morning but had to give up and hold her. She had quite a hard "colic" this p.m. and I couldn't seem to get her eased up whatever I did. It was queer for her to act so, for she had a good movement all by herself this morning. Well, perhaps she'll do better to-morrow. I'm not worrying, for she is as jolly as can be and I think even fatter than when you left. Perhaps she is missing you, like someone else I could mention!

It is fine that you are having such a comfortable trip and such good weather. Do take oh! such good care of your precious old self! What should I do if anything happened to you!

"Patsy" went for a long drive with your father and mother and Mr. & Mrs. Cappe yesterday p.m. They said he behaved very well, and seemed to enjoy himself immensely. He came home much excited and when I

THE CALL TO HARVARD

asked him what he saw he kept clucking away at a great rate. Come to find out they had stopped and watched part of a game of polo, so I guess that was what he meant.

... I am afraid the family will feel hurt at my writing to you when I have neglected them so badly, but somehow I can't help writing to you. I will try to write them tomorrow.

My best love to all. Sister is crying so I must run.

I do love you awfully.

C.

♥ ♥ ♥ ♥ ♥

Christine Reid, Belmont, CA, to Bill Reid, Jr., Brookline, MA
12 March 1905

Christine was probably overly tired when she wrote this short letter, or it was one of her depressive states, something she had from time to time previously when Bill was gone.

Colic! Colic!! Colic!!! Oh Dear! What shall I do with her! She has hardly slept to-day, and when she did sleep it was in my arms! But my! she's fat, and I do believe there's a new wrinkle in her legs. I expect she's a "lettle bit naughty!"

Well, dearie, I am so glad that your trip has been so comfortable. Your note from Ogden came this A.M.

I am so tired that I hardly know what I am writing. Please don't ever go away from me again, Pid—I just cannot stand it.

This is just to tell you that I love you in the same old way.

♥ ♥ ♥ ♥ ♥

Christine Reid, Belmont, CA, to Bill Reid, Jr., Brookline, MA
14 March 1905

Christine looked forward greatly to returning to the East for the next year or so.

Three weeks from to-day and we shall be on our way east! In less than a month we shall be together again! Won't it be great...!!

Julia was rather calling me down for holding [Edith] so much and staying with her all the time, but think of Patsy! I am well repaid for all the trouble I took with him. It is a good investment to devote yourself to them when they're little and I know I shall never regret it....

You have been a dear about writing. It's no use talking, hubbie, you are the best ever anyhow!! In spite of the fact that you are away, that I miss you terribly.... I have a deep peace in the bottom of my heart for all is well between us. I think we both felt rather distressed and disillusioned that our feelings for each other did not stay at "top notch"

187

A Debutante's Passion—A Coach's Erotica

all the time after you came back, but dearie, I don't suppose they ever will exactly. Wouldn't be much use in ever going to heaven if they did, would they? Well I love you with all my might, and how and at least we have had glimpses of what a perfect life together would be.

Take the best of care of your sweet old selfie—Don't let me catch you with a cold or anything when I come. Fact is, I shall be pretty "anxious" myself when I get there. Perhaps I'll be "naughty," how would you like that?

♥ ♥ ♥ ♥ ♥

Christine Reid, Belmont, CA, to Bill Reid, Jr., Brookline, MA
19 March 1905

Christine wrote her husband a negative and sarcastic letter.

My Dearie Boy,

"Sister"' is asleep at this moment, as I will begin a letter to you. It won't be much good, for I have been up so much of the night for the last week that I feel like a starved owl. Just what has struck the "music" I cannot make out, but I suppose I had been boasting about her good behavior at night. I can hear you laugh at that, but you wouldn't laugh if you were here. At present I am waiting as patiently as may be for dinner. Aunt Hattie promised to send up some meat, but as is quite apt to be the case, none has come, and it looks suspiciously like Fast day at the Reid Jr's. Oh well!

I suppose she forgot it, and I don't blame her, only it's a trifle trying, when I went down this morning myself on purpose and offered to go over to the other house myself and get it. But no! she would send it up—so here we are dinnerless. It is Friday, and the thought of the meal you are to sit down to does not tend to make me more resigned. I expect I shall burst with good things when I get there. It is naughty of me to write you this kind of letter, but you will make allowances for my being tired, and it's this or nothing. My head is like a blown egg, and I feel like cuddling in your arms and crying. Why can't Edith behave like an ordinary baby? I disagree with Shakespeare. I'm sure there's something in a name after all, and she's taking after her grandmother. Tell mother that's a joke, she might not know it.

Am glad you enjoyed your stay with Blackhams. So you want me to stay over with them! A few days more or less doesn't make any difference to you does it?

There you see—I am as "blue" as indigo and I'd better shut up before I make you mad.

I love you dearie, tho it may not seem so—will write again when I feel better. I do love you to pieces.
C.

♥ ♥ ♥ ♥ ♥

THE CALL TO HARVARD

Christine Reid, Belmont, CA, to Bill Reid, Jr., Brookline, MA
22 March 1905

Just a little over a week before Christine would travel East, she tried to clear her conscience over her depressing letter writing.

My conscience is punching a hole through me to think of the nasty letter I wrote you last time, but I was dead tired and hardly knew what I was doing. Since then "sister" has been better, and yesterday I don't think she cried once, except for "mum-mum." Patsy has got a cold, and coughs a good deal, and his nose is stuffed up, but he is better to-day, and as it seems to have really cleared off at last, I hope things will go better.
   You dearie boy, I cannot bear to think of you as "blue" and lonely! Try not to be, and we'll have some good times when I get there. . . .
   The "Illustrated Sporting News" with your article has come, and I think it reads awfully well. . . .

♥♥♥♥♥

Bill Reid, Jr., Brookline, MA, to Christine Reid, Belmont, CA
23 March 1905

Bill looked for Christine to join him in Massachusetts, and told her of attempting to get Harry LeMoyne, a flunked-out star athlete, back into Harvard. He had been working on a sheep ranch in Idaho since failing his freshman year, two years before.

It's going to be simply "great" to come home here at night, to find a dear, pretty, loving wife waiting for me, with a kiss, a hug & latter a snuggle. . . . There are others, but I hardly think it proper to mention them to such a young girl, you might not know what I mean. It's pretty nice though.
   I have been hard at work trying to get [Harry] LeMoyne back & feel that I am quite likely to succeed. I now have a pass for him [on the rail] East, a room to stay in in Camb[ridge] & tomorrow I hope to get him tutors & a job. The whole story is too long to tell here but the athletic committee have approved everything I've done. . . .

♥♥♥♥♥

Bill Reid, Jr., Brookline, MA, to Christine Reid, Belmont, CA
25 March 1905

Bill had just been paid nearly $1700, far more than his yearly pay at the Belmont School, and sent money to Christine prior to her travel East. Yet, the letter, surprisingly, said nothing about the loving of Christine when she arrived. She would soon reply.

189

A Debutante's Passion—A Coach's Erotica

Dear C.

Enclosed is a check for $500, which, as near as I can figure it now, will probably pay the $100 we owe Papa (advanced for my trip)—get your ticket, etc., & still leave enough for "on hand."

If it isn't too much trouble—I think it would be a good scheme to keep some of it & then we can see at the end of the year how we figure up. I have sent Dr. Norris $150.00 too.

♥♥♥♥♥

Bill Reid, Jr., Orange, NJ, to Christine Reid, Belmont, CA
26 March 1905

Bill visited his Harvard roommate after attending a large Harvard athletic gathering in New Jersey. It appeared that Bill was mostly interested in telling Christine about Rich and his wife's love life as an opening to a renewal of their own love life.

Girlie darling:

Here I am in New Jersey with Rich. & Eleanor—crazy to have you here too, longing for you, thinking of you, speaking of you & yet perfectly helpless. Imagine Rich with Eleanor in his lap and I itching for you, but alone, imagine Rich. & Eleanor spending tonight together in bed and simply mixing it up as only a boy and girl can—while I—poor me—lie envious and alone in my companionless bed. . . . To know that when I felt like hugging & kissing you, you also were feeling the same way & would have joined in vigorously with me, to know too, that you would be ready & anxious for every possible kind of a good time tonight—has kept me on a fine edge all day. Oh, but I'd just like to have you here now to take you in my arms first, & squeeze you tight against me & then in my lap for a good hugging and a passionate kissing. And perhaps, my hand might get up your dress—um—so warm, & soft!!! And then I'd undress you gradually, kind of teasing myself by taking my time until I had you absolutely stripped. Perhaps you'd have me so—by that time. Then I'd lay you down on the bed & lie on you & hug & kiss you & wiggle and you'd hug me. Then after much perturbation on your part, I'd do again what I so loved at Tahoe—& then ————— Oh bliss & you. You'd "take me in" Oh, so deliciously & we'd squirm a bit & kiss & squeeze & then finally—in each others arms, drop off into heaven for a few seconds. Dear, dear, "how long oh Cataline?" I am positive that as I write now Rich & Eleanor are at it and it fires me all up. My tinder has been getting dryer & dryer and it will be ready to flare up pretty brightly by the time you get here. I feel just like girling tonight—Oh, why aren't we together. Tell me do you think of all these things as I do—& are you as anxious & hot as I? Tell me so.

Yesterday I was on the train from 10 A.M. till 4 P.M.—on my way to Montclair N.J.—where I made a talk before the "Newark Harvard Club."

Arriving in Montclair I went at once to John Reynolds house (he is Pres. of the Club) where I dressed. Then we went to Newark for the dinner (15 min by train)—then after the dinner back to Montclair for the night. This morning Mr. Reynolds drove me over here to Orange & I have been here all day. . . .

There were about 100 men at the dinner including Evert Wendell, a Yale man, a Princeton man, & several speakers besides. . . . The speeches were most of them frightfully long. . . . There was much singing & it added a great deal to the occasion. . . . The Princeton man tried to be eloquent & made to my mind a consummate mess of himself. The Eli did finely. . . . I cut my talk in half & spoke probably 5 minutes in all. I had splendid attention & received a fine send off. . . .

On the menu my "toast"—each speaker had one—was as follows: Toast—"Harvard Football Redivivis" Bill Reid '01. . . .

This A.M. at 10:30 I got to Rich's house where I have spent the day. The home is splendid—trees, lawn, well furnished. Eleanor went to church. Rich & I for a walk. After lunch we went for a 30 mile automobile ride & I wish you could have been—it was simply bully. Rich & Eleanor have been bully to me & I've had a great time. Rich & I had a great old talk. He & Eleanor perform about twice a week & use either a syringe or nothing. . . . Eleanor gives him all he wants he told me. They rather hope for 4 little bootifuls in time. Rich said—the first month or two he had Eleanor every night, frequently two or three times a night & every morning & occasionally during the day. That was great wasn't it. He told me that he & E. were using restraint, but I find that it amounts to waiting till they really want it & then going ahead. In other words having fun anytime they want it. I wonder how long you'd last that way? About one real good wriggle would fix you, I guess. . . .

* Sweet long drawn out.

♥♥♥♥♥

Christine Reid, Belmont, CA, to Bill Reid, Jr., Brookline, MA
27 March 1905

Christine, in good spirits, offered herself fully to Bill, and even apparently kidded Bill about how much she liked California.

You are the dearest boy ever to write so often when you are so busy. . . . It is cold, and I am just comfortably tired, enough to want to snuggle and be "loved." I am going to take a hot bath, and I know after that I shall feel—well—you know how! Don't you wish you were here? I'd guarantee you a good time! Well, it won't be long now, in fact only about a week, less I guess, from the time you get this. Can you be "good" until then? Never mind, dearie, if you can't, I oughtn't to mind I know, but I feel as if "it" all belonged to me, you know. Piggy! I confess. . . .

You asked if I am still nursing! Yes, of course! I must get her east, if possible and I am hoping to keep on through the summer. I shall make a hard fight for it anyhow. . . .

A Debutante's Passion—A Coach's Erotica

Edith and I drove over to San Mateo with Julia this morning. . . We had a fine time. It was a gorgeous day and the view was grand. There's nothing like Cal. after all! (Traitor to my country. Better not tell the family. I do love it here, though. . . !)
I hate the thought of that lonely bed.

♥♥♥♥♥

Christine Reid, Belmont, CA, to Bill Reid, Jr., Brookline, MA
29 March 1905

Christine could hardly wait to see Bill and exchange what they most wanted.

. . . Really I can hardly wait for the time to come when we shall be together again! Last night, I don't know what got into me, but I went over all the delicious details of our meeting and a few spicy details of later on towards bed time. . . . Won't it be bliss though! I feel deliciously embarrassed at the thought. . . .
It has been all I could do to stick it out this long without you! I might make a naughty, naughty pun, but I will refrain, for fear of shocking your tender susceptibilities. . . .
A big hug and kisses and something else (if you want it!) for yourself.

♥♥♥♥♥

Christine Reid, Belmont, CA, to Bill Reid, Jr., Brookline, MA
30 March 1905

Chastised by silence from Bill on loving her in his letter of March 25, Christine was distraught.

Piddie Darling,
The note that came with the check nearly broke my heart, but I deserved it, I know I did. But if I don't get a "loving" one soon, I shall be desperate. I was a bad girl to write you as I did, but I couldn't seem to help it that day. Forgive me, dearie, and love me still, won't you?
Oh Pid! If you shouldn't, I believe I should just collapse. But you do, you must! In future I'll be better, I promise you!
How I wish you were here to take me in your lap and comfort me a little! I am just hungry for you, starving! Please let's never be separated again!
I love you, dearie—
That's all—
C
♥♥♥♥♥

THE CALL TO HARVARD

Christine Reid, Belmont, CA, to Bill Reid, Jr., Brookline, MA
2 April 1905

Soon Christine would be in the East with Bill—at last.

This is the last letter I shall write and you will barely get this before I shall be with you. If all goes well! Your letter from Rich's came last night and I was so glad to get it! My guilty conscience was pinching me and I had a most uncomfortable feeling that you were "mad" with me. I did write you one perfectly horrid letter, and I have regretted it ever since. My dearie boy! I am as wild to see you, and love you and be "loved" and—a few other things! Oh! Piddy, I had a talk with Mrs. Sull the other day, and I am so glad that I don't feel the way she does about it. I will tell you when I see you more about it, but think of never caring one way or the other and rather preferring to go without it! Thank goodness! I'm not built on those lines! I don't see how a woman can really love a man without wanting him to "love" her in the fullest meaning of the word. . . !

I am only too anxious to have all you can give. You dearie boy! I do love you! Read that very long drawn out. . . .

* It won't be long now!

♥ ♥ ♥ ♥ ♥

Christine Reid, note to Bill Reid, Jr., likely Brookline, MA
ca. Spring 1905

Christine had arrived in the East, and one evening she wrote this note to Bill.

Dearest:
I am sorry not to be up, but I have been having a rotten time all day, and am feeling n.g. in consequence. Do come in and see me just for a minute, for I have been looking forward all day long to seeing you.
    I do love you so.
                C.
Come no matter how late it is.

♥ ♥ ♥ ♥ ♥

Christine Reid, note to Bill Reid, Jr.
no place or date

This note might have been written anytime from about 1905 to 1909.

For one whom I love with all my heart and soul—and more & more the longer I live.
    For the dearest, best man in the world.
        X O — O X O O O O   Wifie—

♥ ♥ ♥ ♥ ♥

A Debutante's Passion—A Coach's Erotica

Bill Reid, Jr., Detroit, MI, to Christine Reid, Cohasset, MA
29 August 1905

Christine and Bill had been together since April. Bill decided to visit Fielding H. Yost, the football coach at the University of Michigan. He gives insight into racial relations as they related to William H. Lewis, the first African-American all-American football player in 1892 and a Harvard Law School-educated Negro lawyer in Boston. Lewis, who assisted Reid coaching the Harvard team, would eventually become Assistant Attorney General under President William Howard Taft.

. . . The trip was most enjoyable and many times yesterday afternoon I wished you were along. . . .
    To my great surprise [William H.] Lewis boarded the train at Back Bay—also bound for Detroit. . . . We talked football right along. People look at Lewis in a queer way & I think he felt it a little though I never "let on" & in fact stared back at some of the people with gentle expression. We had supper in the diner together & a "hi beflutin" Boston fellow "looked like Derby" had to sit opposite Lewis. The stranger ignored Lewis' presence entirely & consequently had to keep his eyes glued near the ceiling. It was a very interesting experience all around. I guess that my understanding manner through it all will make Lew. friendlier than ever. . . .
    Yost is a very nice fellow though illiterate & very conceited. By playing the latter card I am getting much of value from him. . . . Lewis is up here at a convention & I may come home with him. Yost won't eat with Lewis & has a Southerner's prejudice. However . . . he is very frank & sensible in speaking of it. We can tide matters over I guess. . . .
    Last night after I was in bed I thought of & prayed for you & the bootifuls & thought also of you alone at Cohasset getting up for Patsy in the night—& my whole heart went out to you. It's only for a couple of nights to be sure—but somehow don't like to be away even that long. I have thought a good deal of our life & relations & can't see why I can't be like other fellows. Well, I love you through & through—sure—. . . .

♥ ♥ ♥ ♥ ♥

Bill Reid, Jr., Detroit, MI, to Christine Reid, Cohasset, MA
30 August 1905

Bill, working hard to make Harvard a winner by beating Yale, discussed football with the highly successful Fielding Yost..

Kind of missed wifie and my cuddle last night. . . .
    Yesterday Yost & I went to a ball game between N.Y. & Detroit & saw several pretty plays as well as a similar number of poor ones. Then we've

had our meals at a different place every time & last night we took a river steamer & rode a couple of hours in the cool. . . .

My trip is already warranted by what I have gotten from Yost. He has told me several things which he has steadily refused to tell anyone else. I have had him so enthusiastic over his own work that he couldn't seem to keep his mouth shut. By asking questions. . . and giving him the impression that he knows it all—he gives me much fatherly advice punctuated with friendly taps on the shoulders. He is the most illiterate fellow—says "he ain't got" or "he hits that man in the slats," etc. But he does know a great deal about football. . . .

I wish I could give you a good old hug & a kind of pressy squeeze. I think of you whenever any pleasure comes that I think you'd enjoy & also when there is no pleasure & I'd like to have you for some. . . .

♥♥♥♥♥

Julia Reid, Belmont, CA, letter to Bill Reid, Jr., likely Cohasset, MA
3 September 1905

Bill's sister, Julia, wanted her brother to know that their father missed having Bill at the Belmont School while he and Christine were in the East.

. . . Papa misses you very, very much. I think he tries not to think much about it, but he seems tired and has said two or three times, "It is about time I was having a little let-up." I think he feels a little deserted and feels that the school really didn't take as much hold on your interest as he hoped it would. . . .

♥♥♥♥♥

Walter Camp, Yale University, to Bill Reid, Jr., Harvard University
10 October 1905

The 1905 football season is probably the most important one in the history of college football, for out of it came a crisis in brutality and morality on the field of play, the creation of the National Collegiate Athletic Association to help reform college football, and the introduction of the "forward pass" to bring about more open play to the game. During the season, representatives of Harvard, Yale, and Princeton, including Walter Camp and Reid, met with Theodore Roosevelt in the White House in an attempt to lead the nation in a more ethical and less brutal type of play. The meeting resulted in a statement, approved by Roosevelt, which was printed in newspapers across America.

I have sent a copy to the president and asked him to notify me of his approval. . . .

"At a meeting with the President of the United States, it was agreed that we consider an honorable obligation exists to carry out in letter and

A Debutante's Passion—A Coach's Erotica

in spirit the rules of the game of foot ball related to roughness, holding and foul play, and the active coaches of our Universities being present with us pledge themselves to so regard it, and to do their utmost to carry out these obligations."

♥ ♥ ♥ ♥ ♥

Ronald A. Smith, ed., *Big-Time Football at Harvard, 1905: The Diary of Coach Bill Reid* **(Urbana: University of Illinois Press, 1994), pp. 272-274, 289.**

9 and 15 November 1905

The tension created by coaching the Harvard football team was nearly more than Bill could take, and he noted this several times in his 440-page diary of the 1905 season. Prior to the Pennsylvania game, he wrote the following.

This being the day of leaving for Philadelphia, I was of course very nervous and in order to occupy my mind as well as possible, I went in town with Mrs. Reid in the morning. . . . at 4 O'clock the men left in a special car from the Square, being cheered off by five or six hundred students. The send off was a most enthusiastic one and pleased the team greatly. . . . [In Philadelphia] when we got back to the hotel I sat up for a long time in order to get so utterly tired out that I could sleep. Dr. Nichols had me take some hot scotch and a warm bath to help the good work along. [The next morning] I made no attempt to get up with the rest of the squad but slept as late as I could, the latter part of my sleep amounting largely to a doze. . . .

[The next week, before the Dartmouth game,] I had various concoctions. . . . [Herbert] White had put one or two sleeping powders in my drink with Dr. Nichols permission, and that was what made me feel so sleepy when bed times comes.

♥ ♥ ♥ ♥ ♥

Wm. T. Reid, Sr., Belmont, CA, to Bill Reid, Jr., Cambridge, MA
1 February 1906

As it turned out, Bill and Christine were together from April 1905 for the next two years, and their letter writing was minimal. However, the question of Bill returning to the Belmont School under the direction of his father and Christine returning to the West coast were much in the elder Reid's thoughts, especially when Harvard' dropping football after the 1905 season was a real possibility because of the brutality and unsavory ethics in the game.

. . . If the [Harvard] board of overseers stand by their decision not to have football next year—which I suspect they will do—then I take your decision [to return to the Belmont School] has got to be made pretty soon. I half wish that they would stick, for I feel very sure, as White does, that it is quite time for you to make up your mind what you are going to do. I have thought a good deal about the pith of White's whole talk with me, and wondered whether it was true or not. It was to the effect that . . . your weakness was your want of decision. One may better make a mistake in deciding wrong than the mistake of not deciding at all. . . .

I should want to turn affairs over to you as quickly as possible, yet I must have a serious interest in things until all debts are paid off. . . .

[Christine had taken the right attitude] that it was her business to fall in with whatever you wanted to do and make the best of it even if it should happen to be something that she did not wholly like; that even if she began by not liking she would end by liking it if you were heartily interested. Nothing could be better than that, except hearty interest to begin with. . . .

♥♥♥♥♥

Bill Reid, Jr., Harvard University, to Wm. T. Reid, Sr., Belmont, CA
26 March 1906

Reid, after coaching the 1905 year at Harvard and losing to Yale, wrote to his father about the problems in returning to the Belmont School and to work under his father again—as he had done from early 1903 to early 1905. He had written earlier to his father, somewhat cautiously as he did not want to hurt his father, and a strong letter came back from his father. Bill claimed that his father was overly sensitive about his previous letter. He was not ready to again submit to his father. In the past year, Bill had kept a 440-page diary on football at Harvard, gone to a White House meeting over football with President Theodore Roosevelt and met with him two other times, dealt with the Harvard Corporation and Overseers over the future of football, replaced Walter Camp as the Secretary of the Football Rules committee, and written articles for several national publications. Orders from his father were not appreciated.

. . . I was then, greatly surprised to see how you took the most unfortunate point of view, in considering everything that I wrote. This very fact—that is simply endeavoring to pretty thoroughly canvas the ground—we have come to an unfortunate misunderstanding into things. . . . My point of view in this whole matter has been this. Our previous experience was not a happy one—at any rate from my standpoint. Before again entering into such an arrangement, it seems to me that we ought in every conceivable way, to sift out all the bumps. If I were dealing with Ginn I should find out clearly, just what was expected of me and just what my relation to him & to others would be. A mistake with Ginn, might cause friction—but friction between one and a stranger isn't comparable to friction between one and his own parents or relatives—since in the former only business ties suffer—while in the latter, family ties and affections are strained. I have then mentioned trifles—or rather what in many cases seem trifles to you—when they mean a great deal to me and to Christine.

I said a few lines above that my experience had not been a happy one—it very probably wasn't evident to you in the degree in which I felt it at any rate—because, at the time I dreaded so much the effect that a complaint or protest might have on you, that I talked only with Mama or else said nothing. There were times however when I said to Christine—"I've simply got to do something else—I can't stand this any longer" to which she would always reply—"Put it through the year anyway & see if things won't right themselves. . .!!

You and I have regarded each other largely as father & boy. . . .

In the matter of the third question—"Your interference in my domestic affairs"—I can see here where you might rightly feel indignant. But here again is where that trouble originated. . . . As far as the baby matter—I felt then & still feel—that it being our baby we should be allowed to bring it up according to our ideas—& that if those ideas don't chime in with those of other people—they ought at any rate to accept our ideas without feeling hurt or ignored. . . .

♥♥♥♥♥

Wm. T. Reid, Sr., Belmont, CA, to Bill Reid, Jr., Cambridge, MA
5 April 1906

Bill had sent his father a letter about the possibility of a partnership. His father repeated Bill's words and felt crushed. This was only two weeks before a much larger eruption, the great San Francisco earthquake, rocked the Belmont School.

. . . The idea of a sub-partnership for you is, as you know, criminally unfair to me. I could not work with or near a man whom I believed to be "criminally unfair. . . ."

♥♥♥♥♥

Wm. Reid, Sr., Belmont, CA, to Bill Reid, Jr., Harvard University
17 April 1906

Bill's father was still upset about Bill's attitude toward working with him and the possibility of turning over the Belmont School to him within a year or two. The letter was written a day before the great San Francisco Earthquake, one that created about $2,000 worth of damages to the chimneys and ceilings of the Belmont School buildings.

. . . I was indignant to have you indicate that you would assume the debt [of the school] if I would turn over the property to you provided it was not serious. . . .

THE CALL TO HARVARD

I have scrupulously kept my hands off from your domestic affairs & I have — oh I said about possibly fifty times—I think a hundred times cautioned Mamma. But in spite of it all you refer to my speaking of the . . . interference when I mentioned the matter just once—never again referring to it in any way. . . .

♥ ♥ ♥ ♥ ♥

Julia Reid, Belmont, CA, to Bill Reid, Jr., Cambridge, MA
5 May 1906

Bill's mother repeated what Bill's father had said to her a couple days earlier.

. . . While he was dressing the other morning he heaved a sigh & when I asked him what he sighed for—he said half jokingly, I am thinking of my sins, & then added—to think of having lived to bring up a family & then to have it all end in failure is mighty depressing. . . .

So your hearty letter of yesterday was full of comfort. . . .

♥ ♥ ♥ ♥ ♥

Bill Reid, Jr., Cambridge, MA, to Harriet Thompson, Providence, RI
9 May 1906

Christine had just given birth to a nine pound daughter, their third child—Christine. One day after, the Harvard governing board decided to again allow football to be played the next season, which would be Bill's last year of coaching football at Harvard. He wanted others to know that their second daughter looked more like his wife than he. He described his own looks, the football question, and the likelihood of returning to the Belmont School in 1907.

. . . [I have an] American eagle nose & elongated Apache face. . . .

With the football question decided on the next day—I felt as though I'd had twins. . . .

We feel that at Belmont, two girls will find it tolerable going where one would find it pretty lonesome. . . .

♥ ♥ ♥ ♥ ♥

Wm. T. Reid, Sr., Belmont, CA, to Bill Reid, Jr., Cambridge, MA
22 May 1906

The negotiations between Bill and his father over returning to the Belmont School were not going well.

I think that your letter of the 13th brought me more sorrow and depression than any other single thing that has come into my life for it

A Debutante's Passion—A Coach's Erotica

seems to me to mark a total failure in my life so far as my relations to you have been concerned. . . .

You say that your coming to Belmont will depend upon my complying with certain conditions and that my agreement to do so must be in writing. . . . I will never do it. . . .

♥♥♥♥♥

Julia Reid, Belmont, CA, to Bill Reid, Jr., Cambridge, MA
27 May 1906

Bill's terse letters demanding his father to put in writing any Belmont School agreement created a schism between Bill and his parents, and Bill's mother had no solution to the divide. The fact that Bill's father had first offered Bill a salary of $1,500 and then lowered it to $1,300 did not help matters.

. . . It is indeed Scylla & Charybidis to choose between, but it seems to me that for you to come up to a possible easing, & perhaps a doing entirely away with the strained relations now existing between you & Papa & between Christine & me—while you not coming lessens the possibility very greatly. . . .

Papa has had a very, very hard year but the school worries, the earthquake, the possible losses next year—all combined have not depressed him as your letters have and as C's attitude has. I suppose Papa has said twenty times that the last three months—"I wish Will were home. . . ."

♥♥♥♥♥

Julia Reid, Lake Tahoe, CA, to Bill Reid, Jr., Cambridge, MA
10 June 1906

Bill's mother had just gone to their Lake Tahoe Summer home when she wrote Bill.

. . . I hated to come away before another letter came from you. I do so long to have you come and let us all with united front strive by unselfish consideration & yielding to create right & happy family relations. As Papa said to me a fortnight ago, nothing would give him more pleasures than to see you & Christine happy in Belmont. Papa, I am sure, will be different just as fast as you & C. will let him. . . .

I am hoping daily for a letter from Christine but I know it is about as hard for her to write letters as it is getting to be for me. Dear child I'd like to put my arms around her & tell her how sorry I am to have made her unhappy. . . .

♥♥♥♥♥

THE CALL TO HARVARD

Wm. T. Reid, Sr., Lake Tahoe, CA, to Bill Reid, Jr., Cambridge, MA
16 July 1906

By summer, the reconciliation between the elder Reids and Bill and Christine was beginning to take place. Bill, only days before, had sent his father $1,000 to help rebuild some of the Belmont School structures damaged by the earthquake.

Your letter of June 10 lifted me as completely as the letter of which I complained depressed me. It was fine in spirit and in expression. . . .

Let us begin at once to plan for next year. We will come up [to Lake Tahoe] as soon as the snow will let us in and stay until Will and Christine want a let-up and then I will go down and take charge, help open school and get it started & then we will stay through Sept. and probably into Oct., and we will at once begin to plan a trip abroad. . . .

I will cooperate and yield upon persuasion but not upon demand. . . .

I do myself an injustice by not explaining. It has always been so and it is a characteristic that I do not defend. It is the same sort of thing that caused me to keep silent and suffer an injustice, when as a boy, by not explaining that a blow that I gave a girl cousin with a cup in a wholly friendly struggle to get possession of it, was an accident, where my mother severely reprimanded me for my meanness.

There is a great danger that in my determination not to make to the charge of your thinking that I am interfering with your home life, you will think me negligent or indifferent or critical for the very reason that I wish to avoid any such charge.

The important thing now is, as you indicated, to call the whole thing off and start anew, with an absolute tabula rasa. . . .

♥♥♥♥♥

Bill Reid, Jr., Cohasset, MA, to Walter Camp, New Haven, CT
28 August 1906

Bill invited Walter Camp, the person most responsible for Yale regularly beating Harvard in football, to come to Cohasset for a couple days, where he could play tennis, golf, and swim.

We are staying in my wife's family's house. . . .

♥♥♥♥♥

Bill Reid, Jr., note likely left at home, to Christine Reid, Brookline, MA
ca. 23 November 1906

Bill was concluding his Harvard football-coaching career, that had drained him physically and emotionally, and he wrote this note to Christine, who had been rather ignored while he was coaching. Soon, they both would be in California to give the Belmont School another try.

201

A Debutante's Passion—A Coach's Erotica

Little Girl:—You can't ever know what a soothing and comforting influence your darling sweetness and affection has had over me, it has been simply ideal. I have never gone through such a trying athletic season before, in my life, and I never could have survived it if it weren't for your love. I know that I haven't been so appreciative as I might—it's not because I haven't appreciated, for I have, but because my mind has been in such a turmoil and I have worried so, that I have been entirely unable to get my mind off of the work.

I love you little one, with all my heart, I adore you, and I am so proud of you that I long to be free so that I may be seen with you more. It's hard—awfully so—to deny myself your company as I've had to do, but it's been for the best and it cannot be helped. Tomorrow night, I shall be free. God bless you & keep you safe.
                              Lovingly, "Bill"
                              ♥♥♥♥♥

Chapter 7

HEADING WEST—AGAIN: "THERE'S A GIRL WAITING TO BE LOVED"

Wm. T. Reid, Sr., Belmont, CA, to Bill Reid, Jr., Brookline, MA
30 December 1906

Wm. Reid, Sr., then 63-years old, told his son that he was looking forward to having Bill and Christine again come to Belmont—that he was in good physical condition and doing very efficient work.

. . .But the greatest factor I suspect has been the let up in the strain between our families. That was just about unbearable, and the thought of having to go out and look for someone upon whom I could shift the burden of the work & to whom I could ultimately turn over the general direction of the school was all but overwhelming. . . .

♥♥♥♥♥

Horatio S. White, Harvard University, to Bill Reid, Jr., Harvard University
19 January 1907

As Bill prepared to continue his California career in helping to administer the Belmont School, the Harvard athletic authorities commended him for his dedication to Harvard athletics, though not success in defeating Yale.

Dear Mr. Reid—The Harvard Athletic Committee, at a meeting held January 18, requested its Chairman to communicate to you its appreciation of the services which you have rendered to Harvard during the period in which you have been acting as head coach of the football team. Those services had not been limited to the technical business of coaching, but have included valuable assistance to the University as its representative on the Football Rules Committee; in collecting and formulating your views and experiences in coaching for the benefit of your successors; and as a spokesman for clean and honorable sport on many public and private occasions. The Committee would cordially bear witness to your fidelity, earnestness, and uniform courtesy, in the execution of your duties in many trying emergencies; and to your successful advocacy of a high standard of conduct and of play, in continuance of the best Harvard traditions.

♥♥♥♥♥

A Debutante's Passion—A Coach's Erotica

Christine Reid, Brookline, MA, to Bill Reid, Jr., New York, NY
ca. 25 January 1907

Christine wrote Bill while he was attending a meeting of the Football Rules Committee in New York City's Murray Hill Hotel. "That man" may refer to Walter Camp, the long-time head of Yale athletics and most important figure on the Rules Committee since the 1870s.

Dearie Boy,
    This is just to tell you that I am thinking of you all the time, and loving you to pieces! The world has been a different place to me since we were "engaged," and I am awfully happy. Don't you think that we are really going to "get there," after all? And don't you think that we are in sight of it?
    There is no doubt whatever but that I am getting to be a perfect baby. It was ages before I could get to sleep last night, and I perfectly hated it. I was freezing cold too! You must never go away again.
    The kiddies are all well. Kitten had her first melons to-day, and such faces. She will learn to like it, though.
    It's snowing hard here, and I hope you are having better weather in New York. Try not get too tired, and don't you dare to sleep with that man!
    My whole heart to you, dearie,
        Yours
        C.
        O X —— O O O X —*
        To be called for Sunday evening.
        ♥ ♥ ♥ ♥ ♥

Bill Reid, Jr., notes to Christine Reid, Brookline, MA
6 March 1907

Christine remained in the East for two months while Bill left to rejoin his father and mother at the Belmont School following two years of coaching football at Harvard. He considered himself a coaching failure, for, even though in his coaching career Harvard won over 90 percent of its games, he lost to Yale in both 1905 and 1906. For Christine, the future would determine if she would live happily when she returned to Belmont. Bill left a couple notes for Christine, the last of which may be Bill's most compelling love letter without details of their sexual life.

I do love you so——-never before so deeply as now. I have treasured you to me as I've gone to and from Cambridge and now as I leave—for eight weeks only—I simply feel my heart, soul and body go out to you.
    I love you awfully, the more so since I told you how I really felt about Belmont, for that evening together tore away every obstacle between us and left us together.

God bless you—dearest I love—l-o-v-e, you.
Cheer up now it won't be long.

♥♥♥♥♥

I have been dreading leaving you—for a long time—and now that the day itself has come, it seems as though I could not stand it. I just ache all over. I know that it is only for a short time before we shall see each other again—but it seems as though it were for ages.

We have grown so much closer during the past two years that even a night away from you seems like a long time, and eight weeks an eternity.

I love you deeply, more deeply than ever in my life before. I feel as though your heart and mine were interwoven, and when I think of going there is a big tug at my heart strings, from all sides.

I am glad that it hurts so to go because it means that we have grown dearer and dearer to each other.

God bless you, you little mother. I have appreciated more and more what a mother you are, and have often to myself thanked God that I had you. I think that reticent as I am, you must have felt my love growing and measuring and must have realized as I do that you have been gradually making me over into more of a family man. It is good, and I love it.

Dear girl, I love you awfully, with all the affection I have, and I don't care where we are, I shall see that you are happy. That means that if we go to Belmont, you are to have things as you want them, and if I can't get them, then we'll come East.

Darling, I shall think of you every minute that we are separated, and shall follow you in love where ever you go, so feel for me when you're lonesome.

Take good care of your dear self and remember that a pair of arms is ready to fold you tight against a living heart—the moment we meet and that a pure love is always surrounding you.
Lovingly, fondly, affectionately, Bill!

♥♥♥♥♥

Christine Reid, Brookline, MA, to Bill Reid, Jr., Belmont, CA
7 March 1907

Christine found Bill's note on her pillow and replied in kind.

My blessed boy,
No one but you would ever have thought of writing all those dear notes, and sending the lovely violets. In spite of you not being here I felt surrounded by you, love, and it was a most delicious feeling. You dear, dear boy, I do love you so! You are the best and dearest husband that ever was!

A Debutante's Passion—A Coach's Erotica

Well, I miss you at every turn, and there is a horrid aching place where my heart used to be. I am glad just the same that you have taken it with you. It was almost more than I could bear when I came here last night, but after feeding the baby, I came back into our room, and found your dear note pinned on my pillow. You darling! How you did think of me! I love you! Can you feel it?
Yours utterly
Christine

♥♥♥♥♥

Christine Reid, Brookline, MA, to Bill Reid, Jr., Belmont, CA
ca. 8 March 1907

While Christine was in Brookline before returning to California, she wrote Bill and suggested that the first night they should take no precautions to prevent a fourth child.

Piddie dearie, don't work too hard and get all done up, will you? I want lots of "loving" when I get there, you know! I think we'll really have to take one chance, don't you. It makes me "thrill at the thought. . . !"

♥♥♥♥♥

Christine Reid, Brookline, MA, to Bill Reid, Jr., Belmont, CA
13 March 1907

Christine remained in the East, her stay to be extended for the wedding of her sister Agnes.

What a good boy you have been to write so often! You would have felt repaid if you could see how I devour every word! I meant to write to you yesterday, but was so "blue" I decided not to. It wasn't very nice of me to feel "blue" because you had arrived in Belmont, and I am not proud of it. I cannot exactly explain just why I felt so, but perhaps you will understand it a little. "You are quite out [of] my reach now," that was it in a way. . . !

Well, I am really to be one of Ag's bridesmaids and am much thrilled at the thought. It means a new dress and hat, so perhaps I ought to refuse, but, as it's probably the only chance I shall ever have and I have never been one before, I cannot resist it. How I wish you could be here. . . !

♥♥♥♥♥

Bill Reid, Jr., Belmont, CA, to Christine Reid, Brookline, MA
14 March 1907

With Christine in Brookline, Bill was lonely when he wrote a 20-page letter to Christine far away on the East coast.

HEADING WEST—AGAIN

... The absolute freedom which you give me in helping myself to your charms is glorious beyond expression—and adds another to the list of endless blessings you have brought me. You are so thrilly when I get in you—too ready to join in that it is simply heaven—& I know it. ...

♥♥♥♥♥

Christine Reid, Brookline, MA, to Bill Reid, Jr., Belmont, CA
16 March 1907

Besides fantasizing about sex, being away had its costs, for letters sometimes were misinterpreted, and both Bill and Christine could become depressed almost immediately by something the other wrote. It is not known who "Bubbles" was or if Bill had met her on the train going West.

You cannot guess how anxiously I am awaiting your first letter from Belmont. So much depends on it! I am wild to hear how it seems to you now, all about our house. ...

Your last letter somehow made me feel awfully far away from you, and it wasn't a bit a nice feeling. Do you like "Bubbles" better than me? She certainly seems to have made a deep impression!

Oh dear! I think being separated this way is perfectly beastly! Do you like it?

Patsy asked me "how do people make people, mama?" But he was quite satisfied when I told him that at first they were very small, smaller than Kitten. ... when I asked him what he wanted for his birthday he of course said "trains," and then added "Be sure to get something for Edith too." He really is the dearest thing. . . !

♥♥♥♥♥

Bill Reid, Jr., Belmont, CA, to Christine Reid, Brookline, MA
ca. 18 March 1907

It was still well over a month before Christine would return to Belmont to be with Bill. He noted how well the house was being furnished and that his salary would be raised by $250 a month. Nevertheless, his mind was on Christine.

... I'm glad you had such a good time at the dance—I'd have loved to see you in your new dress—You do look so sweet in low neck. It would have seemed like old times to have gone with you and to have stolen a few bare neck kisses a la' Beck Hall, and then when we got home I'd have got behind you and felt down over your shoulders—to deliciously soft handfuls—Yi!!!

And now dearest—it's my bed time (would that it were ours) and I must stop. ...

♥♥♥♥♥

207

A Debutante's Passion—A Coach's Erotica

Bill Reid, Jr., Belmont, CA, to Christine Reid, Brookline, MA
                                            ca. 20 March 1907

Bill was writing more regularly than ever.

I miss you. I miss you every minute of the day, and awfully at night. I feel your absence, no matter what I am doing. Oh, but I do love you so—you darling. I worked with a shovel and rake almost all day today and I thought, thought and thought about you and how I should love to go home at night and take you in my lap. . . .

It's morning again—and I love you just as hard—another day of anticipation and thoughts of what I will do when you get here. A kiss, a hug, a passionate squeeze tight against me and at night a sweet * for you. . . .

♥ ♥ ♥ ♥ ♥

Christine Reid, Brookline, MA, to Bill Reid, Jr., Belmont, CA
                                            21 March 1907

It was still over a month before Christine would wend her way West to be with Bill.

. . . Your letters are simply the best things ever, I do love them so! Are you sure you will feel that way when I really get there? I am beginning already to look forward to our "first night," are you? In fact I think I began to do that even before you went almost. Won't it be great. . . ?

♥ ♥ ♥ ♥ ♥

Bill Reid, Jr., Belmont, CA, to Christine Reid, Brookline, MA
                                            24 March 1907

Bill wrote another 20-page letter to Christine, missing her a great deal. He wrote of his first night with Christine in 1902 and the approaching marriage of Christine's sister Agnes.

. . . If Ag and Jim plan to go the Grand Canyon on their honeymoon—they ought to pay a visit afterward. It isn't much farther. Tell Jim to wait a week before he starts because he won't get a chance to give it to Ag. on the train. At the Canyon he'd have excellent opportunities. Poor Ag, she'll be good and sore when Jim has finished the first night. I guess she is likely to refuse him after the first try. I love to think of our first night—and I often think of how darling you were to me—to give me all I cared get—when it hurt you so. You are just about perfect—that's the truth of the matter. . . .

♥ ♥ ♥ ♥ ♥

HEADING WEST—AGAIN

Bill Reid, Jr., Belmont, CA, to Christine Reid, Brookline, MA
25 March 1907

No letter between Bill and Christine was more torrid than this one, but Bill was not sure that the two of them were ready for a fourth child, thus prevention of pregnancy might be necessary.

I have read that letter over and over again, with just time enough between readings to recover from the inexpressible wonder and happiness which it causes me. . . . You could not—sweetheart—have done anything that would bring me on my knees in reverence to you—as you have done in that letter. . . .

As I write, my breath comes in that heavy way which you know so well—when I'm on you, in you, and in the midst of perfect bliss. . . . I ask for nothing in this world—but you. You are everything I most want—nothing else matters. Such a fire as you have silently—perhaps inadvertently—been setting under me—during the past two years—such a hold as you have got. . . .

We've traveled a pretty hard course together and now that the road is smooth I long to glide along with you. . . .

How I'd feel to have you in this room alone with me—first in my arms by the warm bright fire and then in bed. I miss no details, . . . the kissing, your beautiful, warm cheeks and the long, pressing open mouthed kisses, your tongue in my mouth—those delicious and wrenching kisses. Then the kisses with your breasts to mine and hand running up your legs and feeling you—you loving it. Next my putting you on your back on the bed and putting your dress way back—the thrills at the sight of your bare soft legs—and the little crinkles in your clothes. . . . Oh, I have to see them & to think that just a thickness of linen lies between me and heaven. The feeling then as I lie down on you and press in to meet every contour of your body. Oh, but it's perfect—then a hug or two and either a taste or a hurried retreat, for fear of losing control too soon. Meanwhile the gaining desire, the centering of my whole being in the one thought & then the bed itself.

First. . . kisses, hugs, & squeezes & you tight against me. Then, just you there—nothing on. More kisses, kisses all over your face & breasts & then the rarest of all kisses—the heavenly kiss, I do love it so—You are so entrancing and enticing and it is so fine to kiss you where only I may—it's so soft & warm & dear & sweet—I just revel in it. And then I get on top of you—you spread out to give me room & then—I can feel it now—your dear hand takes hold of me—God bless it & helps me in. Ah—as I slip in was ever a fellow happier——heaven. Soft, warm—received with a royal welcome—in, in—I go until we are joined body to body, lips to lips, soul to soul. You wiggle & I watch your delicious movements under me—a rush—a flood of you———- I love it—we have each other—it is heaven on earth—perfection. Oh, girlie I

A Debutante's Passion—A Coach's Erotica

know it all—I can't help thinking of it—perhaps I am weak in this, but I simply can't get over it. . . .

. . . You can't stop me now, and we'll win out this time or bust. . . .

I'd love to take a chance with you—but I'm afraid from the way I feel, that I'd give you such a *ing that it wouldn't be any chance at all—just a dead sure thing. Oh, how I'd like to cut loose in you—such joy & bliss, you love, you—such a dear thing for you to propose.

♥♥♥♥♥

Christine Reid, Brookline, MA, to Bill Reid, Jr., Belmont, CA
27 March 1907

In a letter with several pages missing, Christine revealed her upper-class upbringing and her attitude toward servants, in this case Elizabeth, who would be with them in California.

. . . It is splendid about your salary. . . I am having the time of my life drawing cheques, but I feel as if I was spending a lot of money. This is one good point at Belmont, there isn't so much temptation to spend. . . .

Bill dear, I am sorry to say it but I cannot but feel that you made a great mistake asking Elizabeth to play at the Whist Club. She is a nice girl and all that, but the fact remains that she is a servant and must be treated as such, so she will get a wrong idea of her position. I am awfully sorry that it happened and only hope that she won't be entirely spoilt before I get there. It is a mistake to treat them as in your class I do think, for it only spoils them for their work. However, perhaps there's no harm done, and of course I realize that it was done with the best intentions. . . .

♥♥♥♥♥

Bill Reid, Jr., Belmont, CA, to Christine Reid, Brookline, MA
28 March 1907

Reid's second 20-page letter in three days noted the new furnishings in their Belmont house, including a sofa.

. . . That sofa is going to be one of the greatest pleasures. . . . some day I'm going to * you on it—by the fire. How would you like that?

You ask whether I'll feel so fond of you when you get here. . . ? Well, I guess you'll find me a little worse—if anything—just about what you'll most like on the "first night. . . ."

♥♥♥♥♥

Christine Reid, Brookline, MA, to Bill Reid, Jr., Belmont, CA
31 March 1907

HEADING WEST—AGAIN

Christine was again not looking forward to her trip West, although she would love to be with Bill. Tugging between families had always been present for Christine, and it would not go away.

To-day is Easter Sunday and I wish that we could celebrate it together. As it is, it is a pretty forlorn day for me. . . .

    [Dad and I] have been talking about the trip and it is pretty much of an undertaking when you come down to it. I feel rather appalled! Dad may go as far as Chicago with me and see me safe on board the other train. It is going to be quite complicated taking the Kitten's milk, but I think I'd better do it! The other children will have to do the best they can. I can just imagine how alone I shall feel with all those kiddies. . . .

    This is a horrid letter, but I love you as much as ever all the same. . . .

♥♥♥♥♥

Bill Reid, Jr., Belmont, CA, to Christine Reid, Brookline, MA
1 April 1907

Bill, lonely, wrote another long letter to Christine.

. . . If you were here now you would be mostly undressed lying in my lap in front of the fire, getting hugged & kissed & squeezed & felt—Then I'd take my lovely bride to bed, and we'd both taste of the fruits of a perfect union. . . .

♥♥♥♥♥

Bill Reid, Jr., Belmont, CA, to Christine Reid, Brookline, MA
1 April 1907

Bill was probably right about Christine questioning going West again, but writing about it to Christine may have only increased Christine's anxiety about her move away from her family.

. . . Your letter of March 27th came this afternoon, and I've kept it in my pocket until now, in order to be up here alone with you & the fire. Your last two letters have made me a little glum—partly because of the feeling of dread which seems to cloud up your horizon whenever you think of coming out here, and partly because I feel as though you had found out that you did not really miss me so much after all—and therefore felt that on the whole there isn't much for you here. I suppose that that is all wrong, but I feel as though there were something. . . .

♥♥♥♥♥

Christine Reid, Brookline, MA, to Bill Reid, Jr., Belmont, CA
3 April 1907

A Debutante's Passion—A Coach's Erotica

Christine appeared ready to come West if for no other reason than to take what Bill could offer.

. . . The family were perfectly delighted with your letter to them, and I think feel a great deal more reconciled to my going. It was dear of you to invite them. . . .

Well my dearie, dearie boy, I am loving you hard all the time, so hard that you certainly must feel it at times. You have been such a dear good boy about writing when you are so terribly busy. Take care of yourself, for I want you and "tinker" to be in good shape when I get there. "Tinkerbell" is feeling "right pert. . . ."

♥♥♥♥♥

Bill Reid, Jr., Belmont, CA, to Christine Reid, Brookline, MA
5 April 1907

While Bill thought of Christine, he prepared their home in Belmont for Christine and their children's return, to once again try to make a happy home in California. Bill and Christine's relationship with Bill's parents would be crucial to any success.

When I got home last night from the city I found just the kind of a letter I've been hungering for—one full of love and a delicious passionateness. It set me all a tingle, and I am equal to anything once more. It makes all the difference in the world to me, whether you are with me—and when I feel that you aren't, if it's only for a day—I think—"Well, what's the use. . . ?"

I feel oh so much like "loving" you—great big pressy kisses right on your lovely mouth—tight squeezes breast to breast and wriggles— that's what I'd like to do. And feel you—um, you don't know the sensation of running your hands up the soft legs of a girl like you and feeling her—and knowing from the lusciousness of it all—that she is crazy to lie down, spread out and give you full vent to your passions. I simply can't imagine anything more fascinating than lying on top of you—first with only our bodies from the waist down—touching (while I gloat over the rest of you on my arms) and then lying all over you & kissing & kissing & kissing you. Add to this the absolute exquisiteness of feeling your hand take hold of me and help me in—and the thrills and wrigglings as I go in & in clear up to my body—and it is indeed the seventh heaven. It is enough to make me flood you—just to watch your stomach wriggle and thrust around after I'm in—let alone the feeling itself. I want you to know that I am going to kiss you there long and hard the first night—no matter how you like it. If you knew how I love it—you wouldn't even object. Right up between your legs—it's the softest, sweetest, dearest place that ever was. Just think, I'll be at you in another month. . . .

Papa was up last night & we talked for over two hours. He is planning to go to Tahoe in the first week in June, to return just in time for School. Then, just as soon as school is opened, he expects to return to Tahoe to stay until about October, leaving me alone. He is in dead earnest about getting off, and what I have charge of is really mine. . . . I haven't had a bit of question with Papa over anything. He usually says—"Well, I turn that whole thing over to you—do as you please." That gives me a show & I am taking it.

By August, I shall expect to have everything in ship shape. It's great fun. I know, love, that you'll find it an absolutely different atmosphere. We'll have each other, the children, the house, and our own way of living and doing. Then during the summer we'll be just as close to one another as we can. We'll make little trips & simply devote our time to each other. My finger tips just itch to get around your waist—with a thin dress on—where I can feel your softness "give" as I squeeze. Oh, there are lots of things I have to anticipate doing to you.

Girlie—don't urge me very much to stay in bare. . . . If we do, I know there'll be a baby because I will absolutely fill you full & will get it so far up as to be a sure thing. I love you so for wanting it. . . .

♥ ♥ ♥ ♥ ♥

Bill Reid, Jr., Belmont, CA, to Christine Reid, Brookline, MA
6 April 1907

It was unusual to write two letters in one day. While most of this 16-page letter was devoted to how Bill would make love to Christine, there were sharply focused thoughts on how life in California would be satisfying, not depressing, to Christine in their second attempt to live and work at the Belmont School.

I had no right to expect any letters from you for two or three days, but I "took a chance" at the mail and got a fine letter this morning. . . . I am now a pretty safe proposition for you to tie to, and I am hoping that you will find in me this time—all you want. . . . I feel an awful lot of dear feelings toward you and sympathize with you—something I didn't do much of (at any rate to your way of thinking) when you were here before. This time, I am anticipating having you come right into my arms and lap, to be loved and encouraged when things don't go just right—or else, to get in behind me while I clear up the trouble. No more going it alone—for you—you'll find it all a different proposition.

I have thought a great deal on this subject since you sent me those two or three letters where I felt something was wrong—and I think that I can see how you feel. . . . a dubious future (to you)—not a cheerful prospect to me who lives through difficulties before they arrive. . . . You must not let yourself get depressed about coming, love, because I am positive that we are going to be happier than ever before. I have

213

A Debutante's Passion—A Coach's Erotica

thought every phase of it over and I can't see the slightest possibility of failure. . . . It hurts to feel that you can't feel certain of what I tell you—but it's my fault, I know. Well, new memories & experiences will, I know, obliterate as far as such a thing is possible, all of the old marks. I really love you—this time, and I think I've had enough sense knocked into me to be about 50 % better. . . .

I am crazy to get you down under me—stuffed. . . watching your dreamy looks of pleasure. . . and know that you like it—is inexpressibly dear. . . .

I am glad my letters stir you up—because it will make our enjoyment absolutely perfect when we get together. . . . I adore you saying "I want to be loved, & cuddled &d," that just thrills me all over. Dear, dear girl. . . I love, love, love you.

♥ ♥ ♥ ♥ ♥

Bill Reid, Jr., Belmont, CA, to Christine Reid, Brookline, MA
9 April 1907

Bill was extremely busy and wrote four pages on the difficulties he was having getting rugs that would satisfy Christine in the refurnished home, writing that "I can't get a rug combination that is satisfactory. . . ."

I have been getting so many letters from you lately and they have been in such good spirits that I have walked about on air most of the time. . . .

I have been at this [letter] for two days & two nights. . . . I couldn't get it done—though it isn't a long letter. This morning it was rugs, furniture, etc. with Mama. . . . Before that it was baseball with the 3rd team; after lunch to St. Matthews to see their team play, to see the acetylene gas plant & to see a plumber in San Mateo. Since supper a talk with Howard on the next two or three days work about the place, and so on. Tomorrow morning, I shall go to S[an] F[rancisco] to look at things again. . . .

I'd love tonight to get into bed with you—to get way up in you, & then to lie there and talk with you and hug you & kiss you, in other words to throw my whole self into you. To "come" in you, would seem as natural as kissing you, & both together,—"heaven" itself. You afford so many, many sources for a "good time" that it is simply bliss to be able to "cut loose" with you. You are such a delicious, kissable, huggable, *able little miss that I feel only sorry that I can't do everything that I love to do to you—at the same moment. Kisses to you, dearest all over and big ones in your lovely mouth and delicious breasts and a great big one where none but I may venture. It won't be long now—thank goodness. . . .

♥ ♥ ♥ ♥ ♥

Christine Reid, Brookline, MA, to Bill Reid, Jr., Belmont, CA
10 April 1907

HEADING WEST—AGAIN

What Christine wrote to conclude her letter was what Bill was waiting for.

. . . .Good-bye, dearie boy, remember that there's a girl waiting for a chance to be loved. Will you take that chance? *

♥ ♥ ♥ ♥ ♥

Bill Reid, Jr., Belmont, CA, to Christine Reid, Brookline, MA
11 April 1907

Bill sympathized with Christine's toothaches and dental work, but mostly wanted to tell her how close their house was to completion. Insuring it for $7,000, it was an expensive home.

. . . I don't want to get the bedroom rugs without you, & if we have no rugs the curtains can wait & so if you agree I'll simply get matters comfortable & then we'll do the trick this summer. It will be perfectly delicious to go it together—& at night to be all over, & in each other & love & squeeze & talk it all over. I don't want to buy tables or chairs without you, either. . . .

I love you all the time & feel as though we could almost get along under the trees. . . .

♥ ♥ ♥ ♥ ♥

Christine Reid, Brookline, MA, to Bill Reid, Jr., Belmont, CA
ca. 14 April 1907

Christine, nearly 26 years old, was about ready to leave for her second stay in the West, but would stay until after her sister Agnes got married.

. . . Just think! Ag will be married before you get this, and I shan't see her again. I wish I didn't care so much! I am going to pack her trunk for her to-morrow evening. . . . Her clothes are lovely. . . .

♥ ♥ ♥ ♥ ♥

Bill Reid, Jr., Belmont, CA, to Christine Reid, Brookline, MA
14 April 1907

Bill felt sure that Christine's life at Belmont would be successful working with the elder Reids and little doubted that her sex life would be better than ever.

. . . Papa is letting me do things my own way, and I am enjoying the work immensely. I have absolute control of the men on the place, and give a good many of the permissions and write letters, etc., etc., just as I think best. It's good fun, I tell you. Papa wants to get out of it all, it's very clear. . . .

A Debutante's Passion—A Coach's Erotica

. . . To know that you are crazy for it—to be crazy for it myself and to have such a passionate, pretty and lovable girl to float off into bliss with—is about all I can stand, let alone have her implore me. . . . I feel though we must consider consequences. To tell you the truth, I haven't much respect for your "safe" times when you're normal—I don't think you're ever safe when you're not nursing and that together with the way we shall give it to each other makes me feel almost certain that if you and I simply throw ourselves into each other—we should have another baby. And I'll have more now, but I think it would be something of a catastrophe if you were to be landed just now. I want you to get settled, to meet people, to put in a little time with me exercising, walking, etc. . . . I suppose that you will reproach me for liking to wear something better than to "go it" bare—if you only knew how I long to cut loose with you and to "love" love you in that thorough way which is only possible when we're in bed together, with nothing on and I am way up in you and both of us are wriggling and loving each other for all we're worth. . . . It is a struggle for me to write this, because it would be just heaven itself and I'd so love to make several free trips. . . .

♥ ♥ ♥ ♥ ♥

Bill Reid, Jr., Belmont, CA, to Christine Reid, Brookline, MA
16 April 1907

The wedding of Christine's sister, Agnes, did not mean as much to Bill as to Christine, for Bill was thinking mostly of Christine arriving in California.

. . . Girlie, dearest—if you beg to have me give it to you straight, much more—I shall have to yield baby or no baby—or lose my mind. To feel so hungry for you, to have you implore me & yet to feel that it isn't a safe proposition—just wrenches me all to pieces. . . . What shall I do? I am just as delirious to go it hard the first night as you are and yet I feel as though I were responsible for what happens. . . .

By this time I guess that Jim is satisfied and Ag. mighty sore unless her "stretching" made it easy & then I guess she'd give him all he could stand. . . . Today has meant a great deal more than the wedding day to me. . . . To think that next Wednesday you will be on your way to me makes my heart beat faster. . . .

♥ ♥ ♥ ♥ ♥

Christine Reid, Brookline, MA, to Bill Reid, Jr., Belmont, CA
17 April 1907

Christine remained in Brookline for her sister Agnes' wedding, and following the wedding she wrote Bill.

HEADING WEST—AGAIN

It is now nine o'clock and I suppose there is "something doing" by this time. If only you were here there would be "something doing" in this house as well. Ag was scared to death, I think, and said she was dreading "it," but I tried to cheer her up. She is rather different from me, isn't she? All these last few days I have kept feeling as if it ought to be I who was getting married. . . . A week from to-night I shall be quite well on my way to you. Think of it. . . !

There is a big hug for you, dearie boy, and a big, big, kiss—and something else to follow.

♥ ♥ ♥ ♥ ♥

Christine Reid, Brookline, MA, telegraph post-card to Bill Reid, Jr., Belmont, CA
18 April 1907

The entire telegraph post-card reads as follows:

Remember you have several coming * * * * * I wish I could give them to you now but save them.
Wifie—

♥ ♥ ♥ ♥ ♥

Christine Reid, Brookline, MA, to Bill Reid, Jr., Belmont, CA
21 April 1907

Christine, if not anxious to travel West, wanted again to be with Bill.

It doesn't seem possible that a week from tonight I shall be with you, lying in your arms tight against you! Oh! Won't it be bliss though! It is going to be awfully hard not to teach you to stay in dearie boy, because I do long so to have you and to have it. I shall probably behave very badly and I won't promise to be good about it, because it may be more than I can bear to have you come out. It does seem as if we might have that one time, doesn't it? Do you really care about it as much as I do, I mean does it really make a lot of difference to you? I know it does, but tell me when you see me, won't you. . . ?

Oh Piddie, love me a lot won't you, because it's pretty hard leaving here. Don't think, tho, that I'd stay here with you across the continent. Only be good to me, . . . and love me.

Good-bye my own . . . boy—I will deliver this in person *.

♥ ♥ ♥ ♥ ♥

June 16, '08 —
The Linice —

My dearest husband,
 I am wondering how
you will feel and what you will
think when you read my last letter!
That it will surprise you I have
no doubt! And yet it ought not
to! All day long I have been thinking and thinking and trying to find
an excuse for your talking the you did
with Mrs. Jackson and John for your
apparent [?] I [?] toward her
relation with her husband. Dear,
I really cannot find any! It isn't
as if she were a relation or even a
great friend, for there is absolutely nothing between you to justify your talking so freely on what I cannot
but feel is a most sacred subject. Should you care to have me
speak of our relation to another man,
particularly to one whom I have
not disliked? If not, you should

Chapter 8

MRS. JACKSON—
LAKE TAHOE SUMMER:
"IT'S ALL OR NOTHING FOR ME, DEARIE"

Christine Reid, prior to trip to Lake Tahoe, CA, note to Bill Reid, Jr., likely Belmont, CA

ca. early June, 1908

Following a year in California and a half-dozen years being married, and now with three children, Christine and Bill's life in California was not ideal. Christine was never satisfied leaving the East, and the small irritants of married life grew larger for her and Bill. Their lives would be tested in the next couple months. Christine knew that being separated for a time often radically increased their desire to be together.

As the time draws near for leaving you, my heart fails me and I don't see how I ever made up my mind to do so. I never can realize beforehand how hard it is going to be, and what a terrible large place you hold in my life. At times, when you are provoking (and you know you are sometimes) I try to persuade myself that I don't care, but I do and awfully much too!

In some ways, though, dearie, our separation will be a good thing for us both, for although we are getting adjusted, it is pretty slow isn't it? And when we are not together, we have a chance to think things over, and each realize how much we really do care and how little other things matter. For we do love each other as much as people can, but we still jar and rub each other the wrong way, don't we. . . ? But we're getting there, and far apart each will realize that the other isn't so bad after all. I do love you, dear, with all my heart, and I know that I am interesting enough at times!

Don't worry about the "fellers," I'll take good care of them, and we'll all be there to meet you when you come. Please be careful of your dear old self and don't work too hard.

God bless you dearie, and good-bye.
                Your loving & fat wife—
                      C.

♥ ♥ ♥ ♥ ♥

A Debutante's Passion—A Coach's Erotica

Bill Reid, Jr., San Carlos, CA, telegram to Christine Reid, no address
2 June 1908

Bill likely wanted to quickly respond to Christine's note left for him as she left for Lake Tahoe, and telegraphed her, using code numbers for their bedtime escapades.

Don't give up the ship. All square here. One Four Three.

♥ ♥ ♥ ♥ ♥

Bill Reid, Jr., Belmont, CA, to Christine Reid, no address
8 June 1908

Bill probably thought Christine's comfort in the West was better than it really was.

I wish you weren't going and yet I'm glad that you're going. I shall miss you dreadfully and yet I shall enjoy the fact that you are having a rest and a change. Whenever you leave me, if only for a day, I always feel ashamed of myself for not being a better fellow and husband. You are awfully near and dear to me and your cooperation in the schoolwork is fast bringing us to a rare companionship. I have often thought of it. . . .

♥ ♥ ♥ ♥ ♥

Christine Reid, Lake Tahoe, CA, to Bill Reid, Jr., Belmont, CA
9 June 1908

After Christine told Bill that little Edith accidentally had been hit in the head by a stone thrown by her older brother, Patsy, Christine wished that Bill was at Lake Tahoe.

. . . Oh! it is beautiful up here now. . . just perfection. . . . Edith's little accident has made me feel pretty homesick, and I did so wish that you were here. . . .

♥ ♥ ♥ ♥ ♥

Bill Reid, Jr., Belmont, CA, to Christine Reid, Lake Tahoe, CA
11 June 1908

After a week or so away from Christine, Bill was anxious to be with her again.

It is pretty early to begin talking of what will happen to you when I first get you in bed again—but I think it is safe to say that there will be a pretty far reaching demonstration in the peachy region of my dear little girl. I won't say more—it is too hard on me, but you are in for it—no mistake.

MRS. JACKSON—A LAKE TAHOE SUMMER

 It is hard getting accustomed to an empty house & a solitary bed—but a great satisfaction to think of you all in those beautiful times and to anticipate the good times which we will have together—linked as we will be during them, with the dearest of bonds.
 Good night—little girl—I love you and think of you constantly. . . .

♥♥♥♥♥

Christine Reid, Lake Tahoe, CA, postcard to Bill Reid, Jr., Belmont, CA
11 June 1908

In a short card noting that Edith's head injury was nearly healed and Patsy was having fun with a friend, Stewart, Christine ended her card with their love signal. Another card from Christine near the end of June ended with "One-four-three."

. . . X O O O X O 1-7-3

♥♥♥♥♥

Christine Reid, Lake Tahoe, CA, to Bill Reid, Jr., Belmont, CA
12 June 1908

Life at Lake Tahoe was one of ease for Christine, who had been used to ease for most of her growing up days in the family home in Brookline and the summer home at Cohasset. Still she disliked being away from Bill.

We have been out in the launch nearly all day, and my head is aching. Too much time in the water I guess. . . . Oh! Piddie, do hurry up and come. . . ! It is fine that you have got a new suit. . . . I am glad! I am not quite sure, though, how I like your giving flowers to other women. . . !

♥♥♥♥♥

Christine Reid, Lake Tahoe, CA, to Bill Reid, Jr., Belmont, CA
14 June 1908

Christine closed a long letter telling of fun on the lake and with their kids at Lake Tahoe with the following.

. . . It is fine to think that all is going as you wish it at home, but finer still to think of the time when we shall be together again. I'll try to give you a good time, but of course (?) it will be a great effort on my part!
 Please, dearie, take good care of yourself and don't work too hard.
 Give my love to all, and a great big hug to yourself, from
   Your loving spouse
    C.

♥♥♥♥♥

A Debutante's Passion—A Coach's Erotica

Christine Reid, Lake Tahoe, CA, to Bill Reid, Jr., Belmont, CA
15 June 1908

Christine wrote a blistering letter to Bill for his letter describing a long talk he had with Mrs. Jackson in Belmont. Bill's ability to provoke Christine, and Christine's penchant for jealousy was never clearer. Bill's letter is apparently lost, but it is clear what parts of it disturbed Christine.

Dearest Bill,

If I had answered your letter immediately after reading it, I am afraid I should have written a sharp one and even now I am still awfully upset over it. I loved the first part of it and was feeling very happy until I came to your talk with Mrs. Jackson. In the first place I never have liked her but have tolerated her because Daisy is such a friend of mine and in the second place the idea of you discussing that sort of thing and of swapping filthy stories with another woman is decidedly distasteful to me.

Put yourself in my place and think how you would like it if I sat up until A.M. hr. talking about that sort of thing with, say Herbert White when you were away? Perhaps you will say the case is not parallel, if so, why not? If I remember rightly you were not overly pleased when he let fall one or two questionable things when you were around,—a thing he has never done in your absence. Besides he is one of your best friends and I dislike Mrs. Jackson, and more so now than ever. Would you be willing to have him tell me smutty stories and have me discuss social evils with him,—or any other man for that matter? I must say that I am disappointed in you!

Another thing that I find it hard to believe is your approval of Mrs. Jackson's telling her husband that he might go with any girl he pleased! You consider it generous, do you? Is that's what you could expect of me under like circumstances! Let me disallow you at once! I am not in the least that kind of woman and if that is the kind of thing you admire, you have made a great mistake in marrying me. If I ever knew of your being with another woman, you would never be with me again! And as for my giving my consent to that sort of thing, why, I'd die first! Perhaps you don't care to be loved in that sort of way, but it's the only way I know, and if I can't have you all to myself, why I don't want you at all. I am willing to do my share, but you must do yours, and if I'm not worth more than all other women to you, then your love is worthless to me. This is putting it strongly, but no more strongly than I feel, and I hope in your next letter you will tell me just how you feel about it.

You belong to me, and I know I expect a great deal of you, but I think you will agree that I have sacrificed a lot for you. Oh dear! I do feel so unhappy and miserable, and I would give anything if you were here to hold me in your arms and tell me it was all nonsense. Would you really want me to let you go with other girls? And would you go if I let you?

MRS. JACKSON—A LAKE TAHOE SUMMER

Oh! Piddy dear, please, please tell me that you wouldn't! I feel as if the bottom had dropped out of everything! I am glad you enjoyed your walk with Ethel Jackson so much (at least I ought to be, if I'm not). She is pretty and attractive, but more so to you than to me, I guess. To me she is rather common or cheap, but then—I am perhaps over-particular, and perhaps I like her less because you admire her so much. I am perfectly willing to admit that I am as jealous as I can be, but I cannot help it when I love you as I do.

Perhaps I can care less if I try, and be more like Mrs. Jackson. Shall I try? Be sure to tell me because if I am to get to her state of feelings, not caring whether her husband is with other women or not, I'll have to begin immediately. How about her with other men? Of course it must work both ways, and how would you feel about that part of it?

Oh! Piddy, if you were only here, I'd kiss and hug you and love you to pieces and just make you say you didn't want any one but me! Hurry up and write to me again. I shant be happy again until you do. All day long I have just brooded over it, and my heart just aches. I cannot get over it, or understand how you could have written as you did, and I just cannot bear to think of you sitting up and talking with that damned woman! I hope she won't come up here, I never want to see her again! Please don't discuss me with her any more! I hate her now!

It's no use my writing any more to-night, I get worse and worse. Do you love me or not? I mean the way I love you?

Yours still, C.

♥♥♥♥♥

Christine Reid, Lake Tahoe, CA, to Bill Reid, Jr., Belmont, CA
16 June 1908

Christine stewed over her recent letter for some time and waited for Bill's response.

My dearest husband,

I am wondering how you will feel and what you will think when you read my last letter! That it will surprise you I have no doubt! And yet it ought not to! All day long I have been thinking and thinking and trying to find an excuse for talking as you did with Mrs. Jackson, and also for your apparent point of view toward her relation with her husband. Dearie, I really cannot find any! It isn't as if she was a relation, or even a great friend, for there is absolutely nothing between you to justify your talking so fully or what I cannot but feel is a most sacred subject. Should you care to have me speak of one relative to another man, particularly to one whom I knew or disliked? If not, you should not have allowed her to talk as she did with you. What you said to her I don't know, and perhaps it's as well that I don't, for of course no woman would tell that sort of thing without embarrassment.

A Debutante's Passion—A Coach's Erotica

Oh! Piddy dear, I just cannot get over it, it has haunted me more than you will ever know perhaps, and I cannot but feel that if you make light of it, our love for each other cannot mean to you what it does to me. You are all in all to me, and if I cannot be that to you, I don't wish to be anything at all. Of course my being away from you makes it all the harder to bear, and a heart ache is the worst pain I know. How can you talk in such a way with that woman, I cannot see anything to justify it? Dearie, do you really see any generosity in giving up what you do not care for? Do you think that if Mrs. Jackson really loved Mr. Jackson that she could bear his being with other women, and even wink at it? Is that your idea of love?

Let's have this out now and for all for I never dreamt that you thought a marriage like that ideal! Is my consent all that stands between you going with other women? That's what your letter implies, and yet I cannot believe that you mean that! It's all or nothing for me, dearie. . . . This is the way I feel about it and I am going to make it clear to you now and then we will bury the whole thing if possible. Ever since we were married I have tried to meet you at least halfway, and have tried in every way to do the square thing by you. You say yourself that I am "deliciously responsive" and don't you think that ought to mean a great deal to you? Oh! Piddy, I am so hurt and sore that I hardly know what I am writing! If only you were here to put your arms around me and tell me you do love me, in the only way I want to be loved!

To continue I cannot but feel that having at least tried and in a response, I hope, succeeded in doing the square thing by you, I have a right to expect more of you than perhaps some other women might be entitled to expect of their husbands. What do you think? Have I the right to expect you not to discuss what I might call the relation of the sexes and not to tell indecent stories to other women or not? Does it seem to you that I am asking too much of you or more than you are willing to give? It hurts me, terribly to think of the impression of yourself that you must have left with Mrs. Jackson when you probably told her you thought she was so "generous" to let Mr. Jackson go with other women! "Generous"! That word fairly rankles in my soul! Of course the only conclusion she could come to would be "That's the way he would like to have his wife feel!" I fairly boil at the thought and I never want to set eyes on her again! She had no business to talk as she did to you and you had no right to let her! I cannot, cannot get over it! Oh! But it hurts!

As for Ethel's slapping that officer, you know as well as I do or you ought to, that no man, unless he is a perfect cad, will say "insinuating things" to a girl, unless something that she has said or done seems to justify it. Now I don't say that Ethel did anything, . . . but I do say that in all probability it was her own fault and if I were in her place I'd be far too ashamed ever to mention it particularly to a man, I scarcely knew! That is my point of view!

MRS. JACKSON—A LAKE TAHOE SUMMER

As for Mrs. Jackson's being told those society things by young men! Well, just imagine any young man telling my mother or yours anything like "I couldn't have seen more if I'd paid for it?" Can't you see how that reflects on Mrs. Jackson! I hope she won't come up here with Daisy! I don't see how I could ever bring myself to speak to her, and if I acted as I felt I'd stick a knife in her! She little knows, I suppose, the harm she has done! But if she'd tried, she couldn't have hurt me much more! I despise her from the bottom of my soul!

Now Piddy, perhaps I am taking this too hard, but anything that concerns you does go mighty hard with me as you know and of course I have only what you wrote me to go on. I always knew that Mrs. J. was dirt cheap, but I begin to think now that that is putting it too mildly and that she is perhaps really a bad woman. Of course, I cannot say what her purpose was, or if she really had any, in telling you that nasty story, but I should think her action in so doing was decidedly questionable! If I did not have infinite faith in you, I should be very much more wretched than I am now, if possible.

Where were you when you had this "fine long talk?" Oh! Bill dearest, I don't see how you could, when I was away, and you must have known I wouldn't have liked it? Tell me all about it dearie, you are all mine aren't you?

Perhaps I am foolish, but I cannot think so and would you want me not to care or to feel less strongly about it?

I'll try and write a letter on other lines to-morrow. All is going well here except with me.

Love ever
C.
♥ ♥ ♥ ♥ ♥

Christine Reid, Lake Tahoe, CA, to Bill Reid, Jr., Belmont, CA
17 June 1908

Christine's deep love and some emotional instability did not mix well with anger, a trait Christine admitted she had early in their relationship when she had become engaged to Bill.

My Dearest, sweetest and best-beloved,

All day long I have been struggling with an almost imaginable temptation to come home to you! If I could only, only be with you for even a short time I know the dreadful ache in my heart would stop! Last night I hardly slept at all and have been feeling sick and Oh! so miserable all day! If I could only get to you, touch you, and be held in your arms it would be all right with me again! I never realized before how it was possible to suffer so much! Dearie, am I a perfect little fool? Tell me I am, for I cannot let the leastest part of you belong to any one else for a moment. I do love you so!!

225

A Debutante's Passion—A Coach's Erotica

It has been a cold, raw day and the wind has stirred up my teeth and they have ached, and that has not added to my pleasure. It must be only neuralgia and I hope it will be all right to-morrow. The wild idea of using my teeth as an excuse to fly to you have been running through my mind all day, and it has been a fearful struggle to resist. I have caught myself planning just how I would steal in on you—Would you be glad to see me? How can I ever wait to see you until you will come up here? Oh! Piddy, what shall I do. . . ?

♥ ♥ ♥ ♥ ♥

Christine Reid, Lake Tahoe, CA, to Bill Reid, Jr., Belmont, CA
19 June 1908

In a lengthy letter of all the activity at Lake Tahoe and how well the three children were doing, Christine told Bill what was mostly on her mind.

Lately a certain definition of falling in love has been in my mind a great deal. I need to think it rather exaggerated, but now I know it isn't. It is this—"Falling in love is like running a dagger into one's heart, and then presenting the hilt [handle] to a man to turn and twist as he will." Dearie, you've been turning and twisting your dagger almost more than I could bear these last few days. It will seem funny enough to you to hear that your old "Fatty" cannot sleep and that the very sight of food is distasteful to her! But such is the case nevertheless, and most uncomfortable it is too!! I have never been like this in my life before, and I don't need to tell you that I never want to be again.

Your letter written on the 17th came to-day, and you can imagine how eagerly I devoured it, after a two days' fast. I took to the woods with it, and after reading it, re-reading it, and reading it again, I lay there and dreamed and "loved" you for over an hour. . . .

I have wondered and wondered what your answer will be to my letter. I need not specify which one! I ought to get it tomorrow and I shall be almost afraid but oh, yes, eager to read it when it comes. That you will be surprised at mine, I know, but what more, I do not know. Have you any idea at all when you will come? Make it soon, Piddy, won't you. This being away from you, gets harder and harder, and I never realized how hard it is going to be beforehand! Do you miss me as much as I miss you? I don't mean the fellers but just me! Do you? When you come, I want to go off alone with you without even Patsy. You used to like to be alone with me, do you still? or do I have you? I have sometimes felt that I did. Let's be "pale" again as we used to be when we were engaged, and we'll do some climbing together. That is, if I feel stronger when you come than I do now. I am as weak as a rat at present.

My dearest boy, my heart is as strong as ever, and it beats and beats for you. Come soon—Ever yours, C.

♥ ♥ ♥ ♥ ♥

MRS. JACKSON—A LAKE TAHOE SUMMER

Bill Reid, Jr., Belmont, CA, to Christine Reid, Lake Tahoe, CA
19 June 1908

Bill tried to sooth over the real hurt of Christine because of Bill's conversation with Mrs. Jackson by saying how much he would like to love Christine in person.

. . . Poor little girl I'm awfully sorry that I unwittingly caused you such pain. I could not stand the thought of your having to wait another day before knowing how I felt and so I rode to San Carlos on a wheel just after nine tonight and telegraphed you all that I dared say in a public message. . . .

Little girl, you have no more cause to be jealous than a post has. . . . I have been absolutely true and loyal to you in every way. . . .

You silly little love—I am all yours—every bit—you needn't worry about that. Come over here and let me show you. Get into my lap, let me get my arms around you so that I can press your soft, warm breasts to mine—with coat and vest unbuttoned to get you right against me. Press your warm lips hard and in relaxation against mine and let me breathe into you as I hug and squeeze you, the passionate fondness I feel for you. Feel it, as it pours into you—look into my eyes and read them and see how they glory in you. Let me get my hand up your legs, let me get against you everywhere I can and do all I can to become a part of you. "If this be forgetting, you're right dear and I have forgotten you then."

But this isn't enough—I must be in you—would that I could be now. Way, way, way in and oh if I could only be in, in a dozen different places, one doesn't express it all. What wouldn't I give to have you come passionately over on me wanting me to do it to you and exciting me to distraction. How I'd kiss your mouth, breasts, and oh - - - - - - - -, I loved you saying that you felt then more as though "you owed me than at any other time"—for I just love to do it; it makes me feel as though I were almost a part of you physically. You couldn't have said a lovelier thing to me. I'll think of it day after day. And after it all—this revelry over your dear self and your abandonment to me—to think that there is still left the perfect feeling that comes when I slip in, come down on you and snuggle, I too, have never enjoyed you as I have lately particularly when you lie sideways in my arms, lips to lips, breast to breast my pulsating self way, way in, the dearest sweetest spot on earth—my own spot too—and our hands playing with each other—your holding deliciously my only outside parts—or hugging——-Oh, it is simply perfect. Its no use talking. I can't help thinking about it all & talking about it. If I could only leave off everything and just give it all to you, leave it in, lots of it and way up. I'd say that nothing could ever compare. I'd love to - - - - - you in about ten different ways, indeed until you were almost dizzy with it and could hold no more. I love, love, love to do it, and you know how so well and love it so too that I dwell on the thought all the time. . . .

A Debutante's Passion—A Coach's Erotica

I suppose your jealousy really does hurt you, but I love it even though I've never tried to make you feel that way. . . .

I've tried to set you at rest on that point but seem to have failed. Just what "part" of me have you figured out belongs to anyone else? I suppose unless I can somehow wriggle my whole self up in you, you will never feel safe. . . .

I cannot feel now the effects of my loving you—for in "his" droopy condition he is disappointed. . . . I wish your hand could squeeze him and your fingers rub it over—it is such a perfect feeling.

It will be hard to wait—awfully hard but deliciously tantalizing. I want you without anything on when I come—it is so absolutely sweet to touch you all over. No clothes on you—for me. . . .

Good night you darling—I love you all I can & more—and only you. I am yours now and for eternity. God bless you all—and God watch you for me.

Lovingly and devotedly,
"Piddie"
♥♥♥♥♥

Christine Reid, Lake Tahoe, CA, to Bill Reid, Jr., Belmont, CA
20 June 1908

The Mrs. Jackson incident was in Christine's thoughts, and she was sorry that she had taken it so to heart.

. . . I am a rotten skunk to have hurt you, and I'll try to make it up to you when you come. Oh! Hurry up and come, Pid, nothing is worth while until you do. . . . I've gone back to the days of our engagement or before and feel the same old thrills and pangs of jealousy as I used to then. I do pity you for marrying such a jealous little spit-fire, but you have and I'm afraid the sooner you realize it and make the best of it the better for us both. . . . You have never given me any real cause for jealousy. . . . Perhaps, though, you will admit that my being, well—call it "indulgent" and "responsive" will make up a little for my unreasonableness, and there will be plenty of that sort of thing on hand for you when you come. . . . When you do, I will really let myself go for once—and you'll be shocked and perhaps frightened, see if you aren't?! Do you dread it. . . ?

My blessed boy, let's forgive and forget and I for one, love you harder than ever if possible. You'll find a fiancée and a wife too when you come!

♥♥♥♥♥

Christine Reid, Lake Tahoe, CA, to Bill Reid, Jr., Belmont, CA
22 June 1908

Christine was nearly ready to bury the Mrs. Jackson episode, but not quite.

MRS. JACKSON—A LAKE TAHOE SUMMER

The world looks very bright to me again, and life is once more well worth living. When you come we will go over it all just once and then we will bury it forever, and in the meantime, let's bury it temporarily. I do want to ask just this once more, though, because you haven't answered it—How would you have felt if our positions had been reversed and I had talked and heard such stories from Herbert White. . . !

♥♥♥♥♥

Bill Reid, Jr., Belmont, CA, to Christine Reid, Lake Tahoe, CA
22 June 1908

The Mrs. Jackson crisis appeared to be over, or nearly so.

Two letters today and such dear letters. . . . Everything looks right again. . . .
What you said so deliciously in your second letter made me yearn to get my arms around you and hug you, one of the standing up kind where we press hard together down there while we squeeze, hug and kiss up above. You got me so hot that I was already to give it to you—indeed I doubt whether I could ever get clear in before I would have come. It was a delicious feeling, though I'd liked to have laid you down and gone the limit with you. It is such fun to lie on top of you, clear in—as far as I can reach with the hardest pushing—and sort of fool with you—feel your breasts, kiss them, kiss you, rub against you, get up on my elbows look down & see first our two navels right against each other—then me, absolutely buried in the dearest, sweetest, narrowest little spot—and then our legs wrapped round each other. Oh, girlie, with all that for me backed by your love and faithfulness——You can be as jealous as you want.
I love you in ribboned underclothes and light weight dresses where I can feel you through or can run my hands up your legs or squeeze you against me & feel your soft body. . . against me. . . .
If I get you out in those woods—I'll have your dresses up a whole lot—kissing you, feeling you and - - - - - ing you—Yum—does that last sort of make you wiggle? It does me. We'll just let each other do anything to each other and we'll bind ourselves together as never before. . . .
I think I'll talk news a little now because like the birds and trees it is a little let up and there isn't much more of a "rise" possible in me without a deluge. . . .
I'm yours, all yours & forever. No other girl has a look in. Wish I could get into bed with you—I'd just *fuck* you to pieces. I had to write it—though I made it moderately small. Oh, if you only will cut loose to your limit when I come—afraid!!! so I'll just about pass away if you can improve on our latest good times. . . .

♥♥♥♥♥

229

A Debutante's Passion—A Coach's Erotica

Christine Reid, Lake Tahoe, CA, to Bill Reid, Jr., Belmont, CA
24 June 1908

Christine, who never did get along well with her mother-in-law, blamed her for keeping Bill at the Belmont School, and she wanted Bill's father and mother to cut short their vacation so that Bill could come to Lake Tahoe soon and for a longer time.

All goes smoothly up here and happily too, except for the fact that you are not here. These last two days have been perfect, as to weather. Yesterday after-noon Miss Webb and I took the fellers for a walk over to Blackwood Creek. . . .
    I would be ready for you now if you were here, Pid, and indeed your letters do make me wiggle. . . . We wouldn't need any Vaseline. You'll have to hurry up if you are going to want to kiss me, because if you don't, I am afraid I couldn't allow it. It would be altogether too much of a good thing. My! I wish you were here right now. . . .
    Your mother said that she had thought that they would go back the first of August and let you come up then. I was mad, but had sense enough not to show it. But I said that I thought you ought to have a longer vacation than that. . . . You didn't have any last year. . . . I was silly enough to think that if we all came up here, you'd come soon after us, but—well, you've got to. They've gotten along with Mr. McDougal before and they can again. Anyhow, you've got to be up here on the ninth. I am still baby enough to care about my birthday, and I'll be miserable and wretched if you aren't here! There. . . !
    We'll make up for our separation when you come—it'll be a good one!

♥ ♥ ♥ ♥ ♥

Christine Reid, Lake Tahoe, CA, to Bill Reid, Jr., Belmont, CA
26 June 1908

Christine told Bill how much she missed him, and thanked him for sending candy.

. . . We must sleep out of doors one night anyway. I do want to lie in your arms just out under the stars. We would love to look back on it and for one night it would be delicious. . . .
    O   A good tight one.

♥ ♥ ♥ ♥ ♥

Bill Reid, Jr., Belmont, CA, to Christine Reid, Lake Tahoe, CA
26 June 1908

Christine had been angry with Bill for telling stories with Mrs. Jackson, and Bill replied to her question whether he would be upset with her for

MRS. JACKSON—A LAKE TAHOE SUMMER

staying up and talking with Herbert White. What Bill really wished is that Christine was with him rather than at Lake Tahoe with her father- and mother-in-law.

. . . You have asked me how I would have felt if our positions had been reversed and you had talked and heard such stories from Herbert White. I should not have liked it for several reasons. First, Herbert, although a great friend, is certainly pretty lively when it comes to girls, their legs, shapes and faces and he would be sort of sizing you up as he talked which was not the case & could not be with me & Mrs. Jackson. She does not attract me physically any more than Miss Bennett or Bonnie Bunnelle—and I'd as soon sleep with a piece of pipe as either of them. Second, I do not like the idea of a young girl talking freely with men any how. You may not make a distinction there but I do, as I do also in a number of other points relating to boys and girls. The smoking question for instance—in this practice of having girls learn Spanish dances and then display their legs, etc. to audiences. It's all wrong & any girl who does it ought to know that any fellow of any virility in the audience has had flit through his mind what her probable motions etc. would be. Third, the limits of conversation cannot be arbitrarily set. . . . It's a question of the understanding that exists between people that determines the effects of a given line of talk, not so much the subject or wording.

I do not think that the story part in this case was justifiable—though if with anyone—it was with Mrs. J. I am sorry for this and will not do such a thing again. But I am heartily sick of the whole thing and want to drop it. It has caused me more worry and heart wrenching than the whole thing is worth. . . .

. . . I am sleeping in Papa's room now in his big bed. It is awful to have such a splendid place to lie with you, go empty. We could roll about as we pleased, it's so large. It would be fun to roll over with you with him in, letting him come out if he happened to . . . but sticking him in again at the first opportunity. I wish I could just let go in you without reserve—the warmth & passion due to your delicious legs and their delicate juncture is something which calls for a response of utter abandonment. I ought to stick it way up & then wriggle myself up to "bliss" & then just give up to revelry in you.

Well—it's now midnight. . . I want awfully to see the fellers—I miss you and them constantly. . . .

♥♥♥♥♥

Christine Reid, Lake Tahoe, CA, to Bill Reid, Jr., Belmont, CA
28 June 1908

A Debutante's Passion—A Coach's Erotica

Christine was in the right mood for Bill and told him so.

. . . Our first night together! I have never felt so much like a bride, as I do now, but it's nice to think that I'll have only the terrific pleasure and none of the pain. Won't it be delicious though, Pid. . . ?

I am getting delicious and brown, really like a Cohasset brown, and, if I do say it, it's not unbecoming. Have you any idea when you will come. . . ?

♥♥♥♥♥

Christine Reid, Lake Tahoe, CA, to Bill Reid, Jr., Belmont, CA
29 June 1908

Christine wrote hurriedly and to the point.

. . .This is just a little "loving" to let you know that my heart is full of you and that I long for you always. . . .
   *   I wish I could give it to you right now. . . .

♥♥♥♥♥

Bill Reid, Jr., Belmont, CA, to Christine Reid, Lake Tahoe, CA
30 June 1908

Bill discussed many things, but one thing was really on his mind—Christine, as their wedding anniversary would arrive at about the same time this letter would.

I've been thinking hard all day of my dear little nut-brown bride, rushing over and over again that I might be with her on this our sixth anniversary and planning in a most tantalizing way what I'd do to her if I had her. I just love you all browned up and after a separation of a month or so I know full well what a delicious passion you'd arouse in me. The first thing I'd do I think would be to hug you and kiss you until I got your cheeks red hot—then I'd hug you in my lap and then I'd lay you on the bed, pull your dresses up, kiss you all over your legs and again and again in the dearest spot of all and finally lie flat on you bending in hard against you so as to feel you and have you feel me. I'd rather have you stripped before giving it to you, but I don't think I could wait all day. If my two "girl teasers" ache now, with just writing this, what would happen if we were alive together and I knew that you wanted it as much as I? Girlie, dear, your letter tonight on top of the happiness I already felt just makes me ache in one place for you and get awfully sticky in another. Why can't I fuck you!! It's no use I can't just say "do it" to you—it doesn't half express the squirming and wiggling that I would do if I once got at you. The great difficulty which I face constantly is how to do enough different things to you at the same time, to come anywhere near expressing the passion that all but consumes me.

I guess you'll find yourself on your back about four times during the first morning, a couple of times in the afternoon & about a steady hour of playing with you, kissing you, feeling you & rolling around with you—at night. I don't care how juicy you feel or are—I just love to get down there & sticking my tongue up as far as it will go—it is a most delicious sensation. The ends of my fingers fairly itch to feel you legs and breasts & my breasts, & stomach sort of ripple up with ecstatic thrills at the thought of being pressed hard against you. If I could only just shoot it all right into you & leave it there—what else could we want?

It's a great delight to talk about wanting to come as I do—and know that there is a girl just as crazy to have you—a girl who'll strip for you & do everything she can to add to one's passion—oh, it's glorious. I suppose I'm a regular brute in my passion to get to you—but I do love to fuck you. Nothing compares with being in bed with you—both stripped, me, in so, that our fur is all rubbing together—our arms around each other & our mouths flattened against each other————-and then the dizzy swirl as my boy cream comes rushing up to squirt into you in hot pulsating doses——It is simply Bliss, inexpressible. I am lucky in having a pretty (a beauty), passionate, well built, healthy, loving girl to go to—and you darling, I appreciate it. I love to feel your breasts, to run a hand up your legs & to have you feel me all over. We were made to match—that's all there is to it. I am crazy for you.

The six years have gone fast to me and I am so happy with you. We have had our squabbles & perhaps the flitch of bacon doesn't belong to us but never the less we've had a good time. I'd like to just hug & hug you today to show you how I love you & how happy I am that I've got you.

I have thought a good deal about an anniversary present & it occurred to me that perhaps you'd rather have us order the Davenport, cover & all, as soon as you get back—than have some other thing & not have the Davenport. There is one at Plum's which is just what we want. The springs are fine, upholstered arms, good deep seat, fine height & good fit. If you say so I'll have them reserve it for us. It would be about $140.00 all upholstered & everything. If you'd rather have china plates like Mrs. Hicking, all right, or if there is anything else that you really want—just tell me. I've racked my brain & can find no other solution. Tell me just what you feel. How I'd love to be stripped with you—seven inches up you—in your arms, breast to breast & lip to lip, drinking in the joy of complete abandonment to each other & absolute satisfaction.

I can't tell yet when I can come. I've ordered the sheets ads. printed today. I've investigated the smoke stack matter & am about ready to let a contract there. The tennis courts & roads are all oiled, the uniform question settled, and tomorrow Gilly comes down about the water

A Debutante's Passion—A Coach's Erotica

closets and the hot water heater. I am keeping things moving at a fast clip, I tell you. Would you rather know when I am coming—when I know myself—or would you rather have me just appear? I'll do either way, as you wish.

I received your balsam post card—but it came with the "heart breaker" & I hadn't the spirit to acknowledge it. I wasn't in the mood for it at all—and so simply let it go by.

Well, the oil is on the courts, 2800 gals. & today the contractor began easy work on them preparatory to rolling them with a hot roller. They look well & the contractor is enthusiastic. . . .

Miss Handlin comes down Friday night to talk school with me. She is just back from the East—Don't worry—I'll not elope!!!!

The batch of fish have just come & are beauties. We shall eat them tomorrow. I shall send one to Mrs. O'Neil. It is a good chance to pay her a little compliment that is well earned. . . .

I am going to sleep out of doors with you—only we must go to sleep with me stuck in you. The naps I've had with you that way are among the dearest recollections I have. To do it to you even while we sleep is a delicious thought. . . .

I am glad that the fish are biting & that you are having some luck. I hope that you will get good hauls every time you go out. How would it do for us to go out in the new boat & have a feeling time. It would be great to hear the lap of the water & to feel up each other legs. — Yi, I do love your legs. . . .

The children's enquiring for me is delightful to me. I hope they will all remember. I'm a little afraid of Puss. She must be great hugging.

Poor Yale certainly "caught it" this year—it did me good. I was awfully glad for Wray because this is the first crew he's had upon which he's had 4 consecutive years. It will take the same length of time to do the football, too. . . .

Gee, how I'd push it up—if I had the chance. If you've got any ribbon garters I wish you'd wear them when I come—I love to feel them on you & to take them off or put them on. You've got to let me do whatever I want to you without protest—this time. . . .

♥♥♥♥♥

Christine Reid, Lake Tahoe, CA, to Bill Reid, Jr., Belmont, CA
1 July 1908

For Bill and Christine to be separated for their wedding anniversary was not unusual but was sorrowful.

To-morrow is our wedding anniversary, our sixth one, and I must send you a little message on the eventful day. . . . I wish you were going to be here, so that we might have a celebration worthy of the occasion! I'm sure that we could, and would! We'd take a nice tramp together in the morning, go out in the launch in the after-noon! That in the evening—well! that would be the very best of all! Can you imagine anything better? We'd just love each other to our hearts' content and I'd be "responsive"—never fear. . . . !

Piddy, aren't you going to come for my birthday? I shall be disappointed if you don't. . . .

♥♥♥♥♥

Christine Reid, Lake Tahoe, CA, to Bill Reid, Jr., Belmont, CA
                                                                    3 July 1908

Christine responded to Bill's loving letter of June 30th.

Your anniversary letter was certainly a dandy, and I did love it, but it also was most suggestive, and stirred me up more than was comfortable when you are so far away! A most brilliant idea has come to me, but whether you will think it is feasible or not remains to be seen. However, it won't do any harm to tell you it, anyhow. It would be terribly hard to wait all day for our *, so I suggest we take a comforter and a pillow, find a most secluded and sequestered spot, undress as much as we dare and proceed! What do you think? It would be too awful to have our first —— spoiled by too many clothes and yet,—can we wait until night? You must decide the all-important question, because everything is to be just exactly as you want it. See! Piddy, I must confess that never in my life before have I thought about "it" so much! It's really disgraceful—but tantalizingly delicious! I hope we shan't look too suspicious when other people are around. . . !

. . . I wished all the time and so hard that you were with me, and that we could both be looking forward to a good time that night. Yes, dearie, I may as well confess that I am dying to have you fuck me. (Doesn't it look terrible written out? Do tear up this letter.). . .

There is one thing that is causing me a great deal of worry!?!? You see I go to bed very early up here, and the great question is shall you be ready to go when I am? It troubles me a good deal, especially the first night, for of course I shouldn't want to make you come if you didn't want to. That "make you come" sounds rather suggestive! Well, I guess I'll "make you come" in me. You can come in me long, all night. . . !

♥♥♥♥♥

Christine Reid, Lake Tahoe, CA, to Bill Reid, Jr., Belmont, CA
                                                                 ca. 3 July 1908

Christine again responded to Bill's anniversary letter.

My darling "naughty boy,"
    Suggestive or worse as it was, I want to say that I adored your

235

A Debutante's Passion—A Coach's Erotica

anniversary letter! Thrills ran all over me and I could feel myself getting moist and open for you! You were a perfect darling to write me that dear letter and you may do just whatever you please to me when you come. Strange as it may seem I rather look forward to it.
   * It will be better than it looks.

♥♥♥♥♥

Christine Reid, Lake Tahoe, CA, to Bill Reid, Jr., Belmont, CA
4 July 1908

This Fourth of July letter suggested another reason for Bill to hurry his trip to Lake Tahoe.

There is one thing that I forgot to tell you which I hope will hasten your arrival. That is that I am due on the seventeenth, and that if you don't want to run any risks of having all of our fun spoiled, you must get here before that, long before it because I might come early. Just imagine, Pid, how lonely it would be for you to arrive and find me that way. . . !

Will you please bring all of my nightgowns that you can find. . . . . The ones I brought up are tearing to pieces, and would never stand the strain of being in bed with you. . . !

♥♥♥♥♥

Christine Reid, Lake Tahoe, CA, to Bill Reid, Jr., Belmont, CA
5 July 1908

Christine just learned that Bill would arrive in Lake Tahoe for her 27th birthday on July 9th.

Your letter came this morning, and I am in the seventh heaven of delight in consequence! I was down under the tree reading it as I always retire to the woods so as to be alone with your letters, and when I came to where you said you were coming and what your mother had done, I simply tore up to the house, rushed in and grabbed her! Wasn't it dandy of her, though! I feel as if I know her so much better since we have been up here, and she certainly is a corker. There hasn't been one incident's friction between us all the time, and as you know how hard I am to get on with, that says a great deal! Well, Piddie, to think you will really be here on the ninth! It's too good to be true. . . ! If you approve of my outdoor scheme, I think I will wander round and discover a protective and secluded spot. We really couldn't do it in the house in the day time, it would be awfully brazen! But, perhaps! we'll have another when we go to bed. . . .

You want me to wear a thin dress! Dearie I haven't any up here that would do to wear in the morning. But I'll wear a white skirt

MRS. JACKSON—A LAKE TAHOE SUMMER

and you can take it off when you please. Then in the evening, I'll put on that pleated silk skirt which will be thin and enticing enough I guess with black silk stockings. . . .

Oh! to think you will really be here on my birthday. There'll be a hot time on the ninth all right, won't there. . . ?

♥ ♥ ♥ ♥ ♥

Percy D. Haughton, Boston, MA, to Bill Reid, Jr., Belmont, CA
7 July 1908

The East was not only in the mind of Christine, for Percy Haughton, the Harvard football coach in his first year, wanted Bill to return to Harvard to be his assistant coach for 1908. He invited Reid to come East to check out the situation.

I have talked with Herbert White, who tells me that you are anxious that your wife accompany you on this trip, and I want you to feel that her expenses as well as yours would be included in our arrangement. . . .

If you want Harvard to win next fall, don't say no.

♥ ♥ ♥ ♥ ♥

Bill Reid, Jr., Belmont, CA, to Christine Reid, Lake Tahoe, CA
13 July 1908

Following Bill and Christine's few days at Lake Tahoe, Reid returned to the Belmont School and wrote Christine of his love.

. . . I have had a most delightful time of it and we were together so much that it was almost another honeymoon. It was so good to be able while fishing, to reach out & touch you, to eat with you, kiss you, & walk hand in hand with you. I enjoyed the dear companionship more than I can tell you. You pitched in to give me a good time and I know and appreciate it. . . .

I shall miss you tonight and will long for the long cuddle which we had the last two nights—when you went to sleep with you being in my arms. . . .

I don't think I've ever enjoyed the children quite so much as this time either. They are dandies & you are their mother—God bless you. . . .

♥ ♥ ♥ ♥ ♥

Bill Reid, Jr., Belmont, CA, to Christine Reid, Lake Tahoe, CA
14 July 1908

The next day Bill wrote again about the pile of work awaiting him,

A Debutante's Passion—A Coach's Erotica

including 60 letters to answer, while thinking of Christine.
... I have thought a lot about you all day & though lonely—yet feel a deep satisfaction in our relations. Good night—a kiss & a hug.

♥♥♥♥♥

Christine Reid, Lake Tahoe, CA, to Bill Reid, Jr., Belmont, CA
14 July 1908

Christine reassured Bill of her love.

... Oh! Bill I'll be glad when you come back again! I am feeling all right about "things," dearie boy, so don't worry. You are mine and I will be sensible. If I could only lie in your arms to-night how happy I'd be...!

♥♥♥♥♥

Christine Reid, Lake Tahoe, CA, to Bill Reid, Jr., Belmont, CA
16 July 1908

Bill's and Christine's letters came at a rapid rate.

... You were such a brick to write so soon.... I agree with you that we are closer together than ever before, and I feel awfully happy about it, and shall be happier still when we are once more close together, physically also. I'm a pretty grasping person, you see, but I do like to be where I can touch you whenever I want to....

♥♥♥♥♥

Bill Reid, Jr., Belmont, CA, to Christine Reid, Lake Tahoe, CA
16 July 1908

Bill mentioned a contact from Harvard's Reggie Brown, a football player in the class of 1898.

I am driven to death and cannot write more than a page or so....
  Had a long letter from Reggie Brown about football, etc....
  Well, this is largely a bulletin but I cannot stop.... I love you dearly.

♥♥♥♥♥

Christine Reid, Lake Tahoe, CA, to Bill Reid, Jr., Belmont, CA
17 July 1908

Christine told of the engagement of her best friend, Edith "Tede" Tileston to Fred Eustice, as well as why she did not feel in the mood to write to Bill.

The engagement that I wanted to tell you so much and couldn't is that

MRS. JACKSON—A LAKE TAHOE SUMMER

of Edith Tileston. . . . He doesn't seem the kind of man she would have chosen, does he? I am awfully glad of one thing, and that is that he has loads of money, and she has had to rather skimp since her father died several years ago. . . .

I have "come sick" all night, so will be O.K. when you arrive and quite ready for you I expect. Was I responsive enough this last time? It seemed to me as if I met you half way all night. . . !

♥ ♥ ♥ ♥ ♥

Bill Reid, Jr., Belmont, CA, to Christine Reid, Lake Tahoe, CA
19 July 1908

Still pressured to complete jobs at the Belmont School, he jotted a letter to Christine.

I am still rushed to death. The smoke stack is here and the old one will be taken off & the new one installed on Tuesday & Wednesday. Tomorrow I go to San Jose. . . . The plumbers come on Wednesday. . . . I have. . . four long letters to write to prospectives. . . . You know that I am thinking of you & also that I am awfully hard pressed. . . .

♥ ♥ ♥ ♥ ♥

Christine Reid, Lake Tahoe, CA, to Bill Reid, Jr., Belmont, CA
19 July 1908

Christine gave an interesting account of another couple, who were separated for several weeks.

. . . Mr. George Flint arrived yesterday morning, and if a man didn't seem gladder to see me than he did to see Mrs. Flint, when she had been away three weeks, he could go to hell for all me! Really it was the limit & he didn't even know, & he remarked quite casually, how long she had been away. I felt like slapping him when she is so sweet and attractive. It's lucky she's not like me, isn't it? You are quite right, we do care more than most couples & I'm thankful enough that we do. . . .

I love you all the time and much more than is comfortable, unfortunately. I must cultivate a more easy going nature.

My whole heart to you, dearie, and my soul, if I have any, as well, is in your keeping.

              Your loving but foolish
                  Wife—

o o o o o o o o o o o o o o
(I don't dare to offer you anything more just yet, for I doubt if you are ready for it.) — Let me know!

A Debutante's Passion—A Coach's Erotica

♥ ♥ ♥ ♥ ♥

Wm. T. Reid, Sr., Lake Tahoe, CA, to Bill Reid, Jr., Belmont, CA
21 July 1908

Bill's father advised his son not to take the Harvard football coaching offer proposed by Percy Haughton to be his assistant that fall.

I am of course greatly pleased to have you wanted at Harvard to help in the coaching, but I very much doubt the advisability of your going. Your having been invited to go will of course become known & so you will have the credit of being wanted, while if you go and the team is again defeated as you seem to consider about certain, it seems to me you would be the loser without having been of sufficient service to serve as an equivalent. . . .

    You will not be surprised to know that Mamma says "No" with great vigor. . . .

♥ ♥ ♥ ♥ ♥

Christine Reid, Lake Tahoe, CA, to Bill Reid, Jr., Belmont, CA
21 July 1908

Separation for Christine, as for Bill, seemed to demand the excitement of letters of passion.

. . . I am longing for an old time letter from you, one of the real bad ones. As you see I am quite over our orgy, and ready for another. I am a terror but I know you don't mind. . . .

♥ ♥ ♥ ♥ ♥

Christine Reid, Lake Tahoe, CA, to Bill Reid, Jr., Belmont, CA
21 July 1908

Christine's second letter of the day must have been a joy to Bill.

. . . Please love me hard in your next [letter]! I get starved for it when I am away from you. . . .
    If I acted as I feel like acting I would start for Belmont tomorrow! I'd much rather be there with you, than alone up here. . . . Oh dear! I wish I were where I could "love" you a little anyway. That would be a little let up, wouldn't it? When we're together, not a day goes by that I'd not look forward to lying in your arms at night! I simply adore it and all the cares of the day seem to ship off then, and a feeling of peace comes over me. . . .

♥ ♥ ♥ ♥ ♥

Bill Reid, Jr., Belmont, CA, to Christine Reid, Lake Tahoe, CA

MRS. JACKSON—A LAKE TAHOE SUMMER

22 July 1908

Bill decided to write a very loving letter, but he also wanted Christine to know that he did not appreciate criticism of his letters that asked important questions.

Alone with you at last, even if it is only in the office. How I wish it were at Tahoe or up in our own house! I am in just the mood for a good time with you and it wouldn't take me long to find the way, up your legs and way up between them. I have been rushed, about to death, but I am conscious of quite a desire to go the limit with you and know without looking, that I should shock the knowing ones if I were to walk about in my present . . . condition. . . .

How I wish we could get together tonight—wouldn't it be great to lie together without a thing on—kissing, hugging, and feeling of each other—until a sort of mutual understanding we sought a closer union and a greater expression of our passionate love for each other. . . .

If you were here tonight I'd try to tease you a little by going in and out, by going only half in and by leaning over you & kissing you and your breasts, while only partly in. I should hope to have you reach up, & putting your arms around me, pull me down hard on you, meanwhile bending your waist upwards to run him up the sooner and the farther. . . .

If Edith Tileston comes out, you'll have to agree with her to have a celebration—they in the spare room, we in ours—on the same night. It would be good fun for each couple to know, that it had happened the night before, for sure. I guess that Tede will have poor Fred worn to a whisper in about a week's time. Poor Freddie, but I guess he'll like it as long as he lasts. It's too bad that Tede didn't get a more substantial bed fellow—poor girl. I guess she'll go hungry part of the time.

I have rather reproached myself for using the name for it which you don't like and I shall not do so again in writing—although it is too expressive to get along without when I am actually "gesmuckting" you. . . .

I like to think too of you being on top of me—especially when, as I am about to go in, my legs are spread way apart. That position brings a lot of the real thing to the jumping off point and when it does come, it comes in big spurts. . . .

I don't much enjoy your "call downs" because I have had to write you asking for information. I have done so because I find it hard to get a prompt reply from Papa or Mama & I must have them to keep things up. I daresay that I write you as often if not oftener than any other husband that you can mention, writes to his wife and that when I've a vast deal more to do than any two of them. If you'd rather though I'll send those letters to Papa. . . .

♥♥♥♥♥

Julia Reid (Mamma), Lake Tahoe, CA, to Bill Reid, Jr., Belmont, CA

A Debutante's Passion—A Coach's Erotica

23 July 1908

Bill's mother wrote Bill to try to convince him that returning to Harvard to coach would be a bad decision. She even used some of the Bible, 1 Corinthians, 13, "When I became a man, I put away childish things," to try to dissuade him from leaving the Belmont School.

You must be pleased at the request from Haughton [to coach] but you could not make a greater mistake than to go, it seems to me. Important as athletics are they surely are regarded as belonging to the "childish" things to be put away or put in the background by mature men who have serious interests.

Many things are desirable to be done but not by men who are capable of work of a more enduring nature. . . .

♥♥♥♥♥

Herbert H. White, Thomaston, ME, to Christine Reid, Lake Tahoe, CA
24 July 1908

Herbert White, a close friend of Bill's at Harvard, was trying hard to convince both Bill and Christine to head East and help Harvard on its eternal quest to beat Yale in football.

Dear Christine,

I have been following Percy Haughton's end of his correspondence with Bill in so far as it relates to your both coming east in September. I most earnestly hope you can & Will both come. Please drop me a line and let me know if I can in any way help accomplish that result & if so in what way. We are all well and enjoying a hot summer & a new boat (pictures of Cachalot sent to Bill).

Here is hoping you and yours are well & happy. My best to you & Bill.

       Herbert H. White.

♥♥♥♥♥

Bill Reid, Jr., Belmont, CA, to Christine Reid, Lake Tahoe, CA
24 July 1908

Here is Bill's entire letter a week or so after returning home from his trip to see Christine at Lake Tahoe.

My Own little darling:

It is late and I am tired but I must tell you that I have thought of you often today and loved you. I would give a good deal for a kiss and a cuddle and a good deal more to know that you were to be at my side as I tumble into bed.

I miss the relaxation which always comes when I am with you and

MRS. JACKSON—A LAKE TAHOE SUMMER

the contentment that I always feel in being able to touch you in bed. I wish I could kiss and hug you now, it would do me quite as much good as you, I am sure.

It's only a word—but it shows I'm with you always.

Good bye dearie,
"Bill"

♥ ♥ ♥ ♥ ♥

Bill Reid, Jr., Belmont, CA, to Christine Reid, Lake Tahoe, CA
24 July 1908

In another letter the same day, Bill was more explicit about his love for Christine.

... I would ... spend... the greater part of the night in rolling around with you with nothing on. I should certainly be "all in" too. Already, the thought has brought me to a state of preparation. . . . The delicious part of the day would of course be the evening, when we should be sitting in the big chair before the fire, you with a thin dress on so that I could all but feel your soft body. . . . I love thin dresses, they are so tantalizing, you know there's not much there & that develops the desire to feel, and then up goes a hand. Slipping a hand up your leg is a tantalizing performance too and most limb loosening since one's mind lets go outside matters and relaxes into happy anticipation. I really think that my greatest rest and recreation is fooling with you, because you are the only interest which can make me forget the work here. . . .

How it stirs me up to watch you undress, probably I'd lay you on the bed in process and with your dress clear over your head, would sort of make believe and press in against you hard & passionately, and the delight that a touch down there gives me when in so doing I realize that you are ready & want to guide him in. I always like to think of you as wanting me to do it and as helping me to go the limit with you. And the little pleasure grunts and cries—how they do make me try to get up further and how your struggles and quick breathing do make me laugh as I hold you so that you can't get away. . . .

♥ ♥ ♥ ♥ ♥

Christine Reid, Lake Tahoe, CA, to Bill Reid, Jr., Belmont, CA
24 July 1908

Christine felt sorry for criticizing Bill for writing a letter mostly with questions about the Belmont School and home affairs that needed to be answered. While telling Bill that the fishing at Lake Tahoe was great, it would be even better if he were with her.

Your fine letter has just come, and I am feeling mighty small, uncomfortable,

A Debutante's Passion—A Coach's Erotica

and teary. You know, dearie, that it wasn't the questions I minded, but because there was nothing but questions! I suspect I am horrid and grasping, but I so wanted to be loved and get so hungry for it. If I acted as I feel like acting I would start for Belmont to-morrow! I'd much rather be there with you, than alone up here. . . .

If I had realized how it was going to be, I wouldn't have come up here at all! Now be sure and tell me right away, whether you are coming up again or not, because, if not, we will all come back . . . .

Kitten says often "Papa gone 'way. . . ."

♥ ♥ ♥ ♥ ♥

Bill Reid, Jr., Belmont, CA, to Christine Reid, Lake Tahoe, CA
26 July 1908

Bill took Christine into his confidence on the proposal to go East to help coach again at Harvard, this time under coach Percy Haughton, who ended up as the greatest coach ever at Harvard. If he decided to do this, he would be going against the wishes of both his father and mother.

I had hoped to surprise you with completed arrangements for the enclosed trip—but it does not seem to meet with Papa's approval and so I am going to take you into my confidence. What do you think of the plan?

I feel that if it is distinctly understood that I am to take a vacation after having been here two years without one and after a straight pull all summers—that people will be generous enough to allow me to take it, in whatever way I feel most inclined.

I have loved you very tenderly today and wish you were where I could get hold of you. You are a great comfort and the knowledge that I have you makes me very happy. . . .

I send this thus to give you a chance to think it over & answer. If I do not go East I shall come up again . . . .

♥ ♥ ♥ ♥ ♥

Christine Reid, Lake Tahoe, CA, to Bill Reid, Jr., Belmont, CA
26 July 1908

At the end of her letter on her activities around Lake Tahoe, Christine asked Bill to come to Lake Tahoe soon.

. . . Well, dearie boy, I do wish you'd make up your mind to come and come and share all the fun we're having. I would add fifty percent to it all for me, and I do long to see you and love you and be loved. Please hurry and come.

      Yours lovingly,
       Christine—
* * (one outdoors) & (one in bed.)

MRS. JACKSON—A LAKE TAHOE SUMMER

♥♥♥♥♥
Christine Reid, Lake Tahoe, CA, to Bill Reid, Jr., Belmont, CA
27 July 1908

Christine wrote one of her sweetest letters offering herself fully to Bill, if he would soon come to Lake Tahoe after working all summer at the Belmont School.

Your dear long letter has just come, and I am filled to overflowing with love and longing for you! Won't you please, please, please hurry and come up here? I really am not urging it through selfish reasons, but because I just cannot bear to have you as tired as I know you are. Come up here and let me love you as I so long to do! We will do anything you please and we'll get you thoroughly rested before we go back. . . .

We'll have some tramps together! We'll have some other things together, too, if you want to. Everything is going to be just as you want it. I'll help "him" in with greatest alacrity if he cares to come. Somehow I feel that he does, and I have the thought. . . .

. . . You are planning to be a very bad boy? Now Piddy, be my own dear old boy, and come, come, come! You'll really like it when you do and I'll try to make it interesting, possibly "exciting" for you.

Yours ever, entirely, lovingly, and lastly, but, not lastly, most pleasantly.
Christine—
*   He'll be a dandy! Just you see if he isn't!
♥♥♥♥♥

Bill Reid, Jr., Belmont, CA, to Christine Reid, Lake Tahoe, CA
28 July 1908

Bill had just received the loving letter of Christine and responded in kind.

My own precious Darling:

I had sort of a feeling today that I was about due for a "loving" and I got one tonight. I wish I could make it concrete—my heart is warm for you and longs for you, and I think of you between breaths all day long. I suppose a certain amount of passion underlies it all but it is so much bigger than just that, that it absolutely envelops me. Your frequent and dear letters are the "let up" of the day for me and I love you to pieces for being so good to me.

I am hungry for a good kiss and a hugging and I shouldn't object if you were to pull up your dresses and lie down with me on a bed. It wouldn't be long before we'd be rolling about, over the bed, giving little pleasure grunts and "squiggles" and giving expression to our long restrained affection and passion.

I have always thought that if a fellow worked to the limit, he wouldn't

A Debutante's Passion—A Coach's Erotica

think quite so much of the little girlish nook that it is so delightful to plunge into—but, whether it is the steady thinking of you that does it or an abnormal streak in me, I find myself quite "up in arms" as I write and fully ready to ravish you at the first opportunity. . . .

I cannot leave here until Friday night at the earliest & shall hope to leave then. . . .

♥ ♥ ♥ ♥ ♥

Christine Reid, Mt. Tamalpais, CA, to Bill Reid, Jr., Belmont, CA
ca. 5 Oct. 1908

Bill and Christine had not returned to the East but remained at the Belmont School. Christine had apparently gone to see her Brookline friend Edith "Tede" Tileston. She and her new husband, Fred Eustice, were in California on their way to honeymoon in Japan.

My own darling husband,

Here I am alone up here, having sent the bride and groom off by themselves in the moonlight, and my heart is full of you, and I am loving you Oh! so hard. Before supper we all climbed up on the rocks where you and I sat that evening so long ago, and I wished so much that you were with me. As it was, it was hard enough, and my one pleasure was in my remembrance. Piddy dear! We care much more intensely than they do, and I am so glad for that. I couldn't bear to be loved any the less passionately. I love you just as you are! You are so sweet and dear to me this morning that it just broke me all up. It was been a hard time for you, dearie boy, these last few days, and you have been so brave and fine through it all. I love you for it!

I wish that I could lie in your arms to-night. Not a day passes but that I look forward to it.

God bless you my dear, dear husband.
Sincerely,
Christine
♥ ♥ ♥ ♥ ♥

Chapter 9

THE WESTERN FAMILY CRISIS: "LET'S CLEAR OUT"

Julia Reid, Lake Tahoe, CA, to Wm. T. Reid, Sr., Belmont, CA
                                                         ca. 5 July 1909

After another year working at the Belmont School, Bill's mother wrote an unusually harsh letter to her husband about Bill's relationship to his father and to the Belmont School.

... Don't worry over Will's want of taste about the advertisement. I don't think it strange that he should be carried along by these modern ways of advertising. He will be more conservative as he grows older. Do let him have his positive views and you act on yours. He has got to learn by experience & he is doing so & will continue to do it. He has a lot of fine qualities along with his trying ones, and faith in those will help him get rid of his defects. That is your theory & your doctrine & you ought to practice it on your own son. We have "borned" him and reared him & he is the product of our efforts. If you could look forward ten years I believe you'd see a gratifying result. We have no right to expect as much of him as we have of ourselves. He is very difficult to reach, because he can't bear to be found fault with & never admits he is in the wrong readily though he does often with you in a most hearty way. Generally however he says little or nothing except to defend himself but meanwhile is turning things over in his mind & finally comes to agree with you. So have patience. He is far more receptive with you than with me. We are all too positive—you the least so; I guess the children get it from me; and we are none of us perfect, you the nearest so, therefore you can afford to deal patiently with the rest of us. ...

I took your letters out under the trees to read yesterday, and I opened them without dread—a thing that I have not been able to do for about eight years at least. I have longed for letters yet have dreaded to read them because of so many evidences of your dissatisfaction with me in them, and I have never wished to keep them except some wee portion somewhere which I have torn off.

So I know the deadening effect—fault finding has on Will. Show him your lovely side against his unlovely one.

But you'll cry enough, enough if I say more. ...

♥♥♥♥♥

A Debutante's Passion—A Coach's Erotica

Christine Reid, Cohasset, MA, to Bill Reid, Jr., Belmont, CA
24 July 1909

After about a month vacation at Cohasset, Bill returned to Belmont, while Christine and the three children remained in the East to be with her family. Christine had generally come to the conclusion that living in the West would not work, and that she preferred to live in the East.

Your second letter has just come, and I wonder what you will think of the outburst I sent you yesterday! Well, never mind, that's just the way it all made me feel, and I know you will understand it. After all, as you say, it does not really enter into the question itself, still I do think it should weigh a little in your decision. The fact that your family can think and write in such a way about such a really small thing, proves that they can do it again and I can never get over their telling you that, after all your devotion and hard work, you have been a "hindrance." That sticks in my crop, as you say, and always will. . . .

  Well, my dearie, dearie boy, I love you all the time and hard. We certainly would have a good "cuddle" if you were here, but I won't stir you up with any details. . . . My whole heart to you dearie, a huge hug and all the kisses you might want—also an unmentionable!
(*)

♥ ♥ ♥ ♥ ♥

Christine Reid, Cohasset, MA, to Bill Reid, Jr., Belmont, CA
10 August 1909

Nearly all of Christine's unhappy letter, outlining the problem of staying at the Belmont School, is included. The "Jim" noted is her brother-in-law, married to Christine's next younger sister, Agnes.

My darling old boy,
  It is too, too bad that you are so wretched and unhappy, and I do so wish that there were anyway in which I could help you! But what can I do? Do want me to come out there and stay until the fuss is all over, for I will in a minute if you think it's best for me to come? Sometimes I feel as if I'd have to anyhow for my heart just aches for you out there all alone. Jim and I had just a wee little bit of a talk together last night, your letter depressed me so that I had to talk to someone and he said what I have felt all along, that once the thing is done and we are all settled here in the east, we shall wonder why in the world we didn't cut loose long ago. Dearie, I cannot but feel sure that that is true, often and often you have said, "Well, I can't stand it any longer, let's clear out," and I have sort of backed you up for a while. The same thing has happened to me countless times, of course, and the one thing that kept us was that we did not have these spells at just the same moment.

THE WESTERN FAMILY CRISIS

Dearie, as I have written before, the way looks quite clear before me and I hesitate no longer. You upbraided me for not telling you how I felt and perhaps I should have but please believe that at least I refrained from what seemed to me an unselfish motive. You see the fact is, of course, that I would rather live east and while there seems to be the vestige of a selfish motive I have hesitated to throw the weight of my influence on you to decide you. But I have searched my heart pretty thoroughly these last few weeks, and I realize that if I honestly felt it to be for your best good to stay at Belmont, I would not turn my hand over to keep you here. But I don't feel that it is the right or best thing for you any longer or for the rest of us, and once convinced of that, as I now am, I will say once and for all that I almost beg of you to make your decision at once, plan out what you will say and do and stick to it no matter what follows.

Piddy, I do honestly think that I am advising for your best good and happiness and if not at any rate I am trying to do the right thing by you as far as I can see. I cannot believe that any good can now come of our staying any longer in Belmont. We have got all there is to get out of it, from a selfish point of view. Whether we have added anything to it or not is not for me to say, but at any rate, we did our best, as far as we could and I feel that you have nothing with which to reproach yourself. Don't think that I mean we couldn't have done better but no one is perfect, we were living the hardest years of our life in our relations to each other and the children, and were at best in an exceedingly trying position. What we must do is to regret it as little as possible, what seems to you the wasted time and be everlastingly grateful that we have kept our love for each other unchanged through it all and I cannot but feel all the stronger and deeper for the tough experience that we have lived through together. We have lots to be thankful for dearie boy, and we just must not waste time or energy in useless regrets. We have time before us to redeem everything, and except for lack of money, what more could we want? I have a husband, who I do not hesitate to say calls for the best there is in me, whom I must strive to live up to and whom I love beyond anything in the world. For whom I would do anything, go anywhere, or make any sacrifice.

What can I say more except that he is a man in every sense, and satisfies all my physical demands, and rounds out my life in every way. My greatest wish is to feel that he depends upon me for love, sympathy, comfort and satisfaction, and that I disappoint him in none of these demands. Can I say more, Piddy dear, and what more has life to offer than we still have it in our power to reach? I know what you would say and my answer is ready. A man must have his work and feel it to be worthy of him, and you must force yourself to believe that somewhere here there is a place for you, that is waiting for you and that will be just what you choose to make it. Try to believe that, dearie, it will help you a lot.

A Debutante's Passion—A Coach's Erotica

Piddy, Piddy, how I wish I could just throw my arms around your neck and show you better than words can how deep and true my love for you is. I should like to take you upstairs and lie on the bed with you and gradually arrive at that perfect abandonment of love for which we both long so hard. It would relieve and satisfy us both and oh! how heavenly it would be! I love to give myself up to you so completely, and to feel that you love to have me do so! I would hate it if you didn't want it so much, Pid, and wrong though it may be, I should hate it if we weren't both passionate, and I know you would. There would be a great deal lacking in our love, Bill, if it weren't for that and I'm sure you will agree. It's hard though, when we are not together, and I know it is probably harder for you than for me. But dearie, it's getting pretty uncomfortable for me! There now, I hardly meant to tell you that, but I only want you to know that I really long for you too.

I will get a film for my camera next time I go up to Boston and take some pictures for you of the fellers. They are adorable in bathing. It's too bad the chickens are costing so much, but school opens soon, so I guess you'd better let it go. From then on, they'll have grain only once a day. How are they laying? How I would like to see them and also the garden!

Darling boy, I am so sorry that you feel that we do not "hang together." I will tell you just what the trouble has been. You know how worked I was when you left, I simply was almost beside myself—well,—there was bound to be a reaction and I just got numb and apathetic that was all. Not that I loved you less, but I couldn't suffer like that and it swung the other way, and I felt out of touch with you, and consequently wrote simply newsy, rather of fact letters.

Besides that I carefully avoided the vital question and really intended to, but at too great a cost it now seems. When you begin to think me unsympathetic and doubt my feelings for you, it is time to speak my mind even at the risk of unduly influencing you. So now you have it all! Never have I loved you so deeply . . . and passionately before and I would give the world for even an evening with you. I miss you at every turn, and it is a stab of pain to see Ag and Jim together, and especially when Ag tells me that they've had what she calls a "set to" the night before. But I wouldn't exchange our lot for theirs, they don't love the way we do, and that's the only way for me, and I hope for you. I was talking to the fellers about you and telling them how you were all alone out there. And Pussy went to Miss Rich and said "Can't you go to Belmont and take care of Papa. . . ?" They haven't forgotten you, don't worry.

No more now! I have opened my heart to you this time and you must feel my love for you at every turn or be very blind and dull. It is hard beastly hard for you, dearest one, but a better time is coming, never fear.

THE WESTERN FAMILY CRISIS

    My whole heart to you dearie, X — 0 0 0 0 0 *
(that's the way I feel!)
                      Yours
                      C.

♥♥♥♥♥

Christine Reid, Cohasset, MA, to Bill Reid, Jr., Belmont, CA
                                            13 August 1909

Christine, with Pat (age 6), Edith (age 5), and Christine (age 3) in the East, urged Bill to leave the Belmont School and return to the East.

. . . I looked forward all day to a letter from you, as I felt pretty sad of getting one, two days having passed without any, and each time I thought of it I had a delicious warm feeling round my heart. Then when it came and I sat down to read it with a luxurious feeling,—well, it did seem the last straw. Never mind, though, dearie boy, I am sure I took it harder than it was meant, and I am just going to live along until the next one comes. Just forgive me for being so stupid in expressing it all, and please try to believe that I am not the heartless, unsympathetic witch that I evidently appeared. . . .

Now, dearie boy, forget all I've said on the subject [of leaving the Belmont School and coming East] if you want to. I have infinite faith in you deciding for the best, and I want you to be the one to decide. Please, please don't stop telling me what you think and feel about it, for after this, we shall not be at cross purposes.

I love you always, dearest love, and just as hard as I can.

Here's a tight squeeze for you and anything else that you want, anything. You understand.

♥♥♥♥♥

Bill Reid, Jr., Belmont, CA, to Christine Reid, Cohasset, MA
                                            18 August 1909

Anxious and depressed, Bill and Christine remained apart, separated by the large continent between them and divided over what steps to take in their future together.

. . . Don't you think for a moment, you darling, that all of the heartaches, incidents to a momentary interruption in our loving relations, are on your side, because they make me actually weak in the knees. When anything goes wrong with us, I really do feel a sinking in my knees and an awful torture in my heart. The fact is that I depend on you an awful lot—no one makes any difference to me. What it is hard for me to understand is how you keep your respect for me after the magnificent mess I've thus far made in the way of earning a living. When I think of you and Patsy, and Edith & the baby and recall the fact that we have

A Debutante's Passion—A Coach's Erotica

absolutely no bank account it fires me with a terrific determination to make things "break" right somehow or other——and I'll do it too. There is a certain stimulus in breaking such a situation, and I am determined to score. Your confidence in me and belief in me is a great satisfaction to me and I feel equal to anything. . . .

I am hungry for a chance to get you in my arms, to feel and know that you are near. I go to the mantel and look at your pictures, every time I come into the room and I have with me always the imagination that our cheeks are close together and our lips, one. I can almost feel it and it goes a long ways. If I could only have you in reality. . . .

All of this is having a character building effect on me. I am much more sympathetic with everyone than I was, because the touch of sadness which I feel myself, makes me feel more for others. I feel the greatest sympathy for Papa & Mama—it will blast Papa's last days I am afraid, if this affair ends in my going. I can see it and at table it's hard to eat—it gnaws so at my heart. Then there is Major Hackett—on the threshold. . . . Aunt Hattie thinks she is recovering. . . . In the midst of all this I am raising the question of bringing an axe on Papa!! Is it a wonder, that I feel . . . a deep grasping of my character by this enveloping demand on my heart!!

I told Mama yesterday that I was probably going & why. She said—in a sobbing voice "I am bitterly disappointed" but with no upbraiding in it. She disappeared some after, why, I know full well—to pray and cry. It hurt awfully & my heart has been heavy ever since. Papa knows nothing of it & Mama will not tell. . . .

Mama has said nothing since, I haven't given her a chance, but I notice that she is preparing Papa for it all by many little attentions to him. I tell you Girlie, it is heart rendering & I feel sometimes like slipping silently off and going away, away anywhere—always rushing in your arms.

At present I don't know where I am. I am trying to analyze my feelings. . . . It will be some time before I work through it all. Please do not tell anyone, that I have spoken to Mama. I put it wholly on the one ground that I did not feel sure that it was my work and that four years of it ought to have made that clear. I let out a remark or two on other points, but said in conclusion—"but those are merely details; the one big item is the fact that I have not been happy in the work & do not feel that it is God's call. . . ."

And now, precious little love—let me tell you that I do and have appreciated all along your willingness to do what seems to me best in all this dilemma. I love you deeply for it. The only thing that has been hard for me in it all was the feeling that you weren't opening your heart to me—a feeling that a barrier existed. That is broken down now—& I am with you and now let me kiss & hug you for your desire to save me added pressure & worry. You have been dear to me, but I want to share it all with you—for you are what I love above all else in this world & I can't allow you any secrets. . . .

♥ ♥ ♥ ♥ ♥

THE WESTERN FAMILY CRISIS

Bill Reid, Jr., Belmont, CA, to Christine Reid, Cohasset, MA
25 August 1909

Torn between moving East once again where Christine felt comfortable and staying in the West to help out his father's Belmont School caused tension for both Bill and Christine. Bill signaled his intent to move East only to his mother, but, at the same time, was enjoying more freedom at work and thus pulled to stay in the West.

. . . Tuesday, I told Mama what was in my mind—she cried for two hours in the afternoon. I found her that way when I came up to the house. I gave her a kiss & told her that I was sorry for her and she replied—"I'm sorry for you too—I'm sorry for us all."

Just at present I feel more like staying—not from sympathy—but because on the whole I am getting on pretty well and am rather enjoying the work. I am very busy. I have charge of the new house, am doing all of Major Hackett's work, am seeing people & in general finding much to do. Most of it leaves me to use my own judgment without consulting Papa, & I enjoy the freedom.

The air here is energized with a new life, due to the incoming boys. We had 85 at the first roll call today & we shall be about 97 at roll call tomorrow morning. We have held practically all of our old boys & they seem glad to be back. . . . Every corner is filled, boys are even sleeping in the new Commandant's bed room with him, & one in the Sierra Hall parlor.

I have been pleased at the cordiality of the boys to me—many hunted me up to say "hello" & those whom I saw gave me a very hearty handshake. To-night there has been much singing & good feeling. I cannot begin to give all the names of boys who have asked for you. . . .

♥♥♥♥♥

Bill Reid, Jr., Belmont, CA, to Christine Reid, Cohasset, MA
3 September 1909

The highs and lows experienced by both Christine and Bill may not be unusual in married life. Nevertheless, their dilemma over moving back East or staying in the West would consume much of their lives in the next year. Unfortunately, the letter to which Bill refers in this letter has apparently been lost. The high of this letter would change to depression in others.

With no word from you for about three days, I simply devoured your letter of August 29th when it came this afternoon. I got it just after football practice and although it made me late to supper, I read it over twice before I had even changed my clothes.

It did warm me up so much, and made me feel oh so glad I've got you and so, so contented and happy. It went "right home" and was just

253

what I most wanted and needed. If I could only just hug and kiss you to my hearts content in appreciation of your dear attitude in all that is happening to test my judgment these days, I should indeed feel that my cup was full. Oh!!! but you are dear to me. Every single crisis that develops finds you right "on deck" and I do admire, love and adore you for it beyond my power to express. It makes me positively jubilant—I feel as though I were walking on air. . . .

When I read—"The best that I can do is to say that whatever you finally decide, I'll stand by you, and do the best I can wherever you are"—when I read that, I really think my heart turned clear over in me. . . .

By the time you arrive I expect that Mama & Papa will be in the new house & that would leave us alone again— & how good the word "alone" seems, alone with you, that's what I want. . . .

The pictures of the children were fine!! I just itch to get Pussy in my arms again—she looks so cunning and so dear. Edith with Patsy on the beach is sweet too, and Patsy looks sturdy and well. I am almost ready for another. . . !!

I can't understand how a boy and girl can really love each other and yet "do it" only once a month!! Confound it— I shouldn't feel as though I were even half in love with you if I felt that way. I like to just give myself up to you & have you do the same—and no one can tell me that we aren't fonder of each other for it. . . . I love you in about ten different ways: 1) For your character, 2) For your love of me, 3) For the family you've given me, 4) For your beauty which I greatly enjoy and admire, 5) For your little ways, & methods of expressing yourself, 6) Because you are passionate & love to have me do it to you, 7) Because we've each given up absolutely to the other, 8) Because you have always subordinated your preferences and desires to my career, and 9) Because you are you and satisfy me from every point of view. . . .

I am still a "good boy" and long more than ever for a whole night of it with you a regular hugging, kissing, and - - - - -g night. . . .

♥♥♥♥♥

Christine Reid, Cohasset, MA, letter to Bill Reid, Jr., Belmont, CA
14 September 1909

Christine's stay in the East was lengthy. After telling about a toothache and a "wretched" dental visit and needing glasses to read, she expressed her major reasons for being depressed, feeling that the East should prevail over the West..

. . . I was discouraged just the same and came home "blu" and tired out. A letter from you was the one thing I wanted, but to have you say that I seemed to [be] trying to make up my mind which to choose you or the family, was just too much.

THE WESTERN FAMILY CRISIS

What have I ever said or done to deserve that? But there, I don't suppose I ought to expect you to understand my feeling for my family. You have much of it yourself and don't know what it means. But this I do think that you have seen enough of it to know a little of what it means to me, and to know enough not to say a thing like that. Life isn't so easy for me just now that you can afford to make it any harder! If you had mother saying each day "Isn't there any hope of you staying? Why I had banked on it, and I shall be all alone," and if you felt as I do about her and father, who has done everything in the world for us both, you might know how it feels to think of saying "good-bye" to them all in less than two weeks for an indefinite time. This, too, after my hope had been all raised to staying here. I am crying as I write and I feel you ought to know just how much it stirs me up when you say a thing like that. Have I ever put the family before you yet? When I first read that I must confess it was a temptation to write and tell you that the time had come for you to prove your love, that I had decided to stay east. Would you have come? Piddy, perhaps I ought not to write this way, but I am pretty much on edge now, and it doesn't take much from you to upset me. I love you beyond all else, and cannot but feel that that has been proved over and over beyond all question. Try to be as lenient as you can to me, and I'll try to make it up to you when I come.

I think I'd rather you did not unpack anything until I come, but if you want to, I don't care much either way. It was nice of you to think of it.

It would be nicer for me not to write any more now. I am all unstrung after yesterday and what I have still before me. Forgive me for it all, if you can, you see how well I live up to my quotation, and all will come out right when we are together.

Heaps of love to all, especially to you, who are all the world to me. Please thank your mother for her postal card.

I love, love, love you—
C.

♥ ♥ ♥ ♥ ♥

Bill Reid, Jr., San Francisco, CA, to Christine Reid, Cohasset, MA
20 September 1909

Bill was in San Francisco, attending a meeting of the Pacific Athletic Association, an important group within the leading sport organization at the time, the Amateur Athletic Union. Much of his attention, however, was on Christine and whether she would stay with him at the Belmont School, which she disliked, or would desire to remain in the East.

I am here to attend a meeting of the P.A.A. and have just come in from the Café Bismark where I heard the orchestra play "Fair Harvard" beautifully. I sat down there until they were through and my heart just flew to you for it always does on such occasions, and more especially

A Debutante's Passion—A Coach's Erotica

tonight because I just received your letter in answer to mine expressing fear lest the family was stealing you away from me. To think that it had come just after your trying day at the dentist and that it caused you to cry made me feel awfully sorry I'd sent it and a great pang of remorse because it hurt you. Well, there are no more on the way & there won't be any. You have made your position absolutely clear and I am absolutely satisfied. But in looking back at what I said you must not forget that my family means very little to me & that you are all I have. I thought I felt you slipping away from me a little, & it broke me all up. Call it jealousy, worry, anxiety or anything you please but it was based on the fact that I love you to pieces and simply could not stand the thought of losing any of you.

You asked me in your letter whether if you had said you wouldn't come & had demanded of me that I prove my love by coming to you—what I would have done. I would have come, but as I wrote before I should never have gotten over the disappointment of it. Respect for one's wife must be the basis of any full blooded love & such an action on your part would have dulled a mighty keen edge.

But I shan't discuss that further—for you have acted in the dearest possible way to me and my respect & regard for you could not be greater. I am absolutely contented about it all, and I have already said time after time I am ready to do anything I can to show you that you have made the richest investment that it is possible for a girl to make. I love you to pieces and without one single mental, moral or physical reservation. I wish for nothing more. I am going to see you through on this thing, cost what it may. You have seen every ounce of my love, affection, respect and devotion, and I feel in a different world almost. You & I together, and I am absolutely indifferent to anyone and all else. If I only had you here now to love and kiss and comfort, I would so love to have the chance. I am counting the days now and yet I find that my sympathy for you in leaving gives a little touch of sadness to the thought. My heart goes out to you in one long reach and I long to get you close to me where we can cement our love and give expression to the relationship which exists between us. . . .

I have been elected as an alternate on the board of representatives of the P.A.A. to the A.A.U. or National Amateur Athletic Union. I was also made chairman of the Committee to pass on new applications for admission. It doesn't mean a whole lot of course but I am gratified at it because I entered the association knowing no one & now after six months am formally recognized at the annual election. It indicates that I have made some headway & have some standing. . . .

♥♥♥♥♥

Albert L. Lincoln, Boston, MA, to Bill Reid, Jr., Belmont, CA
12 January 1910

Christine had been in California all fall and over Christmas. Bill's father-in-law let Bill know what he thought of the situation at Belmont for his daughter and Bill. He invited Bill and his family to reside with the Lincolns for some time if they came East.

Your letter dated Dec. 26th but finished later & postmarked Jan'y 3, was received by me Monday morning. It is a very full & complete statement it seems to me of present & past conditions at Belmont as affecting you & Christine & the facts are given in a remarkably dispassionate way. I have read and re-read the letter both to myself & to others—to Mrs. Lincoln & to Jim & my conclusion is inevitably the same & the one which I have already written to Christine, namely that I can see no probability that you & she will ever be continuously happy in Belmont. Much as it would mean to me & Mrs. Lincoln if my conclusion were otherwise, & happy as we may be at the prospect of your moving East to be with us permanently, I cannot help regretting that things have come to such a pass, when I also consider what it means to your own father & mother, & read again the pages you have devoted to that part of this subject.

I recall the anguish I endured when Christine first left us, as it seemed to me then, to pass almost wholly out of our lives, but I felt that we were consulting her happiness in letting her go & I shut my eyes to our own loss & tried not to think of it. Well, Belmont has been tried & I must say that when you & Christine arrived here last Summer I was astonished & startled at the condition of you both. You were free to admit that life at Belmont was impossible under the conditions there for existing, but I now understand that you feel conditions have changed very much for the better as far as you are concerned. The change however does not seem, & you so state in your letter, to have favorably affected Christine, & I think you are ready to stand by her & to admit that she has tried to get into sympathetic relations with the school even if she has not been disposed to enter into its active work, since her return. I do not now believe & in fact am convinced to the contrary, that she can ever be truly happy in the school work & life at Belmont & especially while rearing her children; this I am sure means to you, who I know still love & cherish her, that you cannot be wholly happy in your work there, & the work therefore will surely not be the best of which you are capable.

I haven't a doubt that you can continue the good work which your father has done for the community, and no one appreciates its value more highly than I, but it will be done at the sacrifice of the happiness of your wife & probably of your children. I have been slowly but surely led to the conviction that school life at Belmont & family life such as all our families here are accustomed to & which builds up a home, are incompatible.

If therefore you should decide to remain at Belmont, I shall feel that you are prepared to sacrifice a hope higher than any other earthly object, the happiness of wife & children. I don't mean, dear Bill, that you will intentionally do this, or that you will conclusively agree with me that such will be the result of a decision to remain in Belmont. But such is my conviction.

And now I come to the financial side of the question or as you call it "the business end" of a change: There is no question but what for several years Belmont will pay you better than anything that can be offered to you here—if you accept the offer of $5000—and if you stay I should advise you by all means to accept this offer in preference to the others you mention—altho' this payment I suppose must be dependent on the success of the school; it is certainly liberal but I have no doubt will be justly earned. In this connection let me express the hope that this time the ranch will already be sold—the sale will mean so great a relief to your family, and the proceeds will enable your father to carry out plans he has so long looked forward to.

If you come East there is no question but what a place will be found for you either with Jim, or in a similar concern, but for a year or two you will have to be content with the pay you mentioned, $1,200 a year, which cannot be helped so you are only making a start. If you succeed & I won't allow myself to harbor a doubt on this point—& I have discussed the matter with Jim who knows more about it than I do, & I have too great confidence in your industry, application & capacity for work. I see no reason, given your health, why you should not be wholly self-supporting in a modest way in five years. Barring financial calamity in the business world—which would affect the school also, I think you will be able with some assistance to live independently—that is in a house by yourselves—at the end of two years. In the long run I haven't much doubt but what you will be better off here than in Belmont. This part I have read to Jim & he says I may write that he fully concurs in what I have said. As to help from Mrs. Lincoln & myself, our only wish in life is the happiness of our children & I assure you that whatever we do will be done as much through our affection for you as for Christine & the children. We feel sure we can make you all comfortable as long as you stay with us & I fervently hope you will not let the thought of dependence enter into your mind again after you've once accepted the situation. I realize how a man of spirit feels, but you must remember that we also realize how much it means to have your own family & home & we owe it to you, even looking at it in a selfish way, to make the change as easy as possible for you on the financial side, & this we shall try to do. Whether we can make it up in affectionate devotion & keep you contented & happy you must judge. A great deal more might be written but I hope I have sufficiently covered the ground, & that what I have written may help you to a decision which may result in happy lives for you & Christine & your little ones. Don't let the matter drag any longer. It will reach such a state that you & Christine will be utterly unable to make a sane judgment. Remember that after all you have your own lives to live & are entitled to absolute freedom in your choice. I shall make no personal appeal. My only prayer is that

THE WESTERN FAMILY CRISIS

your mutual decision, & I am more than pleased that you & Christine will come together in this matter, will be for the best interests of you all. . . .

♥♥♥♥♥

Albert L. Lincoln, Boston, MA, to Christine Reid, Belmont, CA
14 January 1910

Christine's father replied to a "delightful" note from Christine, only two days after his long letter to Bill about coming East

. . . By this time my letter on the trying question is half way to you & before this reaches you, you & Bill will be again distracted I fear by what I've written. The business end I'm afraid is what will trouble him as much as anything else, but if you will only make of your minds to stay with us as long as may be necessary, the rest I'm sure will take care of itself & sooner or later Bill will be able to have a home of his own. We are far from worrying about having the Reids again. We only wish we were sure they were coming, and I do feel pretty sure because I think Bill will conclude it the wisest thing to do for all concerned great as will be the disappointment of his mother & perhaps of his father. But the idea of your staying out there alone! Not much. As I wrote Bill, I would not listen to your coming unless you came to us & let us make you as comfortable as possible. But I've written all I ought to on this subject, & while I know you will stick it out if you have to, I fear you'll never be reconciled as long as the family is intact in Brookline, & at times you'll be as unhappy as ever, in spite of your pluck. . . .

♥♥♥♥♥

Albert L. Lincoln, Boston, MA, to Christine Reid, Belmont, CA
5 February 1910

Christine's father again looked at Bill's and Christine's problem and felt confident that the best solution was to move East.

. . . Poor Bill: Your last fine letter to your Ma told of his having finally spoken to his Pa, & I can imagine his state of mind. My heart goes out to you both, for you certainly are in a very trying situation. It seems pretty clear to me that Bill, while not ultimately in sympathy with his work in the School, or with his surroundings, is principally moved to his decision in the matter by his desire to make you permanently happy & I love him for it, & you may be sure we shall do all we can to make it up to him. You see I am feeling pretty confident of the ultimate decision & shall now look forward to seeing you all in May at least. The Cohasset house can be opened & Miss Rick can stay with you as long as possible. . . .

♥♥♥♥♥

259

A Debutante's Passion—A Coach's Erotica

Albert L. Lincoln, Boston, MA, to Wm. T. Reid, Sr., Belmont, CA
11 February 1910

Christine's father replied to a letter from Bill's father and gave his appraisal of a future move East for his daughter and son-in-law.

Yours of 29th ult. was received last Tuesday & I have thought over it very much since then, while the subject matter has hardly been out of my mind since Will & Christine arrived here last summer. Before their arrival, scarcely an inkling had come to me of the situation in Belmont & I confess I was very much affected by Will's depressed condition when he arrived & from which it took several weeks for him to recover. Naturally the matter was talked about & Will simply said he could not go on with the work at Belmont under the conditions which had prevailed thus far & be happy, while Christine said that her family life & her relations with Will had been at times most unhappy, as his work and the way in which he had to do it, had seemed almost to change Will's very nature. In spite of it all however Will, in his desire to be loyal to you & to conquer the work no matter what the result, & Christine in her loyalty to Will, determined to make a further trial.

The School, as I was very glad to learn, started out under most favorable and encouraging auspices & Will seemed to be taking a new interest in his work & to be doing it with far less strain, but not alas! under conditions which seemed to make him wholly happy, nor make conditions which left him anytime for his wife & family, & it was not long before I found that Christine was more discouraged at the outlook than before; so when Will's very full account of the situation came & my advice was asked I could only write as I did in reply. I infer now that he has decided that to stay in Belmont will endanger the happiness of his family & before it is too late. I can fully appreciate the sore disappointment this must be to you & Mrs. Reid who have looked forward to Will following in your footsteps, but you certainly would rather have him leave than to have the school deteriorate from its present high position as it certainly must if he was not happy in the work, and as it might even with best endeavors, when you re-call the tremendous amount of devotion and work you and Mrs. Reid, and Aunt Hattie too, have put into it. Of course you have smoothed the way & Will will step into control of a well finished machine—but one nevertheless that requires the hands, eyes & brain of a skillful master of men to maintain its present position. I don't wish to be taken as doubting Will's ability to fill the place, tho' it would be no discredit to him were I to do so. Without wishing to flatter you, it takes a big man & one I might say born to it, to fill such a position successfully & one I fear who has had more experience with human nature than Will has even had altho' his has been considerable. But this ground which has been more thoroughly threshed over by you & Will & your conclusions on these points would be sounder than mine.

What occurs to me in reply to your letter is this: If the school must be disposed of, it is now admittedly at the highest point of efficiency and prosperity that it has ever reached, & I don't quite understand why, to perpetuate its good work it may be necessary to make a present of it to the man or men willing to carry it out, or a free gift of it after you perhaps, if I understand you, have received something in the nature of an annuity for the remainder of your life. But if this is so, will the case be any better or as good for Will when it may become necessary for him in turn to dispose of it, or for Christine in case he should die or be taken seriously ill? You to be sure have put back a large amount of its earnings into the school which possibly Will may be able to save & invest in something which may always have a full market value. But just think of the self denial & self sacrifice of yourself & family which have enabled you to do this. Will must pay for a great deal which has heretofore been given freely. His expenses will necessarily be heavier than yours, & he will be more distracted from his work by his young children, I suspect, than you have been the past twenty years by your older ones. It is a very grave question then whether on the whole a school is a good form of investment if one is looking forward to a provision for one's old age & from his children. Judging from what you say in your letter it is not, as the investment only has value as a going machine; that is it is a good income producer so long as it runs prosperously, but intrinsically it is likely to fade away if you attempt to realize on it. This consideration also it seems to me might well cause Will & Christine to hesitate, & especially when they consider, as I have said, the amount of self-sacrifice and self-denial the school life involves. Christine has evidently found the prospect beyond her strength, & especially, I think, as she firmly believes that Will can never carry on the task & have anytime to devote to her & the children, & this devotion is something she cannot live without and be happy.

My conclusion from your letter then is this: that there will never be a more favorable time for you or for Will to arrange for the disposition of the school; that if its perpetuation involves the sacrifice of a more comfortable perpetuation of our grandchildren, which I admit must be the case in some respects for a few years at least, this must be faced, & it seems to me quite as easily now as in the future, after Will has put back into it a large part of its earnings in order to keep the school up to its present high standard, as he will have to do. Then too William 3' may be totally unfitted to take the school in his turn & not only your savings but Will's besides must be sacrificed to the perpetuation of the school. It occurs to me that in considering the return, Will is likely to realize from the school there should certainly be deducted a large sum for life insurance in case of sudden death & the then necessary sacrifice of the school by Christine or his children. As I think Will's decision to make a change will stand, for I cannot alter the opinion I have expressed in my previous long letter to him on the subject, & I am sure his domestic happiness will weigh more with him than anything else, I shall hope that the School may be disposed of to better advantage than you seem to fear, & that some man or syndicate of teachers may be found, who will be willing to pay a fair price for the plant as well as for the prestige, standing & goodwill of the School, & that the proceeds may be invested in some form which will

A Debutante's Passion—A Coach's Erotica

make you & Mrs. Reid live happily & comfortably the rest of your lives & then remain to help in the maintenance & education of your grandchildren. Or, may not this be accomplished in some such way as this: Incorporate the School, retaining all of the shares in yourself; find some good man of experience & place him in charge at a fixed salary & a share of the net income, the remaining net income to be paid to you; with an agreement that the shares may be purchased from time to time at a fixed price to be agreed upon in advance between you. Then these shares or whatever may be left of them at the time of your decease could be given by you, if you see fit, to Will, or in trust for the maintenance & education of his children. Or, I should think the School might be leased at a fixed sum with an option given to the lesser to purchase at an agreed price. To give a deed as you suggest, in escrow as it were, to be recorded on your decease, might mean a free gift to some unworthy person, in case you should die within a very short time. I feel confident that such a School as you have founded will find a purchaser on a fair basis.

I have great faith in Will's ability to do well in any position in which he may be placed. He can readily, I am assured, get a start in a respectable business here & his progress ought to be fairly rapid, while I believe he will be much happier than he seems to have been thus far. I think too much however of the calling of a great teacher & educator & of his service to the community not to share with you the keen disappointment this all means, but frankly I no longer feel that Christine brought up as she has been is equal to the sacrifice and effort she has come to see that it means on her part, although I know she will do her best if after all Will decides to remain in Belmont.

Mrs. Lincoln joins me in much love to Mrs. Reid, Aunt Hattie & to yourself. I have written frankly, as I am sure you would wish me to, but I hope nothing to hurt your pride or to injure your feelings.

       Faithfully Yours—
        Albert L. Lincoln

♥ ♥ ♥ ♥ ♥

Chapter 10

EAST OVER WEST: "A CLOUD BETWEEN US IS JUST PLAIN TORTURE"

Undated memo by Bill Reid, Jr., probably written in the Summer of 1909, while he was visiting Christine's parents in Massachusetts

Bill searched the positives and negatives of continuing at the Belmont School, knowing that a move back East would likely be beneficial to both him and to Christine. Yet Belmont and his parents tugged strongly on his entire being.

I drifted into school work largely through force of circumstances. Had I not been through Belmont, I should never have selected teaching as a profession. I can never secure the love & affection of the boys—their respect is all that I hope for. My nature is not a winning one with boys.

I am not literary or scholarly and unless I am at least one or the other I can never be a great success in a broad sense.

I find no enjoyment in associating with the teachers. My friends are all in the East. The constant development of petty irritations plus the endeavor to conciliate one's conscience and standards with the lower standards of the community is such a wrench on nerves as to keep me pretty much on edge much of the time—and being on edge is not the condition to be in in handling boys. Patience is essential & kindliness & both are hard qualities to nurture in the face of irritation. There is no way of getting relaxation from the strain—and it is therefore hard to recuperate. Parents do not admit school teachers on the same basis as they do people in other professions. There is much condescension—a very disagreeable thing when one is doing his best to serve the son and especially so when the mother is a divorcee or a "nouveaux riche."

It is a strain to be everlastingly picking flaws in other people.

There is little more than a bare living to be made in the work.

I have not the missionary spirit to the extent of facing the difficulties & making the necessary sacrifices for the one reward of finding that I am being of service to the community, a boys' school is not a good place in which to bring up girls.

C's [Christine] friends, family & interests are in the East.

The California climate is way ahead of the East.

I own the School plant and am head of it.

In business I should have to start at the bottom. My progress would be slow and the problem of maintaining a family meanwhile would be a serious one.

I own much to my parents, but not to the extent of entering upon a life work—no matter how noble which is not interesting enough to make me willing to forego the difficulties for the satisfaction of the heart, which is the only recompense a school life gives.

A change to ordinary business will seem a great let down to Mama in particular & a great disappointment to Papa—and yet it is better to choose what we can do & want to do with success—than to choose a distasteful work to gratify one's parents.

Belmont is my home & I love the place.

We have a home & own it in Belmont. We have no house here [Massachusetts].

Pat would get a fine education at Belmont & yet be home. He can get a good one too in the East.

What is to become of the school? Where is Papa to get a letup, such as he should have if I took his place?

I am half starved for friends.

I am nervous & it makes me more so. I am at my best when not all wrought up. I need time off every day & diversion. Have not in all five years really loved it. The business end building up is what has attracted me—not the love of the work.

♥♥♥♥♥

Christine Reid, on railroad to Lake Tahoe, CA, postcards to Bill Reid, Jr., Belmont, CA

22 June 1910

After a year in Belmont, Christine took a break from Bill by taking her children, William III [Patrick] (7), Edith [Pussy] (5), and Christine [Kitten] (4), to the eldler Reid's summer home at Lake Tahoe.

Edith says "I hope you'll have a good time. I was a good girl."

Pussy chose this card for you. She has said several times "It's too bad we had to leave Papa!"

♥♥♥♥♥

Christine Reid, Lake Tahoe, CA, to Bill Reid, Jr., Belmont, CA

ca. 24 June 1910

Not all of Christine and Bill's letters were filled to overflowing with their desire for physical love and emotional support, especially when they had just been with each other for a lengthy period of time. Here is nearly an

EAST OVER WEST

entire letter from Christine as she left for Lake Tahoe at the summer home of Bill's parents.

My dearest old "Pid,"

As you already know. . . our trip was safely and comfortably accomplished. The fellers were in bed early, and went to sleep soon after we left the boat at Port Costa. I peeked in once at Pussy and found her flat on her stomach. . . gaping out at the sights through the open window. The others slept all night . . . which was mighty good. They are fine travelers.

You will be horrified to hear that I took off nothing except my outside shirt, not even my shoes! It was really frosty and cold at Truckee but we had [a] hot . . . breakfast, and after strolling about a little, we ate in the living room where there was a fire in the stove. The ride to the Tavern was as lovely as ever and we sat in the open car.

The lake was a bit rough but we all got aboard O.K. and arrived safely at The Pines. Of course you have heard before this that the boat had to be sent to S[an] F[rancisco] to be overhauled. Well, I put Edith and Kitten to bed and the latter had a splendid nap, not waking up until nearly two o'clock. The former of course spent the time looking out of the window, and was rather difficult all day. We had a most delicious dinner of baked trout, green peas and, hold your breath, peach short cake. . . ! After dinner Patsy and Edith had a grand time on the shore.

I can smell chicken cooking at this moment. Later on the fellers came tarring up in great excitement, too old Indians squaws were sitting under the tree and as Edith expressed it "they were lonely and hungry." Your mother gave the fellers each two biscuits to give them & off they went. They seem to have lost their fear of Indians entirely. I lay down on the beach for a while and snoozed and felt quite refreshed. After I went up to the house Edith came up in a state of excitement and did not know whether to laugh or to cry. She had fallen in of course. She was wet up to the shirt so I changed her into overalls and off she went again. They were all in bed early and slept well, but we awoke by five thirty & I simply could not keep them quiet. I turned in myself, after a fine hot bath at 8:30 and slept as long as I was let.

The lake at sunrise was too lovely. I tell you it's a relief to get away from that eternal grind. To-day is much warmer and is perfect.

Duke caught a chipmunk for the fellers and they are thrilled. Your mother is letting them keep it in the meat case for a little while.

Well, my dearie, we all miss you and asked this morning when you were coming. Soon you must. Be good to the turkeys and to yourself, and don't smoke too much or stay up too late and have all the fun you can.

My head is still rather fuzzy but I'll write again to-morrow.

♥♥♥♥♥

A Debutante's Passion—A Coach's Erotica

Christine Reid, Lake Tahoe, CA, to Bill Reid, Belmont, CA
26 June 1910

Lake Tahoe satisfied Christine, and would do so for a while. This time it was a short separation.

Dearest Pid,
　　Here I sit out on the screened porch and it is really too lovely for words. One cannot but feel at peace with the universe. I have been so lazy since I came and haven't done a thing except sit out under a tree and read or go out rowing. . . .
　　Your letter was most welcome. . . .

♥♥♥♥♥

Christine Reid, Lake Tahoe, CA, to Bill Reid, Jr., Belmont, CA
28 June 1910

Christine composed a rather cold letter to Bill, who had indicated that "things were coming" her way.

. . . .Doubtless I am hard to satisfy. . . . Perhaps I am the more sorry as it has meant so much to me through so many dark days. . . .
　　We shall be glad to see you when you come.

♥♥♥♥♥

Bill Reid, Jr., Belmont, CA, to Christine Reid, Lake Tahoe, CA
30 June 1910

Bill wrote a letter to Christine that he would soon be coming to Lake Tahoe, but it contained no indication of love for Christine.

Tomorrow night I start for Tahoe and am therefore quite busy and "het up. . . ."

♥♥♥♥♥

Bill Reid, Jr., Belmont, CA, to Christine Reid, Lake Tahoe, CA
2 August 1910

After a short stay at Lake Tahoe, Bill returned to work at the Belmont School.

"Our house is very clean & very empty, especially our bed. . . ."

♥♥♥♥♥

Bill Reid, Jr., Belmont, CA, to Christine Reid, Chicago, IL
31 August 1910

At the end of the summer, Christine and the three children prepared to go East for an extended stay. Bill wrote a letter for Christine to receive in Chicago before she left. His statement that where they lived was of no great concern may have been true more for Bill than for Christine.

. . . To have day after day pass without a disagreeable word or feeling is as it should be between us and has caused me no end of happiness and satisfaction. I feel as though we were for the first time almost at a point where we understand each other. The absence of little "hold offs" in our relationship has on my side reawakened all the old feelings of fondness and affection. . . .

To me, the future has no bug-bear because if you and I are only happy the place and circumstances do not count for a great deal. I am glad that the "question" has hung fire so long because as matters now stand I feel practically free to decide either way, a thing that up to this time has been impossible. And I can decide without "feelings" which as I told you was what made me afraid to decide before. . . .

♥♥♥♥♥

Bill Reid, Jr., Belmont, CA, to Christine Reid, Cohasset, MA
6 September 1910

Christine and the children traveled East to Cohasset, Massachusetts, while Bill remained in Belmont, having seen them off the day before.

Yesterday was a pretty long day for me and the walk up to and into our house on my return was quite forlorn. . . .

The big empty bed, supper at the other house, the responsibility of being up this a.m. all of them emphasized your going & as I write here there is not a sound in the house. . . .

The balance sheet for the year shows that our net profit for last year was $12,000 which means that every boy over 90 is clear profit. . . .

♥♥♥♥♥

Bill Reid, Jr., Belmont, CA, to Christine Reid, Cohasset, MA
8 September 1910

Bill evidently had written a letter to his father about the conditions at the Belmont School and his poor relationship with his father.

I gave Papa my letter yesterday and I think he has taken it all-right because he has been very cordial today. . . .

I would like to hug you hard tonight & also have a good cuddle. Kiss the fellers for me and remember that I am loving you hard. . . .

♥♥♥♥♥

A Debutante's Passion—A Coach's Erotica

Bill Reid, Jr., Belmont, CA, to Christine Reid, Cohasset, MA
10 September 1910

Bill's letter told of taking the Belmont School boys to a San Francisco parade, where they marched successfully in uniform. He thought of Christine and was awaiting a reply from his father about the letter he recently wrote about the Belmont School situation.

. . . If you had been here last night you'd have got "yours" all right. I wanted to sleep with you in the worst way. The carnival spirit got hold of me & I would have bored in pretty hard. I am sorry you escaped.

Papa & Mama left for Los Gatos at 7:49 today so I am alone in authority. I have had no reply from Papa yet but will probably hear in a day or two. He accepted my criticism of wanting approbation, not criticism—because he had used almost exactly those words in teachers meetings, relative to their attitude toward him & his toward them. . . .

♥♥♥♥♥

Bill Reid, Jr., Belmont, CA, to Christine Reid, Cohasset, MA
12 September 1910

Bill told more about the parade and then later taking four workers at Belmont to San Francisco.

. . . The boys all said they'd never had such a good time before so I feel repaid for my efforts. . . . [However] I have been a cripple ever since for my left foot got all skinned up on the march & on the following day. . . . My new shoes were too narrow & too short for such a hike. . . .

On Saturday, the day after the parade I took Charlton, Bryner, Ross, & McCauley up to the city with me. . . . They chose the baths & fooled around in the water for an hour & a half. When they came out I had a big piece of chocolate layer cake for each. Some of the bathers were the limit. There were six girls in the water with men who felt them all over—the girls shrieking and wriggling.

It was the boldest set of operations I've ever seen. . . .

Well, there is nothing but love left to tell about. I miss you & the fellers very, very much & find the house empty & lonesome. As long, however, as I know that all is well between us & that you are happy there is a great deal to be thankful for. . . .

♥♥♥♥♥

Bill Reid, Jr., San Francisco, CA, to Christine Reid, Cohasset, MA
20 September 1910

Bill had a long talk, again, with his mother about leaving for the East, and announcing to Christine his preliminary decision to move East.

... I had quite a long talk with Mama yesterday about my whole affair here & told her that I felt I should probably go on three grounds:
1. You are not happy here even though willing to stay. (God bless you.)
2. I have not been consistently pleased with the work during four years of trial.
3. I seem unable to cooperate with Papa in a satisfactory way. If I disagree honestly with his policy, he regards me as dictatorial or unloyal. To be loyal & cooperative I must generally agree with him, which means the abandonment of my own opinions. This I am not willing to do. I must be free to think as my judgment dictates.

In addition I feel as though we can not have outside friends much, that the present increase is not enough to let both my family & ours live with any liberality, that there is no definite time in sight short probably of four years in which I can be sure of having charge & lastly the work is one where a person can work himself to death if he is conscientious—which I think I am. It is a case of force yourself to take time off.

Mama agreed that what I said was true. It looks as I shall decide to go, therefore. Do not build on it yet however. I am writing you as I should tell you, what is going on in my mind.

I could just kiss you to pieces for your dear remarks about doing what I decide. Girlie dear, on that basis this affair has got to come out right in the end. Your bully attitude makes me figure your side of it in to a greater degree than ever before & that without effort, or constraint. It makes me feel mighty good to have you stand up to the situation that was in the East & I do about feeling that no one of your acquaintances can pick a flaw in our love or loyalty to each other or fail to admire your "stuff."

I am being good, but last night I had a naughty dream about Pauline Chase. Why, I don't know because I never have admired her—but she floated in on my sensibilities much to my annoyance, but in my dreaming condition, seeming to over power my resistance to her. That is what I hate about being good, I do too much thinking of "legs" etc. & against my will at that. Don't be jealous!! I woke up before anything happened.

It seems a long time to me too, since you left and I am not by any means, adjusted to it. Keeping busy and feeling that you are getting a good rest out of the trip are very good antidotes but do not prevent me from loving you hard & missing you constantly. . . .

♥♥♥♥♥

Bill Reid, Jr., Belmont, CA, to Christine Reid, Cohasset, MA
20 September 1910

Bill sent two letters in one day, attempting to keep up with those coming from Christine.

A Debutante's Passion—A Coach's Erotica

You are a darling to have written to me so often, and I only wish I could get a chance to love you as much as I want to, to show you how much I appreciate it all. Three letters in three days!! is what I am referring to.

    I am awfully glad you are so happy and having such a good time, for it offsets in a large measure some rather blue experiences on my part here. . . . A reaction with Papa which disturbed me, a good deal, although I think I was in the right. It happened this way: Papa has made out some forms for scholarship records which he intends to have printed. He showed them to me & I said that I thought some Mr. McDougal had drawn up were better. . . . In the end he went off into another abuse of my attitude which he said was inconsiderate & dictatorial. When I added that in as much as it was for him to decide what he wanted & that he had decided, I did not see how he could argue that I was dictatorial or could be—he became still more upset. . . . I feel as though this were the beginning of the end with me here, but I shall wait for Papa's answer to my letter before doing or concluding anything. . . .

♥♥♥♥♥

Bill Reid, Jr., Belmont, CA, to Christine Reid, Cohasset, MA
24 September 1910

The proposition of leaving Belmont appeared clearer to Bill than at any time before, but the decision to leave or stay continued to be a most difficult one for him.

. . . Papa handed me his reply to the letter which I wrote him just before you left. . . . It is in fair spirit, but does not go far to any solution so far as Papa's end of it is concerned. As soon as I have answered I will send you his letter and a copy of my reply, which will ignore much and be comparatively brief. . . .

    Whether it is because I have been tired & depressed or not I don't know, but I have felt for over a week pretty well decided to leave here. In his letter to me, Papa speaks of hanging on here for a "year or so" longer which means five years if he sees fit. I am unwilling to go on on that basis.

    What is more I don't see how I am going to avoid getting all in each year owing to the fact that no recreation is available here without great effort & without recreation I simply go stale. . . . There is nothing for us here socially. The change amounts to this: On the grounds of our happiness & a feeling that I am not quite cut out to stand perpetual strain of work as is the case here—shall we throw up $150,000 worth of property & an assured income to enter upon a new business & without previous knowledge of that business? If we do, it is going to be hard sledding for a while at least, & we must cut out all unnecessary expenses even if they be trifling.

If you, knowing this & knowing we are willing to meet that situation—then I will go. I feel more ready & more consistently ready that ever before for this change. With my conservatism, it is hard to make the final journey, but I am ready to do so now—if you are ready to share the consequences with me, I have practically made up my mind to it & shall probably in my answer to Papa, terminate my discussion with him. I would prefer that you say nothing of this to anyone until I send you word that I have done this. The next thing is as to how soon I can go, & that depends on what sort of an opening there is with Jim or can be had with his assistance. After writing my reply to Papa, I shall write Jim & see what he has in mind & then try to adjust myself to circumstances. I wish you would talk with your father & find out how he feels about the probable length of time it will take me to be able to rent a house of our own & in fact anything bearing on the situation that may develop. If I cannot get a position before next summer or Papa cannot let me go before then, I should want to question your coming out here with me until then. If, on the other hand, I can get away at Christmas or thereabouts I don't know as we can afford the added expense, much as I would hate to think of going on here alone. . . .

♥ ♥ ♥ ♥ ♥

Bill Reid, Jr., Belmont, CA, to Christine Reid, Cohasset, MA
25 September 1910

Bill was still rather undecided about leaving, wanting Christine's final advice, but he was certainly not undecided about wanting to love Christine as the days and weeks rolled by.

. . . You are certainly a dear about writing to me and I thoroughly enjoy and appreciate it. Every letter has some dear little thing in it which I love to read and reread. The one today this—"I love you and shall be glad to get back to you even at the price of leaving." That was a dear thing for you to say and it makes me feel very happy. . . . I do love you a powerful lot, and miss you more & more. I would give a good deal in my present perplexed condition to have you here to love & play with. I feel the need for a good loving.

I have my smoking pretty well in hand now I think and aside from an occasional tendency to smoke two cigars a day (which I have done only twice since you left) I do not much miss the rest. I don't see that it makes much difference but I intend to put into you when the time comes is nearly a pure "essence" as I can. My eyes are better I think & probably my stomach, which in time would probably have been injured by my former practice. . . .

Instead of telling Papa in my reply that I am not going to stay, I shall wait for your answer before doing so. If I close the situation with Papa I don't want to reopen it again.

A Debutante's Passion—A Coach's Erotica

I am surely very lonesome—the house seems deserted, & I long for you. The feeling is satisfying nevertheless since it is based on the firm attachment which has lately grown up between us. On some previous occasions I felt concern because I did not feel lonely enough. I dread the thought of having you stay East until I come, if I leave here—it hurts but it is part of our medicine—if we change.

If you or your father feel a question as to my ability to fit in, in the East—say so—remembering that the decision this time is final.

How I wish I could flatten my mouth on yours & tangle myself up with you in bed. It would feel so good way, way up!!

Hugs & kisses to you Dearie, I long for you way beyond a physical longing and am very happy in the feeling. . . .

♥♥♥♥♥

Bill Reid, Jr., Belmont, CA, to Christine Reid, Cohasset, MA
29 September 1910

As Bill edged slowly but closer to leaving for the East, he and Christine seemed to be moving closer to coming together. Time would tell.

. . . I am so, so glad that you are getting so much use of your suit, and I wish Dearie that I could give you all the clothes that your dear little self could wish. It grates on me a good deal to be unable to show you in that way, the appreciation I feel at your loyalty to me. You have stuck, that I never lose sight of and you don't know how much pride and satisfaction it has given me, if you hadn't I don't know where we'd be now. I love, honor, admire and am endlessly grateful to you for it. . . .

I haven't had time to answer Papa's letter yet & I have to word my replies carefully to keep out of word pit falls. I hope to get it done by Sunday night. . . .

This is all, dearie except, more love & more yearning for a good loving.

♥♥♥♥♥

Bill Reid, Jr., Belmont, CA, to Christine Reid, Cohasset, MA
3 October 1910

Walter Camp, the long-time Yale athletic leader and "father" of American football, came to visit the Belmont School and Bill Reid. Camp and Reid observed the annual Stanford-California rugby game, which had recently replaced American football on the two campuses. Bill again stated that he was coming East and wrote that "we are so together now."

. . . The California bleachers cheered Camp & me when we came in. The game was very poor & turned out a tie. Camp told me what he thought but was very non-committal—"eloquently so" the papers put it—with every one else. He doesn't like the game for many good reasons. . . . Between the halves, Camp & I had to make a speech to the bleachers. I pointed out that in injuries, conditioning, type of players, chance for brutality, expense, etc., there was little to choose between the two games & that it was therefore largely a question of personal preference. Then I added that being a matter of personal preference I felt that the boys of the State should be allowed to exercise their preference instead of being compelled to choose Rugby by force of circumstances. . . . What I said seemed to take, for I had more applause as I finished than Walter did. . . .

Camp comes down here tomorrow at 2:51 & stays until 6:30. He is going to help me coach. I think it is mighty nice of him & of course the boys are well set up. . . .

I have four of your letters to answer. I feel as though it were cheating you out of your rights & desserts not to answer them individually. You certainly have been a dear to write so often—it has meant an awful lot to me. . . .

Mrs. Jackson was here only a day or so & then left, so Ethel was all there was. I was very busy & did not see much of her & besides I hardly dared see much of her after my previous experiences. I refer only to the scolding you gave me a couple of years ago. . . .

The fact is that I have decided to leave. I have not had a chance to answer Papa's letter yet—but I shall do so at the first opportunity. . . . You can feel sure however that I shall not again reverse. Whether Papa can now pay us for the house I don't know—if he can't I'm afraid your plan is impracticable, but I hope not. I'd love to get you into a cottage with me, its just what I would dearly like but it may have to be postponed as a part penalty of the change. Camp comes tomorrow . . . so for two days at least I shall be unable to talk or write to Papa. I shall tell Mama my decision tomorrow however.

I don't believe I can possibly get away until Christmas or even later & be fair to Papa. . . .

♥ ♥ ♥ ♥ ♥

Bill Reid, Jr., Belmont, CA, to Christine Reid, Cohasset, MA
7 October 1910

Bill Reid's depressant letter showed signs of something more upbeat as he again decided finally to leave Belmont & move East. Even the lengthy description of the visit of the esteemed Walter Camp's lacked luster. He wrote that he might take a trip East before Christmas to check on job possibilities.

I have just come through three or four of the "fiercest" days I ever spent in my life. I have been tired, blue, discouraged, and harassed and had a haunted feeling which has born down on me so that at times I felt as though I didn't care a continental what happened. I have been worse

A Debutante's Passion—A Coach's Erotica

off than I was in 1906 before the Yale game, and you remember what that was. It seemed as though I should burst with pressure. . . .

When I got home yesterday morning I felt as though I'd been through a keyhole. I finally could stand it no longer & told Mama what I had written you, about going. Her eyes filled with tears & we had a long talk about it all. She said in substance that it was awfully hard for all sides but that she felt that I was probably right. I am too thick in the head to write much of detail but I was tremendously touched by her whole attitude. After lunch I told Papa & said that I was discouraged, blue, & worried about it all. He was fine about it & I was greatly relieved to have let out my feelings to some one. I felt great sympathy for Papa who was simply splendid about it—not a word except of sympathy & help.

Well, he came up last night & we talked until quarter of twelve & practically—yes entirely cleared things up. We had not an unpleasant word. We were in entire sympathy, & Papa said as he left what he hadn't enjoyed an evening so much for 12 years. He said that he felt sorrier & yet at the same time more willing to have me go now, than at any previous time. Sorry because he felt that our relationship was on an excellent basis & because he felt ready to turn over the entire administration of the school to me—limiting himself to the scholarship end of it. He was more willing to have me go now than ever before because relations between us were never better. Had I gone before in ill humor he said that it would have crushed him & he'd never have recovered from it. As it was I went or I go with his blessing.

I tell you Dearie, you don't know what this struggle has cost us all out here. I have never had such a frightful time of it in my life before as this last week. I should have welcomed any relief.

Papa says that we may count on $1000 a year from him & told me again that if I should get into a place where I could get into a fine opportunity that he would back me to the extent of $25,000. . . . Now I don't want him to give us $1000 a year, but if we can have Aunt Mary's cottage & can live in it for my salary say $1200 & 4 or $500 additional I should be willing to take that much. Can we live in that house for a year at that rate. . . ? You cannot do the cooking & care for the children too. You can't stand it & I am not willing for you to try. So you must figure a servant in. . . .

Your last letter seemed a little impatient of my decision. Girlie dear, this whole thing has cost me more than you can ever realize. It has sat on my shoulders like a Harpy for about a year & I have done with it the best I could. I have now arrived safe & sound & with no ill feelings anywhere. . . .

I wish you were here with me to talk things over & to kiss & hug, for I crave the feeling of having you in my arms & lap; pressed against me, & to kiss & hug.

♥ ♥ ♥ ♥ ♥

EAST OVER WEST

Christine Reid, Brookline, MA, to Bill Reid, Jr., Belmont, CA
10 October 1910

Christine tried to reassure Bill of her love, the same day Bill wrote from California his most depressing and unsympathetic letter to Christine.

. . . Things will straighten out all right and we are going to be happier than ever before. You'll see. I love you quite terribly much, you dear old boy, I long to be in your arms to lie close and hand against you (and him) and then——well, I want that terribly. So you see, it's the same old story, after all. . . .

♥ ♥ ♥ ♥ ♥

Bill Reid, Jr., Belmont, CA, to Christine Reid, Cohasset, MA
10 October 1910

Bill was in deep depression while determining when he would depart for East. He had received unsympathetic letters from Christine, which were apparently discarded. He would soon regret sending this correspondence.

Since I last wrote, two letters have come from you which have troubled me deeply. . . . I have tried three times now but with the same result—I could not bear to send any of them. It may be due to the frightful depression I am just struggling out of, but those letters seem to me so lacking in sympathy and consideration that I find myself wondering if anything is any longer worthwhile. I have got to a point where I don't care much what happens. . . .

I am losing all I have gained by seven years of effort, have nothing saved because I expected by now to be in charge with a larger salary, am leaving my father in the hole, have nothing but an indefinite future to look to, have my family taken away, an absolutely empty house to live in—and then you put it up to me that under these conditions, I have a fair chance to see how I like the work. It isn't a square deal.

Then as regards the time it has taken me to reach a decision and the impatience which you have expressed at the delays—it seems to me that your own vacillation, when you only had to decide whether you'd be happy here or not without assuming the responsibility of carrying the support of the family on your shoulders in case a change was needed, thus it seems to me ought to have rendered you not only tolerant but warmly sympathetic. Instead—you say—"If you love me don't discuss the question anymore." If I can't even turn to you in this situation I don't see what there is left. . . . I owe quite as much to my family as you do to yours and I am not going to break my father's and mother's hearts. . . .

A Debutante's Passion—A Coach's Erotica

Finally, you say—"I cannot but compare my married life to that of all my different friends and they have all had such a peaceful and sheltered existence, compared to mine." That strikes me as rather a hard commentary, when I am in a hole, and especially when I am in an endeavor to make you happier. I realize that I have made a mess of things and that you would probably have been much better off if you had thrown your lot in with some Eastern fellow—and have been doing my utmost to recover. It therefore comes hard to have all this pointed out to me at the time the strain is greatest. . . .

My heart goes out to you in the tenderest way in spite of everything, and I would give the world to hold you in my arms and love you. I have looked for the words "kiss," "hug," "sit in your lap" in the last fifteen letters—I am hungry for it—but it hasn't appeared. . . .

If I could only have you here to fix this all up—to hug you, & kiss you, & squeeze you & just feel you against me & with me, it would save the worry and anxiety of these next two weeks.

Tenderly,
"Bill"

♥♥♥♥♥

Bill Reid, Jr., Belmont, CA, to Christine Reid, Cohasset, MA
11 October 1910

Bill had written the most negative letter of that fall just the day before. It would be one that he would regret for a long time. The next morning, Bill felt remorse for his previous letter.

. . . When we are not in harmony it is next to impossible for me to work. . . . It hurts to be so far away and to have to wait so long to hear. I feel better today, probably because I feel as though I had unloaded my feelings, but it hurts to think that I have poured them into you. . . .

I would like to take you in my arms and hug you and have you in my lap, and then in bed. I feel as though just one evening of this sort would end this situation and I want it—so, so much. My arms ache to be around you and my heart longs for you.

♥♥♥♥♥

Bill Reid, Jr., Belmont, CA, to Christine Reid, Cohasset, MA
13 October 1910

Bill had made his decision to go East, but he was unhappy with the situation with Christine and her attachment to her family. He began his letter uncharacteristically with "Dear Christine."

Mama has not yet shown me your letter to her, but Papa says she intends to do so. . . .

I have been chosen by the English Department of Stanford as one of the judges in one of the important prize contests to be held there in November. The subject of the essays will be "The Ethical Aspects of Intercollegiate Rivalry." I have accepted. . . .

I hope that I shall cheer up & develop a little more enthusiasm than I have at present. . . .

The feeling steals over me too, that back there as you are with your family and friends, I am rather out of it—You seeming to be rather swallowed up by your surroundings and influenced by your environment. I feel as though in this affair it were more a question of your family, you & me rather than just you & me. As a result of everything that has transpired I am "up in the air" & do not find myself on solid ground. . . .

This letter is hardly worth sending but is the best I can do just now.

♥ ♥ ♥ ♥ ♥

Bill Reid, Jr., Belmont, CA, to Christine Reid, Brookline, MA
16 October 1910

In Bill's attempt at justifying his downbeat letter of October 10th, he wrote the longest letter in years, 28 pages. He compared the depressing feeling he was experiencing with his worst football coaching days at Harvard. Christine, he said, was contributing to his deepening depression. Yet, he wrote of his passion for Christine.

. . . I have felt very conscience stricken since yesterday morning because I have figured that my upset letters must have arrived and that without a chance for me to see you and love you in sort of atonement. . . . I . . . got your fat letter. . . . [It] warmed me up both in heart & passion. Tired as I was, your closing remarks about "first night" were too much for me. . . . I wanted you & could not for the life of me get out of my mind the mental picture of you lying in bed with nothing on and inviting me with eyes and the general pose of your body to satisfy an almost unbearable desire. I knew that if you had been here under the circumstances and I had felt of you that I would have found you hot and juicy. . . & I could not stand it. . . .

. . .The conditions of the last three weeks, with the loneliness of everything, has borne me down as nothing else I've ever experience not excepting my worst football days. . . .

The tone of your last two letters was a great pleasure to me because I read in them an undercurrent of love and sympathy which I had felt was lacking in many previous ones. I felt as though it were you alone & not you egged on by environment & possibly Agnes. I may be unfair to Agnes in this—but I have felt as though she were advising this as that action on your part. I want you, dearie, to deal with me & no one else. This is our affair & it's up to us to handle it & we can.

A Debutante's Passion—A Coach's Erotica

Your suggestion that we begin all over again suits me to a T. & I will join hands & also other parts of our anatomy on that basis. If Aunt Mary lets the house go, I think as I wrote in my definitive announcement that your castles-in-the-air will prove to have pretty good earthly foundation. . . .

I haven't forgotten the little bench at the side of Aunt Mary's house either—where I first kissed you. I can recall now, feeling your loose hair by your forehead brush against my cheek as I got nearer & nearer to the final leap to a kiss. Those were great old days. Look inside of your ring for a reminder. . . .

About Papa's buying the house I think I have already written of the most feasible & reasonable plan. He owed Aunt Hattie $10,000 which he felt is honor bound to make up to her because an investment she made at his advice failed. This he has paid, together with 4 or $5000 left on the new house. He is now debt free, but the first payment on the ranch is about exhausted. The next one comes next year early. If he pays us up gradually & gives us an equivalent . . . it seems to me that he is not only doing the square thing, but the handsome thing. I was greatly pleased to have you end up your proposal & remarks with—"I don't mean to be horrid & I leave all that sort of thing to you." Because your expression "It seems hard to be cheated out of all that" wasn't after all a very pleasant thing for you to say of my father. I will land things right if you will just be patient with me, feel confidence in me and give me time. . . .

Are we going to "let loose" that first night? I am crazy to & know that I can give you such a time as you have never yet had. But what about the consequences? I can feel now the contentment with which I should turn over to sleep after having turned loose way up in you & deluged you with my stored up vitality. It seems as though I couldn't bear not to be "natural." The thought of leaving everything in is fascinating to me—despite consequences. I will guarantee a successful evening from all points of view or of touch. Do not leave this letter around as it would make fine gossip for the maid. . . .

Church today—especially the singing seemed to have almost a sacred significance to me—largely I guess because I was thinking so of you & seemed to be so in tune with you. . . .

♥♥♥♥♥

Bill Reid, Jr., Belmont, CA, to Christine Reid, Brookline, MA
19 October 1910

The agony of the October 10th letter remained with Bill. The ranch, which had caused such financial stress to Bill's father for a dozen years, had been sold, but still could default back to the elder Reids.

I am expecting a letter from you within the next three days, in answer to my awful one, and it is no fun. . . . Your last two letters were perfectly

EAST OVER WEST

dear and you unconsciously covered many things that I took up in my letter. . . . I am sorry that I ever sent the old thing although at the time it seemed to me the only way to clean things up. . . .

The people who bought the ranch are now offering it for sale, which looks as though they had had a row. We are absolutely protected however as unless they make the payments they forfeit all that they have already made & the property comes back to us. We sold that at just the psychological moment. . . .

I prefer to come. . . about January eighteenth. . . that. . . will be a help to Papa that I owe him and will give me a more satisfied feeling. . . . I dread Christmas. . . without you, but I really think this is the best plan. . . .

♥ ♥ ♥ ♥ ♥

Bill Reid, Jr., Belmont, CA, to Christine Reid, Brookline, MA
21 October 1910

Bill hoped his relationship with Christine would improve, and he would soon join her in married bliss, while trying to forget the October 10th letter.

I am dreading tonight's mail a great deal because I feel almost positive that your letter will come then. . . . I . . . only wish I could ignore the whole thing. . . .

. . . It won't be so long at worst before I have you in my arms and your dream of not being always away from one family or the other, will be realized. I miss you every moment but the relief at having everything settled and without ill-feeling or a break in my family is so great that I feel willing to put up with almost anything in the actual carrying out of my plans. . . .

♥ ♥ ♥ ♥ ♥

Bill Reid, Jr., Belmont, CA, to Christine Reid, Brookline, MA
22 October 1910

Christine's response to the October 10th letter arrived. Following a telegram to Christine, Bill waited, unsuccessfully, for Christine's reply, and he sat down to compose his apology for his October 10th letter.

Today has seemed almost interminable to me because your letter came and with it the deepest remorse. To think that I hurt you so and to have you tell me to decide what I want to do about it almost makes my heart stop beating. As if the thing I most wanted wasn't to get you in my arms and sit and love you for eternity. I feel just as though my insides had all been removed and only a shell remained. To be at this distance and so helpless almost drives me frantic and everything

A Debutante's Passion—A Coach's Erotica

I have done has been in a sort of stupor and by the greatest tax on my will power. I have spent my spare time alone in our bed room just thinking and thinking and worrying. A more miserable fellow it would be hard to find.

Girlie dear, I don't suppose I can undo all I've wrought but I will try awfully hard if you will forgive me. You are all I've got, and I do depend on you so. It seems as though I should never get out of trouble, first in one place and then another. . . .

You have stood by me out here in what was almost a "hell" to you and you did all that I could ask to make it go. . . .

I can't answer your letter seriatim, it's too horrible for that. . . . You darling, I know that you are not mercenary, unsympathetic or hard hearted, but your letters caught me all unstrung, down and out, and I could not raise myself from my depression. . . . I am sorry, sorry dearie that I wrote the letter. It does not represent my feeling or estimate of you at all—down in your heart, you know it too. All I can say is that I hope you will make an undeserved allowance for the condition I was in at the time. I want you as you are and by heavens when we get together we'll stick. All that I have thus far said is based on the supposition that you are willing to take me. . . . I am heart broken at what I have done and beg you forgiveness.

♥ ♥ ♥ ♥ ♥

Bill Reid, Jr., Belmont, CA, to Christine Reid, Brookline, MA
23 October 1910

Bill received a telegram and letter from Christine, which immediately turned his depression to an immediate jubilation.

. . . Certainly I cannot love you more fully than I do just at this minute. I just think & think of you and long for a hard, hard hug and a long drawn out kiss. I'd like to get your cheeks in my hands turn your mouth up and just go to it. . . .

Don't worry about the "anxious to be loved" idea with which you close. You'll be loved all right enough—so hard in fact that it is almost painful to me. But I love the pain. . . .

The days have been glorious & the moon large & red as it was at Tahoe and it has been most tantalizing. There is just enough "sting" in the air to make lying together snug and warm. I think often of your coming over with the scissor position and with you & me pressed together and it is thrilly. I often wonder if I am vulgar in all this—and yet to you—with whom I have a right to all these things—it seems as though it were merely an overflow of love which emphasizes my passion for you. What do you think about it. . . ?

♥ ♥ ♥ ♥ ♥

EAST OVER WEST

Bill Reid, Jr., Belmont, CA, to Christine Reid, Brookline, MA
26 October 1910

Bill's life crisis continued. The day after his 32nd birthday, Bill contemplated coming East, as a representative of the Pacific Athletic Association, to the annual meeting of the Amateur Athletic Union and being with Christine for a short time. He also indicated that Dr. Edward Nichols, in charge of Harvard baseball, had invited Bill to coach the baseball team. Certainly the amount of pay, knowing what little Bill might make initially coming East, would make Bill consider the position.

. . . Yesterday was my thirty second birthday and I do so long to have you here to celebrate it with me. I feel as though I'd been shut off from hugs and kisses long enough and from other "nice little girlish features" without having a girless birthday too. . . . As I look back on the 32 years of my life, it seems to me to be largely a story of "might have beens" and does not for ten years seem to have amounted to much. I am determined however to make up for it in the next ten & to make up for my failure to make you happy. . . . I am going to make this thing "go" and by heavens I'll make you happy yet. . . .

The meeting [of the Amateur Athletic Union] is in N. York, on Nov. 19, the day of the Yale game. What tempted me awfully was needless to say the chance of folding my arms around your dear self. I had a vision of taking you to the Yale game, going on to New York—spending the night with you or in you there & then coming back to Boston for a day to see Jim & your Father before my return. It is a frightful temptation but I can't yet reconcile myself to the situation from all sides. . . .

[Dr. Nichols wrote:] "If you will look over the five names on the baseball committee, Wendell, Frothingham, Garcelon, the Capt. & I, you will see that I am to run the baseball situation. We want a coach from the middle of February to the end of June and a moderate amount of time in the fall. We will pay $2,500 or $3,000 if we get the right man. Would you take it temporarily or permanently in connection with any work you may get here? If you would, it would settle our troubles, and it might help you out, either temporarily or until you get something permanent."

At present, I don't think it would be at all wise to consider it. Mixing into athletics, besides the strain on me, would I think give me a black eye with any first class firm. I haven't talked with Papa yet about it, but shall do so today. Whether I take it or not, it makes me feel pretty good to have my coaching thought enough of to come after. I have always felt that the letter handed me by the Athletic Committee after I left the eleven in 1906 was not wholly representative, but more specially a case of "Well, he won't be back & we'll make this as much of a boost as we can. . . ."

♥ ♥ ♥ ♥ ♥

A Debutante's Passion—A Coach's Erotica

Bill Reid, Jr., Belmont, CA, to Christine Reid, Brookline, MA,
28 October 1910

Bill sent a short letter empathizing with Christine, whose younger sister Louise was in the hospital for some undisclosed malady, which was likely severe depression.

. . . Just sort of cuddly snuggling with you would be so delicious. I feel particularly like it because I sympathize so keenly with you in Louise's troubles. I wish I could be there to help. . . and to relieve you in such occasions as I could with the fellers. You simply must get a nurse—that's a necessity. If you don't I'm afraid you'll break down and then where would we be. . . .

♥♥♥♥♥

Bill Reid, Jr., Belmont, CA, to Christine Reid, Brookline, MA
29 October 1910

Bill attempted to put a sympathetic voice to all that had happened in the fall of 1910.

. . . One thing you can count on, I will not allow anything to disturb our relations. . . .

Now I size things up this way. When you went East you were in doubt as to what I was going to do, you had the children to look after and we had our little affair. Since then Louise's trouble has come or it has been impending right along. All of these things have conspired to make it very, very hard both physically, mentally & emotionally.

Now my going is settled. Only the date remains & I expect Jim's answer to my letter to give some light on that. At any rate the decision has been made. Then our affair has been straightened out. So there remains Louise & the children. . . .

Your moving must have been very hard and here again I wish I could have been there to hug you & kiss you between times & in the evening to have taken you in my lap before the fire and loved you to pieces. In bed too, I would have rubbed your back and petted you and tried to cheer you up. Poor little girl, it is hard. . . .

♥♥♥♥♥

Bill Reid, Jr., Belmont, CA, to Christine Reid, Brookline, MA
30 October 1910

Bill and Christine's wavering passion for each other was probably influenced by their insecurities and penchant for days of depression. It was time for Christine's melancholy to be addressed.

... My heart reaches out to you in all of this depressing worry over Louise, and I long so to get you in my arms and comfort you. ...

With the question settled & ourselves together—at any rate I am with you—we must now resolutely & cheerfully face the future feeling that we are in sight of the end of our troubles. Cheer up little girl—we are going to be all right. I am ready for anything and anxious to do for you. ...

♥♥♥♥♥

Bill Reid, Jr., Belmont, CA, to Christine Reid, Brookline, MA
31 October 1910

Bill kept paying for his earlier treatment of Christine.

It seems to me that I do very little thinking now-a-days except about you. ... I think of you in the house & with the fellers & want so much to be with you. It isn't passion for my sympathy with you overshadows that. It is simply love—and a longing to be at your side where I belong. ...

♥♥♥♥♥

Bill Reid, Jr., Belmont, CA, to Christine Reid, Brookline, MA
2 November 1910

As Christine's empathy for Bill pined, it was devouring the heart of Bill as he awaited his return to the East.

... I am glad that you have told me that you do not feel right toward me because as you say I should not want you to write me anything that you do not feel. But just the same I have missed your love dreadfully and have hoped that each letter would bring some indication of a return of your old feelings. I realize that it is my fault. ... I feel pretty much of an outcast. But I am coming nevertheless for I do want to see you. ...

Jim's offer to you of a nurse was mighty nice, but I see no reason why we cannot employ our own. ... If we have got to have assistance I want Papa and Mama to give it and not Jim. I feel pretty sensitive on that point. ... I want you to have whatever help you need, as I wired you, and I'll pay for it if I have to play Sunday ball. ...

I am a little afraid that feeling as you do my writing of my fondness for you may be annoying rather than helpful and so I am going to hold myself in as best I can until I know. ... As for May Lewis or any of the rest of them, I don't want to hear about them. I don't care about them at all—it is you I want. If I am not decent enough for you, I wouldn't last at all with them. I don't want you to think of other girls that way. I am satisfied as it is and I'd go single before I took any of them. ...

I have definitely given up the New York trip as I do not feel that I can afford the time. Jim's answer has just come stating that he is to consult Mr. Read with regard to a position with the firm and that the sooner I can get on the better. . . . Papa will probably go East in a week or so & I will have to look after things. It is possible that I may leave here in time to be in Boston by Christmas. . . . A great deal will depend on whether you want me and in Papa's trip. He must be back before I can start. I can't go & feel that you are going to be cold to me or that you are indifferent to my coming. I could not stand it and my work would be a failure too. . . .

I love you dearly and long to have you in my arms & lap. I shall be patient & hopeful and ready for you when you want me. . . .

♥ ♥ ♥ ♥ ♥

Bill Reid, Jr., Belmont, CA, to Christine Reid, Brookline, MA
4 November 1910

Never had Bill written so many letters in such a short period of time. He was trying to save his marriage.

My heart is very warm for you this morning and I just must send you a line. If you only could come here to straighten things out—what a welcome you would get. I can feel now how my heart would thump while I was waiting for the head-light of your train. . . .

♥ ♥ ♥ ♥ ♥

Bill Reid, Jr., Belmont, CA, to Christine Reid, Brookline, MA
5 November 1910

Bill was fighting the good battle to keep Christine as his loving wife.

Your dear, dear letter expressing such regret at your forgetting my birthday and closing with an appeal to me to help you "get back" reached way, way down into every nook and corner of my heart. It took hold so that I felt as though I was bleeding there and I finally had to seek relief in another night message.

I am so anxious to get you back. I long & long for a word from you that shows that you feel once again as you used to. Why, why did I write that awful letter [of October 10th]. It doesn't represent my feelings or estimate of you at all. Your letters reached me at a time when I was almost frantic with strain. . . . You know that if I had spoken to you that way that I should have been utterly miserable all day (if I lasted that long) and that we should have loved it out that night. . . . To think that I have wounded you so cuts me all up and I am ready to make any atonement that you require. I have no complaint to make only a determination to make it up to you during the rest of my life. . . .

I am going to get you back. I am no quitter and will do anything to make you happy again. I am getting an awful punishment and it is eating me up, but so long as I can stand up, I shall struggle on for you. . . .

    I had a talk with Papa last night and he says that he will pay us $12,000 for the house when we need it & want it, but that he would rather wait a little longer if it is convenient to us. Meanwhile he says that he will give us $1200 a year—$100 a month, & whatever else we may need besides. As the $1200 is more than double the income from the $12,000, it seems to me that we are mighty well off.

    When I come will you live with me? If sleeping with you and all that that implies is distasteful I will sleep anywhere else you want. It is you that I want to do for. I am at your service. . . . I am sure that I can make the little cottage a house & I long for the time when I shall come in from the day's work to take you in my arms. . . . .

    You will find out one thing whatever happens and that is that you have married a fellow who will never "give up. . . ."

♥ ♥ ♥ ♥ ♥

Bill Reid, Jr., Belmont, CA, to Christine Reid, Brookline, MA
6 November 1910

Bill's feelings of regret kept "piling up" in Christine's mailbox.

. . . It is horrid without you & I miss you so. . . .

    I am hoping for a letter tomorrow and if you do not feel easier in your mind toward me in your next couple of letters I am coming to you. . . . You need me and if you aren't relieved, I am coming to take you in my arms. . . . Good night, darling, I need you so. . . .

♥ ♥ ♥ ♥ ♥

Bill Reid, Jr., Belmont, CA, to Christine Reid, Brookline, MA
7 November 1910

A short letter about packing Christine's clothes, and being sorry that they couldn't be new ones, allowed Bill to send his love.

. . . If I had you here I'd want to hold you close to me all day and all night. I would just about devour you. . . .

♥ ♥ ♥ ♥ ♥

Bill Reid, Jr., Belmont, CA, to Christine Reid, Brookline, MA
8 November 1910

As Bill prepared for his move East and as his father began making inquiries about someone to take Bill's place at the Belmont School, Bill had to deal with Christine's melancholy.

A Debutante's Passion—A Coach's Erotica

... If only I could feel that you felt right, and could find the dear little loving messages which I used to look forward to so—I should be as happy as I can be at such a distance from you. As it is I am awfully worried and feel at times as though I simply cannot stand it. It is bad enough under any circumstances to be so far way, but to have a cloud between us is just plain torture. ...

♥♥♥♥♥

Albert L. Lincoln, Boston, MA to Bill Reid, Jr., Belmont, CA
9 November 1910

Bill had written his father-in-law about returning to the East, and Mr. Lincoln responded, indicating some of Christine's problems as well as those of her younger sister Louise.

I am very glad to learn that you will probably come on here before Christmas. Under all the circumstances your decision to give up Belmont seems to me wise, hard as it will be for you to break away from all its associations and to leave your mother & father. I never imagined it would be such a strain on Christine to live away from her family & to leave her associations here, but we must face the fact that it has been a constant strain upon her & had she not been so much stronger than Louise I fear the result might have been the same. ... Christine looks well most of the time, her backache has practically ceased & her digestion is such that she no longer "puts" her food, but for all that it is plain to see that she is feeling a strain & I feel that she truly needs you by her side for the support, comfort & solace which a wife must get from a husband whom she truly loves & who loves her in return. Men little appreciate how much little attentions mean to a woman, but I'm sure you must realize by this time how dependent Christine is upon them & I think she is quick to respond. ...

Mrs. Lincoln & I only regret that we cannot have you all at 61 Walnut Place, but Geoffrey Jr., will have to come there & a place must be ready for Louise when she has sufficiently recovered to leave Dr. Stedman's. The latter gives us encouraging reports last evening. She is sleeping finely, ... eating well & beginning to take an interest & he said her progress had been remarkably good. She is still too weak, nervously, to talk much & she is not able to write. It will take time & care. ...

By the way, I think it was my fault that Christine said anything about your Pa paying something for your house. I remarked that probably the house was worth to the School all it cost & as it was legally your Pa's, he might feel, if it really did add value to the estate, like repaying at least the $8,000 I had put into it. ...

Please give my love to your Pa & Ma & I hope they'll forgive Christine whom I suppose they will hold largely responsible for their disappointment as regards the school.

♥♥♥♥♥

EAST OVER WEST

Bill Reid, Jr., Belmont, CA, to Christine Reid, Brookline, MA
9 November 1910

Bill discussed a football game on the 19th with Alameda which he thought would be very difficult, but he had a good team at the Belmont School.

. . . This is to be my last year of coaching and my last game, and I am awfully anxious to win it. It will be a great relief when it is over. . . .

♥ ♥ ♥ ♥ ♥

Bill Reid, Jr., Belmont, CA, to Christine Reid, Brookline, MA
11 November 1910

Bill was offered a bond salesman position through his brother-in-law's efforts. Finally deciding to return to the East, he told Christine that he would not consider coaching again. He wanted Christine to tell her acquaintances that she had returned to the East for good, with or without Bill, not just for an extended visit.

You simply must not keep things quiet any longer. I didn't realize that it would be at all hard for you supposing that it would be assumed that you were merely visiting your family as you have done heretofore. My only reason for wanting it kept quiet was because I was afraid it would get out here before we announced. . . .

I just tossed & tossed in bed last night and feel more like a skeleton than a man. Such absolute anguish as the whole thing has caused me gives me a pretty good idea of why some men take to drink. I won't of course but I never have been as tortured before. My present plan is to come to you for a few days anyhow—leaving here the night of the Alameda game—if there is a train. It is a big expense but I'd give every single thing I have for just a minute with you. My coming will put off Papa's trip but I don't believe I can live through a month more of this. It is simply killing me. . . .

I am glad you spoke to Jim as you did about the baseball. I wrote him today about it. You may say that I am absolutely through with coaching of any sort. This is final & I will not go out even if permission were granted by my employers. I am going to knuckle down to business and try to give you the home & freedom which you have so long been deprived of. That is my goal and nothing can deflect me from that line. I am going to bore in with absolute fierceness & if you will only come to my arms I will make a big success of it. . . .

My heart goes out to you and I cannot but believe that the Lord will answer my prayers for you. That little period every night when I implore divine help and wisdom and courage is the only little respite in all the long hours as they drag on. . . .

♥ ♥ ♥ ♥ ♥

A Debutante's Passion—A Coach's Erotica

Bill Reid, Jr., Belmont, CA, to Christine Reid, Brookline, MA
13 November 1910

Bill was determined to compete for financial success and a happier marriage with Christine.
. . . I think you will find my point of view changed in a great many respects when you see me. I don't believe I'll measure much short of those fellows whose wives you have felt were getting what your dear heart craves. You will get it all in big measure see if you don't. We are going to be awfully happy & I know it. . . .
You may get a telegram from me about the time this reaches you asking how you feel. My idea is this, if you are still unhappy, I am coming to see you for a few days—I can't bear it any longer. I must feel that we are together. When that is accomplished, the dawn of what I believe will be the happiest part of our lives will be at hand. I can work like a Trojan if my heart is at peace and I am coming back entirely convinced that it is wisest for me as well as for you, as you need not feel in even a remote way that it is up to you. I feel as though things are beginning to clear up & consequently more cheerful. . . .

♥♥♥♥♥

Bill Reid, Jr., Belmont, CA, to Christine Reid, Brookline, MA
14 November 1910

Bill was still not sure where Christine stood in relation to him, particularly because of things that he had done and said in the past.

I feel dreadful to think that you have so long remembered things which I have said to you in impatience and which do not in the least represent my feelings toward you. . . . I do not blame you dearie, for in a measure discounting what I say, on the ground that I have said the same things before and yet have not lived up to it,—you have grounds for such a feeling—but if ever again I say anything to wound your dear heart my name is not Bill Reid. You are very sensitive and I am rough and you have taken literally much that I did not mean. I ought to have realized it before—but I do now—and little girl—there will no more of it. . . .
Don't you dare to mention the word failure to me again. . . . You haven't failed and I don't want you to think for a minute that I think so for I don't and never have. You have stuck to me through a regular "hell" and I am going to make up to you for it. . . .
If I can, I shall leave here in time to reach Boston before Christmas, but don't build on it. . . . When you move into Aunt Mary's get all the help you need & spare yourself, and you must have a cook & nurse at any rate until I get there. . . .
I am devoting my spare time to arithmetic dealing with percentage, interest, stocks, bonds, etc., so as to have some basis of work in the

office. I am such a green horn. . . . I am in this to win and win I will. That home which you consider so far off is going to materialize if I have to work all night to make up for my late start. . . . We will go higher than Freel's Peak if I have to pick you up in my arms and carry you. Don't you feel it . . . ?

I am so delighted with Jim's telegram making a definite offer that it is hard for me to sit still long enough to write. To think that I have a start and to me, what is best of all, that I shall have you in my arms in a little over a month is too delicious for words. . . .

I will let the bed-room set go as you suggest although I hate to think of any other bed as ours. That was so comfy & roomy and so much has happened in it. . . .

♥♥♥♥♥

Bill Reid, Jr., Belmont, CA, to Christine Reid, Brookline, MA
15 November 1910

The entire letter of Bill to Christine is included, written as he prepared for his journey to the East.

My darling Wife:
Today has been an unusually busy one for me but that has not prevented my thoughts from traveling Eastward at every opportunity. To you has gone love, sympathy and courage and everything else that my fondness for you can suggest as likely to be of help.

Everything is so definite now and so much has been cleared up that I feel as though we have struck smooth weather and a good breeze again. Except for being actually there everything is as favorable as it can be and my state of mind is such that I am feeling very enthusiastic.

We were afraid that Mama had pneumonia yesterday afternoon but it finally developed into one of her fainting spells from which she rallied in fine shape and we are now entirely easy. She sat up in bed today & read and talked and it will be hard to keep her in bed tomorrow.

I am getting a lot of rivets ready and when I get East I am going to rivet you to me so that you'll know that we can't be slipped apart any more as has been the case every time you've been East. I am already half dreading leaving you for my first day's work—it seems as though when I do get you, I shall want you with me every minute.

I have written to Jim today but did not get a chance to write to your father. I shall do so tomorrow if I do not go to the city which I think is very probable. I have got to go to a P.A.A. [Pacific Athletic Association] meeting tomorrow night & shall probably go up, come back & then go up again.

We have had just one rain since last May and the weather has been perfect. If it holds out this week we shall have the roof on the new house [for school boys] and the concrete walls up in front of the main house. The night is clear and moonlight with just a tingle in the air. Just the sort of a cozy snuggle with me longing for it. Never mind, it will be only a month and then—what a loving you're due for.

I have decided to learn Bridge if you want me to and I will turn in with you on anything else which will yield you my companionship. I am out for blood in this deal and you are not going to be disappointed in me again.

I am sending you a check for $50.00 more so that you won't feel that you have got to count every cent and also for you to get that nurse with. I want you to get Miss Rick if you can to take the children for a week & then go off for a visit to Tede's, Dorrie's or elsewhere. You can then rest, get good sleep and not have the fellers on your mind. Don't say you can't do it, just do it. It will do you good and gratify me immensely.

I am wearing out everything old I've got so that I should not have to bring back any more than possible. Mama has had Mrs. Smith make me a half dozen pairs of short drawers of splendid material, and three heavy night gowns so I am fixed in those two respects for a year at least.

I shall start packing just as soon as the Alameda game is over on Saturday so as to get things we are likely to need on the way. I don't see but that we are going to be very coy and I look forward to our cottage with great pleasure.

There is no use talking dearie, you are the whole show to me, and I am beginning like the boys to count off the days. Don't worry, I'm in fine fettle and I am going to make you dreadfully happy.

What a loving you'd get this minute if I could just lay hands on you. Good night and affection unlimited.
Fondly, "Piddie"
♥ ♥ ♥ ♥ ♥

Bill Reid, Jr., Belmont, CA, to Christine Reid, Brookline, MA
16 November 1910

Just a month or so after being at his depths of despair, Bill moved to near ecstasy after receiving a telegram from Christine. However, Bill's father would arrive in Boston a month before Bill, attempting to find a replacement for Bill at the Belmont School, and his visit would be a disturbance to Christine.

My darling little Girl:
I am just this minute back from the city for the second time today and it is late so I shan't write much but I cannot wait till morning to tell you how happy your telegram, with its loving message, has made me. You dear, dear thing, how I wish I could smother you with kisses to show you how near you are to me. It has put new energy into me and I have whistled all the way up from the station I felt so happy. Miss Wakelee

took the message & wrote it on her typewriter so that I hadn't the least idea what was in the envelope until I began to read. I have the slip in my pocket and read it over constantly all through I know it by heart. The one seven three was so much more than I dared hope for that my heart just bounded with joy. Your name, which I love, signed to the message does look so good and sounds so like it used to with the ring in it that I fairly ate it up.

I do feel so happy over it all that I can hardly settle down. "Things" have developed so fast in the last four days that I can hardly realize it. I'll hang on here till Christmas alright but what's more I'll hang on to you when I once lay my hands on you—till doomsday.

The only "out" about the whole situation is that I can't get at you now. Such a loving as I'd give you, you've never had and such a closeness as I should get to you. Kisses would be too ordinary to count. Hugs, squeezes, arms around your neck, cheek against cheek, in my lap, just wrapped up in my whole being that's what would happen to you.

Surely, dearie, my prayers have been answered and ten fold—all in my estimation because I had faith. I shall not miss my prayers again so long as I live.

Papa has his ticket for Friday and tomorrow, just think of it, I shall pack his trunk with our things, the first installment. Isn't it exciting and bully?

Girlie, with you with me, they can't stop me—I am bound to score. Everything has worked out so beautifully & it seems to me that our sky has hardly a cloud in it. I feel as though I had dined on nectar, only better. You blessed little girl.

Goodnight, "Pid"

♥ ♥ ♥ ♥ ♥

Bill Reid, Jr., Belmont, CA, to Christine Reid, Brookline, MA
17 November 1910

It took little to kill Bill's joyous spirit, as had happened in the past. Just as he was about to travel East, Christine had penned some less-than-loving statements.

. . . But our relations are my one big concern. Your letter last night, if I had not that telegram in my pocket, would have added almost more than I could bear, dear as it was. To have you still cold toward me, even though you feel sympathy and interest in me, just gnaws away at my heart. I am not blaming you, as I realize that it is my just reward, and I cannot complain, but it just about does me up. I don't feel that it is in my power to love you or sympathize with you any more than I am doing. Every action of affection, love, devotion and sympathy in me is centered on you. . . .

♥ ♥ ♥ ♥ ♥

A Debutante's Passion—A Coach's Erotica

Bill Reid, Jr., Belmont, CA, to Christine Reid, Brookline, MA
20 November 1910

Bill kept up his stream of letters to Christine, missing only a few days.

Well, dearie one month from today and I shall be on my way to you. I feel as though this whole distressing experience has really brought Christianity to me and that there is fullness to me and that there is a fullness to my heart and a sympathy in it which I have never before experienced. . . .

My dearest love to you, darling and my closest sympathy. I need you & you need me and we've got to get together. . . .

♥♥♥♥♥

Bill Reid, Jr., Belmont, CA, to Christine Reid, Belmont, CA
23 November 1910

Looking forward to being with Christine by Christmas, Bill could be more optimistic than a month before.

. . . No mention has yet been made of salary to me—but I am not worrying. The chance is what I want and I'll make myself valuable. . . .

Good old days!! and yet they won't compare with my Christmas this year. Such a celebration as it will be—and all of it with the consciousness that we'll never separate again. . . .

I am determined that your home shall be the dearest that ever was. Wait & see if I don't put those other fellows in the shade—Jim & Herbert included. Perhaps I shan't have so much means, but heavens there'll be love and harmony and tenderness. . . .

♥♥♥♥♥

Christine Reid, Brookline, MA, to Bill Reid, Jr., Belmont, CA
5 December 1910

In one of the few existing letters from this period, Christine expressed a lack of need for her father-in-law to come for a visit to the Lincolns while he was on a recruiting trip to fill Bill's position at the Belmont School.

I am . . . anxious, for I have certainly given you some mighty miserable times and I am awfully sorry. The letter that came from you this morning did me a world of good. You won't have to stick to me through hell, I trust, but it certainly was dear of you to say you would. . . . Well, dearie, it's just as you say, we've got to get together and then we'll make a go of it somehow. I have got to live alone through these next three weeks somehow and then we'll be together physically at least, and to both of us that means a great deal, doesn't it? I feel now as if I were getting over a long illness, I am so weak and nervous. But I think I am on the upward trail and I hope to have got the better of my depression before you come. . . . One of the pictures that you took of our house is perfectly splendid and makes me homesick for it all. Oh Piddy darling! Have we made a mistake leaving it all? If only things had gone better there!

Your father came last night and is looking well I thought, although he says he is not awfully well. . . . Father was here so they talked mostly school. . . . For my mind it is a risky experiment taking out an Eastern man for a school like Belmont. . . . It is a different proposition entirely from the Eastern schools. . . .

Bill dear, we just will begin over and I feel ready to do my share. . . . Love me all you can, dearie, if you still can and we'll both believe and trust that once physically together (does that sound good to you?) the rest will come. . . .

♥ ♥ ♥ ♥ ♥

Christine Reid, Brookline, MA, to Bill Reid, Jr., Belmont, CA
8 December 1910

Christine had had trouble with Bill's father on the West Coast, and it apparently continued when he had recently visited Brookline.

Dearest Bill,

I had planned to write you a letter last night but your father came to supper and spent the evening and left me in a mood where I felt it was nicer not to write. He tried to talk to me about our relatives, etc. and then criticized my attitude. It does no good to talk with him, but he means well and it probably won't do any harm. I don't know why I am writing all this as I didn't intend to when I started. I sent you a telegram on Sunday but received no answer. Why, I wonder!

We have had a fine snow storm and the fellers are having the time of their lives. They went coasting up at mother's yesterday and came home wet to the skin, but so happy! They are all O.K. to-day, as no harm was done. I shall write a real letter to-night if possible and hope to do better.

Yours
C.

♥ ♥ ♥ ♥ ♥

Christine Reid, Brookline, MA, to Bill Reid, Jr., Belmont, CA
8 December 1910

Christine wanted to correct her earlier letter that day about a statement she made about her father-in-law.

On thinking it over I doubt if I made it clear that it was my attitude towards him not towards you that your father criticized. He seemed to feel rather disturbed that I would not let him get "closer to me" & he expressed it. I told him that I was sorry, but that I doubted very much whether all this talking it over did any good. I said that I had learnt not to depend on sympathy and to stand on my own feet in so far as possible, and that discussing things was not very much in my line. . . . . He did adore the children. . . .

[On Bill coming East] Certainly we are not engaged, nothing of the sort! We haven't much more than just met, but I will stretch a point and come to meet you when you arrive, but you mustn't perceive too much on my doing so! I do hope you will try to get here before Christmas. . . . I don't want to be a total wreck before a possible suitor.

♥♥♥♥♥

Bill Reid, Jr., Belmont, CA, to Christine Reid, Brookline, MA
9 December 1910

Bill was nearly back to writing his loving letters to Christine, as he again felt her love for him.

. . .You little old precious—another letter today—when I didn't expect it and such a dandy too—three straight and a loving for me in everyone—maybe I don't feel like a King. I have just devoured these last letters, but how I will devour you. . . .

When I get there. . . you are in for a loving such as no girl ever experienced and it'll keep up well after we're gone to bed, & way up at that. Oh, how I do long to feel it slipping in and up and to watch you as I do it. We will never have experienced so absolute a union before. . . . Being together physically does mean a lot to us and to me it's the sweetest relation we have, for it combines love, affection, passion, union and an utter surrender such as nothing else can. When I am clear in and lying with you close against me and in my arms and with kisses passing & hugs and little fascinating movements—I can't conceive of anything dearer. . . . I feel shaky at the bare thought. Perhaps I won't satisfy that feeling—just as often as you want & oh, so passionately. A week on the train tired as I am, will fix me up and the six weeks of straight abstinence will bring me to you swiftly, piping hot. Just go ahead and "bank" on anything you please—I'll surpass it all. . . . Once "physically together" & it will be all up with your blues—see if it doesn't. If I could just give it to you three or four times and leave it in, you'd get nourishment from it—that's an absolute fact. But you are dead right on that, you're not in condition to run any risks & besides we must find ourselves first. . . .

Do you remember that night while we were engaged & how naughty we were? I can feel you tight against me now—with the same little thrills that went over me when I felt your bare legs (just a little of them) touch mine. Whew—it makes me wriggle. How we ever stood it without just going to it, I don't see. I couldn't stand it now. . . . I am head over heels in love with you and simply existing till I get to you. . . .

♥♥♥♥♥

EAST OVER WEST

Bill Reid, Jr., Belmont, CA, to Christine Reid, Brookline, MA
11 December 1910

All seven pages of this letter were devoted to loving Christine when he would arrive in the East. It was triggered by Christine's telegram, just received, and her remembrance of Profile House on the second night following their wedding.

You never will know what a joy your telegram inviting me to a feast that should surpass Profile House was to me. . . . I guess that you will blush when you read my reply--which, if I do say so myself--is a gem. I don't think anyone else will "catch on" but you will see it plain as day. Didn't you like the words "spread," & "served several times" and "are you game"? And the "hot & ready," wasn't that a pippin? Did you get the "lady fingers" idea too? I can just feel you holding me & squeezing me now & I positively ache. . . .
    Girlie dearie, I've waited faithfully long and hard, and now to have you simply write me in your inimitable and fascinating way to do anything I want to you--oh, it's heavenly. . . .
    I almost hope I miss connections because then I'll only have half the torment that I can see you are so gleefully planning to subject me to. . . . It will be the dearest reunion that ever was. . . . I have been positively uncomfortable all day and am sure I am an inch larger than I ever was--will you like that. . . ? I'm afraid that just the moment I feel myself slip in to that delicious little haven, so warm & hot, I shall come & in great big spurts--all of this is as near heaven & ecstatic bliss as I ever hope to get. Your bare arms, hot cheeks, your little wriggles & your quick breath--how they do inflame me. . . .
    I'm afraid my letter is too exultant in tone & perhaps too plainly put, but you'll forgive me I know when you consider that I have been cut off without even hope of having you--for almost 20 weeks. . . .
    I shall be almost delirious with you when we are absolutely together & to think that we can lie on the bed & play with each other on the day after the first night. . . .

♥ ♥ ♥ ♥ ♥

Bill Reid, Jr., Belmont, CA, to Christine Reid, Brookline, MA
12 December 1910

Bill did not keep up the intensity of his letter of the day before, but he felt the need to send some news of what was going on in his life in the West.
My darling little Girl:
    It is too bad that Papa came along to talk matters over with you just when he did, and I am very sorry but pleased to see that you kept your balance so well. I tried to head him off from just such a discussion but my letter could not have reached him in time as it had to be forwarded.

295

A Debutante's Passion—A Coach's Erotica

Never mind, dearie, he tried to help, remember that and then forget the whole thing. We are together and that's all we want—now we'll settle our own affairs as we think best. We are going to be oh so close and dear to each other and we mustn't let anything ruffle us. I am writing in a most comfortable way you see because I have your dear telegram in my pocket and I know that this is just a temporary thing with you. I am so, so happy and am anticipating being with you and have you with me and by my side. I love you dreadfully and the thought of being with you again is too dear for expression.

I am very sorry about that telegram—the reason I did not answer was because I thought as I said before that it was sent principally to ease up the two letters which had just arrived. How happy the message made me I have already told you—it was dear of you to send it & I appreciated it keenly.

Not much has happened today except that tomorrow I expect to have everything packed. I am afraid you'll have to do all of our Christmas shopping as I cannot bring anything and have not the time to shop anyhow. I am still up to my ears in work & shall be until train time Sunday. I played tennis for a little while this afternoon. Mr. Damon & I against Mr. Hatch & Mr. Himman. They won the first-set 6-0 & then we braced & took three straight. I felt so happy over you dear thing, that I simply could not lose. My first exercise for a week & a half & it did me good.I have just come up from the gymnasium, after an interval of an hour after having played on the Senior Basketball Team against Hopkins Hall. We were beaten 12-9, the score being tied 8-8 at the end of the first half. We outplayed them in every way except in fouls—on which they won. They only made one basket from the floor. Of course I was fouled freely, but I threw all the fouls they made but one & spoiled several baskets from the floor. Mr. Meddick the coach played with Hopkins & made all of their points, so that after all we did pretty well. I am all in of course, but it did me good & the boys enjoyed it.

Poor Mama feels dreadfully and half cries all the time she is up here. She has been a perfect brick and I feel for her. First came my leaving then Charlie's trouble & now Mrs. Sleeper's going. She knew that before but it all centers at this time. Then Papa is away and that isn't pleasant, particularly when I am leaving. . . .

♥♥♥♥♥

Bill Reid, Jr., Belmont, CA, to Christine Reid, Brookline, MA
14 December 1910
The barrage of letters continued from Bill to Christine.

I have only 2 1/2 days here now & then I shall be on my way to you, you darling. I am coming with the steadfast purpose of "making good" to you, and also in business. You have given me great help during the

last two weeks and I shall see if I can't boom things for you. I know I can help and by golly I do love you.
♥ ♥ ♥ ♥ ♥

Bill Reid, Jr., Belmont, CA, notes to Christine "Lincoln," Brookline, MA 13 December 1910

The following two notes, one based on courting Christine a decade before, were probably included in his letter of December 14th.

Dear Miss Lincoln:

I had such a nice time with you on Situate Beach day before yesterday that I thought it only fair to contribute something to your happiness and so I am sending these violets to take the place of those that got so mushed up that evening. We must go driving again one of these days & I would suggest following some of those by-roads in Harve's Woods. If you like the idea, set a date & I'll be there. I shall call tonight & shall hope to find you in.

Very Sincerely, W. T. Reid, Jr.,
♥ ♥ ♥ ♥ ♥

My Precious Little Darling:

These blossoms are for you to wear when you come to meet me. They are poor substitute for the love I feel for you, but they will show you that I am thinking of the dearest little girl in all the world and longing to kiss and hug her and shield her from the world. My whole heart to you Dearie—all, all, all of it, and it's a big one.

Lovingly, "Bill"
♥ ♥ ♥ ♥ ♥

Bill Reid, Jr., Belmont, CA, to Christine Reid, Brookline, MA 15 December 1910

Bill was on a high as he attended going away parties in Belmont and awaited going East to start a new life with Christine.

I wish you might have been here these last few days and this evening, for everyone has been so good that I only need you to share it with me to make my happiness complete. . . . The townspeople, the eleven, the school, and the faculty have all given me something. . . . As I leave, to have people so cordial and hearty about it, makes me feel for the first time as though I am as capable as the next man. With my half finished football at Harvard and failure staring me in the face here for two years, I began to wonder whether I wasn't a failure & so all of this has infused me with new life. . . . There is a beautiful moon tonight and I would so love to sit with you in my lap quietly hugging and kissing you

A Debutante's Passion—A Coach's Erotica

and talking it all over. I feel half robbed of it all without you and I hope that I can carry the spirit of the whole thing to you when I arrive. . . .

Three wagon loads of boxes, barrels & crates are in the freight car at Belmont and another & the last will go about noon tomorrow. . . . My anticipation almost obliterates my sadness at the going, and I can now appreciate better your "torn in two" feelings. . . .

♥ ♥ ♥ ♥ ♥

Bill Reid, Jr., Belmont, CA, note to Julia Reed Reid, Belmont, CA
17 December 1910

Bill wrote a final note to his mother before going East. His comment about Christine not being well may have been truer, in the long run, than Bill knew.

Mother dear:

These blossoms are just a wee attempt at a recognition of all that you have done for me from the cradle up. As I grow older I realize more & more what you have done for me. During these hard months I think that I have at last found what you have worked so hard to bring into my life—the spirit of God. I call it the new religion from "Together" because it has been the first glimpse of anything that has meant a satisfying of my inner self. I have never been very affectionate to you or Julia or Papa but I have felt a great deal & my heart goes out to you all. If my conscience were not clear I could not stand it, for my going is a severe wrench. I have given to love the boys and the work and I feel that my experience here will afford me an entrance to many things in life which I should otherwise have missed.

Do not worry about C and me, we are going to be closer than ever and I shall be patient as long as I have her. She loves you, but please remember that she is not well & do not attach too much weight to her sluggish condition of heart. She has suffered more keenly than we have known.

God's blessing be on you. Your life shall be my Northern Star and my love for you is deep and lasting.

      Good night & peace be with you.
         Lovingly, "Will"
         ♥ ♥ ♥ ♥ ♥

Chapter 11

HARD TIMES: "YOU ARE A HOUSEHOLD AREN'T YOU?"

Bill Reid, Jr., Brattleboro, VT, to Christine Reid, Brookline, MA
1 February 1911

Bill was traveling in the East in his new position as bond salesman for the Boston-based William A. Read and Company. His early optimism about success was touched by reality, and gloom pervaded his being. The entire depressing letter to Christine at their home at 25 Harvard Street in Brookline is included.

Dearest little Girl:

I wish you were here tonight for I am very tired and lonely. I haven't had even a nibble until today and have met about 150 strangers so far. I don't believe the banks here would buy from anyone—in fact one of the Trustees told me that his bank hadn't bought for 4 or 5 years. I shouldn't mind if I could make at least an occasional sale, but this empty game bag is becoming very annoying.

I have been industrious and thorough and feel much easier when I go into a bank or private house, but I feel blue over the failure to sell. I suppose the second or third trip I may pick up some business, but this first time round certainly is the limit.

I feel just like a quiet little lap talk and we'd have it if you were here. You have been a perfect brick in not complaining about my being away, and I am working my head off to give you & the kids what I want for you. Your whole attitude is a great stimulus to me and I am able to fight off with fair success the glum feelings that come as time passes with nothing to show for my work.

I hope Pussy is OK & that you are not too tired. I went to bed at two last night & was up at 6:30 to take my train. In consequence I am pretty tired now.

Will you please have Farley press my every day suit & my blue one—the latter only in case his price is reasonable. Tell him that if he will make me a good price for a year or by the month, I will consider it. I should judge that one suit a week with an additional one once every two weeks is about what I need. That would get my dress suit & blue serge pressed once in two weeks. But see what he offers.

A Debutante's Passion—A Coach's Erotica

I love you dearie & shall hope to see you Friday night though probably not at supper. I am too far away to get back at a reasonable hour on the Boston & Maine.

Lovingly,
Bill
♥♥♥♥♥

Bill Reid, Jr., Winchendon, MA, to Christine Reid, Brookline, MA
28 February 1911

Bill began his letter to Christine in failure mode, but after a talk with his brother-in-law, Jim, he saw a greater possibility of bond sales.

My Winchendon sale did not materialize on Monday as I had hoped and so I came up here to find out why. I expected to spend the night here but fortunately ran across two of the big men in my sale on the train, and am thus enabled to go on to Bellows Falls tonight. I don't expect to do any business there or in Brattleboro but I must go to keep up my acquaintance. Sales look pretty slim just now and I don't see any prospect ahead for the balance of the week. The Winchendon sale will come off in a day or so I feel confident & will be for 5000. I had hoped for 10,000 but it was a question. . . .

My talk with Jim on Monday was quite encouraging. He intimated that he was going to give me a little better territory or add to mine saying that he was going to give the best places to the best salesmen. As I have sifted this territory pretty carefully & don't see much possibility of many more sales with our present list of bonds & a rather poor market—I shall welcome additional ground. As it is I have to offer about the same things on my second trip as on my first. Don't mention this to Ag., it's simply between us.

Enclosed is Papa's February check. Mine from the office will be along in a day or so. I don't know how I stand but am afraid that with shoes, hat, theatre, etc., out of it, it may be cut down. I thought I'd prepare you for the worst if the worst happens. My new rubbers are completely worn out & I had to throw them away—isn't it disgusting.

Well, I think of you & the fellers when I feel in need of motive power & I find that it gets me through some pretty bad looking drifts. This plodding about with only an occasional chance for business is certainly very trying at times. Still no one has sold anything to speak of this week & Geoffrey not for 10 days—so I suppose I can't kick.

Take good care of yourself & please see a doctor about the monthly difficulty. It is very important and a delay now may mean serious complications later. . . .

♥♥♥♥♥

HARD TIMES

Bill Reid, Jr., Greenfield, MA, to Christine Reid, Brookline, MA
7 March 1911

Bill was now into his second month of bond sales, and one gets some of the feeling produced by Arthur Miller's play, "Death of a Salesman," in which Willie Loman sustained himself with false illusions of material success.

Monday started off in better shape than any I have yet had as I stand a good chance of a sale there before the week is over. There I have a good chance with a private customer.

Today I found a possible sale for about April 1st & then plodded all day until 4:30 just about quitting time. I was pretty tired and rather blue but following a motto I have of "Keep Moving" & as a result fell into a $5000 sale. This put quite a different aspect in the day. The biggest satisfaction however came from the fact that the Treas. of the bank turned down my offer & I made the sale over his head with the Pres. of the bank.

Tomorrow I shall move on to North Adams unless something interferes.

Dear little girl, I think a whole lot about you as I plod along and I want you to know that I don't intend to have you weighing every penny as you are having to do any longer than I can help it. I feel all this very keenly and the feeling presses me forward under all circumstances.

Yesterday in Fitchburg, a man recognized me from my back & asked me if I wasn't Bill Reid. That's the first time that has ever happened to me.

I had a rather good sleep last night and ate a solid breakfast & am cutting down on smoking & late hours. One has to be cheerful & bright in this business & plenty of sleep is essential.

I called on Jennie last night & tonight I call on Dr. Twitchell—Harvard man—whom Jennie spoke to regarding me. This is another step in my acquaintance chain here & later on may mean business. . . .

Well—take good care of yourself & do see the doctor. It isn't fair to me or the kids to let your trouble go uncared for.

♥♥♥♥♥

Bill Reid, Jr., Fitchburg, MA, to Christine Reid, Brookline, MA
12 March 1911

Bill was caught between his desire to be with Christine and the need for returning to the road for a better financial future.

I felt a big lump in my throat as I left you this afternoon and it was hard to go. I felt as though I were halfway deserting you and actually started back before I got to the gate. I decided to go ahead however upon reflecting that a 6:40 train from Boston meant getting up at five—not that I was unwilling to make that effort to be with you—which I should have thoroughly enjoyed doing—but because it meant routing you out of your sleep of which you get little enough as it is. This sounds poorly as I read it over—but what I have tried to say is that it was my consideration for you and not convenience for myself that decided me. . . .

I have changed hotels here & find this one much nicer, in fact, very nice. I wish you were here to occupy a very comfortable double bed—it looks inviting.

Much love if you want it, from Hubbie.

♥♥♥♥♥

Bill Reid, Jr., Gardner, MA, to Christine Reid, Brookline, MA
14 March 1911

The pressure to attain financial security dominated this letter.

I have had another pretty good day. My trip to Athol and a conference with Dearborn whom I went to see there, ended in Jim's selling 350 shares of stock at $160 a share or over, a total of $56,000 worth. This should net between $1000 and $1500 to the firm. Besides this, I sold one bond to the bank and have succeeded in having a special meeting of the Investment Com. called for tomorrow night to consider a purchase of 5,000 or 10,000 Bos. & Northern bonds. It all hangs on one man's say so as all of the rest have definitely committed themselves, I shall go back to Orange at noon tomorrow to try & put on the finishing touches before the meeting. If this goes through I shall be tickled to death as I have already sold 10,000 of the bonds & this will be a second buy. It is about an even chance. . . .

My new rules have improved my general condition greatly—earlier hours at both ends and less smoking. . . .

♥♥♥♥♥

Bill Reid, Jr., Orange, MA, postcard to Christine Reid, Brookline, MA
15 March 1911

Bill kept Christine informed of some success in the bond business.

Dear C:
Another pretty good day. Bank here or rather in Orange took 5000 . . . which was what I was working for. On to Williamstown tonight. . . .

♥♥♥♥♥

Bill Reid, Jr., location unknown, to Christine Reid, Brookline, MA
8 May 1911

Bill had some success in selling bonds, but he was still only eking out a living and working very hard, while being away from home and Christine and the family. Christine, who was having her own problems of happiness, was about to take off for New Hampshire to be with friends Susie and John Noble in East Jeffrey, New Hampshire. The entire letter is included.

My dear little Girl:
I am very happy at the thought of the little outing which you are to have and want you to go in for anything that will contribute to your happiness.

You have had a pretty tough time of it and have stood up to the racquet like a real suffragette and it is now up to you to "forget it" while you are away.

You have had a heap of disagreeable things to do and have done them so faithfully. I have appreciated them even if I haven't always spoken about them and have felt a lot of sympathy for the many sacrifices which you have had to make to keep within the little which I have earned. It has spurred me on and I am determined to make a success of things before I am done.

I know that you want a masculine man and that it must be a humiliation to you to see other's earning so much more, just as it is a humiliation to me to have you have to weigh expenses & wear other's clothes. Well—its not going to last that's all and things have got to go.

The enclosed ten dollars is a little personal contribution on my part to your spree. Where it came from makes no difference—it won't be deducted from next month's check. This is to be spent for whatever you choose except in the way of household expenses. Furthermore it is to be spent on this trip. It is strictly fun money—nothing else. Remember!

Now, sail in & enjoy yourself—forget the speckled beauties at home & tend to those in the brooks, forget dish towels and handkerchiefs and the provoking husband—forget it all & enjoy yourself.

I shall enjoy my week with the thought of your pleasure and in the feeling that slowly but surely you are coming back to me in your old way. I long for it and want it and will do my share, & more.

Your greeting at the door tonight and once before warmed me up—it's what I need & want. Don't force it but let it come when you feel it.

This is a queer note—foolish, serious, but with an undercurrent of feeling which I can't express.

My best to Susie & John & my whole self to you.
               Fondly,
               Bill.

♥ ♥ ♥ ♥ ♥

Bill Reid, Jr., Greenfield, MA, to Christine Reid, East Jeffrey, NH
11 May 1911

Bill just had the biggest week in selling bonds ($27,000) since he began the job a few months before. Christine was not feeling well and not acting too kindly toward Bill, for some unknown reason.

A Debutante's Passion—A Coach's Erotica

I have been thinking a great deal of you since you waved your farewell in Fitchburg and I hope that you are having the bully time that you so richly deserve.

Thus far I have had the busiest week of the year and have sold something every day. The total is $27,000 in all—my biggest week of the year. If I can pull off a sale tomorrow I shall feel pretty good. . . .

There is a banquet of bond men in Boston tomorrow, Friday night, and I have been chosen as one of four to represent the house. . . . It is on the firm which is very nice. . . .

I have felt that we are getting together and with friction eliminated as it has been, have been conscious of more and more affection between us. I like to hug you whenever I see you & to kiss you when I dare, knowing that it is more or less distasteful to you. Don't peeve over this, it's meant for a joke.

I am in good shape for a set to if you feel like it when you get back. I've been good as indeed I have with one exception ever since I have been out.

Make the most of your trip & don't hesitate to do what you feel like doing because of expense. You are out for a rest & I want you to get it from every possible angle.

Please tell Susie & John that I am under great obligations to them for what they have done & cannot thank them enough.

A big hug & kiss to you Dearie and my heart's best. . . .

♥♥♥♥♥

Bill Reid, Jr., Athol, MA, to Christine Reid, Brookline, MA
ca. 22 May 1911

Success in bond sales remained tenuous at best.

. . . I am feeling pretty glum this morning and not much account. I haven't a prospect in sight and what I sell amounts to practically nothing. I feel as though Jim had greatly overestimated me in giving me Providence & Worcester and am afraid I shan't come up to expectations. I find it hard to press a sale when a man doesn't want to buy or to talk with enthusiasm about a bond which I wouldn't buy myself. Well, I shall plug along & do the best I can but I don't see much ahead. . . .

♥♥♥♥♥

Bill Reid, Jr., North Adams, MA, to Christine Reid, Brookline, MA
23 May 1911

It didn't take much to discourage Bill, just a day of no bond sales. He poured out his woe to Christine.

Not a sign of a sale today. . . . I haven't even had a toe-hold anywhere, and have come to the conclusion that I am a big dub. . . .

I wish you were here with me because I should get a lot of comfort out of loving you. A hurdy gurdy has been playing outside and the music seemed to make it worse. I am in a blue funk and homesick. I am staying with it of course but it's hard to go three or four days without a smell of a market & yet keep up a cheerful front in passing on to further disappointment. It may be part of the business to go on this way, but it wears on my nerves and spirits to be doing nothing but adding expense. I've gone at it hard enough to get something at least. Don't mention this to anyone—it is just my inner most feelings which are for you only. I do want to get ahead—I've got to & this desert market smacks of failure to me whether it is so or not. I am ready to work but I can't stand unproductive work.

I've made a grand mess of things thus far and I don't feel at all sure yet that I have found my grove. Meanwhile time is passing and I am getting darned uneasy.

I want to feel that I am on the way and that you & the fellers are in line for what I intend you shall have, and until then when I can feel things moving to my satisfaction, I can't help worrying about it.

I don't want to add to what you are carrying but I must write, and this is what is in my mind. I would love to have you here in my lap & to snuggle up close—it would help a whole lot.

♥♥♥♥♥

Wm. T. Reid, Sr., Belmont, CA, to Bill Reid, Jr., Boston, MA
12 October 1911

After Bill was away from California for nearly a year, his father wrote to him about the bond sales business as well as his own Belmont School, to which, he hoped, Bill might still return.

... I think that you have thus far done surprisingly well. I couldn't have done anything like as well. ... I have great respect for the sand you have shown under the circumstances. It is the kind of stuff that will make or break and now that you have fairly passed the worst stress of it all I think your future is pretty fairly assured. ...

I every now and then feel a very strong regret that you are not here. If you were, I feel confident that I should feel easy to go away at will and stay away pretty nearly at will. Oh well, I suspect that it was about the best thing that could be done. ...

♥♥♥♥♥

Wm. T. Reid, Sr., Belmont, CA, to Bill Reid, Jr., Boston, MA
31 October 1911

Bill's father, for a decade and more, gave Bill advice on what he should do in life. He continued in the quest for his son to do better than his father had

A Debutante's Passion—A Coach's Erotica

done as Headmaster of the Belmont School, just as Christine hoped that Bill would become a greater financial success.

I am a little sorry, or a good deal sorry, to have you raise the question whether the bond business is going to be your forte or not. I have many times wished that you had gone into railroading. I think that offers one of the finest fields possible. It calls for judgment, untiring industry and great executive ability. . . . I also believe that you would make a decided success in finance, if you get far enough along to get a controlling voice in some strong house . . . .

♥♥♥♥♥

Wm. T. Reid, Sr., Belmont, CA, to Bill Reid, Jr., Boston, MA
10 November 1911

Bill's father wrote again to see if there was a possibility of Bill returning to help run the school. He indicated that the school for 1910-11 had a net return of $12,000, probably the highest income in its history.

. . . Hinman said a few days ago "If I go home next summer, I think that I shall go out of my way to see Will. I want to see him mightily. I declare I wish he would come back. I hope he will succeed where he is and he will of course but this is his logical work and would be a fine opening for him," etc. Major Kirk said something of the same kind. I am sure you will be glad to know of the feeling. . . .

I have never ceased to regret the necessity of your going, wise as it probably was, for you this year had $4000 and a certain portion of the net profits besides & I think that you would probably have felt the rubbing of the harness less & less and you would of course have made a success of it. But I dare say that is all gone by and over of coming back. I however remember you once saying that you would be glad to know if there should be a possibility of raising the question. I am not going to use a word of persuasion or even suggestion. Indeed I doubt whether it would be wise for you to come but you will know whether things have so changed as to make it worth while to raise the question in the way of saying what if there should be an opening? I leave it in this general way. . . .

♥♥♥♥♥

Julia Reid, Belmont, CA, to Bill Reid, Jr., Brookline, MA
19 May 1912

Bill and Christine had been living together in the East for nearly a year and a half, but their life was not one of happiness. Bill's mother addressed the dark side of their relations in an effort to be helpful.

I feel helpless in the face of what you & C are going through. . . . I may not be able to say anything helpful, but I hope I shall not hinder where I want to help.

I cannot doubt that C. is just as sore-hearted over the shadow that has fallen over you both as you are & I feel sure she would give a great deal to get back to where you were ten years ago, just as I know you would.

One thing you told Papa [that] she said or felt explains many of her feelings from the first of your stay in Belmont. She resented your "trying to bring her up." Speaking of Jim & Agnes once she said to me that "Jim never tried to make Ag over but took her just for her own self."

Now we all tried to have C. our own way in many things when she was here & you often protested in her behalf. I'd give a good deal to have my chance with her over again. C. has reason to feel your patience & your efforts & for feeling that you want to & are trying to have the old feeling for her, but isn't it evidently effort & not spontaneity—has love returned to your heart any more than she says it has to hers—or rather has it not failed to revive in your heart just as she says it has failed to revive in hers (or words to that effect) and evident that C. is making some effort also.

When you feel as you do sometimes, your thoughts must send out an untoward influence & must reveal themselves to some degree.

You wrote of C's saying she did not know you disliked the kind of dog she got & adding if you would give her the money she would get another, & then you said this "shut you up as tight as a chain." If you could have met this thoughtless and inconsiderate remark by putting your arms around her & saying "I wish dear I could give you a hundred times what I have to give for it makes me miserable all the time to think how many things you would like to have that I cannot afford to get for you." I believe she would have responded & felt ashamed & blamed herself as she used to do before you were married when you generously met her ill temper or sullenness.

Your one wish then was to prove to her that you loved her—& to make her happy—& not to make her good or try to change her. She has ill temper to contend with & you have a disposition to sulk & to upbraid in tone if not in words that you have to contend with. I have a similar fault & I know it is a real stumbling block, just as temper is to C.

If you could have at once given her the extra fifty & said—"I'm glad of this especially for your sake dear." I think it would have stirred a chord in her heart—whereas your not even telling her of the raise proclaimed your feeling of estrangement & so most likely intensified hers.

You can be generous in such ways easier than she can earnestly trying to overcome yourself & to change in the little ways where she wants to change.

If you can only do some such things sometimes I am sure you will sometimes at least win response.

If I could have telegraphed you last week & felt sure that you & you only would receive it I would have urged you not to sever relations with

A Debutante's Passion—A Coach's Erotica

your friends by refusing further invitations because the risk was too great. I am glad enough of your sensitiveness to such expressions as you quote but as Papa said to me & as he intended to say to you & perhaps did—such expressions probably prevailed in your early cut shorts, would likely be harmful rather than helpful. . . .

♥♥♥♥♥

Julia Reid, Belmont, CA, to Bill Reid, Jr., Boston, MA
26 March 1913

Bill's mother wrote to Bill and not to both Bill and Christine, addressing her letter to the Boston bond office, not to their home in Brookline.

I enclose a draft for $2000, though when Papa realized that it was for stocks, he said perhaps you'd better invest only $1000 but do as seems best. The money was not drawing interest so if you don't use it nothing is lost.

♥♥♥♥♥

Julia Reid, Belmont, CA, to Bill Reid, Jr., Boston, MA
29 April 1913

Bill's mother again wrote to his Boston bond office, Wm. Read & Co, to criticize another of Bill's traits.

. . .Whether you are sick or driven with work or offended at my last letter, taking you to task for not trying to regain the love of reading you once had, I would like just a word.
    . . . I sent Christine 2 doz artichokes Apr. 8, but they went to Brooklyn N.Y. & a tracer was sent—& we were notified & I sent word to throw them away.

♥♥♥♥♥

Christine Reid, Brookline, MA, to Bill Reid, Jr., Greenfield, MA
ca. 20 May 1913

While Bill was on the road attempting to sell bonds, Christine wrote a lackluster letter, indicating what was apparently missing in a happy marriage. She was inquiring about going to Jeffrey, New Hampshire with friends for the weekend on their farm. Bill wrote on the back of the envelope, probably for a telegram: "Letter just received. Go if possible. I heartily approve Jeffrey trip."

Dearest Bill,
Susie Knoble has just called up and wants me & you up to the farm with them Friday noon and stay over Sunday. They want you too, but I suppose you would rather go to Cohasset or Marblehead. I told Susie I

would think it over or else crawl out of Marblehead & perhaps go there later. Another trouble is that little Jimmy [a nephew] is pretty sick and I think Ag rather depends on seeing me every day. Unless he's better I don't know that I ought to go away for a long, but I'd love to see the farm again & have you see it and the country there. Would you feel like coming up on Sat.? I wonder when I can hear from you! What will you say if you come home & find I've gone to Jeffrey! If I do, I'll leave explicit directions for you.

All goes well here & Pat is bustling with health & spirit.
Much love,
C.
If you think necessary, telephone me at six p.m.
♥ ♥ ♥ ♥ ♥

Julia Reid, Lake Tahoe, CA, to Billy [Pat], Edith, and Christine Reid, Brookline, MA

17 June 1913

Bill Reid's mother looked forward to having her grandchildren come to Tahoe Pines, the elder Reid's house at Lake Tahoe.

It makes me laugh to think of seeing you all tumble around here again. Take good care of your Mamma & help her all you can on the way out here so she won't get tired.
♥ ♥ ♥ ♥ ♥

Julia Reid Willard, Santa Barbara, CA, to Bill Reid, Jr., probably Boston, MA

21 July 1913

Bill's sister wanted to know if Bill and Christine were still together. She began her partially missing letter in a direct manner.

My dear Will—We had a very nice letter from you yesterday and I was awfully glad to get it. You are a household aren't you. . . ?
♥ ♥ ♥ ♥ ♥

Julia Reid, Belmont, CA, to Bill Reid, Jr., and Christine Reid, Boston, MA

11 August 1913

Bill had visited his parents at Lake Tahoe with his children, while Christine remained in the East. Bill's mother thought he was rather sloppy in appearance.

. . . I am going to send you $25 towards a good made to order suit.

I was proud of you this summer but ashamed of your clothes & your

A Debutante's Passion—A Coach's Erotica

hats & your cravats & your shirts. You didn't seem to belong to your children to judge from your appearance & theirs. I can't send the money yet—both banks and savings bank as well are drained dry. But I will send some as soon as the new boys pay & the $100 will go at the same time—so you can count on it by Aug. 25th.

Your visit will furnish lovely memories for the whole coming year. I wouldn't have missed it for anything.

♥ ♥ ♥ ♥ ♥

Christine Reid, Cohasset, MA, to Bill Reid, Jr., Greenfield, MA
ca. 13 August 1913

The contrast between some of Christine's loving letters of the early 1900's and those of a half-decade later are apparent.

Dearest Bill,

Am so glad that you are feeling so perky! Pat is really better. He would certainly do well as a living skeleton in a side show. However, I do hope he'll pick up now. Ag very kindly sent him for a little ride in her car yesterday and I think it did him a lot of good.

I played some tennis yesterday with Louise Richardson, K. Higginson, and E. Founcend and we had a great time, but surely am rotten.

Ag and I are going up to Boston to-day to see the "Ino Dochie" pictures & to dine with Dad & Mother. This pen is the limit!

I may try to get a dog for Pat.

Take care of yourself & don't work too hard.
With much love,
C.

♥ ♥ ♥ ♥ ♥

Julia Reid, Belmont, CA, to Bill Reid, Jr., and Christine Reid, Boston, MA
17 August 1913

Bill's mother was never diplomatic in her correspondence with Bill, and probably was one reason why Christine did not get along with her, nor travel to see the Reids on the West coast.

The memory of your visit is a daily pleasure to me & brings a sort of content whenever I think of it in this busy week preceding School. . . .

I am afraid I used too many capitals in speaking of your clothes, Will—& too few in speaking of you—for about you I feel only pride & affection & your clothes didn't match you & they didn't match the appearance of your family either. . . .

Belmont people all regret C. did not come too. Those who knew her wanted so to see her & the few at school wanted to meet her. Mrs. Clark took a great liking to you.

I have a number of enlargements made from films C. lent me but will keep the films a little longer as I shall probably have another set of the enlargements. These I shall send to the children soon to be hung in their rooms.

We are hoping daily for a letter from some of you.

Charlie [son-in-law] continues to feel so down that Julia is anxious. Don't mention it to them. It has lasted over a month now, while generally those periods have lasted not over a week. . . .

♥♥♥♥♥

Julia Reid, Belmont, CA, to Bill Reid, Jr., and Christine Reid, Boston, MA
25 August 1913

Bill's mother wanted to tell Bill and Christine what they might do for their children, but for once asked them if they wished to hear her opinions.

My dear Will & Christine:

I didn't get the money off as soon as I promised & I hope you have not been inconvenienced by it. It has been a very busy time & the days have been too short. I didn't want to send the draft without a word & yet I wish now I had for I feel too hurried this morning to write. We've had to get a new teacher as there are 9 classes in High School Mathematics. The number of boys is not as large as at first thought—several old ones dropped out to go to work & two new ones left the second day because of homesickness, so we have only 100 instead of 105. . . .

Give much love to C & the children. Oh I see so many tendencies in children here that could have been checked earlier, that I can only pray that you & C will seek divine guidance in training yours. They are all so very different & so lovely in different ways & each has a temperament needing different handling.

Lovingly
Mamma

If you and C. both wish to I will tell you what I feel about each— Perhaps it might help as an outside view. In any case it can be ignored.

♥♥♥♥♥

Christine Reid, Cohasset, MA, to Bill Reid, Jr., Athol, MA
ca. 17 September 1913

Marital troubles were not by now new to Bill and Christine, and this letter about the health of Pat, age 10, showed concern for Pat, but little for Bill.

Dearest Bill,

Pat had one of his same old colds yesterday and so I sent for Dr. Osgood, who stands very high here. I told him that Pat's general condition was very poor and that I wanted his blood tested. Then I told him about his tendency to colds, etc. He was certainly awfully thorough and I liked the way he "took hold" as you would say. He says that Pat is anemic, his blood is only 60 where it should be 100, which of course shows that he's badly run down. Dr. Osgood says that if, as he thinks, Pat has chronic bronchitis, there is a vaccine that will cure him of that tendency. Of course nothing is sure as yet. He says there is no need to worry, but actually I have not been very happy about it and am rather blaming myself for not having a doctor sooner, but I did what I felt was best at the time & I guess that's all a person can do. Pat had a fine night last night and is feeling much better this morning, has a good appetite, etc., but it was not the cold that worried me. I am afraid the trip west was not the best thing in the world, but that is over now so we won't think about it. Dr. Osgood is coming again this morning, and I'll know more about that. He thinks that dreadful whooping cough is at the bottom of it all, as I have felt always. That winter will never cease to be a nightmare to me!

My mind is so full of Pat that there is no room for anything else. He will come out all right, this I'm sure.

I hope that you are having a good week.
Much love,
C.

♥ ♥ ♥ ♥ ♥

Julia Reid, Belmont, CA, to Bill Reid, Jr., Boston, MA
ca. 29 September 1913

Bill's marital troubles continued, and his mother tried to help him in his relations with Christine.

You must know you are in my thoughts & prayers many times a day. I have not written—but silence is sometimes wiser.

I don't see any help for things except regeneration. That is all that will accomplish what Begbie calls the Miracle.

One thing I would suggest though & that is—if you feel you have not C's love—caresses would better be withheld in the main. Instead confine yourself to thoughtful unselfish attentions & patience & good humor.

When caresses come to be missed under these circumstances it may cause a wish for them & revive affection & love.

Kisses, etc., from one I didn't love would alienate rather than draw me—this however is only my own feeling perhaps.

Just send a few half dozen lines each week—don't feel that you must write at length—when under such a strain.

Cultivate sleep & avoid stimulants or narcotics. . . .

♥ ♥ ♥ ♥ ♥

HARD TIMES

Julia Reid Willard, San Francisco, CA, to Bill Reid, Jr., Boston, MA
9 June 1914

Bill's older sister wrote to congratulate Bill on his salary hike.

Some days ago Mamma let me read a letter of yours in which everything seemed to be going your way and I was awfully glad to hear it. It is certainly pretty nice having another raise when you felt that you had reached the limit for this kind of work. I hope though, that there may be some position open to you in the office so that you won't have to be on the road. . . .

♥♥♥♥♥

Wm. T. Reid, Sr., Belmont, CA, to Bill Reid, Jr., Boston, MA
20 June 1914

Bill's father told of Bill's mother's illness in which she could eat only soft foods, and of Julia's (Bill's sister) judgmental attitudes toward Bill. He discussed Bill's drinking habits.

I have felt nothing short of admiration for your whole attitude for the last six months or so. You have handled matters better than I could have done. I am as much surprised at your consideration and patience with Julia as at anything else. It seems almost impossible for her to keep from dictums that she of all persons should keep clear of. . . . She would have made a mess of your affairs if she had been in your place. But then so should I, I fear. But no matter about that. Your level-headed restraint has filled me with admiration and the result justifies my admiration. I couldn't have done as well. Indeed I fear that I should have failed.

As so I hesitate to advise in the matter of your hardly knowing what to do about the social glass, and so I am going to say that I think that you can stand by your guns & not only win out but add to the respect in which you are held, to make it inoffensively clear that there are limits beyond which you will not go. And by that I mean this. So limit your taking of wine or cocktails as to make it clear that nothing is going to endanger your habits or your poise. I do not hesitate to take wine or occasionally a cocktail and yet I am regarded as very nearly a teetotaler. . . .

♥♥♥♥♥

Wm. T. Reid, Sr., Belmont, CA, to Bill Reid, Jr., Brookline, MA
6 October 1914

Bill's father still hoped that Bill might return to the Belmont School and help him out. This time there was the possibility of the Belmont School merging with the St. Matthew's School in San Francisco.

A Debutante's Passion—A Coach's Erotica

. . .[Major Kirk] said that if you should be laid off for six months you might be willing to come out & give us a lift—adding "That would give us a great boost." I'd like it of course but I suspect that it is out of the question. If there is any chance for it let me know. . . .

♥♥♥♥♥

Wm. T. Reid, Sr., Belmont, CA, to Bill Reid, Jr., Brookline, MA
17 October 1914

Bill's father again mentioned the possibility of school mergers, giving the pros and cons. He ended his letter with a comment about Christine, who was seven months pregnant.

Let us know how C gets along. It is a great delight to us to know that she keeps in good spirits.

♥♥♥♥♥

Wm. T. Reid, Sr., Belmont, CA, to Bill Reid, Jr., Brookline, MA
29 October 1914

Bill's father, age 71, regretted not spending more time with Bill and Julia in their upbringing, and he saw that Bill and Christine were spending time with their children. He also commented on the naming of the forthcoming child after Charles Willard, the husband of Bill's sister.

. . . I wish that you & C knew how eagerly both Mamma and I are looking forward to the new baby that is coming into your home. I wonder if Mamma ever wrote C or you at all as she spoke to me of the letter in which C spoke of naming it Julia if it proved to be a girl or Charles if a boy. I didn't appreciate at the time that she meant Charles Willard and some days later I asked Mamma whether the Charles was to be after Charlie Williams. I should like to see Charles Willard if the baby should be a boy & should be named after him. I can't think of anything that would be likely to give him more pleasure. . . .

But your and C's attitude toward the children only causes me regret that Mamma and I gave you and Julia so little of the home. The fact is there has been too little of sentiment in Mamma's life and mine—too much of the grind. . . .

♥♥♥♥♥

Wm. T. Reid, Sr., Belmont, CA, to Bill Reid, Jr., Brookline, MA
13 December 1914

Bill Reid's father discussed his school and its future as well as Bill's financial future.

I have ample reason for feeling very happy over the outlook. Nothing could make me feel happier except substituting your name for his. However your position is probably wise—the only course to take.

Let me, if I can finally set at rest your feeling chagrin because I am contributing something toward carrying you to the point of getting squarely on your feet, as you are sure to do in the end. Remember that it is not a burden to us but a pleasure. Your getting on your feet means more to both Mamma and me than anything that can now come into our lives. When you tell me what you are doing for your children I feel a regret that I wish I might now atone for because I did not contribute more than I did to make your boyhood a happy one. My only & my great consolation is that in spite of it all, is the promise of your career to my greatest pleasure.

♥ ♥ ♥ ♥ ♥

Bill Reid, Jr., Brookline, MA, telegram to Mr. & Mrs. Wm. T. Reid, Sr., Belmont, CA

17 December 1914

Christine and Bill now had their fourth and last child, Charles (Chilly), to go with Patrick (age 11), Edith (age 10), and Christine (age 8). Christine was 33 and Bill was 36 years old, when they telegraphed Bill's parents, naming the child after the elder Reid's son-in-law, Charles Willard. Would their life be happier in the future?

We are four. Charles Willard Reid arrived early today. Christine exceptionally well.

♥ ♥ ♥ ♥ ♥

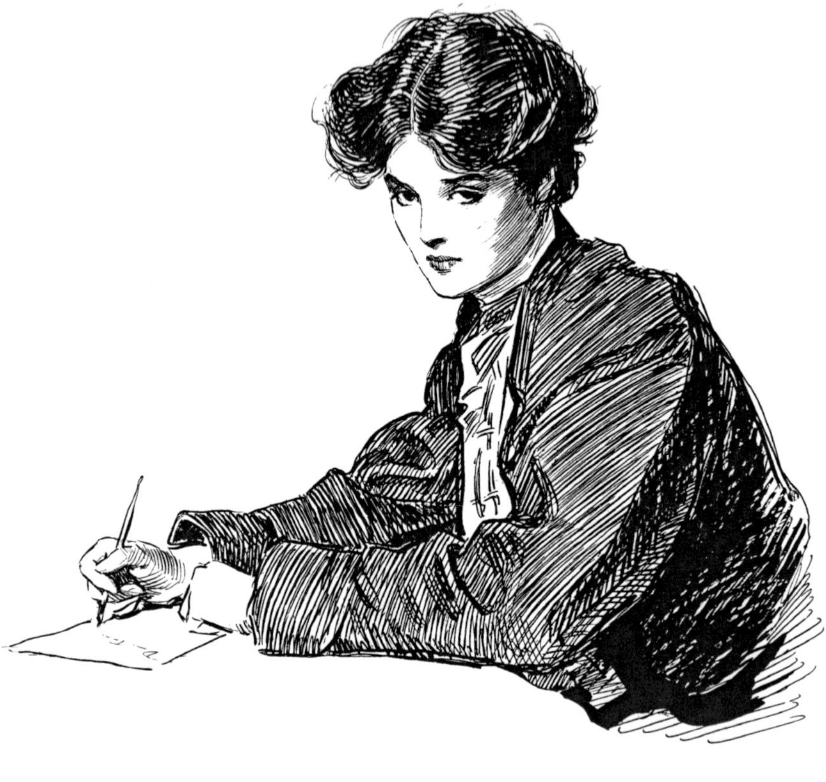

Chapter 12

THE END OF A LOVE AFFAIR AND A LIFE: "THIS ISN'T A LOVE LETTER"

Wm. T. Reid, Sr., Belmont, CA, to Bill Reid, Jr., Brookline, MA
                                                          10 January 1915

Bill's father was hoping that Bill would write on a regular basis, wanting to hear especially about Christine and Bill's new baby, Charles or "Chilly."

Let us know a little more about the baby. Is he in good shape & does he seem to like his new life? It gives us great pleasure to know how well C is getting along, and in how good spirits she keeps. That leads us to hope that baby too is getting along pretty well.

♥♥♥♥♥

Wm. T. Reid, Sr., Belmont, CA, to Bill Reid, Jr., Brookline, MA
                                                          29 April 1915

Bill's father wanted his son's family to come West and, among other things, see the 1915 San Francisco International Exposition, marking the opening of the Panama Canal.

Is there is any earthly use, discussing the matter of coming? I suspect that C would hesitate a long time before starting out with the baby & you would hesitate to come without her. Still talk it over—My! but we would like it. I am about as eager to see the baby as I can be. . . . Oh but I'd like to see the whole bunch of you. I do hope that C can be kept out of work or worry that will interfere with her sleep and good spirits. She can't afford to get any setback, neither can you. Well, tell the whole bunch, every last single one of them, Billy, Edith & Pussy as well as C that nothing would make us all so happy as to have you turned loose here & give us a chance to run you over & over again to the Exposition grounds.

♥♥♥♥♥

Wm. T. Reid, Sr., Belmont, CA, to Bill Reid, Jr., Boston, MA
                                                          11 November 1915

A Debutante's Passion—A Coach's Erotica

Bill and Christine stayed East throughout the summer. That fall, Bill's father offered to help buy a building lot for Bill and Christine in Brookline near Christine's parents. He believed the lot to be $17-18,000. He was to write Christine about his proposal, including paying $8,000 for the house Bill and Christine built at the Belmont School the previous decade.

[I will] turn over whatever I can spare in cash & have you put it into bonds or whatever she wishes. I of course purposely wrote her instead of you. You may turn over if you like the Sugar bond you have. Mamma thinks you have one of $2000 or two of $1000 each. I think she is mistaken and that you have but one of $1000. I think that I can send two and may be more the two thousand now at any time that you like.

. . . I'll pay up the entire $8,000 that was put in the [Belmont] house as soon as I can. It may be possible to pay it all at once. I'll write to C on same mail & she will then open up the subject. I'll write her that I have written you about it.

♥ ♥ ♥ ♥ ♥

Christine Reid, Lake Tahoe, CA, to Bill Reid, Jr., probably Cohasset, MA
26 June 1916

Christine finally made the trip West. Bill remained East, presumably to attend to building their new house. Christine took her four children to Lake Tahoe and Bill's parents' summer home, Tahoe Pines. She sent motherly love, especially regarding 13-year-old Pat's injury, but little wifely love.

Dearest Bill,
    Pat slipped and fell on the sharp edge of a stump yesterday afternoon, and cut a horrid gash in his shin, right down to the bone! He walked into the room as I was putting Charles to bed and said, "Mother, I've cut my leg, but it isn't bad!" Well, I took one look, and I saw it was a horrid deep one. So I tore over to the Smilies' and got Howard in his automobile, and in the meantime Nell and your mother put some bandages on Pat's leg and tied it up. Then we drove over to Tahoe City. . . . The doctor. . . put iodine on too and that hurt terribly. Pat had a pretty good night and his leg is not as bad to-day, but he is in bed. I tell you I was proud of him, but then, I always am.
    The baby had a bad night, so I am pretty much all in to-day.
    Will write to-morrow.
                Much love
                    C.

♥ ♥ ♥ ♥ ♥

Christine Reid, Lake Tahoe, CA, to Bill Reid, Jr., Cohasset, MA
5 July 1916

THE END OF A LOVE AFFAIR AND A LIFE

Christine and Bill exchanged 12th wedding anniversary letters, but in her next letter there was little to do with being married, except for comments about their children and their activities at a local festival.

Your letter arrived promptly on the very day, and I was delighted to get it. . . . Your mother has a box of our wedding cake which she put at my place at dinner, but I thought I'd much rather save it until you could be here too, so it is still unopened. It will probably not be edible. . . !
    The weather is glorious and just right and the lake is calm.
    Well, my dear, I surly do miss you, but I think I have written myself out.
               Lots of love
                        C.
♥ ♥ ♥ ♥ ♥

Julia Reid, Belmont, CA, to Miss Christine Reid, Brookline, MA
5 October 1916

Bill's mother sent a note to Bill and Christine's youngest daughter, Christine, age 10, noting their new house at 25 Harvard Street in Brookline.

These are wonderful times for you children—a big new house & a new yard and new neighbors and I guess some new hearts, for Edith wrote me you and she hadn't quarreled yet & were not going to so that makes up the most wonderful time of all.
    But how did it happen that one member of your family [a doll?] got left behind at Belmont! I don't know his name but he looked so forlorn & frightened when Nakamura picked him up from the floor behind the red couch in your room. I told him not to cry for I would send him back to you as soon as I could. Did you miss him?
    You must draw me a plan of your yard & the street, and the different floors of the house. Send me a plan of the yard first. Ask Billy if he can spare time to help you measure the yard & also show just where the house stands & how much room it takes from the yard. If he can't, perhaps Edith will. I should like it very much. Be sure & show which way is east. . . .
♥ ♥ ♥ ♥ ♥

Julia Reid Willard, Coronado Beach, CA, to Bill Reid, Jr., probably Brookline, MA
30 December 1916

Bill's sister Julia wrote of her concern for Bill's over-smoking.

. . . I know you were conscious of the fact when you were out here, that I was exercising great self-restraint in not saying a word about my being unhappy over your smoking, and I managed to hold on to myself when I wrote the birthday letter. . . .

A Debutante's Passion—A Coach's Erotica

You admit, Will, that your friends think you smoke too much, for you said last summer that Jim Dean said an occasional glass wouldn't hurt you as much as the smoking you do.

You know how it hurts Mama, you know that it hurts my pride, you know that Christine wishes you would give it up.

♥♥♥♥♥

Bill Reid, Jr., Hartford to Boston RR, to Wm. T. Sr., & Julia Reid, Belmont, CA

13 April 1917

Bill's last letter to his parents before his mother died was 15 pages long, likely arriving only a day or two before her death and shortly after the U.S. entry into World War I.

I seem to have recovered from a period of lassitude into which I plunged a month or so ago and now feel splendidly. It is therefore a great pleasure to be writing to you again for I feel like it and have much to say.

I have lived up to my resolve on smoking from Jan. 1 to April. First I did no smoking in the mornings. On April 1st, I cut myself down to one smoke after lunch & then no more until after supper. . . . I am feeling much better for it—splendidly in fact & with plenty of sleep. . . .

I am very happy now that war is here because I feel that we're at last lined up where we long since belonged. . . .

C. . . is taking a course in war cooking—the preparation of nourishing food in quantity at a cheap cost. We have two or three of the dishes a week & they are very palatable. . . . C expects to help with cooking at camps, etc. . . .

I wish I could enlist, but I cannot stop work. I am almost 39 & am badly flatfooted. If it comes to a point where one is in my position. . . I shall go. I don't believe however that there will be a chance of it before it is all over. . . . I am on the Committee that is raising funds in Boston to send 3 ambulances to France. . . .

I guess I will tell you in just two words what I am doing to help the Gov't, "Secret Service." I am in it & helping to organize it. This is confidential of course, but I think you are entitled to know. "Nuff Ced."

C & I have been out to dinner several times & with people I very much like so it was very enjoyable. . . .

Miss Bond, the cripple whom C has always taken a great interest in, was told a week or so ago that she would probably lose her hearing & was all broken up on top of her invalid condition. C went in to see Dr. Claire Blake one of the best in Boston & C's cousin & he agreed to examine her & treat her. Then C got the L's [Lincoln's] auto & went after Miss Bond. She was much affected & broke down. Then to cap the climax, the doctor says that he thinks

THE END OF A LOVE AFFAIR AND A LIFE

he can save her hearing. It is this sort of thing that fits C in a class by herself. . . .

Momma, don't let this war get on your nerves. There is bound to be a great deal connected with it that is not desirable, but the net result will be a big step ahead for the world & humanity. . . .

There, I've covered the ground & have written steadily for over 3 hours & enjoyed every minute of it. I have felt . . . guilty at the long hiatus. . . .

Can't you come on this summer & visit us? You can come instead of going to Tahoe & if I can sell a decent number of bonds, I'll help with the expenses. Your stay would offset in expense much if not all of your traveling expenses. . . .

♥♥♥♥♥

Bill Reid, Jr., Brookline, MA, to Wm. T. Reid, Sr., Belmont, CA
22 April 1917

Upon hearing that his mother died at the age of 70, Bill wrote this letter to his father.

Heaven itself is a better place now. Well done thou good and faithful servant, enter thou into the joy of thy Lord. We must be thankful for our long and privileged companionship with mother and for the merciful relief from the patient, courageous struggle, and for the heritage of memories beautiful so filling our thoughts. My heart goes out to you and Julia. Keep up your courage. Will write again later.

Will.

♥♥♥♥♥

Christine Reid, Brookline, MA, to Wm. T. Reid, Sr., Belmont, CA
9 May 1917

Following the death of Bill's mother, his father decided to come East to visit. Christine was gracious in her letter to him.

Dear Father Reid,

Just a line to tell you how glad we all are that you are coming to make us a visit. I feel sure that it will do you a lot of good, and it will be so nice for you all to come together. Bill is perfectly delighted, and we shall do our best to make you comfortable.

Affectionately,
Christine

♥♥♥♥♥

Bill Reid, Jr., Worcester, MA, to Wm. T. Reid, Sr., possibly Belmont, CA
6 July 1917

A Debutante's Passion—A Coach's Erotica

The trip East must have been good for both Bill and his father. William, Sr., had lost both his wife and daughter, Julia, to an unknown cause. Never before did Bill appear to be so happy to have had his father with him. It is not known how Christine felt about the visit, though it might have been easier on her not to have to deal with Bill's mother.

My dear Father:
    Your visit with us has meant more to me than I can possibly express. It has been as near perfect as anything could be and has brought me great happiness and peace. Your whole attitude has been wonderful, with good cheer, a fine sense of the whole situation, and a lovely attitude toward everyone and everything predominating. I am very proud of you and my heart smiles at this good bye.
    I want you to hurry and do three things.
1. Incorporate the School.
2. Take $50,000 in cash.
3. Deed it over leaving the selection of head-master to someone else—meaning the Trustees.
    Then & soon—pack up & come to us. I want & need your company & you need ours. This is the place for you and it is your duty to us to come.
    As to the school, there must be a break in the end—make it now & come! Mamma & Julia would both wish it and you know we do.
              God bless You,
                  "Bill"

♥♥♥♥♥

Christine Reid, Brookline, MA, to Bill Reid, Jr., Belmont, CA
25 December 1917

Bill went to see his father before Christmas. Christine sent a luke-warm letter to Bill., not knowing when he would return East.

Well Christmas is nearly over and I have missed you at every turn! Last night was the worst of all, it seemed as if I had no heart to fill stockings and I certainly had none to go out and sing carols!
    It is quite a while since I last wrote but I had the feeling all the time that you might be on your way back. Charlie's trying to reach you on the train seemed to me as if for some reason they did not want you out there. I am most eager to hear how things are, but you mustn't bother to write long letters!
    The children seemed pleased with their presents. . . . Of course we all, except Charles, went to mother's for dinner and it certainly seemed horrid not to have you there. We had grape juice and drank to your safe return. . . .
    The firm has sent you a check for $60, which I enclose. If you felt like putting some into your overcoat I should not shed a tear! Perhaps it's luck I can't cash it!

THE END OF A LOVE AFFAIR AND A LIFE

Well, my dear, this is a rambly letter and I'm not saying any of the things you want to hear except that I do certainly miss you.

♥ ♥ ♥ ♥ ♥

Christine Reid, Brookline, MA, to Bill Reid, Jr., Belmont, CA
29 December 1917

Christine's letters lacked the spark of a decade before when she was writing Bill in Belmont from her home in Brookline.

My dearest boy,

You first letter from Belmont came this morning and I was so glad to get it and to hear that things are, on the whole, so encouraging. I was so afraid that you might not find them so.

Indeed I cannot imagine Belmont without your mother, or Charlie without Julia, and that part of it must have been very hard for you all. I am awfully pleased that your father was so glad to see you, because I couldn't help being a little afraid he might not be. Wouldn't it be splendid if you could sell the school. . . !

Pat is third in his class this time and had such a high average that he got "honorable mention." This means that he will receive rank in the whole school of 200. Pat thinks he will be about 30 or thereabouts. As Country Day graduates enter college better than any other, I think even you must be almost satisfied!

I enjoyed your postals in route very much and it is splendid that you had such a fine trip and especially such a warm one.

My hands are too cold to hold the pen any longer! We all miss you terribly and the evenings especially are forlorn enough. It is terrible to have no one to "pick on" . . . !

♥ ♥ ♥ ♥ ♥

Christine Reid, Brookline, MA, to Bill Reid, Jr., Belmont, CA
31 December 1917

Bill was helping his father as he worked on selling the Belmont School, which he had run for over three decades. Bill certainly knew how to antagonize Christine, as her return letter indicates in its entirety.

My dear old Boy,

What in the world can I possibly have said to upset you so? I have tried and tried to think but I cannot! It's true that I did not write for quite a while, but I sort of thought you might be coming back on account of Charlie's telegram and also I was fearfully busy! Mother was in the house with a cold and I had all her Christmas shopping to do as well as my own. The children were writing each day and I was sure you would make allowance for what you must know would be a hectic time for

A Debutante's Passion—A Coach's Erotica

me. I am very sorry and won't let so long a time go again, but what in the name of goodness are you asking to be forgiven for? You've got me guessing, but whatever it is you are forgiven so do cheer up! I had just said to Jim that I was feeling so happy over your first Belmont letter, because you had found things apparently so much better than you expected and had enjoyed the trip so much. Then the telegram, and leaks in the pipes and still way below zero here! It is to laugh!

Never mind! Cheer up, the children are all well, & it can't stay 14 below forever; I have given up opening a window and we are thinking how lucky it is that you are not here. Oh! how you'd hate it!

I am enclosing two checks, you see I was the guilty one and found the one for the fellows in the drawer of my desk, after all.

We are not doing much but sit close to the fire & try to keep warm. Now do be sensible and have all the fun you can. Love from us all, — lots from me.

C.
♥♥♥♥♥

Christine Reid, Brookline, MA, to Bill Reid, Jr., Belmont, CA
1 January 1918

Little things apparently were magnified when the love of Christine for Bill lacked the intensity of years gone by. Bill wanted it; Christine lacked it.

. . . You are no doubt wondering why I have never mentioned your Christmas telegram! Well the reason is because your writing of having sent one in the letter I received to-day was the first I ever heard of it. It was nice of you to send it, and I am sorry it never arrived, so please forgive me seeming unappreciativeness! No doubt we are a queer family, but you are the first and only person to accuse me of lack of affection for each other! In fact most people joke us about being as crazy about each other. However, that's neither here nor there.

I haven't recovered from your telegram yet! and I keep wondering what in blazes it was all about and what I've said or you've said or done to cause such an upheaval! It certainly was a bolt from the blue. . . !

On reading over your letter I find that you did not imply as I thought that we as a family did not care for each other and I take all that back & please just forget it. I am afraid I am too lazy to rewrite it. . . .

Your letter. . . came this A.M. and I wish for your sake that I could write the kind of letter you would like, but I just plain can't. But I do love you, dear, and you must have faith in me.

Yours,
C.
♥♥♥♥♥

THE END OF A LOVE AFFAIR AND A LIFE

Christine Reid, Brookline, MA, to Bill Reid, Jr., Belmont, CA
4 January 1918

A lengthy cold spell apparently made Christine even colder than usual to Bill.

Still zero weather and I begin to think my hands are as frozen as everything else. . . !

It is dreadful not having our double windows on but of course you couldn't expect a man to put them on in this kind of weather! I guess the coal we have burnt trying to keep warm would have more than paid for having them put on.

I am still wondering about that telegram!

Well, dearie, I'll try to do better next time. All I can think of is the cold. . . !

♥♥♥♥♥

Christine Reid, Brookline, MA, to Bill Reid, Jr., Belmont, CA
11 January 1918

Christine believed that Bill was jeopardizing his bond sales position as he continued his stay in California to help his father dispose of the Belmont School. She was not about to leave for California to be with him.

I am so afraid that you will think we don't understand the situation or are not sympathetic! We are, but you did not tell me that you had agreed to be back in the office on the 15th! It is a terribly hard position for you but I really think if you made that agreement you ought to keep it whatever you may decide to do later. The firm is tiding you over an almost impossible situation and you certainly owe them your loyalty now. It is a perfect shame that things are as they are but after all there probably is almost no chance of a sale now. . . . Don't think that I wouldn't stand by you, for I would, but I feel that your duty now is to the firm. If you chose to give up your position that is another matter. . . . However that is up to you, but I shouldn't feel that I could leave the children at present. They depend upon me more than you realize, perhaps, and I think need me very much. . . !

♥♥♥♥♥

Christine Reid, Brookline, MA, to Bill Reid, Jr., Belmont, CA
20 January 1918

Christine had not written for over a week, but she was upset that Bill had not returned to his Boston job in bond sales, jeopardizing their lifestyle. She hoped that Bill's father would soon consolidate the Belmont School with another or sell it so that Bill could return to his position.

A Debutante's Passion—A Coach's Erotica

I expect that you are having a fit over my failure to write and I know I am a very naughty girl! You must be lenient, tho', for as you know it is like pulling teeth for me to write a letter even to you and besides my arm has bothered me a lot. However that doesn't excuse me and I apologize. . . !

Everyone asks when you are coming back and I feel like a chump to have to say, I haven't the least idea! I hope you have written to father in regard to the mortgage, because he said yesterday he didn't understand why he had not heard from you. . . .

The coal situation is very serious and apparently there is not much prospect of its improving. We have plenty of stove but very little furnace. However, we'll hope for the best but it's one thing to order it and another thing to get it. . . .

Well, dearie, this isn't much of a letter. I'd write a better one if I could.

♥♥♥♥♥

Christine Reid, Brookline, MA, to Bill Reid, Jr., Belmont, CA
ca. 26 January 1918

Bill continued on in California with his father. It was sometimes difficult to tell if Christine was upset with Bill or just making fun of him.

Dearest old Kid,

Just a line to go with the enclosed because I fear from the outset you will expect a letter. I shall write one soon!

I was sorry as soon as I sent you that whinny letter but it is really dreadful not to have some one to "pick on." No wonder you look fat in the picture!

Have all the fun you can! But don't forget old crosspatch.

♥♥♥♥♥

Christine Reid, Brookline, MA, to Bill Reid, Jr., Belmont, CA
1 March 1918

This is the last preserved letter sent to California, as zestless as the previous, before Bill return East. She noted, among other things the sale of the Belmont School and, apparently, the death of the son of the owner of Bill's bond firm.

I wanted to write you once more anyhow to congratulate you on really selling the school. I am proud of you and feel that you have done a mighty good job. I know that when it came to the point you must hate to have it go and although I suspect you think me unsympathetic. . . . But you incline as to brood over thinking that I must hit the level somehow. So try to believe that I know it is hard and that I do feel for both you and your father. I suppose you have not made any definite plans for him yet.

THE END OF A LOVE AFFAIR AND A LIFE

I am writing to the music of coal being put in and as we were entirely out for a day or two, it is a welcome sound. . . .

Curtis Read was killed abroad. He was a naval aviator, and all they know is that there was an accident. I believe he was Mr. Read's favorite son. Isn't it awfully sad? Two of the other boys are aviators too. The war is beginning to come home to us. . . .

I expect any moment to hear you've started and it's hard to write feeling that you may not get it. . . .

Much love to your father & Charlie—last but not least yourself—

♥♥♥♥♥

Christine Reid, Brookline, MA, to Bill Reid, Jr., San Francisco, CA
ca. 4 October 1918

Bill was again in California visiting his father, who was apparently living with Bill's brother-in-law, Charles Willard. This is the only preserved letter of the previous half-year and is one of Christine's cheeriest letters of the decade. It is included in full. The influenza discussed is the great Flu Epidemic of 1918 that killed millions during World War I. Evidently their two girls, Edith and Christine, aged 14 and 12, were staying at the Lincoln's Cohasset summer home.

Dearest Boy,

You have hardly been gone twenty-four hours but it seems a year! I had all I could do to keep from running up the hill after you but as I knew I should arrive looking like a waterfall I refrained. The house seemed so empty last evening, was dreadful. Pat gave me a little concert on the Victor, but I felt awfully lonely and went to bed when he did. To-day is a lovely bright clear day and it seems as if it must improve the influenza.

We had a scout meeting this morning and put through a lot so I felt as if it were not time wasted. I am taking care of baby this afternoon so Auntie B is coming to supper. Also to Sunday dinner. I had a talk with mother this morning and all is going well down there. Edith wants to come home, but Pussy is as happy as can be.

Well, dearie boy, I would have liked to have you crawl in last night. Please take the best of care of yourself.
       Lots of love
        C.
Here comes Charlie.

♥♥♥♥♥

Christine Reid, Brookline, MA, to Bill Reid, Jr., San Francisco, CA
8 October 1918

Christine was upbeat towards Bill and having fuel during World War I.

A Debutante's Passion—A Coach's Erotica

Your Chicago letter came yesterday. I loved the card! What made you think I wouldn't. . . ?

The wood came yesterday & is all stacked up. We've never had such a lot before. It is thrilling!

Well, dearie, I love you & miss you. Be careful of yourself.

♥♥♥♥♥

Christine Reid, Brookline, MA, to Bill Reid, Jr., San Francisco, CA
13 October 1918

Christine wrote a short letter, anxiously awaiting a letter from Bill on his arrival in California.

Baby was asking for you this morning saying "I like Pa, I want him come home!" I rather thought I might hear of your arrival yesterday but I guess it was a little too soon, probably to-morrow. . . .

Albert writes that he & Martha have "got it bad" as "bad as Christine & Bill" so you see what our reputation is.

This isn't a love letter & I fear you'll be disappointed but it carries lots of love just the same. Be careful of your good old self.

    Lovingly
     C.

♥♥♥♥♥

Christine Reid, Brookline, MA, to Bill Reid, Jr., San Francisco, CA
18 October 1918

Christine wrote another positive letter, even as the Flu Epidemic of 1918 was going on and which evidently was keeping the schools closed. She appeared not to be depressed, nervous, or upset. The "Jim" noted is her brother-in-law, married to her sister Agnes.

Dearie Boy,

Two fine letters from you and I did not mean to let yesterday go by without writing to you, but it went. However, the children have written so you did not suffer. If the schools don't open soon, I shall be a wreck! Jim said at breakfast that I reminded him of a rabbit, with all the little rabbits clamoring around, but it is when we have the whole neighborhood here that the real fun begins. However, I'd rather have the house the rendezvous, so of course I must pay the penalty. Well, we've had the excitement of a lovely leak over our bathroom which came down even into the lavatory. It was some flood & the pipe was literally rotten. The children had been playing in the attic so of course I blamed it on them, and I sputtered and the fur flew. Then Mr. Mildowney arrived and, as he expressed it, "the children had a perfect alibi" so I've had to apologize to each child in the neighborhood and I got them

THE END OF A LOVE AFFAIR AND A LIFE

some doughnuts for a peace offering. But the ceiling in our bathroom is a sight to behold! So be prepared and don't scold for I really am not responsible. . . .

I am delighted to hear that your father is so well and so comfortably situated. Give him lots of love from us all. . . .

To-night, [Jim] and I and the Prontys are dining either at the Plaza or the Country Club. I don't know when I have been so gay. . . .

When do you start back? But perhaps you will start before you can answer this.

It is cold here but we are getting along without the furnace. Have we had all the furnace coal that we are entitled to? It looks very little.

Well, my dear, my hands are frozen, but my heart is warm! Take care of yourself.

Success to your work!

A big hug & a squeeze.

♥ ♥ ♥ ♥ ♥

Bill Reid, Jr., Hartford, CT, to Wm. T. Reid, Sr., probably Berkeley, CA
19 December 1918

World War I was over, and Bill had returned to the East. He responded to his father's letter, even suggesting that his father begin writing a memoir.

It did seem so good to receive a letter from you,—the first I have had since I reached home from the West. It wasn't because of your generous remembrance to us all—that was to be sure very delightful—but because I have missed you and because the old familiar hand-writing looked so natural and so good, and then your graceful way of saying things is always a delight to read. If you don't write oftener—even a postal—I'll have to apply your old medicine to me at college and shut off on your allowance. . . .

Don't forget that if you feel like coming East to live with us—you are most welcome at any time, indeed nothing would give us more pleasure or satisfaction. With the school matters all settled, there would be no possible cause for friction of any sort, and you would have company from some of us and at the same time be able to do just as you pleased. . . . Christine wants you—we all do. . . .

♥ ♥ ♥ ♥ ♥

Wm. T. Reid, Sr., Berkeley, CA, to Bill Reid, Jr., Brookline, MA
20 April 1919

After telling Bill that Bill's letter gave him great pleasure, Bill's father asked if the family would be coming to Lake Tahoe in the summer.

. . . I am anxious to know whether Christine's plan to come to Tahoe for the summer is promising. If it is I want it rounded out by your coming

A Debutante's Passion—A Coach's Erotica

also. Your ultimatum to me about my tendency to limit my personal expenditures I am going to act upon, & so I am going to tell you to set aside $1,000 for my personal gratification. This money to be spent in bringing you folks to Tahoe for the summer. When can you leave? If you can't leave with C & the children, send them along when convenient & follow them when you can, but let me know as soon as you know when they can come so that I may have things ready at Tahoe. . . .

I am gratefully conscious all the time of my good fortune in selling Belmont for cash and then relieving myself of all concern about investment by putting it in your hands. . . .

♥♥♥♥♥

Bill Reid, Jr., Boston, to Wm. T. Reid, Sr., Berkeley, CA
16 May 1919

Bill told his father that he was to again coach Harvard baseball, beginning on Monday, at a salary of $1,000 for the remainder of the season. It was, Bill said, a bad year and prospects were poor. He asked again for his father to move East.

[I shall] take charge to try & save the situation. . . .
    Is it true that you have got to move—June 1st. . . ?

♥♥♥♥♥

Bill Reid, Jr., on the way to California, to Christine Reid, probably Brookline, MA
12 August 1921

This is the last preserved letter by Bill to Christine, and is included in its entirety. It is rather upbeat and sensitive to Christine's needs.

My dearest little Wife:
I feel very selfish to be going off for a vacation without you and especially when you have earned one so much more than I. If it weren't for the fact that father must be looked after, I wouldn't go at all. It is a hard pull to leave you with the load you are carrying and the only satisfactory thing about it is that I won't be gone long. I shall be constantly wishing you were with me to do this or that thing.

I realize fully what a big job you are doing this summer, and so cheerfully and well! You are doing us all proud and as George Sears so truthfully said are the only one in the family except your father, who has made good. I don't know what your mother, father, or Louise would do without you.

With all the work, I never saw you looking prettier or more fascinating.

We have our little squabble due principally to the fact that we are both of executive temperaments, but we really agree pretty definitely on essentials and that is the big thing.

THE END OF A LOVE AFFAIR AND A LIFE

I want you to take it as easy as you can and to take trips when you can. You must have an eye to your own health and nervous energy.

I can't take kisses enough with me to last, and you will have to stand for a good loving when I get back. In the meantime take care of yourself and if you don't feel like writing don't do it, I will understand.

With lots of love,
"Pid"

♥ ♥ ♥ ♥ ♥

Edith (Didie) Reid, Smith College, MA, to Christine Reid, Brookline, MA
11 February 1924

There is no preserved family correspondence for two and a half years from 1921 to 1924. However, Edith, the eldest daughter of Bill and Christine, wrote home as a 19-year-old student at Smith College, the last known letter from Edith to her mother.

Dearest Mother,

Thanks a lot for your 2 letters & card. It was good to hear from you & to know you are enjoying yourself. Exams weren't so bad, though I did work pretty hard of course. Still you couldn't work all day & it was sort of a free & easy life, just to know you could stop studying when you felt like it. I feel sure that I passed all but chemistry, as the flunk notes are supposed to be out within a wk. after the exam. I have had none so far, but a wk. has not yet gone since the chem one. I know definitely that I passed French & Hygiene & a week has passed since the English, Latin, & Spoken Eng. ones, so I guess I made them too. Not bad, c'est-cepas?

Moreover, Miss Townsend (basketball coach) seemed to be quite interested as to how my exams went which bodes well for at least 1 of 3 teams, for if you get a deficiency you can't play of course. Several of my worst opponents are out of it since mid-years! K's are too. The way we cheered each other.... It made the boys laugh when they came up. "Our nice friendly spirit" etc. & that brings me to this week-end.

It was just great! & the boys seemed to be having a good time too. Pat [Edith's older brother], George [his Harvard friend], & the 2 "squeaks" came up. Kirby didn't have money enough to get here or something. "No kiddin, Pat. I'm out 100 & something. I'd like to, but I venture to say I can't do it" etc. K & I had everything fixed up pretty well. We met them on the 2:44 & then took them for a short walk over the grounds before supper. They were much impressed by the river, boat-house, etc. We had supper at the "Mary Mary" tea room. (K & I almost ruined ourselves as the boys had just enough money to get back on!!) They all had 2 orders of things & so on. Dear me! Pat seemed tired, but enjoyed the change & ate plenty anyhow. George kept saying, "Why this is a great place up here! From the way you talked about it, I thought it was way up on a barren hill & that the girls cried all the time & — why it's wonderful here & they all look so happy!" They were quite scared

A Debutante's Passion—A Coach's Erotica

at first, but we didn't introduce them to a soul at the start & before they left, George at least quite enjoyed being stared at. We had reserved tables at all 3 meals.

After supper, we took them over to a toboggan slide which they set in every yr. near the pond. It's wooden & has 2 tracks that meet at the bottom & then go along a track walled in with snow for a good ways. It was all ice when we got there & we stood & watched others come down at first. The slide & pond were all lighted up & it was a great sight—just right. As we stood there, these toboggans would shoot past us so fast it was like a roller-coaster. Hats flew off & the people shrieked & all the rest. They were going 50 miles an hr., we found out later. A man had some apparatus there to time them. Well, you can imagine how we felt as we stood in line with a toboggan we got at the boat house from a man there. The whole college had turned out & the town too. All the toboggans for rent were gone as well as those owned by the College (big ones for six or seven!) We got the next to the last after waiting in a line for it! Well to continue. At the top of the slide there was sort of gang plank on which you put the toboggan & then a man boosts the rear end up & slides you off at a terrible rate. The boys were a bit nervous & kept telling us what to do etc. We piled on—Wee at the end & K & I somewhere in the middle, then off we shot. Wow! I never saw anything to beat it. We just tore down yelling like mad to the very end of the slide where we hit the embankment & sailed sideways along it at a ghastly angle then tipped over at the end. We got up speedily for others were coming after us & there were several accidents that night (We saw 1 girl get hit & run clean over by a toboggan with 4 or 5 on it. She was more or less O.K. though). Well we went up & down several times getting spilled pretty often & getting bruised & bumped on the way down very often. Wee got a hard-ride from sitting on back, but when put on front, lost his hat which flew by my face like a whirlwind. Gee, you ought to have seen us! Too bad Poo [Edith Reid's youngest sister] wasn't there too.

"Well," said George on the way home, "we have nothing like this at Harvard." We sat around & got warm at my house where people took turns staring much to George's glee. Then they went to bed. Had breakfast with them at the White House at 11 next A.M. & then took them for a walk till dinner. . . . Had lunch at 2 at the Snack Box & then went sleighing till 4. Ruth & Leslie came, but not Mary. We drove ourselves &, though it was cold, had a good time & the horse went well on the way home at least. After that (I couldn't eat again, though the boys might have. It seemed as though all we did was to eat & eat & then eat some more & Wee was always hungry) I took Pat in to see my room, "Cracky" coming too. Pat was much appreciated by her. Later on, we took them to the station all very appreciative & talking about "the next time we come up!" "Poor

THE END OF A LOVE AFFAIR AND A LIFE

Kirby! He'll be so sore, when we tell him" etc. Gee, it was fun & K was thrilled because, out of a clear sky, Pat said, "I'll write you after mid-yrs, Brother K." (Don't pass this on!!)

Pat & George may come up for the spring dance if Pa will let them (or Pat at least). I hope they can, for another girl up here is having Henry Stetson [whom Edith married in 1927] & she said to K, "don't you think Edie & Henry ought to have a date together!" but it would be a hard thing to manage I'm afraid unless I fuss too. K. wants Pat up & what George & I thought if they'd come, we would ask the other 2 out to Sunday breakfast perhaps. By the way Henry wrote & said to be sure & let him know when "I got off on parole" again, so that was nice too.

Well, I guess you're wondering where I got the time for all this. We just got a cut given us in Latin! First for me this yr. I've got to stop here though, for the time's about up & anyhow my news is too. So goodbye. I'll write again eventually. The spring dance is March 1st & may have news then if not before. Give my love to your fellow travelers & tell Uncle Ed the floor is always safe to sleep on anyway.

Lots of love,
Didie

One more thing. George caught K's roommate leaning over the banister to see him & the rest & he peered up at her much to her alarm & his amusement for her hair was all down, etc. We also saw one at my house & said, "I see you!" & pointed up.

♥♥♥♥♥

Christine Reid, Woodstock, VT, to Bill Reid, Jr., Cohasset, MA
ca. 12 July 1924

This is Christine's last preserved letter to Bill, written while she was on a trip to see her 18-year-old daughter, Christine (Poo or Pussy) and her 9-year-old son, Charles (Chilly) at their summer camps.

Dear Bill,

I set forth alone with Edward to see Pussy, as Ag & Doche preferred to stay here and prowl among the antique shops. It was a perfectly glorious day, by far the best so far, and it was a lovely ride all the way. Part of it was high above the Connecticut River and simply wonderful!

We could see the camp in the distance as we came along looking like toy tents on the hillside. Pussy was playing tennis as we drove in and gave me her own peculiar call. She seemed glad to see me and is looking extremely well and is apparently very happy.

The hillside, where the tents are, is very steep, almost like going up the side of a house and their tent is quite well up above the Lake or more properly "pond." It was only a marsh once but is now a real pond. Esther greeted me cordially, also one of the Dewsomes. The other was in bed,

A Debutante's Passion—A Coach's Erotica

but I paid her a little call & she told Poo she'd like to see a "home-face." She has never entirely recovered from the Schick [diphtheria-immunity] test and her arm has a horrid place on it like a big black & blue spot. Poo took me over to the main building and I had a nice chat with "Hobie" and met "William" & others. Then Poo and I took our lunch and climbed up behind the camp and I told her all the news I could think of. The camp is really very attractive, as camps go, & I think Poo is getting a lot out of it. I have the feeling that Esther is a tiny bit homesick but I may be mistaken.

We go cross country to-morrow on our way to see Chilly and I hope to find him as cheerful & contented as Poo.

We may not get back until Tuesday, but I begin to hanker for my own friends. What a fool I am.

Love to all

Wifie

♥♥♥♥♥

Christine L. [Poo] Reid, Boston, to Christine L. Reid, West Roxbury, MA
12 December 1924

Christine Williams Lincoln Reid would never receive this letter from her youngest daughter, Christine. Between August and December, Bill's wife must have had a severe medical condition, such as deep depression, for she was living at the Weld Farm Homestead in West Roxbury, Massachusetts, not far from her home in Brookline. The Weld Farm Homestead was likely a home for those in need of lengthy medical care. The letter was written the day before the fateful day, December 13, 1924, when 44-year-old Christine ended her life, evidently at the Weld Farm Homestead. Young Christine, at the time, was attending the Boston Museum of Fine Arts School. The entire letter to her mother, "Maga," is included.

Dear Maga,

I thought I'd write you a letter because I haven't seen you for so long, and I know you'll like to hear all the news. The dance at Esther's was perfectly splendid. I only had to sit down once for a short time without a partner! Very unusual for me! I know lots of the boys and met one or two. Aunt Gaga went in town with me and we got a dress at Slattery's of awfully pretty yellow. Then I had a very splendiferous half curl at Madame Alary's and then I was the "grandest tiger in the jungle." I got Billy four pairs of good woolen stockings and will get him more if he needs them after Christmas at a mark-down probably. Mrs. Jack, an aunt of Martha's living up Upland Rd., has asked me to a dinner before the Brattle Saturday night. Isn't that nice of her! The Brats are great this year but the first of Friday's was very slow! But then we, none of us, knew more than four or five boys and they are all Freshmen. Chilly got the prize for the best manners at school the other day, a Nabisco. I guess

THE END OF A LOVE AFFAIR AND A LIFE

he sometimes leaves most of them at school for he still feeds his tie quite generously. He was as good as gold about the shampoo. Would like to give him Dr. Doolittle's Circus which I have for him here. I am giving him "Wild Animals I Have Known!" Must go to bed now!

Lots & lots of love from Poo.

♥♥♥♥♥

Brookline Chronicle

18 December 1924

The obituary appearing in the Brookline newspaper was inaccurate in several statements, and it did not reflect much of Christine's 44 years of life. In only one letter of Christine's did she ever mention the Girl Scouts or her church, and there is no mention in the obituary of her life in California, a central episode in the life she lived.

Mrs. Christine Williams Reid, wife of William T. Reid, Jr., died suddenly last Saturday at the family home at 14 Hawthorn Road. Mrs. Reid was born in Brookline, the daughter of Albert L. Lincoln, and had resided here all her life. She had been for many years active in and prominently identified with the Girl Scout movement and gave largely of her time to this work. She was also actively interested in the undertakings of the First Parish Church of which she had long been a leading member. Besides her husband, she is survived by her father, two sisters, and a brother.

♥♥♥♥♥

[CRL monogram]   Mary made pancakes tonight!

Dear Maga,

I thought I'd write you a letter because I haven't seen you for so long and I know you'll like to hear all the news. The dance at Esther's was perfectly splendid & only had to sit down once for a short time without a partner! very unusual with me!

Epilogue

LIFE AFTER CHRISTINE: "HOW FAR SHORT I HAVE FALLEN"

When Christine took her life, she left with Bill four children, William III (Patrick), aged 21, Edith (Didie), aged 20, Christine (Pussy, Poo), aged 18, and Charles (Chilly), aged 9. The *Brookline Chronicle* obituary read:

> Mrs. Christine Williams Reid, wife of William T. Reid, Jr., died suddenly last Saturday at the family home at 14 Hawthorn Road. Mrs. Reid was born in Brookline, the daughter of Albert L. Lincoln, and had resided here all here life. She had been for many years active in and prominently identified with the Girl Scout movement and gave largely of her time to this work. She was also actively interested in the undertakings of the First Parish Church of which she had long been a leading member. Besides her husband she is survived by her father, two sisters, and a brother.

It is questionable that she died at home, and we certainly know that she had not resided in Brookline her entire life for she and Bill lived at the Belmont School for about five years in the first decade of the twentieth century. The day before Christine died, her youngest daughter, Christine, attending the Boston Museum of Fine Arts School, wrote to her mother at the Weld Farm Homestead, West Roxbury, Massachusetts, about five miles from Brookline. And she began, "I thought I'd write you a letter because I haven't seen you for so long and I know you'll like to hear all the news." Evidently Bill's wife had been there for some time for young Christine often saw her younger brother, Chilly, at home in Brookline. Likely Christine was being treated at the Weld Farm Homestead, needing a lengthy stay for her health.

Three years after Christine's death, her daughter, Christine, recorded for the first time in her diary her feeling about her mother's death:

> Momma died on December 13 in 1924, and things will never be the same again. How could they be? She was the center of our family life, and the staunch mainstay

of our existence. She was too good for our world. . . , but the loss is sometimes more than I can bear. I wish I could more adequately fill her place, particularly for Papa and Chilly. Chilly is just twelve years old, and the very best of younger brothers. I come next in age, and then comes Edith who is a year and a half older than I, and then Pat, who will be twenty-four this coming March. We shall lose Edith this summer, for she is engaged to Henry Stetson, and they are planning to get married in July.

Bill Reid was despondent after the death of his 44 year-old wife, Christine, who apparently committed suicide. Whether Christine was a manic depressive or was merely depressed at times, can be left to psychologists to ponder. Bill, from childhood, had always been sullen in his own way, and his penchant for suffocating Christine psychologically must have contributed to her tendency toward unhappiness. Bill's mother was probably correct when she once wrote Bill saying that he always wanted to make Christine into his image of what a woman should be, rather than letting her be herself. He may never have learned how much he could hurt Christine with his cutting remarks. Even in his early married life when he made derogatory remarks to Christine and promised never to do so again, he would return to his old ways. Bill could write the most beautiful love letters when he was away and missed Christine, but when he was with her, he would often irritate her with his exacting ways.

A couple months after Christine's death, Bill's uncle, his father's brother, living in Ridgewood, Mississippi, invited Bill to come for a visit. From his reply, it is difficult to determine how much Bill was grieving, but it was likely a great deal.

I would like very much to make such a visit but my position here makes it out of the question for me to go away for such a length of time, and particularly at the present time when I had the misfortune to lose my wife during last December, and now have the added burden of the sole care of my four children.

Bill's father had died two years before (his mother had died in 1917), and the invitation by his Uncle George to come for a visit was not accepted.

Bill's life would remain somewhat unfulfilled, something he would refer to a number of times in the future. All four children were in school when Christine died. The three older children were in institutions of higher learning, Patrick at Harvard, Edith at Smith College, and Christine at the Boston Museum of Fine Arts School, while Charles (Chilly) was in grade school. Bill would remain in bond sales while residing in Brookline, his home for the next half-century.

EPILOGUE: LIFE AFTER CHRISTINE

All the children had a trust fund, upon which they could draw on the earnings once they had reached the age of majority. By the 1960s, the value of these trust funds was well over $1,000,000. Nevertheless, as he approached his 50th reunion of graduation from Harvard, he wrote his youngest daughter, Christine, of his failure in life. Responding to a Father's Day card, he wrote: "From time to time—to appraise my life—& as I have done so, & realize how far short I have fallen from the hopes of 50 years ago—I sometimes feel pretty low." Yet he felt blessed with children and grandchildren. "If I have accomplished nothing else—that is at least more—by far—than many other parents have been able to do, and then I think of the joy which the knowledge of all this would bring to your good mother—which indeed she may know—& that is a great satisfaction—as you children are her heritage to me."

Bill remarried in 1931 to Connie Hinchman, but this apparently did not bring great joy to his life. Bill reported to a friend that he was lonely, and his friend replied to Bill's circumstances: "You can readily understand that emptiness there is when your children marry and leave your home, your wife gone, your father—the last touch gone too—nothing to cling to but trouble, and as the parson said 'it's raining too.'" Bill's eldest, son, Patrick, wrote to his younger brother early in World War II, and warned his brother about their father. "If you want peace, Chet," Patrick warned his brother, "for God's sake keep out of that house next year. It's getting worse & worse."

Bill remained close to Harvard through the years, and at times reminisced about his role in Harvard athletics, some positive and some negative. Bill's often pessimistic thinking resulted in his feelings of failure over the years. Two years after Christine's death, he sent in a life's account for the Harvard Class of 1901 25th Anniversary Report. In those intervening 25 years, he emphasized his two years of coaching the Harvard football team in 1905 and 1906. "In the end," he wrote, "we were beaten again [by Yale], and by the same score as before. My disappointment was, of course, very great, and for a time I looked upon the two years as a failure. . . ." At about the same time as his quarter-century report, he revealed for the first time to a writer from the Boston *Herald* how he helped save football at Harvard following the 1905 season. That was the time when brutality and unethical play threatened the game at Harvard and across the nation, and President Theodore Roosevelt telegraphed him: "Come dine with me and talk over football." Two decades later, Bill was still revealing how he was responsible for having 19 Harvard rules introduced by various members of the Football Rules Committee and thus saved the game for not only Harvard but for America. "I was able to put this across. . . . For instance Yale backed the ten yards [for a first down]. . . and the forward pass [introduced for the first time]. . . ."

As Bill grew into old age, Harvard was never far from his mind. He remained active with the Harvard baseball team well after World

A Debutante's Passion—A Coach's Erotica

War II, assisting the coaching, especially of catchers. His football accomplishments came to be recognized, when at the age of 91, he was elected into the College Football Hall of Fame as a Pioneer member. When Bill was interviewed by the *Washington Post* in 1970, six years before his death, he remembered coaching and the 1905 season as clearly as if he were recording his thoughts during the season. If only Harvard could have beaten Yale, and if he could only have had Christine at his side, one can conjecture that he would have considered his life to have been a success.

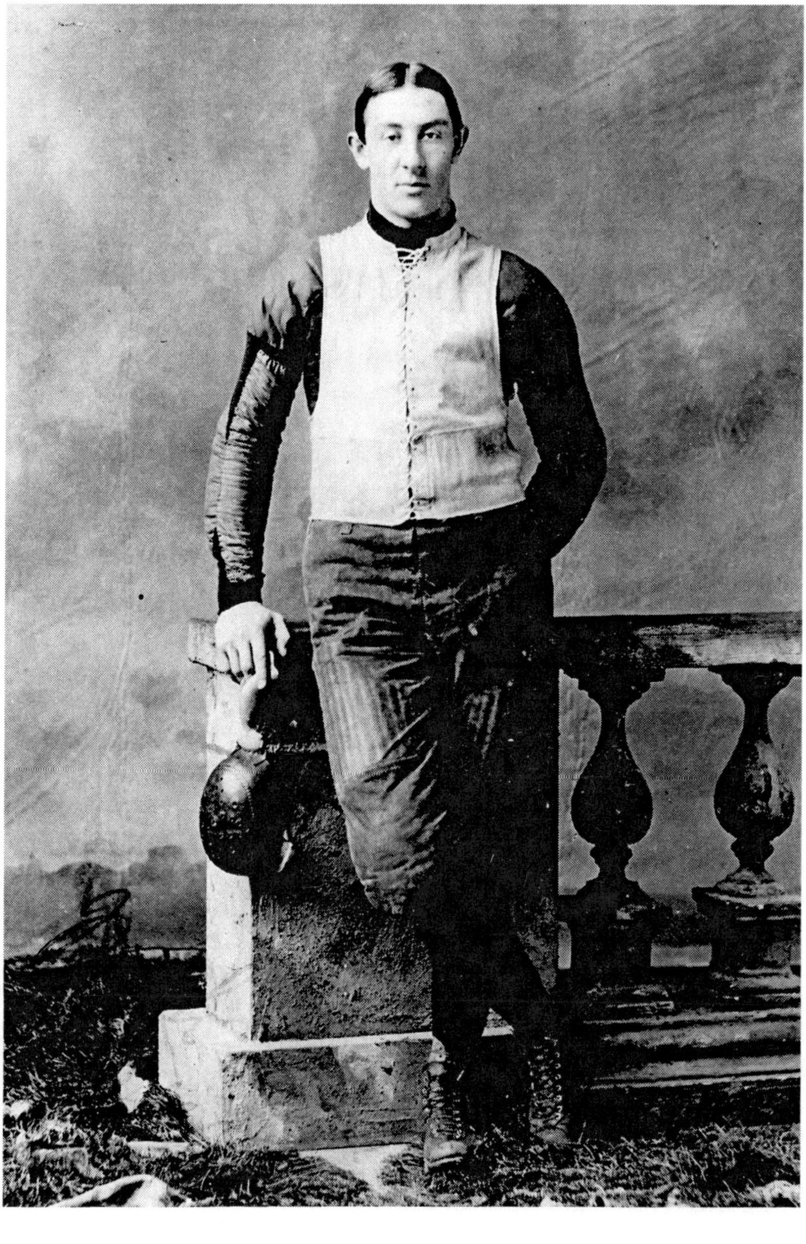

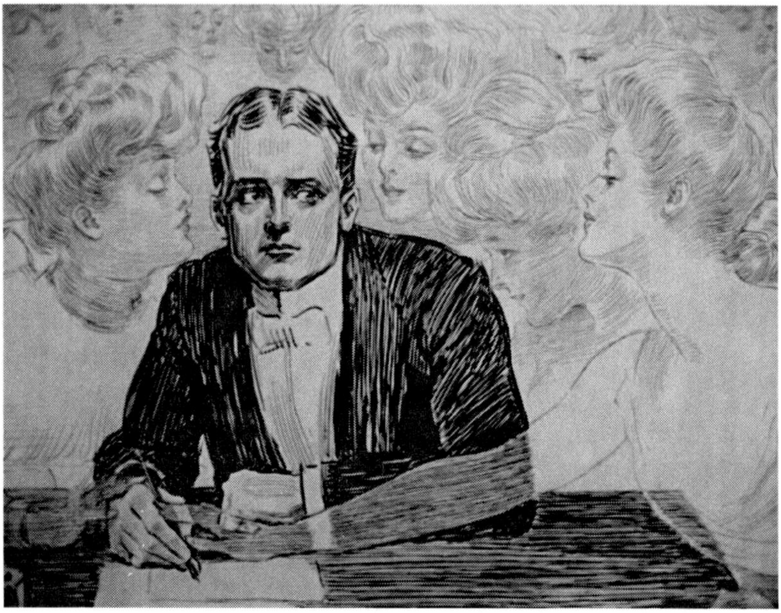

TIMELINE

November 8, 1843 — William Thomas Reid, Sr., father of Bill Reid, Jr., is born in Jacksonville, Illinois.

November 20, 1846 — Julia Frances Reed (Reid), mother of Bill Reid, Jr., is born in Jacksonville, Illinois.

June 1868 — William T. Reid, Sr., graduates from Harvard University.

August 16, 1870 — William T. Reid, Sr., and Julia Frances Reed are married.

August 10, 1871 — Julia Reid (Willard), sister of Bill Reid Jr., is born in Newport, Rhode Island. She marries Charles Willard in about 1898.

October 25, 1878 — Bill Reid, Jr., is born in San Francisco.

October 10, 1879 — Christine Lincoln's parents are married.

July 9, 1881 — Christine Williams Lincoln is born in Brookline, Massachusetts, child of a prominent Boston lawyer father and socialite mother.

June 1881 — William T. Reid, Sr., becomes President of the University of California.

March 14, 1885 — William T. Reid, Sr., resigns as President of the University of California, a victim of politics at the state level and the governing board.

August 5, 1885 — William T. Reid, Sr., becomes owner and headmaster of the Belmont School, a boy's preparatory school, in Belmont, California.

January 2, 1896 — The father of Bill Reid, Jr., writes his first letter of advice to Bill, age 17, about girls and life in general during Bill's junior year at the Belmont School.

September 1897 — Bill Reid, Jr., begins his freshman year at Harvard.

TIMELINE

November 19, 1898 Bill Reid, Jr., stars in Harvard's 17-0 football victory over Yale by scoring two touchdowns. Christine Lincoln attended the game but did not know Bill at the time.

December 17, 1898 Bill Reid, Jr., is given a full-page photo in a football uniform in the Christmas issue of *Harper's Weekly*.

February 1900 Bill Reid, Jr., and Christine Lincoln begin a lifetime of correspondence.

March 1, 1900 Bill Reid, Jr., invites Christine Lincoln to the Harvard Hasty Pudding dinner and dance.

August 23, 1900 Bill Reid, Jr., returns East from California to be with Christine a short time before she leaves for Europe, and to ask her to marry him.

September 10, 1900 Bill Reid, Jr., and Christine Lincoln are unofficially engaged.

September 11, 1900 Christine Lincoln begins an eight-month trip to Europe and Egypt.

September 12, 1900 Christine Lincoln meets a French artist, Henry Niorr, on board the steamer to England, a meeting that would cause turmoil for both Bill and Christine.

December 6, 1900 Christine Lincoln says a solitaire would be a preferred engagement ring.

December 18, 1900 Bill Reid, Jr., is elected Second Marshal by the senior class at Harvard only days after he was invited by the captain to coach the 1901 football team.

March 30, 1901 Christine Lincoln writes a more complete letter of the steamer affair that took place on the previous September 12th on the way to England.

June 24, 1901 Bill Reid, Jr., captains the Harvard baseball team to a final victory over Yale, concluding an 18-2 season record.

TIMELINE

June 1901 Bill Reid, Jr., graduates from Harvard University

September 3, 1901 The Christine Lincoln and Bill Reid, Jr., engagement is announced in the newspaper.

Fall 1901 Bill Reid, Jr., coaches the Harvard football to an undefeated season including a 22-0 victory over Yale.

July 2, 1902 Bill Reid, Jr., and Christine Lincoln are married in Brookline, Massachusetts and then honeymoon in Europe until December.

September 1902 Christine Reid announces to her parents and in-laws that she is pregnant.

January 1903 Bill Reid, Jr., begins a position as Assistant Headmaster of the Belmont School in California, working for his father.

March 17, 1903 William T. Reid, III (Patrick), is born to Christine and Bill Reid in Belmont, California. He dies on July 27, 1987.

July 9, 1903 On her 22nd birthday, Christine Reid writes her parents a depressing letter about life in California and weaning young Pat.

January 4, 1904 Bill Reid, Jr., is invited to be the next Harvard football coach by Captain Dan Hurley. Reid declines, but accepts the next year.

June 18, 1904 Christine Reid writes one of her sexiest letters to Bill after being away in the East visiting her parents for well over a month.

December 1, 1904 Edith Williams Reid (Didie) is born to Christine and Bill Reid, Jr., in in Belmont, California.

March 1905 Bill Reid, Jr., becomes the head football coach at Harvard for the second time with an enormous salary of $7,000.

TIMELINE

October 9, 1905 — Bill Reid, Jr., and another Harvard representative, and representatives of Yale and Princeton meet with President Theodore Roosevelt to attempt to lead colleges in more ethical and less brutal football.

January 12, 1906 — Bill Reid, Jr., becomes a central figure in the creation of the National Collegiate Athletic Association as he withdraws from the old Football Rules Committee to help form a new one that helps reform football.

May 8, 1906 — Christine Lincoln Reid (Pussy, Kitten) is born to Christine and Bill Reid in Brookline, Massachusetts. She dies in April 1990.

March 1907 — Bill Reid, Jr., begins his second term as Assistant Headmaster at the Belmont School. Christine and children soon join him.

June 13, 1907 — Bill Reid, Jr., writes an undiplomatic letter to Christine telling of an intimate talk with a Mrs. Jackson while Christine was vacationing at the Reid summer home at Lake Tahoe.

July 7, 1908 — Bill Reid, Jr., is invited by Percy Haughton to assist him in coaching Harvard football that fall. Reid declines.

Summer-Fall 1909 — Christine Reid and her three children remain in the East for an extended stay after Bill Reid, Jr., returns to work at the Belmont School.

January 12, 1910 — Christine Reid's father invites Bill and Christine to return to the East and live with them to begin life again away from California.

September 1, 1910 — Christine Reid and the three children journey East to be with her family, awaiting a decision by Bill to leave Belmont and begin a new life.

October 10, 1910 — Bill Reid, Jr., writes a regrettable and depressing letter to Christine, who remains in the East with their three children.

TIMELINE

December 17, 1910	Bill finally leaves the Belmont School to be with his wife and children in Brookline, Massachusetts, beginning a new life as a bond salesman.
December 17, 1914	Charles Willard Reid (Chilly) is born to Christine and Bill Reid in Brookline, Massachusetts. He dies on December 17, 1943
April 21, 1917	Julia Frances Reed Reid, Bill's mother, dies in Belmont, California at age 70.
December 1917- March 1918	Bill Reid, Jr., visits his father to help him sell the Belmont School.
December 17, 1922	William T. Reid, Sr., dies in Berkeley, California.
December 12, 1924	Christine Reid's daughter, Christine, writes the last known letter to her mother, just before her mother's death.
December 13, 1924	Christine Reid dies at the Weld Farm Homestead in West Roxbury, Massachusetts, most likely a suicide.
August 20, 1931	Bill Reid, Jr., marries Connie Hinchman.
1969	Bill Reid, Jr., is voted into the College Football Hall of Fame.
September 28, 1976	Bill Reid, Jr., dies at age 97 in Brookline, Massachusetts.
December 1994	The Bill Reid, Jr., diary of the 1905 football season at Harvard is published as *Big-Time Football at Harvard 1905: The Diary of Coach Bill Reid*, ed. Ronald A. Smith (Urbana: University of Illinois Press).